Comme... Gospel of John

❖c⊃❖

Chapters 1–5

THOMAS AQUINAS IN TRANSLATION

ST. THOMAS AQUINAS

Commentary on the Gospel of John

❧co❧

Translated by
†Fabian Larcher, O.P., and
†James A. Weisheipl, O.P.

With introduction and notes by
Daniel Keating and Matthew Levering

Chapters 1–5

The Catholic University of America Press
Washington, D.C.

Library of Congress Cataloging-in-Publication Data
Thomas, Aquinas, Saint, 1225?–1274.
[Super Evangelium S. Joannis lectura. English]
Commentary on the Gospel of John / St. Thomas Aquinas ;
translated by Fabian Larcher and James A. Weisheipl ;
with introduction and notes by Daniel Keating and Matthew Levering.
p. cm. — (Thomas Aquinas in translation)
Includes bibliographical references and index.
ISBN 978-0-8132-1723-9 ((first vol.) paper : alk. paper) —
ISBN 978-0-8132-1733-8 ((second vol.) paper : alk. paper) —
ISBN 978-0-8132-1734-5 ((third vol.) paper : alk. paper)
1. Bible. N.T. John I, 1–18—Commentaries.
I. Larcher, Fabian R. (Fabian Richard), 1914–
II. Weisheipl, James A.   III. Keating, Daniel A.
IV. Levering, Matthew, 1971–   V. Title.   VI. Series.
BS2615.53.T5513 2010
226.5'07—dc22   2010005230

CONTENTS

COMMENTARY ON THE
GOSPEL OF JOHN

ACKNOWLEDGMENTS

Our first thanks go to Dr. David McGonagle of the Catholic University of America Press for recognizing, as early as 2001, the need to bring St. Thomas Aquinas's *Commentary on John* back into print. His consistent support for this project has been the *sine qua non*. In the late 1990s and early 2000s, Matthew Levering corresponded regularly with and visited Fr. Pierre Conway, O.P., and Thomas Gallagher. Years ago Fr. Conway—a dear friend of the main translator, the late Fr. Fabian Larcher, O.P.—and Mr. Gallagher had spearheaded the first publications of English translations of Aquinas's biblical commentaries, and both men enthusiastically supported this project. Since that time both Fr. Conway and Mr. Gallagher have passed on to God. May the Lord bless them abundantly! The English translation first appeared in two volumes, published in 1980 (Magi Books) and 1999 (St. Bede's Publications), respectively. When the estimable St. Bede Publications stopped publishing earlier in this decade, Matthew Levering gained approval from the Dominican Fathers to seek a republication of the work with the Catholic University of America Press. A friend of Daniel Keating's, David Eldersveld, scanned the text into a Word document, and Daniel and David checked it for typographical errors; many thanks to David for his work. We are grateful to Dean Michael Dauphinais of Ave Maria College, and then of Ave Maria University, who approved faculty research grants that supported the project. We owe thanks to Sarah Surmanski, now a novice in the Dominican Sisters of Mary, Mother of the Eucharist, and then an Ave Maria College undergraduate, who did a great deal of work on the patristic citations and the citations of the Gospel of John in the *Summa theologiae*. John Boyle made a number of suggestions regarding the notes and introduction that greatly improved the result. Guy Mansini, O.S.B., served as a master translator when two brief passages were found in the Latin text that had been overlooked by Frs. Larcher and Weisheipl. Jörgen Vijgen checked the citations of the Gospel of John in the *Summa theologiae* and saved us from a number of errors. He also found one of the untranslated sentences. To these three long-standing friends, our debts of gratitude continue to mount. We thank God for the privilege of working together on this project; may it be a service to his Word.

INTRODUCTION

St. Thomas Aquinas's faithful scribe, Reginald of Piperno, append-
ed the following remark to the original manuscript of the *Lectura super
Ioannem*:

> Here therefore is what I, Friar Reginald of Piperno, of the Order of
> Preachers, at the request of certain companions and particularly at the
> order of the reverend Father Lord Provost of Saint-Omer, have gath-
> ered together in following Friar Thomas Aquinas—just like—just like
> he who gathers the grapes [left] after the harvest. Please God that it is
> not too inadequate to the work.[1]

From this note, scholars have gathered that the *Super Ioannem* is Reginald's *reportatio*, or course notes, on Aquinas's lectures on the Gospel of John. Jean-Pierre Torrell estimates that Aquinas delivered these
lectures before students at the University of Paris between 1270 and
1272, shortly before Aquinas's death but while he was still at the peak
of his powers. Torrell argues that Aquinas probably never revised Reginald's *reportatio*.[2] As Thomas Prügl observes, nonetheless, "The quality of these notes was so remarkable that they were accepted by the
University of Paris as an exemplar, that is, an official copy serving as
an authentic text for further copying."[3] Torrell judges the *Super Ioannem* to be among Aquinas's most valuable biblical commentaries:
"It would be a bit foolish to try drawing up a ranking of Thomas's
best scriptural commentaries, but it is certain that we could classify
this one as among the most fully finished and most profound that he
has left us."[4] In the best passages of the *Super Ioannem*, "Thomas reveals himself . . . as one of the contemplatives of whom St. John is the
model."[5]

---

1. Quoted in Jean-Pierre Torrell, O.P., *Saint Thomas Aquinas*, Vol. 1: *The Person
and His Work*, trans. Robert Royal (Washington, D.C.: The Catholic University of
America Press, 1996), 198–99.
2. Torrell, *Saint Thomas Aquinas*, vol. 1, 199.
3. Thomas Prügl, "Thomas Aquinas as Interpreter of Scripture," in *The Theology of Thomas Aquinas*, ed. Rik Van Nieuwenhove and Joseph Wawrykow (Notre
Dame, Ind.: University of Notre Dame Press, 2005), 386–415, at 390.
4. Torrell, *Saint Thomas Aquinas*, vol. 1, 200.
5. Ibid., 201.

Biblical Commentary and *Sacra Doctrina*

If we follow Torrell's time frame, we find that at the height of his career Aquinas was—among other projects—lecturing regularly on the Gospel of John, commenting on the works of Aristotle, and composing the *tertia pars* of the *Summa theologiae*.[6] These concurrent projects illustrate how integral Scholastic theologians considered philosophical inquiry and biblical commentary to be for the transmission of *sacra doctrina*. In this regard, Nicholas M. Healy has well described the high Scholastic understanding of the Master's task: "The pedagogical function of theological inquiry is to train readers of Scripture so that they read it more profoundly and with less error, in order that they may go forth into the world and preach the gospel. The best kind of training is that whereby students discuss Scripture under the authority and guidance of the master, using reason and dialectic."[7] Aquinas's intense labor served this integration of scriptural exegesis with "reason and dialectic" and "theological inquiry."

To Healy's description of the Master's task, one might add the goal of contemplation. The Master must lead the student to understand how the various topics of theological inquiry have their place under the rubric of the study of the triune God. Understood as sapiential contemplation of God, *sacra doctrina* aims not merely at understanding Scripture per se, but at an intellectual (and affective) union with realities taught by Scripture, so as to attain a foretaste of beatific contemplation. As Aquinas explains, "the purpose of this science [*sacra doctrina*], in so far as it is practical, is eternal bliss."[8] Likewise he states that *sacra doctrina*, as a particular body of knowledge or *scientia*, "proceeds from principles established by the light of a higher *scientia*, namely, the *scientia* of God and the blessed."[9] Scripture reveals these principles and enables human minds to participate somewhat in God's own knowledge even prior to the beatitude enjoyed by the blessed in heaven. This participation requires intellectual reflection that is enlightened by faith, humbled by charity, and disciplined by philosophical reasoning.

To place a strict separation between the biblical commentaries and the *Summa theologiae* would therefore be a mistake. Not only is Scripture the primary source of "scientific" and sapiential expositions of theology, but also the discussions found in the biblical commentaries

---

6. See ibid., chapter 12, for discussion of the commentaries on Aristotle's works.

7. Nicholas M. Healy, "Introduction," in *Aquinas on Scripture: An Introduction to His Biblical Commentaries*, ed. Thomas G. Weinandy, O.F.M. Cap., Daniel A. Keating, and John P. Yocum (New York: T. & T. Clark, 2005), 12.

8. *Summa theologiae* [hereafter, *ST*] I, q. 1, a. 5.

9. *ST* I, q. 1, a. 2. He later adds, "Sacred doctrine derives its principles not from any human knowledge, but from the divine knowledge, through which, as through the highest wisdom, all our knowledge is set in order" (I, q. 1, a. 6, ad 1).

recur throughout the *Summa theologiae*. In fact, Prügl points out, the difference between the biblical commentaries and the *Summa theologiae* is "modest,"[10] because Scripture is *sacra doctrina* and thus itself possesses an ordering wisdom that Aquinas, like other high Scholastics, sought to illumine by the method of *divisio textus*.[11] Prügl goes on to say, "The 'advantage' of the *Summa* lies in the fact that its endeavors are not tied to the continuous text of a biblical book; its topics are instead 'freely' arranged according to the requirements of the theological discipline [*secundum ordinem doctrinae, non secundum quod requirebat librorum expositio*]."[12] As set forth in a *Summa*, the ordering wisdom of the biblically revealed principles should possess a distinct clarity— which explains why Aquinas carefully revised his *Summa theologiae* but not his biblical commentaries. Yet, no high Scholastic theologian gave up the task of commenting on Scripture. As Torrell says, "The great systematic works have monopolized attention. But 'to read' Scripture was the first task for the master in theology, and therefore also for Thomas."[13] Understanding St. Thomas thus calls for uniting scholarship on his *Summae* with scholarship on his biblical commentaries. Torrell affirms, "If we wish, therefore, to get a slightly less one-sided idea of the whole theologian and his method, it is imperative to read and use in a much deeper fashion these biblical commentaries in parallel with the great systematic works."[14]

Scholarly Study of Aquinas's Biblical Commentaries

When Torrell wrote those words in 1993, there existed no book-length study, so far as we know, of Aquinas's *Lectura super Ioannem*. There did not even exist a full French or English translation of the *Super Ioannem*. Since that time, fortunately, the situation has changed rather significantly.[15] Clearly, this surge in interest in Aquinas's biblical com-

10. Prügl, "Thomas Aquinas as Interpreter of Scripture," 403.
11. On this point, see ibid., 401–2.
12. Ibid., 403–4. The quotation is from the Prologue to the *prima pars* of the *ST*.
13. Torrell, *Saint Thomas Aquinas*, vol. 1, 55.
14. Ibid.
15. Pim Valkenberg's study of Aquinas's use of Scripture in the *ST*, originally published in 1990, received a much larger print run in 2000 under the title *Words of the Living God: Place and Function of Holy Scripture in the Theology of St. Thomas Aquinas* (Leuven: Peeters, 2000). Book-length studies of Aquinas's commentaries on the Psalms, on the Letter to the Ephesians, and on the Letter to the Hebrews have appeared, by Thomas F. Ryan (2000), Christopher T. Baglow (2002), and Antoine Guggenheim (2004), respectively. See Thomas F. Ryan, *Thomas Aquinas as Reader of the Psalms* (Notre Dame, Ind.: University of Notre Dame Press, 2000); Christopher T. Baglow, "Modus et Forma": *A New Approach to the Exegesis of Saint Thomas Aquinas with an Application to the* Lectura super Epistolam ad Ephesios (Rome: Pontifical Biblical Institute Press, 2002); and Antoine Guggenheim, *Jé-*

mentaries in general and the *Lectura super Ioannem* in particular marks a major step, even if only a preliminary one, toward the accomplishment of Torrell's goal that scholars learn to "read and use in a much deeper fashion these biblical commentaries in parallel with the great systematic works." Around the same time, the second and final volume of the English translation of the *Super Ioannem* finally appeared in 1999, nineteen years after the publication of the first volume.[16] Unfortunately, almost immediately after its appearance, this second volume joined the first one in going out of print, having sold out its print run. In recent years, those who led the original effort to publish English translations of Aquinas's biblical commentaries have passed to the Lord: one thinks especially of Fabian Larcher, O.P., Pierre Conway, O.P., and Thomas Gallagher, publisher of Magi Books, who spent his last years editing the 1999 volume of the second half of the *Super Ioannem*.

The present republication of the English translation of Aquinas's *Lectura super Ioannem* corresponds with growing scholarly attention to the commentary and validates the important work of Fabian Larcher and his contemporaries. In preparing this republication of Fr. Larcher's translation (whose first eight chapters were corrected by James Weisheipl, O.P., for the 1980 edition), we have corrected typographical errors, clarified a few translation problems, and added one short section from the commentary on chapter fifteen, lecture three, that was missing from the original edition. We have also added a prologue attributed to St. Jerome with a commentary by St. Thomas, translated by Becket Soule, O.P. This was not part of the volume published by Fr. Larcher in 1980. The prologue does not appear in any of the extant works of Jerome (and so its authenticity is questionable), but the text

*sus Christ, grand prêtre de l'ancienne et de la nouvelle alliance. Étude du Commentaire de saint Thomas d'Aquin sur l'*Épître aux Hébreux (Geneva: Parole et Silence, 2004). Thomas G. Weinandy, O.F.M. Cap., Daniel A. Keating, and John P. Yocum edited *Aquinas on Scripture: An Introduction to His Biblical Commentaries* (2005), a collection of essays covering the majority of Aquinas's commentaries. With particular focus upon the *Lectura super Ioannem*, Pierre-Yves Maillard published a study of the vision of God (2001) and Denis-Dominique Le Pivain a study of the Holy Spirit's action (2006); Michael Dauphinais and Matthew Levering edited a collection of essays, *Reading John with St. Thomas Aquinas* (2005), which also contains a lengthy bibliography of publications treating Aquinas's biblical commentaries. See Pierre-Yves Maillard, O.P., *La vision de Dieu chez Thomas d'Aquin. Une lecture de l'In Ioannem à la lumière de ses sources augustiniennes* (Paris: Vrin, 2001); Denis-Dominique Le Pivain, F.S.S.P., *L'action du Saint-Esprit dans le commentaire de l'évangile de saint Jean par saint Thomas d'Aquin* (Paris: Téqui, 2006); and Michael Dauphinais and Matthew Levering, *Reading John with St. Thomas Aquinas: Theological Exegesis and Speculative Theology* (Washington, D.C.: The Catholic University of America Press, 2005).

16. St. Thomas Aquinas, *Commentary on the Gospel of Saint John*, trans. Fabian Larcher, O.P. and James A. Weisheipl, O.P., 2 vols. (Albany, N.Y.: Magi Books, 1980; Petersham, Mass.: St. Bede's Publications, 1999).

has been traced back to the sixth century and several medieval authors (St. Bonaventure, St. Albert, Hugh of St. Cher, Nicholas of Lyra, and St. Thomas) attribute it to Jerome. We are including Jerome's prologue and Aquinas's commentary on it primarily because the latter sheds further light on Aquinas's overall estimation of the Gospel of John.

The most significant addition we have made is to situate Aquinas's *Commentary on John* more clearly and directly in relationship to his patristic sources and to his *Summa theologiae*. When Aquinas quotes a patristic author, we provide the full citation of that source in either the Patrologia Latina or Patrologia Graeca (but we have not done this for the many allusions where he does not cite his source).[17] We have also noted when the patristic source that Aquinas cites appears in the *Catena aurea* (which is his own collection of patristic texts on the four gospels). Similarly, without claiming to have caught every instance, we note where a given verse from the Gospel of John appears in the *Summa theologiae*, thereby enabling both a direct comparison of Aquinas's discussion of the verse in his *Super Ioannem* with his use(s) of the verse in the *Summa theologiae*, and an appreciation of which verses from the Gospel of John are deemed by Aquinas to be most important for his theological reflection in the various parts of the *Summa*.

Since the *Super Ioannem* itself contains a large amount of speculative theological reflection, we have also noted discussions of the same or similar themes in the *Summa theologiae*, so as to assist readers in moving from the commentary to the *Summa*. In general, these are not *loca parallela* in the traditional sense. Instead, these notes point the reader to further speculative background in the *Summa* regarding a particular theme that appears in the *Super Ioannem*. The *Summa* aims at enabling theologians to read Scripture well, and so the insights of the *Summa* are often presumed in the commentary. Our notes, while not exhaustive, seek to identify key places where this is so. In addition, when Aquinas refers to councils, heresies, or lesser-known figures, we have provided an explanatory note giving information about the person or event in question. So as to avoid confusion, we should also observe that we have kept the Vulgate numbering of the Psalms.

Fr. Larcher's translation is based on the Parma, Vivès, and Marietti Latin editions of the *Commentary on John*.[18] It is not, however, based upon a critical edition of Aquinas's *Super Ioannem*, since none exists.

17. We have attempted to identify as many of the patristic sources as possible. For this task, the English edition of the *Catena aurea* has been indispensable, and the footnotes from the French edition of Aquinas's *Commentary on John* have been gratefully mined in order to identify many of the original sources: Thomas D'Aquin, *Commentaire sur l'Évangile de saint Jean*, vol. 1, introduction and trans. M.-D. Philippe (Paris: Les Éditions du Cerf, 1998).

18. See "A Note to the Reader," in St. Thomas Aquinas, *Commentary on the Gospel of St. John*, part II (Petersham, Mass.: St. Bede's Publications, 1999).

The Leonine edition of Aquinas's *Super Ioannem* has not appeared and—from what we can foresee—will not appear for some years. Since the variations in the extant texts (thirty-three complete and thirteen incomplete surviving manuscript copies) of the *Super Ioannem* are relatively few, it is to be hoped that the eventual publication of the Leonine edition of the *Commentary* will require only slight adjustments in this English edition.

Spiritual and Literal Senses

In the *Lectura super Ioannem*, Aquinas employs the spiritual sense relatively rarely. Not all chapters in his commentary contain even one example of the spiritual sense. This does not mean, however, that Aquinas disdained the spiritual sense. Thomas Prügl observes that "any attempt to reduce his exegesis to a wrestling between the spiritual and literal sense would represent a gross misunderstanding of his concerns. The discussion of different senses in Scripture illustrates merely one aspect of his exegesis."[19] Rather than seeking in his exegesis to prioritize one sense over another, Aquinas is concerned throughout his exegesis, as Prügl goes on to say, "with the most important task of theology: encountering the ultimate and greatest mystery of faith, God and the ways in which He reveals Himself to humanity for our salvation."[20] The encounter with "God Teaching" is at the heart of Aquinas's exegetical work, and the literal and spiritual senses of Scripture serve this encounter.

An example of this appears in Aquinas's commentary on Jn 20:17, "Jesus said to her [Mary Magdalene], 'Do not hold me, for I have not yet ascended to the Father; but go to my brethren and say to them, I am ascending to my Father and your Father, to my God and your God.'" The difficulty consists in understanding why Christ told Mary Magdalene not to hold him. After all, Aquinas points out, the very opposite is found in other post-Resurrection accounts, for instance Lk 24:39, "Handle me, and see; for a spirit has not flesh and bones" (no. 2516). In Matt 28:9, similarly, Mary Magdalene and the other women were allowed to take hold of the risen Christ's feet. These instances suggest that in addition to the literal meaning of Jesus' words to Mary Magdalene in Jn 20:17, there is a meaning that the Holy Spirit seeks to teach believers.

What meaning might this be? Why would Christ tell Mary Magdalene, at this meeting, not to hold him? Aquinas offers two "mystical reasons" from Augustine (no. 2517). Augustine's mystical readings presuppose the literal sense, namely, that Christ is a teacher, which Mary

19. Prügl, "Thomas Aquinas as Interpreter of Scripture," 391–92.
20. Ibid., 406.

Magdalene proclaims him to be in the preceding verse. Christ therefore speaks here in order to teach Mary Magdalene, and those who believe in him, an important truth. Augustine's first mystical reading presents Christ as teaching through mystical symbolism, as Christ does often in the Gospel of John. If we read Christ's words, in their context, as mystical teaching, Mary Magdalene could symbolize "the Church of the Gentiles, which was not to touch Christ by faith until he had ascended to the Father" (no. 2517). Jesus may intend to teach us through mystical symbolism a truth about the Church, whose permanent center is Israel to whom Christ preached in the flesh. Augustine's second mystical reading suggests that "touch is the last stage of knowledge: when we see something, we know it to a certain extent, but when we touch it our knowledge is complete" (no. 2517). Mary Magdalene may know Jesus to a certain extent, but not yet know him fully as the divine Son. Jesus would then be teaching her how to know him. She should not think that she already knows him fully ("hold" or "touch" him) in the limited sense that she now sees him; she must seek to see him spiritually.

Augustine, followed by Aquinas, in this way presents the encounter between Jesus and Mary Magdalene as a spiritual or mystical instruction concerning how Mary Magdalene must learn to know Jesus, understandable (and therefore interpretable) only in faith. Aquinas summarizes Augustine's second interpretation:

> Thus Christ says, "Do not hold me," that is, do not allow what you now believe of me to be the limit of your faith, "for I have not yet ascended to my Father," that is, in your heart, because you do not believe that I am one with him—yet she did believe this later. In a way Christ did ascend to the Father within her when she had advanced in the faith to the point of believing that he was equal to the Father (no. 2517).

Such mystical interpretations, Aquinas makes clear, do not compete with the literal sense, but illumine it. In this case, he draws the literal sense from John Chrysostom. Chrysostom supposes that Mary Magdalene, seeing Jesus, thinks of him simply as a man who, having died, has now risen from the grave to return to his former bodily life. Such a response on Mary Magdalene's part would not be surprising. On this reading, Jesus' instruction to Mary not to hold him "was like saying: Do not think that I have a mortal life, and can associate with you as before: 'Even though we once regarded Christ from a human point of view, we regard him thus no longer' (2 Cor 5:16)" (no. 2518). Similarly, Jesus' remark that "I have not yet ascended to my father" would explain why he was in this transitional state, visible to her as if continuing his mortal life. The transitional state belonged to his desire to teach his followers: "For before he ascended he wanted to strengthen in the hearts of the

apostles their faith in his resurrection and in his divinity" (no. 2518).
The mystical or spiritual sense, in short, builds upon and manifests the literal sense, namely, that Christ is the Teacher, both before and after his Resurrection. This literal sense corresponds with Aquinas's understanding of Scripture as a privileged mode (because its principal author is the Holy Spirit) of *sacra doctrina*. To cite Prügl again: "Aquinas views Scripture as a part—indeed, a central part—of this encompassing project of transmitting divine knowledge, which starts in God's wisdom, continues in the revelation of the incarnate Logos, arrives at the apostles as main witnesses of Christ's deeds and words, and is eventually transmitted from the biblical authors to the interpreters of Scripture."[21] The mystical sense here arises from and deepens Aquinas's keen appreciation of Christ, in the literal sense, as the Teacher of *sacra doctrina*.[22] That there is a mystical sense comes from the fact that Christ, by the Holy Spirit, teaches both literally, at the level of the interchange between himself and Mary Magdalene, and spiritually, using that historical interchange as symbolism for further teaching about realities such as the Church or the act of faith.

Aquinas often uses the spiritual sense without dividing it into allegorical, moral, and anagogical, preferring to call it simply the "mystical" sense. He is nonetheless aware of the division. For instance, he proposes an allegorical reading of Jn 1:35 (no. 281) and of Jn 1:38 (no. 290), as well as a moral reading of Jn 1:38. As we will see below, he cites Origen on the anagogical sense of Jn 2:22 (no. 415). He has no hesitation in specifying and employing the different senses.

Regarding the literal sense in the biblical commentaries, a question that frequently arises is whether Aquinas allows that a particular biblical passage can have more than one literal sense. Certainly, Aquinas denies that any merely human exegete can so fully apprehend the literal sense of certain biblical passages as to exclude further literal senses. As we will see, therefore, he frequently places side by side, without deciding between them, quite different interpretations of the literal sense, generally taken from the Fathers. As Thomas Prügl states, however, Aquinas also affirms that "the meaning remains rooted in the text and must not be arbitrarily separated from it by the interpreter."[23] Aquinas further holds that the creedal articles of faith, as set forth by the Church's Magisterium, impose definite limits on the range of possible literal interpretations.[24]

---

21. Ibid., 392.
22. See also Michael Sherwin, O.P., "Christ the Teacher in St. Thomas's *Commentary on the Gospel of John*," in *Reading John with St. Thomas Aquinas*, 173–93; Michael Dauphinais, *The Pedagogy of the Incarnation: Christ the Teacher According to St. Thomas Aquinas*, Ph.D. dissertation, University of Notre Dame, 2000.
23. Prügl, "Thomas Aquinas as Interpreter of Scripture," 395.
24. Thus one might need to qualify Prügl's remark that for Aquinas "the in-

Aquinas's Sources

Parallel Biblical Texts

An extraordinary profusion of "parallel" biblical texts characterizes Aquinas's *Lectura super Ioannem*, which whenever possible seeks to interpret Scripture through Scripture. This profusion of parallel texts displays how Aquinas conceives of the richness of the realities depicted in Scripture. He ranges throughout the Old and New Testament with a freedom that is possible only for one who believes that the realities of faith are present and active throughout history, preparing for and/ or fulfilling the work of deification in Christ through the Holy Spirit. Brevard Childs considers Aquinas's citation of parallel passages as a sophisticated form of "intertextuality," wherein "a catena of verses without commentary . . . prompts the reader to reflect on the nature of the reality undergirding these different witnesses."[25]

We can take as a representative example, among so many, Aquinas's commentary on Jn 1:16–18, "And from his fullness have we all received, grace upon grace. For the law was given through Moses; grace and truth came through Jesus Christ. No one has ever seen God; the only Son, who is in the bosom of the Father, he has made him known." His commentary on these verses runs somewhat more than four thousand words in total.

To what other biblical passages does Aquinas refer in order to elucidate these three verses from John's Gospel? With regard to grace (Jn 1:16 and 1:17), Thomas refers to Stephen in Acts and to the Virgin Mary in Lk 1:28. He crosslists texts about the Holy Spirit from 1 Cor 12:11, Jl 2:28, Rom 8:9, and Wis 1:7. He also cites passages that have to do with God's grace in Sir 24:26, Eph 4:7, Prov 4:2, Rom 3:1, Rom 6:23, Rom 11:6, and Zech 4:7. With regard to Moses and Christ (Jn 1:17), he compares Christ and Moses by recourse to Deut 6:4, Deut 34:10, Is 33:22, 2 Cor 3:9, Heb 7:19 (twice), Heb 10:1, and Rom 6:6, as well as Jn 14:6 and 18:37.

Lastly, with regard to the question of whether any human being or angel has ever seen God (Jn 1:18), Aquinas turns to Ex 33:20, Is 6:1, Is 45:15, Prov 30:4, 2 Sam 6:2, 1 Tim 6:16, Matt 5:8, Matt 18:10, Matt 22:30, 1 Jn 3:2, Gen 18:1–3, Gen 32:30, Wis 13:5, Rom 1:20, Job 36:25, Job 36:26, Jer 32:18, 2 Cor 5:8, and 2 Cor 12:3, as well as Jn 4:24 and

---

terpretation of Scripture is never final because the Holy Spirit imbues the texts with a degree of vitality that continues to affect the Church in ever new ways and at all times" (396). Truths taught *de fide* by the Church do constitute, for Aquinas, definitively truthful interpretations of Scripture. Though such interpretations are not final in one sense because they can develop in depth, they are final in another sense in that they can never be contradicted.

25. Brevard Childs, *The Struggle to Understand Isaiah as Christian Scripture* (Grand Rapids, Mich.: Eerdmans, 2004), 160.

17:3. He investigates Christ's unique knowledge of God by means of Ps 2:7, Ps 109:3, 1 Cor 2:11, Matt 11:27, Is 52:6, Heb 1:1, and Heb 2:3.

In short, in his treatment of three verses from the Gospel of John, Aquinas cites three of the four Gospels, eleven of the twenty-seven books of the New Testament, and thirteen books of the Old Testament, including three of the five books of the Pentateuch as well as texts from the historical books, the prophets, the psalms, and the wisdom literature. Obviously some of these "parallel" biblical passages have more clear application than others, a point that is particularly in evidence with regard to the Old Testament texts. Even so, it could be shown that almost every one of the texts employed by Aquinas has a clear theological relationship with the verses from John 1.

While such a profusion of parallel biblical passages does not occur equally for every three verses of the Gospel of John, nonetheless we have here an accurate portrait of Aquinas's effort to read Scripture by means of Scripture. These parallel biblical passages differ from the ones chosen by Albert the Great in his commentary on John; unless we are mistaken, many of them are original to Aquinas himself.

Patristic Commentary

One of the hallmarks of Aquinas's biblical commentaries is his liberal citation of the Fathers. Especially for his era, Thomas's access to, and use of, the Greek Fathers is particularly noteworthy. In the early 1260s, Pope Urban IV asked Thomas—then resident in Orvieto—to provide a Gospel commentary based upon the Latin and Greek Fathers. Though Urban lived to see only the first volume completed (in 1264), Thomas went on to finish this massive project, a work known to us as the *Catena aurea* (the "Golden Chain").[26]

In the Introduction to the 1997 reprint of the English edition of the *Catena aurea*, Aidan Nichols observes that "the patristic research represented by the *Catena aurea* is, for its time, staggering."[27] Thomas cites more than fifty authors in the four-volume commentary, mostly from the patristic era, but also from the medieval period, including the *Glossa Interlinearis* and the *Glossa Ordinaria*. He undoubtedly took many of his citations from earlier collected *catenae* of patristic citations, but it also appears that he had access to complete commentaries as well. When compiling the *Catena aurea* on John, Aquinas relied principal-

26. For Aquinas's use of the Church Fathers, see Leo J. Elders, "Thomas Aquinas and the Fathers of the Church," in Irena Backus, ed., *The Reception of the Church Fathers in the West: From the Carolingians to the Maurists*, vol. 1 (Leiden: E. J. Brill, 1997), 337–66.

27. Aidan Nichols, "Introduction to the 1997 Republished Edition," *Catena Aurea* (Southampton, U.K.: Saint Austin Press, 1997), v; English edition first published in 1841, ed. John Henry Newman.

ly on a few select authors. He cites far fewer sources overall (approximately sixteen) than he does in the *Catena* for the Synoptic Gospels, and he depends largely on three authors: Origen, Augustine, and John Chrysostom.[28]

Origen. The practice of line-by-line commentary on the Gospel of John in the patristic period had a curious beginning. Though we find individual references to John's Gospel in the anti-Gnostic writings of Irenaeus (c. 180), the first recorded commentary on the fourth Gospel comes from the Valentinian Gnostic teacher, Heracleon, toward the end of the second century. Prompted in part by Heracleon's work, Origen of Alexandria undertook his own massive commentary on John, composing thirty-two books between the years 230 and 242. It is Origen who has preserved fragments of Heracleon's work, refuting the Gnostic's interpretations in the context of his own commentary. In turn, Origen's commentary had an enormous influence on subsequent interpretation of John in both the East and the West.

Scholars surmise that Origen never finished his commentary on John's Gospel, but instead ended at Jn 13:33—worn out, perhaps, by having devoted more than three hundred pages to Jn 1:1–29.[29] From the thirty-two books that originally made up Origen's commentary, only books 1, 2, 6, 10, 13, 19, 20, 28, and 32 survive in Greek.[30] It is not surprising, then, that thirty-six of Aquinas's eighty-five references to Origen appear in his discussion of chapter one of John's Gospel. Of the remainder, thirteen appear in his discussion of John 8, eleven in his discussion of John 13, nine in his discussion of John 4, six in his discussion of John 2, and four in his discussion of John 11. The remaining few are scattered in various chapters, and refer at times not to

28. Aquinas does not appear to have had access to the full-length commentaries on the Gospel of John by Theodore of Mopsuestia (c. 410) and Cyril of Alexandria (c. 425–27). Theodore's commentary, available in full only in Syriac translation, represents the epitome of Antiochene biblical commentary, a close and careful adherence to the plain sense of the text, but with little exploration of wider biblical connections and themes. Cyril's massive commentary on John, the largest extant commentary from the patristic period, presents a Christological interpretation of John, and is commonly judged to represent the finest theological commentary on John among the Greek Fathers. In the West, citations of John appear in the more significant Latin Fathers (Tertullian, Novatian, Cyprian, Hilary, Ambrose, and Jerome), but the only full-length treatment of the fourth Gospel comes from the pen of Augustine. For the history of the Fourth Gospel in the Latin Fathers, see Douglas J. Milewski, *Nos Locus Dei Sumus: Augustine's Exegesis and Theology of John 17 in the Light of* In Evangelium Iohannis Tractatus *CIV–CXI* (Rome: Institutum Patristicum Augustinianum, 2000), 61–84.

29. See Ronald E. Heine, "Introduction," in *Origen: Commentary on the Gospel According to John Books 1–10*, trans. Ronald E. Heine (Washington, D.C.: The Catholic University of America Press, 1989), 7.

30. Ibid., 8.

Origen's commentary on John but to other texts of Origen. There are no references to Origen in Aquinas's discussion of John 5–7, 9, 14, and 16–20.

When Origen's name does appear, we find a wide variation in Aquinas's appraisal of Origen's interpretations. On the one hand, approximately ten percent of the references criticize Origen's position, often in strong terms. Discussing the affirmation in Jn 1:1 that "the Word was God," for example, Aquinas observes,

> We should note that Origen disgracefully misunderstood this clause, led astray by the Greek manner of speaking. It is the custom among the Greeks to put the article before every name in order to indicate a distinction. In the Greek version of John's Gospel the name "Word" in the statement, *In the beginning was the Word*, and also the name "God" in the statement, *and the Word was with God*, are prefixed by an article, so as to read "the Word" and "the God," in order to indicate the eminence and distinction of the Word from other words, and the principality of the Father in the divinity. But in the statement, *the Word was God*, the article is not prefixed to the noun "God," which stands for the person of the Son. Because of this Origen blasphemed that the Word, although he was Word by essence, was not God by essence, but is called God by participation; while the Father alone is God by essence. And so he held that the Son is inferior to the Father (no. 58).

Against Origen's position, Aquinas provides a lengthy argument from St. John Chrysostom. Aquinas goes on to pair Origen with Arius, since both denied the full divinity of the Son (no. 126).[31]

Nonetheless, the great majority of Aquinas's references to Origen in the *Super Ioannem* treat him as a highly valuable interpreter. Given that Origen devoted significant portions of his commentary to critiquing the views of Heracleon, a disciple of Valentinus, Aquinas draws upon Origen to criticize Gnostic readings of the Gospel of John. With regard to Jn 1:3, for example, Aquinas observes that some thinkers had interpreted the phrase "without him nothing was made" as if "nothing" were a substantial reality. Following Origen, Aquinas describes in some detail the view of Valentinus, who held this position regarding Jn 1:3:

> [Valentinus] affirmed, as Origen says, a multitude of principles, and taught that from them came thirty eras. The first principles he postu-

31. Aquinas also denounces Origen for his denial of the full divinity of the Holy Spirit (no. 74), for teaching that the Son is the subordinate instrument of the Father (no. 75), for speculating that Christ's soul preexisted his body (no. 467), and for asserting that all would be saved (no. 486). The strength of the charges against Origen stem not just from indications in his own writings, but from later condemnations of exaggerated Origenist teaching in his followers in the fourth, fifth, and sixth centuries.

lates are two: The Deep, which he calls God the Father, and Silence.
And from these proceed ten eras. But from the Deep and from Silence,
he says, there are two other principles, Mind and Truth; and from these
issued eight eras. Then from Mind and Truth, there are two other principles, Word and Life; and from these issued twelve eras; thus making a
total of thirty. Finally, from the Word and Life there proceeded in time,
the man Christ and the Church. In this way Valentinus affirmed many
eras previous to the issuing forth of the Word (no. 80).

The Gnostics also taught that the Father of Jesus Christ is different
from the God of the Old Testament, and that evil is a substance (and
coprinciple with good). In commenting upon Jn 8:19 and 8:44, Aquinas cites Origen for help in refuting both these positions.

Origen provides an important source for Aquinas's use of the spiritual sense of Scripture as well. Aquinas's commentary on John 2 offers an example of this influence. Discussing Jn 2:19, where Jesus
says "Destroy this temple, and in three days I will raise it up," Aquinas
states that Origen "assigns a mystical reason for this expression, and
says: The true body of Christ is the temple of God, and this body symbolizes the mystical body, i.e., the Church" (no. 404). Likewise, Aquinas accepts Origen's anagogical reading of Jn 2:22, where the evangelist relates, "When therefore he was raised from the dead, his disciples
remembered that he had said this" (no. 415). Origen finds in this verse
the promise that after our resurrection from the dead, we will understand things that before our resurrection are obscure to us. Again,
commenting on Jn 4:21, Aquinas adopts Origen's explanation that Jesus' discussion of worship with the Samaritan woman may mystically
be interpreted as showing that "the three types of worship are three
kinds of participation in divine wisdom," namely, erroneous worship,
the Church's imperfect worship, and the perfection of the heavenly
Jerusalem. Such examples of Aquinas's use of Origen on the spiritual
sense of Scripture could be multiplied.

As regards the literal sense, Aquinas frequently cites Origen posi-
tively. Regarding Jn 1:2 in relationship to 1:1, Aquinas states: "Origen gives a rather beautiful explanation of this clause, 'He was in the
beginning with God,' when he says that it is not separate from the
first three, but is in a certain sense their epilogue" (no. 63). According
to Origen, followed by Aquinas, the clause points back to "In the beginning" (1:1), "was God" (1:1), and "was with God." Similarly, interpreting Jn 1:3–4, Aquinas notes that Augustine, Origen, and Hilary of
Poitiers each give a different meaning to the Greek. Whereas the mod-
ern Revised Standard Version has "that was made. In him was life,"
Aquinas accepts the reading "What was made in him was life" (no.
89f.). He then observes that Augustine constructs the sentence "What
was made in him" / "was life," whereas Origen constructs the sentence

"What was made" / "in him was life." The theological differences that these constructions imply enable Aquinas to reflect fruitfully on the variety of possibilities within the literal sense of the text. Again, interpreting Jn 1:10, "He was in the world," Aquinas praises Origen's literal reading of this verse as being about creatures' presence in the Word: "Origen uses an apt example to show this, when he says that as a human vocal sound is to a human word conceived in the mind, so is the creature to the divine Word; for as our vocal sound is the effect of the work conceived in our mind, so the creature is the effect of the Word conceived in the divine mind" (no. 135). Just as with the spiritual sense, examples of Aquinas's appreciation for Origen's literal reading could easily be multiplied.

Augustine. Augustine's commentary on John, which Aquinas possessed in full, is a constant presence in Aquinas's own commentary.[32] The first chapter of Aquinas's *Super Ioannem* cites Augustine more than forty times, and this reliance continues throughout each chapter of the *Super Ioannem*. Augustine provides a central source for the literal sense (inclusive of technical theological discussions), as well as the spiritual sense.

Although Aquinas generally places Augustine's interpretation side-by-side with other patristic interpreters such as Chrysostom, Origen, and Hilary,[33] at times he draws upon Augustine's commentary in a more exclusive fashion, especially when the biblical text involves a theme that has particular significance in Augustine's theology. Thus, for example, Aquinas's discussion of Jn 1:1, "In the beginning was the Word," draws heavily and at times exclusively upon Augustine's commentary in seeking to explain the meaning of the term "Word" (see nos. 25–29)—although Aristotle and John Damascene are also present here. A similar representative example of reliance on Augustine's commentary is Aquinas's discussion of "Peace I leave with you; my peace

32. The *Tractates on the Gospel of John,* written between 406 and 421, treat the entire Gospel against the backdrop, first of the Donatist, and then of the Pelagian, controversies. The dating of the *Tractates* is debated, but there is general agreement that they should be divided into two distinct groupings: the first group, *Tractates* 1–54, makes regular reference to the Donatists, and is dated either c. 405–408 or c. 411–414; the second group, *Tractates* 55–124, shows a Pelagian background, and is dated c. 416–418. See John W. Rettig, *Tractates on the Gospel of John: 1–10,* Fathers of the Church 78 (Washington, D.C.: The Catholic University of America Press, 1988), 23–31, for a summary of the scholarly debate over the date of the *Tractates.*

33. See, for example, the commentary on Jn 16:14, "I did not say these things to you from the beginning, because I was with you," where Aquinas develops two possible explanations of the literal sense from Augustine, but then offers a different account from Chrysostom (no. 2081). Repeatedly, Aquinas pairs the interpretations of Augustine with John Chrysostom and others, without choosing between them.

I give to you" (Jn 14:27). Aquinas has in view Augustine's theology of "peace," which plays such a crucial role in Augustine's anthropology, political theory, and eschatology. In order to explore its theological ramifications, Aquinas devotes a distinct "lecture" in his commentary to the first half of Jn 14:27.

According to Augustine's famous definition, employed here by Aquinas, "Peace is nothing else than the tranquility arising from order" (no. 1962).[34] Following Augustine without explicit attribution, Aquinas observes that human beings exhibit a threefold "order." The soul and body should be properly ordered, as happens when the intellect directs the will and the intellect and will direct the sense appetites; the person should be rightly ordered to other created persons by the bond of love; and the person should be rightly ordered to God by loving God above all things. Given this threefold order, "peace" is also threefold, as Aquinas affirms through biblical quotations: interior (with oneself), with one's neighbor, and with God.

In its full meaning, it is clear that even the followers of Christ, on earth, do not enjoy perfect "peace." Aquinas recognizes this tension: "The saints [true Christians] have this peace now, and will have it in the future. But here it is imperfect because we cannot have an undisturbed peace either within ourselves, or with God, or with our neighbor. We will enjoy it perfectly in the future, when we reign without an enemy and there can never be conflicts" (no. 1962). Thus Aquinas, following Augustine, proposes that when Jesus describes "peace" in two ways—"Peace I leave with you, my peace I give to you"—Jesus is describing two degrees of peace, imperfect and perfect. Without peace, the fruit of the grace of the Holy Spirit, Jesus' followers would be unable to be sanctified on earth, and would remain entirely unjust (disordered) in themselves, in relation to other created persons, and in relation to God. Aquinas cites Augustine to the effect that "one cannot gain the inheritance of the Lord who is unwilling to observe his covenant, nor can he have a union with Christ if he lives in strife with a Christian" (no. 1962).

In addition to this imperfect "peace," the second way of describing "peace"—"my peace I give to you"—indicates a second sense of "peace," namely, the perfect peace that we will enjoy in heaven. Jesus characterizes this peace as "my peace" because it is perfect, just as his peace has always been perfect. As Aquinas notes, "He always had this second kind of peace, because he was always without conflict" (no. 1963). Yet, is the "peace" that Jesus leaves with us (the first way of describing peace) also Jesus' peace? Drawing a connection between this text and Jn 16:33, "in me you shall have peace," Aquinas affirms the unity of Christian peace. The distinction between imperfect and per-

34. See *ST* II-II, q. 29, a. 2.

fect peace does not exhaust Jesus' meaning: "According to Augustine, both statements can refer to the peace of this time. Then Christ is saying, 'Peace I leave with you,' by my example, but 'my peace I give to you,' by my power and strength" (no. 1963).

In Augustinian fashion, therefore, Aquinas interprets this biblical verse first in terms of the distinction between earthly and heavenly "peace," and second in terms of Christ's efficacious example and grace as giving us "peace." While Christ is the author of our peace in both this life and the next, in the next life we enjoy peace in the same way that Christ possesses it, whereas in this life we do not enjoy peace in this way. For Aquinas and Augustine, in short, it is important to recognize variations on the meaning of "peace" in interpreting this text. Otherwise, one will end up being forced either to deny that followers of Christ receive peace—to deny that any real sanctification occurs at all—or else, by imagining that we are expected as Christians to display on earth Christ's perfect peace, to despair at our pitiful condition and to fear that no one is saved because all are hypocrites.

Though Aquinas most often employs Augustine's exegesis to undertake the literal theological interpretation that we have seen above, he also turns to Augustine to present the spiritual sense. As a representative example of this practice, one might note Aquinas's interpretation of Jn 5:2. Here the evangelist describes the Sheep Pool in Jerusalem as having "five porticoes." The literal sense of this verse, Aquinas says, simply conveys the structure of the pool which enabled the priests to "stand and wash the animals without inconvenience" (no. 704). The number five, however, prompts a search for the mystical sense of the verse. Just as he so often does for the literal sense, Aquinas sets forth the spiritual interpretations of Chrysostom and Augustine: "In the mystical sense these five porticoes, according to Chrysostom, signify the five wounds in the body of Christ; about which we read: 'Put your hand into my side, and do not be unbelieving, but believe' (Jn 20:27). But according to Augustine, these five porticoes signify the five books of Moses" (no. 704). In this way Aquinas exhibits, as the mystical sense of the five porticoes, Christ's fulfillment of the Torah by his Passion.

John Chrysostom. We have already noted that Chrysostom appears in Aquinas's *Super Ioannem* with a frequency that rivals that of Augustine. This is not surprising, because Aquinas drew heavily upon Chrysostom's biblical commentaries in his *Catena aurea* as well. As Torrell remarks, "The last chapters of his [Aquinas's] commentary on Saint John are a rewriting of the *Catena*,"[35] and indeed the entire commentary is stamped by the *Catena*'s influence.

Unlike Origen, Chrysostom is not in need of doctrinal correction;

---

35. Torrell, *Saint Thomas Aquinas*, vol. 1, 139.

and unlike Augustine, whose theology so deeply influenced the medieval *distinctiones* and *quaestiones*, Chrysostom rarely provides the basis for an extended theological discussion whose main lines appear also in the *Summa theologiae*. Instead, Aquinas values Chrysostom for his ability to draw forth a profound theological insight from what at first seems an unremarkable observation. Commenting for instance on Nicodemus's question, "How can a man be born again when he is already an old man?" (Jn 3:4), Chrysostom observes that Nicodemus understands Christ's words carnally and therefore makes a foolish objection. From this point, which is quite clear in the Gospel, Chrysostom proposes that likewise "all the reasons brought forth to attack the things of faith are foolish, since they are not according to the meaning of Sacred Scripture" (no. 437). Human reason must be illumined by faith in order to understand Scripture's teachings truly; faith saves human reason from foolishness. Both a hermeneutics for biblical interpretation and an account of the relationship of faith and reason follow from Nicodemus's misunderstanding.

Similarly, discussing the Virgin Mary's request to Jesus at the Wedding at Cana (Jn 2:3), Chrysostom asks why she had not urged him to do miracles before this time. After all, the angel had told her to expect that he would be powerful (Lk 1:32–33). Aquinas notes that Chrysostom answers that she waited until the time was ripe. While true enough, this insight hardly goes far enough. Yet Chrysostom finds in her waiting, and in her request for a miracle at Cana, the evidence that she embodies the perfection of Israel. Because "Jews demand signs" (1 Cor 1:22), her request for a miracle flows from her perfect Jewishness (no. 346). She reveals herself to be the mother of the Messiah precisely as the perfection of "the symbol of the synagogue, which is the mother of Christ" (no. 346). Chrysostom's commentary also demonstrates an attentiveness to the working of ordinary minds. For example, regarding Jesus' promise that the Father will give the Holy Spirit "to be with you for ever" (Jn 14:16), Chrysostom explains that "one could say that our Lord said these things to dispel a certain physical interpretation they might have. They could have imagined that this Paraclete, which was to be given to them, would also leave them after a while by some kind of suffering, like Christ" (no. 1914). If the Messiah, whom they had expected to reign forever on earth, was leaving, then certainly they might have wondered whether the Paraclete would also eventually depart. In his commentary on Cana and on the Paraclete, we find Chrysostom's rich ecclesiology, whose lineaments—as regards its attention to Israel and to the Holy Spirit—Aquinas adopts.

Heretics and Heterodoxy

The role of the early Church's central heretics in Aquinas's *Lectura super Ioannem* should not go unmentioned. Thus Aquinas repeatedly refers to the theology of Arius, whose views naturally come up relatively frequently in Aquinas's patristic sources, such as Augustine and Hilary of Poitiers (see no. 1879). Arius appears not only where we would expect it—namely, in the discussion of the Word in chapter one of the Gospel, which contains eight references to Arius that combat the denial that the Son is fully divine—but he receives attention throughout the commentary. For example, commenting on Jn 12:27, where Jesus says "Now is my soul troubled," Aquinas points out that Jesus thereby refutes "the error of Arius and Apollinarius. For they said that Christ does not have a soul, and in place of his soul they substituted the Word" (no. 1654). Similarly, discussing Jesus' statement that "he who receives me receives him who sent me" (Jn 13:20), Aquinas also brings in Arius: "Arius used this text in the following way to help support his own error: the Lord says that he who receives him receives the Father; and so the relationship between the Father who sends and the Son is the same as that of the Son who sends and the disciples. But Christ who sends is greater than the disciples who are sent" (no. 1794). Against the logical conclusion that the Father is greater than the Son, Aquinas follows Augustine in appealing to Jesus' two natures and role as Mediator. Again, when Jesus instructs Mary Magdalene to tell his disciples that "I am ascending to my Father and your Father, to my God and your God" (Jn 20:17), Aquinas warns against Arius's interpretation. He points out that Arius interpreted the words "my Father and your Father" as evidence for the notion that "God is the Father of the Son in the same way that he is our Father, and that he is the God of the Son in the same way that he is our God" (no. 2520). In response to Arius's reading, Aquinas notes that Jesus is asking Mary Magdalene to "go to my brethren" (Jn 20:17). Thus he is speaking as man, and emphasizing his unity with the disciples in his humanity. Without question, "in his human nature he is subject to the Father as a creature to the Creator" (no. 2520).

Also present, though less frequently (in part because they lived after the deaths of Aquinas's key patristic sources), are heterodox figures such as Apollinarius, Nestorius, and Eutyches.[36] Commenting on Jn 1:14, for instance, Aquinas asks "why the Evangelist did not say that the Word assumed flesh, but rather that 'the Word was made flesh.' I answer that he did this to exclude the error of Nestorius" (no. 170), in other words, to exclude any possibility of holding that the Virgin Mary is mother solely of the human nature, not mother of God. The problem with Nestorius's heresy, Aquinas observes, is that "it would mean that God did not become man, for one particular *suppositum* cannot be predicated of another. Accordingly, if the person or *suppositum* of the

36. Other heretics who make appearances in the *Super Ioannem* include Sabellius, Eunomius, and Ebion, to name only a few.

Word is different than the person or *suppositum* of the man in Christ, then what the Evangelist says is not true, namely, 'the Word was made flesh'" (no. 170). Aquinas likewise takes up Nestorius's views in interpreting Jn 2:19, where Jesus says, "Destroy this temple, and in three days I will raise it up." Nestorius, Aquinas says, argues from this verse that "the Word of God was joined to human nature only by an indwelling, from which it follows that the person of God is distinct from that of man in Christ" (no. 400). In response, Aquinas notes that the Person of the Word does not indwell the human nature as in a temple, because the divine Person is the Person of the human nature. For his part, Eutyches comes up also in the context of "the Word became flesh" (Jn 1:14). Aquinas holds that Eutyches's effort to blend the divine and human natures in Christ does not do justice to the Evangelist's earlier affirmation that "the Word was God" (Jn 1:1) (no. 166). It would be a crude understanding of the Incarnation to suppose that the divine nature changed into flesh.

Aristotle

Thomas Prügl observes, "When his scriptural commentaries are compared not only to Albertus Magnus but also to his own *Summae*, Aquinas employs even quotations from Aristotle quite sparingly."[37] By our count, Aquinas quotes Aristotle directly only in chapters 1, 2, 4, 10, 12, 15, 19, 20, and 21. This is not of course to say that Aquinas's commentary is not influenced by Aristotelian concerns, about causality, for example. The quotations of Aristotle show the range of his influence.

For example, in his discussion of the name "Word" (Jn 1:1), Aquinas begins by quoting Aristotle's *On Interpretation* concerning vocal sounds: "To understand the name 'Word' we should note that according to the Philosopher vocal sounds are signs of the affections that exist in our soul" (no. 25). He goes on to ask what the vocal sound "Word" signifies. Drawing again upon Aristotle, he states, "Now there are three things in our intellect: the intellectual power itself, the species of the thing understood (and this species is its form, being to the intellect what the species of a color is to the eye), and thirdly the very activity of the intellect, which is to understand" (ibid.). Having concluded that the vocal sound does not signify any of these, he argues following Augustine that the "Word" must be understood analogously through the "interior word," namely, that "which the one understanding forms when understanding" (ibid.). Employing Aristotle's account of the operation of the intellect in concepts and judgments, Aquinas explains that "the Philosopher says that the notion [*ratio*] which a name signi-

---

37. Prügl, "Thomas Aquinas as Interpreter of Scripture," 399.

fies is a definition. Hence, what is thus expressed, i.e., formed in the soul, is called an interior word. Consequently it is compared to the intellect, not as that by which the intellect understands, but as that in which it understands" (ibid.). In his exegetical exposition of Jn 1:1, in short, Aquinas draws together Aristotle and Augustine.

Similarly, Aristotle provides an important source for the insights into human action that abound in Aquinas's commentary. In particular, we find Aristotle's *Rhetoric* as a valued source. Interpreting Jn 12:27, "Now is my soul troubled. And what shall I say?" Aquinas remarks that "it is natural to deliberate about what to do when one is perplexed. So the Philosopher says in his *Rhetoric* that fear makes a person take counsel" (no. 1656). Likewise, commenting on Pilate's scourging of Jesus, he proposes that Pilate did this so as to soothe the anger of those Jews who wanted Jesus put to death: "For it is natural for our anger to subside if we see the one we are angry at humiliated and punished, as the Philosopher says in his *Rhetoric*" (no. 2372). With regard to the risen Lord's remark to Peter that "when you were young, you girded yourself and walked where you would" (Jn 21:18), Aquinas says that such self-will "is characteristic of the young, as the Philosopher says in his *Rhetoric*" (no. 2629). Aquinas also cites Aristotle to explain Jesus' comment to his disciples that "[i]f you were of the world, the world would love its own" (Jn 15:19). People who commit the same sin hate each other: "As the Philosopher says, potters quarrel with one another," out of greed and envy in business (no. 2036).

Aristotle also plays a role in discussions of politics, both ecclesial and secular. Aquinas suggests that the risen Lord asks Peter, "Do you love me more than these?" (Jn 21:15), because it is fitting that the leader possess greater love: "as the Philosopher says in his *Politics*, it is the natural order of things that the one who cares for and governs others should be better" (no. 2619). This "natural order" applies, or should apply, to the bishops of the Church. Commenting on the difference between the good shepherd and the hireling, Aquinas also turns to Aristotle: "the good shepherd looks to the benefit of the flock, while the hireling seeks mainly his own advantage. This is also the difference between a king and a tyrant, as the Philosopher says" (no. 1402). Aristotle also has an influence upon a more mystical interpretation of the biblical account of Christ's Passion. Aquinas finds it to be fitting that Christ died between two thieves, because this manifests Christ's coming role as Judge: "it is the function of the judge to be in the middle of the parties; so the Philosopher says that to go to a judge is to go to the middle. Christ was also placed in the middle" (no. 2417).

Aquinas uses Aristotle's theory of carnal generation to explain the difference between creation and graced sonship (nos. 160–61), in light of Jn 1:12–13, "But to all who received him, who believed in his name, he gave power to become children of God; who were born, not of blood nor of the will of the flesh nor of the will of man, but of God." He employs Aristotle's account of motion and change to discuss the original goodness of the devil (no. 1246), in light of Jn 8:44, "He [the devil] was a murderer from the beginning, and has nothing to do with the truth, because there is no truth in him. When he lies, he speaks according to his own nature, for he is a liar and the father of lies." He uses Aristotle's arguments against astrology to deny that Jesus' statement that "my hour has not yet come" (Jn 2:4) implies that fate controls Jesus' deeds (no. 351). He draws on Aristotle's understanding of material bodies to argue that the risen Lord's ability to move through closed doors was miraculous rather than the property of a glorified body (no. 2527). And he takes up Neoplatonic and Aristotelian arguments to make the claim that "every creature possesses some likeness to God, but it is infinitely distant from a likeness to his nature" (no. 947).

Lest one receive the wrong impression, we might close this section with Aquinas's point that "the wisdom of no philosopher has been so great that it could keep men from error; rather, the philosophers have led many into error" (no. 854).

The *Glossa Ordinaria*

How much does Aquinas's *Super Ioannem* draw from the *Glossa ordinaria*?[38] The chapters of Aquinas's commentary quote regularly from the Gloss, but not frequently. To give examples from the early chapters: chapter one, by far the longest chapter of the commentary, contains six references to the Gloss; chapters four and five, three references each; chapter two, two references; chapters three, six, and seven, one reference each. Chapter eight contains no direct references to the Gloss. Sometimes Aquinas takes an argument from the Gloss, as in chapter one, where he writes regarding "In the beginning was the Word" (Jn 1:1), that "this verb 'was,' according to the Gloss, is not understood here as indicating temporal changes, as other verbs do, but as signifying the existence of a thing" (no. 40). At other places he adopts a "parallel" biblical passage used by the Gloss, as in chapter seven (no. 1110). Still elsewhere he takes a quotation from Augustine (no. 411), or a timeline for Jesus' deeds (no. 498). In short, while the Gloss certainly contrib-

---

38. The production of the standard Medieval Gloss of the biblical text is associated with the school of Anselm of Laon (1100–1130) and the figure of Gilbert of Auxerre. Though it has been common to see the Gloss as the merging of two separate works (the marginal Gloss and the interlinear Gloss), it is now commonly judged that both the marginal and the interlinear notes are from the same school. For the history of the *Glossa Ordinaria*, see Beryl Smalley, *The Study of the Bible in the Middle Ages*, 3rd ed. (Oxford: Blackwell, 1983), 62–66; and E. Ann Matter, "The Church Fathers and the *Glossa Ordinaria*," in *The Reception of the Church Fathers in the West*, vol. 1, 83–111.

utes to Aquinas's *Super Ioannem*, his *Catena aurea* is much more conse-
quential, as will be apparent from the footnotes to the text.

Conclusion

At all points in Aquinas's *Lectura super Ioannem*, we should keep in
mind his understanding that *sacra doctrina*, in its various modes, leads
us back to "God Teaching." To be drawn into "God Teaching" is the act
of the contemplative. For Aquinas, St. John is the master contemplative, and Aquinas's own theological and exegetical procedure seeks to
imitate St. John's contemplative power. How does St. John's Gospel
lead us to union with the triune God, and thus to salvation? Behind
all the interpretations of particular passages, we would submit, stands
this question. In reading John with St. Thomas Aquinas, we seek not
solely knowledge, but faith's knowledge that is, like the Word himself,
filled with love.

ABBREVIATIONS FOR PATRISTIC
AND MEDIEVAL SOURCES

Alcuin

Comm. in S. Ioannis Evang.	*Commentaria in sancti Ioannis Evangelium*

Ambrose

Comm. in ep. ad Cor. primam	*Commentaria in epistolam ad Corinthios primam*
Expos. Evang. sec. Luc.	*Expositio Evangelii secundum Lucam*
Hex.	*Hexaemeron*

Anselm

Mon.	*Monologion*

Augustine

Conf.	*Confessiones*
Con. Faust.	*Contra Faustum*
De agon. chris.	*De agone christiano*
De bapt. parv.	*De baptismo parvulorum*
De bono conj.	*De bono conjugali*
De civ. Dei	*De civitate Dei*
De cons. Evang.	*De consensu Evangelistarum*
De div. quaest. 83	*De diversis quaestionibus octaginta tribus liber unus*
De Gen. ad litt.	*De Genesi ad litteram libri XII*
De nat. boni	*De natura boni*
De oper. mon.	*De opere monachorum*
De praed. sanct.	*De praedestinatione sanctorum*
De Symb.	*De Symbolo*
De Trin.	*De Trinitate*
Ep.	*Epistolae*
Enarr. in Ps.	*Enarrationes in Psalmos*

Enchir.	*Enchiridion de fide, spe et caritate*
Quaest. ex Novo Test.	*Quaestiones ex Novo Testamento*
Quaest. in Evang. sec. Matt	*Quaestionum septemdecim in Evangelium secundum Matthaeum*
Quaest. vet. et novi Test.	*Quaestiones veteris et novi Testamenti*
Serm. de Scrip.	*Sermones de Scripturis*
Serm. de symb. ad catechum.	*Sermo de symbolo ad catechumenos*
Serm. supposit.	*Sermones suppositii*
Tract. in Io.	*Tractatus in evangelium Ioannis*

Bede

Hom. XIII in dom. sec. post Epiphan.	*Homilia XIII in dominica secunda post Epiphaniam*
In S. Ioannis Evang. expos.	*In S. Joannis Evangelium expositio*
In S. Matthaei Evang. expos.	*In S. Matthaei Evangelium expositio*

Chrysostom

Hom. in Io.	*Homiliae in Ioannem*
Comm. ad Gal.	*Commentarius in Epistolam ad Galatas*

Cyprian

De unit. Eccl.	*De unitate Ecclesiae*

Didymus

De Spir. Sanc.	*Interpretatio libri Didymi de Spiritu Sancto*

Dionysius

De coel. hier.	*De coelesti hierarchia*
De div. nom.	*De divinis nominibus*
De ecc. hier.	*De ecclesiastica hierarchia*
De myst. theol.	*De mystica theologia*
Ep.	*Epistolae*

Erigena

Comm. in S. Evang. sec. Io.	*Comm. in S. Evangelium secundum Ioannem*
Hom. in prol. Evang. sec. Io.	*Homilia in prologum S. Evangelii secundum Ioannem*

Eusebius

HE   *Historia ecclesiastica*

Gregory the Great

XL hom. in Evang.   *XL homilia in Evangelia*
Ep. V ad Theoc.   *Epistola V ad Theoctistam*
Hom. in Ezech.   *Homiliarum in Ezechielem*
Mor.   *Librorum moralium*
Reg. pastor. liber   *Regulae pastoralis liber*

Hilary

De Trin.   *De Trinitate*
Liber de Syn.   *Liber de Synodis*

Jerome

Comm. in Matt.   *Commentaria in Evangelium S. Matthaei*
Expos. in quat. Evang.   *Expositio in quatuor Evangeliorum*
In Evang. sec. Ioan.   *In Evangelium secundum Ioannem*
Praef. in Pent.   *Praefatio in Pentateuchum*

John of Damascus

De fide orth.   *De fidei orthodoxae*

Leo the Great

Serm.   *Sermones*

Origen

Comm. in Io.   *Commentaria in Evangelium Ioannis*
Comm. in Matt.   *Commentaria in Evangelium secundum Matthaeum*
De Prin.   *De Principiis*

Peter Lombard

Collect. in Epist. Pauli   *Collectanea in Epistolas S. Pauli*
In Ep. I ad Tim.   *In Epistolam I ad Timothaeum*

Theophylact

Enar. in Evang. S. Ioannis   *Enarratio in Evangelium Ioannis*

Thomas Aquinas

Expos. in Ps.	*Expositio in Psalmos*
Expos. super Job	*Expositio super Job ad litteram*
Sent.	*Scriptum super Sententiis*
ST	*Summa Theologiae*
Super Eph.	*Super Epistolam B. Pauli ad Ephesios lectura*
Super Rom.	*Super Epistolam B. Pauli ad Romanos lectura*

Commentary on the Gospel of John

Chapters 1–5

PROLOGUE TO THE
GOSPEL OF JOHN

I saw the Lord seated on a high and lofty throne, and the whole house was full of his majesty, and the things that were under him filled the temple. (Is 6:1)

1. These are the words of a contemplative, and if we regard them as spoken by John the Evangelist they apply quite well to showing the nature of this Gospel. For as Augustine[1] says in his work, *On the Agreement of the Evangelists*: "The other Evangelists instruct us in their Gospels on the active life; but John in his Gospel instructs us also on the contemplative life."

The contemplation of John is described above in three ways, in keeping with the threefold manner in which he contemplated the Lord Jesus. It is described as high, full, and perfect. It is high: *I saw the Lord seated on a high and lofty throne*; it is full: *and the whole house was full of his majesty*; and it was perfect: *and the things that were under him filled the temple.*

2. As to the first, we must understand that the height and sublimity of contemplation consists most of all in the contemplation and knowledge of God: "Lift up your eyes on high, and see who has created these things" (Is 40:26).[2] A man lifts up his eyes on high when he sees and contemplates the Creator of all things. Now since John rose above whatever had been created—mountains, heavens, angels—and reached the Creator of all, as Augustine[3] says, it is clear that his contemplation was most high. Thus, *I saw the Lord.* And because, as John himself says below (12:41), "Isaiah said this because he had seen his glory," that is, the glory of Christ, "and spoke of him," the Lord *seated on a high and lofty throne* is Christ.

Now a fourfold height is indicated in this contemplation of John. A height of authority; hence he says, *I saw the Lord.* A height of eternity; when he says, *seated.* One of dignity, or nobility of nature; so he says, *on a high throne.* And a height of incomprehensible truth; when he says, *lofty.* It is in these four ways that the early philosophers arrived at the knowledge of God.

---

1. *De cons. Evang.* 1. 5; PL 34, col. 1045–46.
2. See *ST* II-II, q. 180, a. 4.
3. *De cons. Evang.* 1. 4; PL 34, col. 1045.

1

3. Some attained to knowledge of God through his authority, and this is the most efficacious way. For we see the things in nature acting for an end, and attaining to ends which are both useful and certain. And since they lack intelligence, they are unable to direct themselves, but must be directed and moved by one directing them, and who possesses an intellect. Thus it is that the movement of the things of nature toward a certain end indicates the existence of something higher by which the things of nature are directed to an end and governed. And so, since the whole course of nature advances to an end in an orderly way and is directed, we have to posit something higher which directs and governs them as Lord; and this is God.[4] This authority in governing is shown to be in the Word of God when he says, **Lord**. Thus the Psalm (88:10) says: "You rule the power of the sea, and you still the swelling of its waves," as though saying: You are the Lord and govern all things. John shows that he knows this about the Word when he says below (1:11), "He came unto his own," i.e., to the world, since the whole universe is his own.

4. Others came to knowledge of God from his eternity. They saw that whatever was in things was changeable, and that the more noble something is in the grades of being, so much the less it has of mutability. For example, the lower bodies are mutable both as to their substance and to place, while the heavenly bodies, which are more noble, are immutable in substance and change only with respect to place. We can clearly conclude from this that the first principle of all things, which is supreme and more noble, is changeless and eternal.[5] The prophet suggests this eternity of the Word when he says, **seated**, i.e., presiding without any change and eternally: "Your throne, O God, is forever and ever" (Ps 44:7); "Jesus Christ is the same yesterday, today, and forever" (Heb 13:8). John points to this eternity when he says below (1:1), "In the beginning was the Word."

5. Still others came to knowledge of God from the dignity of God; and these were the Platonists. They noted that everything which is something by participation is reduced to what is the same thing by essence, as to the first and highest. Thus, all things which are fiery by participation are reduced to fire, which is such by its essence. And so since all things which exist participate in existence (*esse*) and are beings by participation, there must necessarily be at the summit of all things something which is existence (*esse*) by its essence, i.e., whose essence is its existence. And this is God, who is the most sufficient, the most eminent, and the most perfect cause of the whole of existence, from whom all things that are participate existence (*esse*).[6] This dignity

---

4. See *ST* I, q. 2, a. 3.
5. See *ST* I, q. 9, a. 1; I, q. 10, a. 2.
6. See *ST* I, q. 3, a. 4.

is shown in the words, *on a high throne*, which, according to Diony-
sius,[7] refer to the divine nature. "The Lord is high above all nations"
(Ps 112:4). John shows us this dignity when he says below (1:1), "the
Word was God," with "Word" as subject and "God" as the predicate.

6. Yet others arrived at knowledge of God from the incomprehensibility of truth. All the truth which our intellect is able to grasp is finite,
since according to Augustine,[8] "everything that is known is bounded
by the comprehension of the one knowing"; and if it is bounded, it is
determined and particularized. Therefore, the first and supreme Truth,
which surpasses every intellect, must necessarily be incomprehensible
and infinite; and this is God.[9] Hence the Psalm (8:2) says, "Your greatness is above the heavens," i.e., above every created intellect, angelic and human. The Apostle says this in the words, "He dwells in unapproachable light" (1 Tim 6:16). This incomprehensibility of Truth is
shown to us in the word, *lofty*, that is, above all the knowledge of the
created intellect. John implies this incomprehensibility to us when he
says below (1:18), "No one has ever seen God."[10]

Thus the contemplation of John was high as regards authority, eternity, dignity, and the incomprehensibility of the Word. And John has
passed on this contemplation to us in his Gospel.

7. John's contemplation was also full. Now contemplation is full
when someone is able to consider all the effects of a cause in the cause
itself, that is, when he knows not only the essence of the cause, but
also its power, according as it can extend out to many things.[11] Of this
flowing outward we read, "It overflows with wisdom, like the Pishon,
and like the Tigris in the days of the new fruits" (Sir 24:35); "The river of God is full with water" (Ps. 64:10), since the divine wisdom has
depth in relation to its knowledge of all things. "With you from the beginning is wisdom, who knows your works" (Wis 9:9).

Since John the Evangelist was raised up to the contemplation of the
nature of the divine Word and of his essence when he said, "In the beginning was the Word; and the Word was with God," he immediately tells us of the power of the Word as it extends to all things, saying,
"Through him all things came into being." Thus his contemplation was
full. And so after the prophet had said, *I saw the Lord seated*, he added
something about his power, *and the whole house was full of his majesty*, that is, the whole fullness of things and of the universe is from
the majesty and power of God, through whom all things were made,
and by whose light all the men coming into this world are enlightened.
"The earth and its fullness are the Lord's" (Ps 23:1).[12]

---

7. *De coel. hier.* 13. 4; PG 3, col. 304C.   8. *De civ. Dei* 12. 18; PL 41, col. 368.
9. See *ST* I, q. 16, aa. 3, 5–6.   10. See *ST* I, q. 12, a. 7.
11. See *ST* II-II, q. 180, a. 5.
12. See *ST* I, q. 45, a. 5; I-II, q. 109, a. 1.

8. The contemplation of John was also perfect. For contemplation is perfect when the one contemplating is led and raised to the height of the thing contemplated. Should he remain at a lower level, then no matter how high the things which he might contemplate, the contemplation would not be perfect. So in order that it be perfect it is necessary that it rise and attain the end of the thing contemplated, adhering and assenting by affection and understanding to the truth contemplated. Job (37:16) says, "Do you not know the path of the clouds," that is, the contemplation of those preaching, "how perfect they are?" inasmuch as they adhere firmly by affection and understanding to contemplating the highest truth.

Since John not only taught how Christ Jesus, the Word of God, is God, raised above all things, and how all things were made through him, but also that we are sanctified by him, and adhere to him by the grace which he pours into us, he says below (1:16), "Of his fullness we have all received—indeed, grace in return for grace." It is therefore apparent that his contemplation is perfect. This perfection is shown in the addition, *and the things that were under him filled the temple*. For "the head of Christ is God" (1 Cor 11:3). The things that are under Christ are the sacraments of his humanity, through which the faithful are filled with the fullness of grace. In this way, then, *the things that were under him filled the temple*, i.e., the faithful, who are the holy temple of God (1 Cor 3:17) insofar as through the sacraments of his humanity all the faithful of Christ receive from the fullness of his grace.[13]   *Key Analysis*

The contemplation of John was thus full, high, and perfect.

9. We should note, however, that these three characteristics of contemplation belong to the different sciences in different ways. The perfection of contemplation is found in Moral Science, which is concerned with the ultimate end. The fullness of contemplation is possessed by Natural Science, which considers things as proceeding from God. Among the physical [natural] sciences, the height of contemplation is found in Metaphysics. But the Gospel of John contains all together what the above sciences have in a divided way, and so it is most perfect.[14]

10. In this way then, from what has been said, we can understand the matter of this Gospel. For while the other Evangelists treat principally of the mysteries of the humanity of Christ, John, especially and above all, makes known the divinity of Christ in his Gospel, as we saw above. Still, he does not ignore the mysteries of his humanity. He did this because, after the other Evangelists had written their Gospels, heresies had arisen concerning the divinity of Christ, to the effect that Christ

13. See *ST* III, q. 8, a. 1; III, q. 62, aa. 1–3.
14. See *ST* I, q. 1, a. 2.

was purely and simply a man, as Ebion and Cerinthus falsely thought.[15] And so John the Evangelist, who had drawn the truth about the divinity of the Word from the very fountain-head of the divine breast, wrote this Gospel at the request of the faithful. And in it he gives us the doctrine of the divinity of Christ and refutes all heresies.

The order of this Gospel is clear from the above. For John first shows us *the Lord seated on a high and lofty throne*, when he says below (1:1), "In the beginning was the Word." He shows secondly how *the house was full of his majesty*, when he says, "through him all things came into being" (1:3). Thirdly, he shows how the *things that were under him filled the temple*, when he says, "the Word was made flesh" (1:14). The end of this Gospel is also clear, and it is that the faithful become the temple of God, and become filled with the majesty of God; and so John says below (20:31), "These things are written so that you may believe that Jesus is the Christ, the Son of God."

The matter of this Gospel, the knowledge of the divinity of the Word, is clear, as well as its order and end.

11. Then follows the condition of the author, who is described above in four ways: as to his name, his virtue, his symbol, and his privilege. He is described as to name as John, the author of this Gospel. "John" is interpreted as "in whom is grace," since the secrets of the divinity cannot be seen except by those who have the grace of God within themselves: "No one knows the deep things of God but the Spirit of God" (1 Cor 2:11).[16]

As concerns his virtue, John *saw the Lord seated*, because he was a virgin; for it is fitting that such persons see the Lord: "Blessed are the pure in heart" (Mt 5:8).[17]

He is described as to his symbol, for John is symbolized by an eagle. The other three Evangelists, concerned with those things which Christ did in his flesh, are symbolized by animals which walk on the earth, namely, by a man, a bull calf, and a lion. But John flies like an eagle above the cloud of human weakness and looks upon the light of unchanging truth with the most lofty and firm eyes of the heart. And gazing on the very deity of our Lord Jesus Christ, by which he is equal to the Father, he has striven in this Gospel to confide this above all, to

15. Ebion was the purported founder of the Ebionites, a Jewish-Christian sect of the early Church. According to the evidence provided by Irenaeus, Origen, Hippolytus, and Tertullian, the Ebionites rejected the writings of Paul, accepted only the Gospel of Matthew, followed all the prescriptions of the Jewish Law, and (notably for Aquinas here) rejected the divine status of Jesus. Cerinthus was an early Gnostic teacher (first–second century) credited with teaching that Jesus was a mere man on whom the "Christ" descended at his baptism. His views were denounced by Polycarp and Irenaeus, and Eusebius later wrote that the Apostle John composed his Gospel in order to refute the teachings of Cerinthus.

16. See *ST* I-II, q. 109, a. 1.

17. See *ST* II-II, q. 152, a. 4.

the extent that he believed was sufficient for all. Concerning this flight
of John it says in Job (39:27): "Will the eagle," that is, John, "fly up
at your command?" And further on it says (39:29), "His eyes look far
away," because the Word of God is seen in the bosom of the Father by
the eye of the mind.

John is described as to privilege since, among the other disciples of
the Lord, John was more loved by Christ. Without mentioning his own
name John refers to himself below (21:20) as "the disciple whom Jesus loved." And because secrets are revealed to friends, "I have called
you friends because everything I have heard from my father I have
made known to you" (below 15:15), Jesus confided his secrets in a
special way to that disciple who was specially loved. Thus it says in Job
(36:32-33): "From the savage," that is, the proud, "he hides his light,"
that is, Christ hides the truth of his divinity, "and shows his friend,"
that is, John, "that it belongs to him," since it is John who sees the
light of the Incarnate Word more excellently and expresses it to us,
saying "He was the true light" (below 1:19).[18]

Now the matter, order, end and author of this Gospel of the blessed
John are clear.

18. See *ST* I, q. 20, a. 4.

PROLOGUE OF SAINT JEROME

I. This is John the evangelist, one of the disciples of the Lord; he was chosen by God to be a virgin, whom God called away from a wedding although he was willing to marry.

II. A double testimony of John's virginity is given in the Gospel, both since he was said to be beloved by God above the others, and because the Lord, while hanging on the cross, commended his own mother to him, so that a virgin might serve a virgin.

III. Furthermore, the Evangelist clearly manifests in the Gospel that he himself was beginning a work on the incorruptible Word, for he alone testifies that the Word became flesh and that light was not comprehended by darkness. He placed first the sign which the Lord did at a wedding, showing what he himself was, to demonstrate to the readers that where the Lord is invited, the wine of the wedding ought to cease: and also that all things instituted by Christ might appear new, now that the old things have been changed. Moreover, he wrote this gospel in Asia, after he had written the Apocalypse on the island of Patmos, so that the one who is noted as the incorruptible beginning at the beginning of the canon in Genesis, might through a virgin be described also as the incorruptible end in the Apocalypse, since Christ says: I am alpha and omega.

IV. And this is John who, knowing that the day of his death had come, after his disciples were called together in Ephesus, disclosed Christ through many signs, and descending into the place dug out for his burial, was gathered to his fathers after a prayer, as much a stranger to the pain of death as to the corruption of the flesh.

V. He wrote the gospel after all the others; and this was due to a virgin. We have explained in detail, however, neither the order in which the books were written, nor how they were arranged, so that, when the desire to know has been granted, the fruit of labor might be reserved to those who seek, and the magisterial teaching to God.

THE EXPOSITION OF SAINT THOMAS
ON THIS PROLOGUE

I

12. In this Prologue, Jerome intends to explain two things, namely, the author of the Gospel, and to show that it was fitting for him to write this Gospel.

Therefore it is divided into two parts: in the first he describes John with respect to his life, in the second, with respect to his death, where he says [n. 20], *And this is John*.

He makes two points in the first part: first, he describes the author of the work, with respect to the gifts granted to him in his life; second, he shows John's suitability for writing the Gospel from these things [n. 16]: *Furthermore the Evangelist clearly manifests in the Gospel*.

He does two things regarding the first of these points: first, he commends the author; second, he gives the proof [n. 15]: *A double testimony of John's virginity is given in the Gospel*.

13. For he describes the author's name, saying *This is John*, that is, the one in whom is grace; "by the grace of God I am what I am" (1 Cor 15:10). Then he describes his office, when he calls him *the Evangelist*; "The first will say to Zion: Behold, I am here and I shall give an Evangelist to Jerusalem" (Is 41:27). Thirdly, he describes his dignity, when John is said to be *of the disciples of the Lord*; "I shall make all your children to be taught by the Lord" (Is 54:13). Fourthly, he describes John's virtue of chastity, when he is called *a virgin*. Fifthly, he describes John's election: *He was chosen by the Lord*; "You have not chosen me" (Jn 15:16). Sixthly, he describes the manner of John's call, when he says that *God called him away from a wedding*, that is, from the wedding to which Jesus was invited with his disciples, where he changed the water into wine.

14. But Matthew writes that John was called with James his brother from the boat, and not from a wedding (Mt 6:21).

We answer that the callings of the apostles were different. At first they were called to intimate acquaintance with Jesus, but finally they were called to discipleship, that is, when they followed Jesus after they had left their nets. Thus we should understand what Jerome says to be about the first type of call, by which John was called to intimate acquaintance with Jesus away from the wedding; but what Matthew writes should be understood to be about the final call, by which Jesus called John from the boat with James his brother, namely, when they followed Jesus after they had left their nets behind.

II

15. Next, when Jerome says, *a double testimony of John's virginity is given in the Gospel*, he commends John's virginity by two signs.

First, as a sign of greater love. Jerome speaks with respect to this *double testimony of his*, that is, John's, *virginity given in the Gospel*, that is, in the words contained in the Gospel, *in that he was said to be beloved by God above the other disciples*: "This is the disciple who testifies of these things and wrote these things" (Jn 21:24). The reason for this special love was his purity, which calls forth to love, as it is written in Proverbs: "Whoever loves pureness of heart on account of the grace of his lips, will have the king for his friend" (Pr 22.11).

He proves the same thing by a second sign, that of Christ's entrusting his mother to John, when he says *the Lord*, while he was hanging on the cross, *commended his own mother to him*, that is, to John (Jn 19:27), *so that a virgin*, namely John, *might* appropriately *serve a virgin* mother.

III

16. Then, when he says, *Furthermore, the Evangelist clearly manifests in the gospel*, etc., he shows that it was fitting for John to write the Gospel, and this is so for four reasons.

The first reason has to do with the beginning of the Gospel, which starts with the incorrupt Word, about which it is fitting to investigate only what is incorrupt. Jerome refers to this when he says *Furthermore, manifesting*, that is, John, *in the Gospel that he himself was beginning a work on the incorruptible Word, for he alone testifies that the Word became flesh and that light was not comprehended by darkness*.

17. The second reason concerns the beginning of miracles.

For John composes the order of the miracles beginning with that miracle which God showed at the wedding, namely, when he changed water into wine (Jn 2:1-11), in which the wine at the wedding was exhausted when the new wine, namely, that of virginity, was restored. Jerome refers to this when he says *in placing first*, at the beginning of the other miracles, *the sign*, that is, the miracle, *which the Lord did in a wedding, he shows what he himself was*, that is, a virgin, *to demonstrate to the readers that where the Lord is invited the wine of the wedding*, that is, the enjoyment of marriage, *ought to cease: and also that when the old things have been changed*, that is, the old water has been turned into new wine, *all things instituted by Christ might appear new*; that is to say, when men have turned to Christ, they must put off the old man and put on the new, as it is said in Col 3:10, and in Rev 21:5: "Behold, I make all things new."

18. On the other hand, it seems for this same reason that, when he says that when the Lord was invited the wine of the wedding must cease, whoever loves God must abstain from marriage: therefore it is not permitted to marry.

I respond that a person is called by God in two ways: according to the common grace, it is not necessary for the wine of the wedding to cease in this way; and according to the special summit of contemplation: the wine of the wedding ought to cease in this fashion. The Apostle gives the reason for this: "The married woman cares for how she may please her husband," and therefore there must be an obstacle to the act of contemplation, "but she who is unmarried cares for how she may please Christ" (1 Cor 7:34).

Or we may say that for those who love God and possess him through grace, the wine of the wedding must cease from the effect of the wine, that is to say, it does not cause drunkenness by carnal pleasure. This effect can be so great and can be experienced with such force that there may be mortal sin even between the married.

19. The third reason concerns the order of the composition of the book.

For this Gospel was written after all of the other books of Sacred Scripture had been composed. For although the canon of Scripture begins with the book of Genesis and concludes with the Apocalypse, this Gospel was written at the request of the bishops of Asia after John was recalled from the island of Patmos in Asia. Nevertheless, it was not placed at the end, even though it was the last book to be written. From this the fittingness of writing the gospel is shown *so that in the beginning of the canon,* that is, of Sacred Scripture, when we read, "In the beginning God created the heaven and the earth," *the one who is noted as the incorruptible beginning in Genesis might be described also through a virgin in the Apocalypse as the incorruptible end,* with respect to the order of the books, not with respect to the order of Scripture.

IV

20. Then, when Jerome says, **And this is John**, he described the author and makes two points.

First he commends John's death, and, second, he concludes from this the fittingness of this Gospel's order, where [n. 22] *He wrote the gospel after all the others.*

21. The privilege of John's death was wonderful and special, for he felt no pain in death; and this took place by God's action so that the

one who was a complete stranger to the corruptions of the flesh might
be exempt from the pain of death.

V

22. He shows appropriateness of the author to faith, saying, *He
wrote the gospel after all the others.*

We may consider two orders in the books of Sacred Scripture, namely, one as the order of the time in which the books were written, and
the other as the order of the arrangement of the books in the Bible.

CHAPTER 1

LECTURE 1

1 In the beginning was the Word; and the Word was with God; and the Word was God. 2 He was in the beginning with God.[1]

23. John the Evangelist, as already indicated, makes it his principal object to show the divinity of the Incarnate Word. Accordingly, his Gospel is divided into two parts. In the first he states the divinity of Christ; in the second he shows it by the things Christ did in the flesh (2:1). In regard to the first, he does two things. First he shows the divinity of Christ; secondly he sets forth the manner in which Christ's divinity is made known to us (1:14). Concerning the first he does two things. First he treats of the divinity of Christ; secondly of the Incarnation of the Word of God (1:6).

Because there are two items to be considered in each thing, namely, its existence and its operation or power, first he treats the existence of the Word as to his divine nature; secondly of his power of operation (1:3). In regard to the first he does four things. First he shows when the Word was: *In the beginning was the Word*; secondly where he was: *and the Word was with God*; thirdly what he was: *and the Word was God*; fourthly, in what way he was: *He was in the beginning with God*. The first two pertain to the inquiry "whether something exists"; the second two pertain to the inquiry "what something is."

24. With respect to the first of these four we must examine the meaning of the statement, *In the beginning was the Word*. And here three things present themselves for careful study according to the three parts of this statement. First it is necessary to investigate the name *Word*; secondly the phrase *in the beginning*; thirdly the meaning of the Word *was in the beginning*.

25. To understand the name *Word* we should note that according to the Philosopher[2] vocal sounds are signs of the affections that exist in our soul. It is customary in Scripture for the things signified to be themselves called by the names of their signs, as in the statement, "And the rock was Christ" (1 Cor 10:4). It is fitting that what is within our soul, and which is signified by our external word, be called a "word." But whether the name "word" belongs first to the exterior vo-

---

1. St. Thomas quotes Jn 1:2 in *ST* I, q. 41, a. 3.
2. Aristotle, *On Interpretation* 1; 16a3–4.

12

cal sound or to the conception in our mind, is not our concern at present. However, it is obvious that what is signified by the vocal sound, as existing interiorly in the soul, exists prior to the vocal expression inasmuch as it is its actual cause. Therefore if we wish to grasp the meaning of the interior word, we must first look at the meaning of that which is exteriorly expressed in words.

Now there are three things in our intellect: the intellectual power itself, the species of the thing understood (and this species is its form, being to the intellect what the species of a color is to the eye), and thirdly the very activity of the intellect, which is to understand. But none of these is what is signified by the exterior vocal word: for the name "stone" does not signify the substance of the intellect because this is not what the one naming intends; nor does it signify the species, which is that by which the intellect understands, since this also is not the intention of the one naming; nor does it signify the act itself of understanding since to understand is not an action proceeding to the exterior from the one understanding, but an action remaining within. Therefore, that is properly called an interior word which the one understanding forms when understanding.[3]

Now the intellect forms two things, according to its two operations. According to its operation which is called "the understanding of indivisibles," it forms a definition; while according to its operation by which it unites and separates, it forms an enunciation or something of that sort.[4] Hence, what is thus formed and expressed by the operation of the intellect, whether by defining or enunciating, is what the exterior vocal sound signifies. So the Philosopher[5] says that the notion (ratio) which a name signifies is a definition. Hence, what is thus expressed, i.e., formed in the soul, is called an interior word. Consequently it is compared to the intellect, not as that by which the intellect understands, but as that in which it understands, because it is in what is thus expressed and formed that it sees the nature of the thing understood. Thus we have the meaning of the name "word."

Secondly, from what has been said we are able to understand that a word is always something that proceeds from an intellect existing in act; and furthermore, that a word is always a notion (ratio) and likeness of the thing understood. So if the one understanding and the thing understood are the same, then the word is a notion and likeness of the intellect from which it proceeds. On the other hand, if the one understanding is other than the thing understood, then the word is not a likeness and notion of the one understanding but of the thing understood, as the conception which one has of a stone is a likeness of

3. See ST I, q. 27, a. 1.
4. See ST I, q. 85, a. 5.
5. Aristotle, On Interpretation 2; 16a20–16b5.

only the stone.[6] But when the intellect understands itself, its word is a likeness and notion of the intellect.[7] And so Augustine[8] sees a likeness of the Trinity in the soul insofar as the mind understands itself, but not insofar as it understands other things.

It is clear then that it is necessary to have a word in any intellectual nature, for it is of the very nature of understanding that the intellect in understanding should form something. Now what is formed is called a word, and so it follows that in every being which understands there must be a word.

However, intellectual natures are of three kinds: human, angelic and divine; and so there are three kinds of words. The human word, about which it is said in the Psalm (13:1): "The fool said in his heart, 'There is no God.'" The angelic word, about which it is said in Zechariah (1:9), and in many places in Sacred Scripture, "And the angel said to me."[9] The third is the divine word, of which Genesis (1:3) says, "And God said, 'Let there be light.'" So when the Evangelist says, *In the beginning was the Word*, we cannot understand this as a human or angelic word, because both these words have been made since man and angel have a cause and principle of their existence and operation, and the word of a man or an angel cannot exist before they do. The word the Evangelist had in mind he shows by saying that this word was not made, since all things were made by it. Therefore, the word about which John speaks here is the Word of God.

26. We should note that this Word differs from our own word in three ways. The first difference, according to Augustine, is that our word is formable before being formed, for when I wish to conceive the notion of a stone, I must arrive at it by reasoning. And so it is in all other things that are understood by us, with the sole possible exception of the first principles which, since they are known in a simple manner, are known at once without any discourse of reason. So as long as the intellect, in so reasoning, casts about this way and that, the formation is not yet complete. It is only when it has conceived the notion of the thing perfectly that for the first time it has the notion of the complete thing and a word. Thus in our mind there is both a "cogitation," meaning the discourse involved in an investigation, and a word, which is formed according to a perfect contemplation of the truth. So our word is first in potency before it is in act. But the Word of God is always in act. In consequence, the term "cogitation" does not properly speaking apply to the Word of God. For Augustine[10] says: "The Word of God is spoken of in such a way that cogitation is not included, lest

---

6. See *ST* I, q. 85, a. 1.
7. See *ST* I, q. 87, a. 1.
8. *De Trin.* 9. 5, no. 8; PL 42, col. 965. See also *ST* I, q. 34, a. 2.
9. See *ST* I, q. 55, a. 2.
10. *De Trin.* 15. 16, no. 25; PL 42, col. 1079; cf. *Catena aurea*, 1:1a.

God Unchangeable

anything changeable be supposed in God." Anselm[11] was speaking improperly when he said: "For the supreme Spirit to speak is for him to
look at something while cogitating."[12]

27. The second difference is that our word is imperfect, but the divine Word is most perfect. For since we cannot express all our con-
ceptions in one word, we must form many imperfect words through
which we separately express all that is in our knowledge.[13] But it is
not that way with God. For since he understands both himself and everything else through his essence, by one act, the single divine Word is
expressive of all that is in God, not only of the Persons but also of creatures; otherwise it would be imperfect. So Augustine[14] says: "If there
were less in the Word than is contained in the knowledge of the One
speaking it, the Word would be imperfect; but it is obvious that it is
most perfect; therefore, it is only one." "God speaks once" (Jb 33:14).[15]

28. The third difference is that our word is not of the same nature
as we; but divine Word is of the same nature as God. And therefore it
is something that subsists in the divine nature. For the understood notion which the intellect is seen to form about some thing has only an
intelligible existence in our soul. Now in our soul, to understand is not
the same as the nature of the soul, because our soul is not its own operation. Consequently, the word which our intellect forms is not of the
essence of our soul, but is an accident of it. But in God, to understand
and to be are the same; and so the Word of the divine intellect is not
an accident but belongs to its nature. Thus it must be subsistent, because whatever is in the nature of God is God. Thus Damascene[16] says
that God is a substantial Word, and a hypostasis, but our words are
concepts in our mind.

29. From the above it is clear that the Word, properly speaking, is
always understood as a Person in the Divinity, since it implies only
something expressed by the one understanding; also, that in the Divinity the Word is the likeness of that from which it issues; and that it
is co-eternal with that from which it issues, since it was not first formable before being formed, but was always in act; and that it is equal to
the Father, since it is perfect and expressive of the whole being of the
Father; and that it is co-essential and consubstantial with the Father,
since it is his substance.

It is also clear that since in every nature that which issues forth and
has a likeness to the nature from which it issues is called a son, and
since this word issues forth in a likeness and identity to the nature

11. *Mon.* 63; PL 158, col. 208.
12. See *ST* I, q. 14, a. 7; I, q. 34, a. 1, ad 2.
13. See *ST* I, q. 13, a. 4.
14. *De Trin.* 15. 14, no. 23; PL 42, col. 1076; cf. *Catena aurea*, 1:1a.
15. See *ST* I, q. 34, a. 1, ad 3.
16. John of Damascus, *De fide orth.* 1. 13; PG 94, col. 857.

from which it issues, it is suitably and appropriately called a "Son," and its production is called a generation.[17]

So now the first point is clear, the meaning of the term *Word*.

30. There are four questions on this point, two of them from Chrysostom.[18] The first is: Why did John the Evangelist omit the Father and begin at once with the Son, saying, *In the beginning was the Word?*

There are two answers to this. One is that the Father was known to everyone in the Old Testament, although not under the aspect of Father, but as God; but the Son was not known.[19] And so in the New Testament, which is concerned with our knowledge of the Word, he begins with the Word or Son.

The other answer is that we are brought to know the Father though the Son: "Father, I have manifested your name to the men whom you have given to me" (below 17:6). And so wishing to lead the faithful to a knowledge of the Father, the Evangelist fittingly began with the Son, at once adding something about the Father when he says, *and the Word was with God*.

31. The second question is also from Chrysostom.[20] Why did he say *Word* and not "Son," since, as we have said, the Word proceeds as Son?

There are also two answers to this. First, because "son" means something begotten, and when we hear of the generation of the Son, someone might suppose that this generation is the kind he can comprehend, that is, a material and changeable generation. Thus he did not say "Son," but *Word*, which signifies an intelligible proceeding, so that it would not be understood as a material and changeable generation. And so in showing that the Son is born of the Father in an unchangeable way, he eliminates a faulty conjecture by using the name *Word*.[21]

The second answer is this. The Evangelist was about to consider the Word as having come to manifest the Father. But since the idea of manifesting is implied better in the name "Word" than in the name "Son," he preferred to use the name *Word*.

32. The third question is raised by Augustine[22] in his book *Eighty-three Questions*; and it is this. In Greek, where we have "Word," they have "Logos"; now since "Logos" signifies in Latin both the "notion" and "word" [i.e., *ratio et verbum*], why did the translators render it as "word" and not "notion" since a notion is something interior just as a word is?

I answer that "notion" [*ratio*], properly speaking, names a concep-

17. See *ST* I, q. 27, a. 2; I, q. 34, a. 1.
18. *Hom. in Io.* 2. 4; PG 59, col. 33; cf. *Catena aurea*, 1:1a.
19. See *ST* I, q. 33, a. 3.
20. *Hom. in Io.* 2. 4; PG 59, col. 34; cf. *Catena aurea*, 1:1a.
21. See *ST* I, q. 27, a. 2.
22. *De div. quaest. 83*, q. 63; PL 40, col. 54; cf. *Catena aurea*, 1:1a.

tion of the mind precisely as in the mind, even if through it nothing exterior comes to be; but "word" signifies a reference to something exterior. And so because the Evangelist, when he said "Logos," intended to signify not only a reference to the Son's existence in the Father, but also the operative power of the Son, by which, through him, all things were made, our predecessors preferred to translate it "Word," which implies a reference to something exterior, rather than "notion," which implies merely a concept of the mind.[23]

33. The fourth question is from Origen,[24] and is this. In many passages, Scripture, when speaking of the Word of God, does not simply call him the Word, but adds "of God," saying, "the Word of God," or "of the Lord": "The Word of God on high is the foundation of wisdom" (Sir 1:5); "His name is the Word of God" (Rev 19:13). Why then did the Evangelist, when speaking here of the Word of God, not say, "In the beginning was the Word of God," but said *In the beginning was the Word?*

I answer that although there are many participated truths, there is just one absolute Truth, which is Truth by its very essence, that is, the divine act of being (*esse*); and by this Truth all words are words. Similarly, there is one absolute Wisdom elevated above all things, that is, the divine Wisdom, by participating in which all wise persons are wise. Further, there is one absolute Word, by participating in which all persons having a word are called speakers. Now this is the divine Word which of itself is the Word elevated above all words. So in order that the Evangelist might signify this supereminence of the divine Word, he pointed out this Word to us absolutely without any addition.[25]

And because the Greeks, when they wished to signify something separate and elevated above everything else, did this by affixing the article to the name (as the Platonists, wishing to signify the separated substances, such as the separated good or the separated man, called them the good *per se*, or man *per se*), so the Evangelist, wishing to signify the separation and elevation of the Word above all things, affixed an article to the name "Logos," so that if it were stated in Latin we would have "*the* Word."

34. Secondly, we must consider the meaning of the phrase, *In the beginning.* We must note that according to Origen,[26] the word *principium* has many meanings [such as "principle," "source," or "beginning"]. Since the word *principium* implies a certain order of one thing

23. See *ST* I, q. 34, a. 3.
24. *Comm. in Io.* II. 4, no. 37; PG 14, col. 116B; cf. *Catena aurea*, 1:2. Citations of chapter and paragraph numbers for Origen's *Commentary on St. John* follow the critical edition in *Sources Chretiénnes*, 5 vols (Les Éditions du Cerf, 1966–1992).
25. See also *ST* I, q. 34, a. 2.
26. *Comm. in Io.* I. 16–17, nos. 90–105; PG 14, cols. 49B–53C; cf. *Catena aurea*, 1:1a.

to another, one can find a *principium* in all those things which have an order. First of all, order is found in quantified things; and so there is a principle of number and lengths, as for example, a line. Second, order is found in time; and so we speak of a "beginning" of time, or of duration. Third, order is found in learning; and this in two ways: as to nature, and as to ourselves, and in both cases we can speak of a 'beginning": "By this time you ought to be teachers" (Heb 5:12). As to nature, in Christian doctrine the beginning and principle of our wisdom is Christ, inasmuch as he is the Wisdom and Word of God., i.e., in his divinity.[27] But as to ourselves, the beginning is Christ himself inasmuch as the Word has become flesh, i.e., by his Incarnation. Fourth, an order is found in the production of a thing. In this perspective there can be a *principium* on the part of the thing generated, that is, the first part of the thing generated or made; as we say that the foundation is the beginning of a house. Another *principium* is on the part of the generator, and in this perspective there are three "principles": of intention, which is the purpose which motivates the agent; of reason, which is the idea in the mind of the maker; and of execution, which is the operative faculty. Considering these various ways of using the term, we now ask how *principium* is used here when it says, **In the beginning was the Word.**

35. We should note that this word can be taken in three ways. In one way so that *principium* is understood as the Person of the Son, who is the principle of creatures by reason of his active power acting with wisdom, which is the conception of the things that are brought into existence.[28] Hence we read: "Christ the power of God and the wisdom of God" (1 Cor 1:24). And so the Lord said about himself: "I am the *principium* who also speaks to you" (below 8:25). Taking *principium* in this way, we should understand the statement, **In the beginning was the Word,** as though he were saying, "The Word was in the Son," so that the sense would be: The Word himself is the *principium*, principle, in the sense in which life is said to be "in" God, when this life is not something other than God. And this is the explanation of Origen.[29] And so the Evangelist says **In the beginning** here in order, as Chrysostom[30] says, to show at the very outset the divinity of the Word by asserting that he is a principle because, as determining all, a principle is most honored.

36. In a second way *principium* can be understood as the Person of the Father, who is the principle not only of creatures, but of every divine process.[31] It is taken this way in, "Yours is princely power (*principium*) in the day of your birth" (Ps 109:3). In this second way one

27. See also *ST* I, q. 42, a. 3.
28. See *ST* I, q. 34, a. 3.
29. *Comm. in Io.* I. 19, nos. 116–17; PG 14, col. 57A; cf. *Catena aurea*, 1:1a.
30. *Hom. in Io.* 2. 3; PG 59, col. 33; cf. *Catena aurea*, 1:1b. See also *ST* I, q. 34, a. 3.
31. See also *ST* I, q. 33, aa. 1 and 3.

reads *In the beginning was the Word* as though it means, "The Son was in the Father." This is Augustine's[32] understanding of it, as well as Origen's.[33] The Son, however, is said to be in the Father because both have the same essence. Since the Son is his own essence, then the Son is in whomsoever the Son's essence is. Since, therefore, the essence of the Son is in the Father by consubstantiality, it is fitting that the Son be in the Father. Hence it says below (14:10): "I am in the Father and the Father is in me."

37. In a third way, *principium* can be taken for the beginning of duration, so that the sense of *In the beginning was the Word* is that the Word was before all things, as Augustine[34] explains it. According to Basil[35] and Hilary,[36] this phrase shows the eternity of the Word.

The phrase *In the beginning was the Word* shows that no matter which beginning of duration is taken, whether of temporal things which is time, or of aeviternal things which is the aeon, or of the whole world or any imagined span of time reaching back for many ages, at that beginning the Word already was. Hence Hilary[37] says: "Go back season by season, skip over the centuries, take away ages. Set down whatever you want as the beginning in your opinion: 'The Lord possessed me in the beginning of his ways, before he made anything'" (Prov. 8:22). But what is prior to the beginning of duration is eternal.[38]

38. And thus the first explanation asserts the causality of the Word; the second explanation affirms the consubstantiality of the Word with the Father, who utters the Word; and the third explanation affirms the co-eternity of the Word.

39. Now we should consider that it says that the Word *was* (*erat*), which is stated in the past imperfect tense. This tense is most appropriate for designating eternal things if we consider the nature of time and of the things that exist in time. For what is future is not yet in act; but what is at present is in act, and by the fact that it is in act what is present is not described as having been. Now the past perfect tense indicates that something has existed, has already come to an end, and has now ceased to be. The past imperfect tense, on the other hand, indicates that something has been, has not yet come to an end, nor has ceased to be, but still endures. Thus, whenever John mentions eternal things he expressly says "was" (*erat*, past imperfect tense), but when he refers to anything temporal he says "has been" (*fuit*, past perfect tense), as will be clear later.

---

32. *De Trin.* 6. 2, no. 3; PL 42, cols. 924–25.
33. *Comm. in Io.* I. 17, no. 102; PG 14, col. 53A–B.
34. *De Trin.* 6. 2, no. 3; PL 42, col. 925.
35. *Hom.* 16. 1; PG 31, col. 474C; cf. *Catena aurea*, 1:1a.
36. *De Trin.* 2. 13; PL 10, col. 60D; cf. *Catena aurea*, 1:1a.
37. Ibid.
38. See *ST* I, q. 42, a. 2.

But so far as concerns the notion of the present, the best way to designate eternity is the present tense, which indicates that something is in act, and this is always the characteristic of eternal things. And so it says in Exodus (3:14): "I am who am."[39] And Augustine[40] says: "He alone truly is whose being does not know a past and a future."

40. We should also note that this verb *was*, according to the Gloss,[41] is not understood here as indicating temporal changes, as other verbs do, but as signifying the existence of a thing. Thus it is also called a substantive verb.

41. Someone may ask how the Word can be co-eternal with the Father since he is begotten by the Father: for a human son, born from a human father, is subsequent to his father.

I answer that there are three reasons why an originative principle is prior in duration to that which derives from that principle. First of all, if the originative principle of anything precedes in time the action by which it produces the thing of which it is the principle; thus a man does not begin to write as soon as he exists, and so he precedes his writing in time. Secondly, if an action is successive; consequently, even if the action should happen to begin at the same time as the agent, the termination of the action is nevertheless subsequent to the agent. Thus, as soon as fire has been generated in a lower region, it begins to ascend; but the fire exists before it has ascended, because the motion by which it tends upward requires some time. Thirdly, by the fact that sometimes the beginning of a thing depends on the will of its principle, just as the beginning of a creature's coming-to-be depends on the will of God, such that God existed before any creature.

Yet none of these three is found in the generation of the divine Word. God did not first exist and then begin to generate the Word: for since the generation of the Word is nothing other than an intelligible conception, it would follow that God would be understanding in potency before understanding in act, which is impossible. Again, it is impossible that the generation of the Word involve succession: for then the divine Word would be unformed before it was formed (as happens in us who form words by "cogitating"), which is false, as was said. Again, we cannot say that the Father pre-established a beginning of duration for his Son by his own will because God the Father does not generate the Son by his will, as the Arians held, but naturally: for God

---

39. See *ST* I, q. 2, a. 3.

40. *De Trin.* 5. 2, no. 3; PL 42, col. 912. On the eternity of God see *ST* I, q. 10.

41. The Gloss was the standard Medieval commentary on the Bible, drawn largely from citations of the Church Fathers. Though the texts of the Fathers were gathered over many years, it was the school of Anselm of Laon (1100–1130) that was largely responsible for composing the Gloss. It was finished by the mid-12th century.

the Father, understanding himself, conceives the Word; and so God the Father did not exist prior to the Son.[42]

An example of this, to a limited degree, appears in fire and in the brightness issuing from it: for this brightness issues naturally and without succession from the fire. Again, if the fire were eternal, its brightness would be coeternal with it. This is why the Son is called the brightness of the Father: "the brightness of his glory" (Heb 1:3). But this example lacks an illustration of the identity of nature. And so we call him Son, although in human sonship we do not find coeternity: for we must attain our knowledge of divine things from many likenesses in material things, for one likeness is not enough. The Council of Ephesus says that the Son always coexists with the Father: for "brightness" indicates his unchangeability, "birth" points to the Word himself, but the name "Son" suggests his consubstantiality.[43]

42. And so we give the Son various names to express his perfection, which cannot be expressed by one name. We call him "Son" to show that he is of the same nature as the Father; we call him "image" to show that he is not unlike the Father in any way; we call him "brightness" to show that he is coeternal; and he is called the "Word" to show that he is begotten in an immaterial manner.[44]

43. Then the Evangelist says, *and the Word was with God*, which is the second clause in his account. The first thing to consider is the meaning of the two words which did not appear in the first clause, that is, *God, and with*; for we have already explained the meanings of "Word," and "beginning." Let us continue carefully by examining these two new words, and to better understand the explanation of this second clause, we must say something about the meaning of each so far as it is relevant to our purpose.

44. At the outset, we should note that the name "God" signifies the divinity concretely and is inherent in a subject, while the name "deity" signifies the divinity in the abstract and absolutely. Thus the name "deity" cannot naturally and by its mode of signifying stand for a [divine] person, but only for the [divine] nature. But the name "God" can, by its natural mode of signifying, stand for any one of the [divine] persons, just as the name "man" stands for any individual (*suppositum*) possessing humanity. Therefore, whenever the truth of a statement or its predicate require that the name "God" stand for the person, then it stands for the person, as when we say, "God begets God."[45] Thus, when it says here that *the Word was with God*, it is necessary that *God* stand for the person of the Father, because the preposition *with* signifies the distinction of the Word, which is said to be *with God*. And although this preposition signifies a distinction in person, it does not sig-

42. See *ST* I, q. 42, a. 2.   43. See *ST* I, q. 27, a. 1.
44. See *ST* I, q. 34, a. 2, ad 3.   45. See *ST* I, q. 39, aa. 4–5.

nify a distinction in nature, since the nature of the Father and of the Son is the same. Consequently, the Evangelist wished to signify the person of the Father when he said *God*.

45. Here we should note that the preposition *with* signifies a certain union of the thing signified by its grammatical antecedent to the thing signified by its grammatical object, just as the preposition "in" does. However, there is a difference, because the preposition "in" signifies a certain intrinsic union, whereas the preposition *with* implies in a certain way an extrinsic union. And we state both in divine matters, namely, that the Son is *in* the Father and *with* the Father. Here the intrinsic union pertains to consubstantiality, but the extrinsic union (if we may use such an expression, since "extrinsic" is improperly employed in divine matters) refers only to a personal distinction, because the Son is distinguished from the Father by origin alone. And so these two words designate both a consubstantiality in nature and distinction in person: consubstantiality inasmuch as a certain union is implied; but distinction, inasmuch as a certain otherness is signified as was said above.

The preposition "in," as was said, principally signifies consubstantiality, as implying an intrinsic union and, by way of consequence, a distinction of persons, inasmuch as every preposition is transitive. The preposition "with" principally signifies a personal distinction, but also a consubstantiality inasmuch as it signifies a certain extrinsic, so to speak, union. For these reasons the Evangelist specifically used here the preposition "with" in order to express the distinction of the person of the Son from the Father, saying, *and the Word was with God*, that is, the Son was with the Father as one person with another.

46. We should note further that this preposition *with* has four meanings, and these eliminate four objections. First, the preposition *with* signifies the subsistence of its antecedent, because things that do not subsist of themselves are not properly said to be "with" another; thus we do not say that a color is with a body, and the same applies to other things that do not subsist of themselves. But things that do subsist of themselves are properly said to be "with" another; thus we say that a man is with a man, and a stone with a stone.

Secondly, it signifies authority in its grammatical object. For we do not, properly speaking, say that a king is with a soldier, but that the soldier is with the king. Thirdly, it asserts a distinction. For it is not proper to say that a person is with himself, but rather that one man is with another. Fourthly, it signifies a certain union and fellowship. For when some person is said to be with another, it suggests to us that there is some social union between them.

Considering these four conditions implied in the meaning of this preposition *with*, the Evangelist quite appropriately joins to the first clause, *In the beginning was the Word*, this second clause, *and the*

Word was with God. For if we omit one of the three explanations of, *In the beginning was the Word* (namely, the one in which *principium* was understood as the Son), certain heretics make a twofold objection against each of the other explanations (namely, the one in which *principium* means the same as "before all things," and the one in which it is understood as the Father). Thus there are four objections, and we can answer these by the four conditions indicated by this preposition *with*.

47. The first of these objections is this. You say that the Word was in the beginning, i.e., before all things. But before all things there was nothing. So if before all things there was nothing, where then was the Word? This objection arises due to the imaginings of those who think that whatever exists is somewhere and in some place. But this is rejected by John when he says, *with God*, which indicates the union mentioned in the last of the four conditions. So, according to Basil,[46] the meaning is this: Where was the Word? The answer is: *with God*; not in some place, since he is unsurroundable, but he is with the Father, who is not enclosed by any place.

48. The second objection against the same explanation is this. You say that the Word was in the beginning, i.e., before all things. But whatever exists before all things appears to proceed from no one, since that from which something proceeds seems to be prior to that which proceeds from it. Therefore, the Word does not proceed from another. This objection is rejected when he says, *the Word was with God*, taking "with" according to its second condition, as implying authority in what is causing. So the meaning, according to Hilary,[47] is this: From whom is the Word if he exists before all things? The Evangelist answers: *the Word was with God*, i.e., although the Word has no beginning of duration, still he does not lack a *principium* or author, for he was with God as his author.

49. The third objection, directed to the explanation in which *principium* is understood as the Father, is this: You say that *In the beginning was the Word*, i.e., the Son was in the Father. But that which is in something does not seem to be subsistent, as a hypostasis; just as the whiteness in a body does not subsist. This objection is solved by the statement, *the Word was with God*, taking "with" in its first condition, as implying the subsistence of its grammatical antecedent. So according to Chrysostom,[48] the meaning is this: *In the beginning was the Word*, not as an accident, but he was *with God*, as subsisting, and a divine hypostasis.

50. The fourth objection, against the same explanation, is this. You say that the Word was in the beginning, i.e., in the Father. But what-

46. *Hom.* 16. 4; PG 31, col. 479B; cf. *Catena aurea*, 1:1b.
47. *De Trin.* 2. 14; PL 10, col. 61; cf. *Catena aurea*, 1:1b.
48. *Hom. in Io.* 4. 1; PG 59, col. 46–47; cf. *Catena aurea*, 1:2.

ever is in something is not distinct from it. So the Son is not distinct from the Father. This objection is answered by the statement, *and the Word was with God*, taking "with" in its third condition, as indicating distinction. Thus the meaning, according to Alcuin[49] and Bede,[50] is this: *the Word was with God*, and he was "in" the Father by a consubstantiality of nature, while still being "with" him through a distinction in person.

51. And so, *and the Word was with God*, indicates: the union of the Word with the Father in nature, according to Basil; their distinction in person, according to Alcuin and Bede; the subsistence of the Word in the divine nature, according to Chrysostom; and the authorship of the Father in relation to the Word, according to Hilary.

52. We should also note, according to Origen,[51] that *the Word was with God* shows that the Son has always been with the Father. For in the Old Testament it says that the word of the Lord "came" to Jeremiah or to someone else, as is plain in many passages of sacred Scripture. But it does not say that the word of the Lord was "with" Jeremiah or anyone else, because the word "comes" to those who begin to have the word after not having it. Thus the Evangelist did not say that the Word "came" to the Father, but was "with" the Father, because, given the Father, the Word was with him.

53. Then he says, *and the Word was God*. This is the third clause in John's account, and it follows most appropriately considering the order of teaching. For since John had said both *when* and *where* the Word was, it remained to inquire *what* the Word was, that is, *the Word was God*, taking "Word" as the subject, and "God" as the predicate.

54. But since one should first inquire what a thing is before investigating where and when it is, it seems that John violated this order by discussing these latter first.

Origen[52] answers this by saying that the Word of God is with man and with God in different ways. The Word is with man as perfecting him, because it is through him that man becomes wise and good: "She makes friends of God and prophets" (Wis 7:27). But the Word is not with God as though the Father were perfected and enlightened by him.[53] Rather, the Word is with God as receiving natural divinity from him, who utters the Word, and from whom he has it that he is the same God with him. And so, since the Word was with God by origin, it was necessary to show first that the Word was in the Father and with the Father before showing that the Word was God.

---

49. *Comm. in S. Ioannis Evang.* 1; PL 100, col. 745.
50. *In S. Ioannis Evang. expos.* 1; PL 92, col. 638.
51. *Comm. in Io.* II. 1, no. 8; PG 14, col. 105C; cf. *Catena aurea*, 1:1b.
52. Ibid., no. 10; PG 14, col. 105D; cf. *Catena aurea*, 1:1c.
53. See *ST* I, q. 34, a. 2, ad 4.

55. This clause also enables us to answer two objections which arise from the foregoing. The first is based on the name "Word," and is this. You say that *In the beginning was the Word*, and that the Word was *with God*. Now it is obvious that "word" is generally understood to signify a vocal sound and the statement of something necessary, a manifesting of thoughts. But these words pass away and do not subsist. Accordingly, someone could think that the Evangelist was speaking of a word like these.

According to Hilary[54] and Augustine,[55] this question is sufficiently answered by the above account. Augustine says that it is obvious that in this passage "Word" cannot be understood as a statement because, since a statement is in motion and passes away, it could not be said that *In the beginning was the Word*, if this Word were something passing away and in motion. The same thing is clear from *and the Word was with God*: for to be "in" another is not the same as to be "with" another. Our word, since it does not subsist, is not "with" us, but "in" us; but the Word of God is subsistent, and therefore "with" God. And so the Evangelist expressly says, *and the Word was with God*. To entirely remove the ground of the objection, he adds the nature of being of the Word, saying *and the Word was God*.

56. The other question comes from his saying, *with God*. For since "with" indicates a distinction, it could be thought that the *Word was with God*, i.e., the Father, as distinct from him in nature. So to exclude this he adds at once the consubstantiality of the Word with the Father, saying, *and the Word was God*. As if to say: the Word is not separated from the Father by a diversity of nature, because the Word itself is God.

57. Note also the special way of signifying, since he says, *the Word was God*, using "God" absolutely to show that he is not God in the same way in which the name of the deity is given to a creature in Sacred Scripture. For a creature sometimes shares this name with some added qualification, as when it says, "I have appointed you the God of Pharaoh" (Ex 7:1), in order to indicate that he was not God absolutely or by nature, because he was appointed the god of someone in a qualified sense. Again, it says in the Psalm (81:6): "I said, 'You are gods'"— as if to say: in my opinion, but not in reality. Thus the Word is called God absolutely because he is God by his own essence, and not by participation, as men and angels are.

58. We should note that Origen disgracefully misunderstood this clause, led astray by the Greek manner of speaking. It is the custom among the Greeks to put the article before every name in order to indicate a distinction. In the Greek version of John's Gospel the name

54. *De Trin.* 2. 15; PL 10, col. 61; cf. *Catena aurea*, 1:1c.
55. *Tract. in Io.* 1. 8; PL 35, col. 1383.

"Word" in the statement, *In the beginning was the Word*, and also the name "God" in the statement, *and the Word was with God*, are prefixed by an article, so as to read "the Word" and "the God," in order to indicate the eminence and distinction of the Word from other words, and the principality of the Father in the divinity. But in the statement, *the Word was God*, the article is not prefixed to the noun "God," which stands for the person of the Son. Because of this Origen[56] blasphemed that the Word, although he was Word by essence, was not God by essence, but is called God by participation; while the Father alone is God by essence. And so he held that the Son is inferior to the Father.[57]

59. Chrysostom[58] proves that this is not true, because if the article used with the name "God" implied the superiority of the Father in respect to the Son, it would never be used with the name "God" when it is used as a predicate of another, but only when it is predicated of the Father. Further, whenever said of the Father, it would be accompanied by the article. However, we find the opposite to be the case in two statements of the Apostle, who calls Christ "God," using the article. For in Titus (2:13) he says "the coming of the glory of the great God and our Savior Jesus Christ," where "God" stands for the Son, and in the Greek the article is used. Therefore, Christ is the great God. Again he says (Rom 9:5): "Christ, who is God over all things, blessed forever," and again the article is used with "God" in the Greek. Further, in 1 John (5:20) it says: "That we may be in his true Son, Jesus Christ; he is the true God and eternal life." Thus, Christ is not God by participation, but truly God. And so the theory of Origen is clearly false.

Chrysostom gives us the reason why the Evangelist did not use the article with the name "God," namely, because he had already mentioned God twice using the article, and so it was not necessary to repeat it a third time, but it was implied. Or, a better reason would be that "God" is used here as the predicate and is taken formally. And it is not the custom for the article to accompany names used as predicates, since the article indicates separation. But if "God" were used here as the subject, it could stand for any of the persons, as the Son or the Holy Spirit; then, no doubt, the article would be used in the Greek.

60. Then he says, *He was in the beginning with God*. This is the fourth clause and is introduced because of the preceding clause. For from the Evangelist's statement that *the Word was God*, two false interpretations could be held by those who misunderstand. One of these is by the pagans, who acknowledge many and different gods, and say that their wills are in opposition. For example, those who put out the fable of Jupiter fighting with Saturn; or as the Manicheans,[59] who

56. *Comm. in Io.* II. 2, nos. 17–18; PG 14, col. 109A–B.
57. See *ST* I, q. 34, a. 1, ad 1.
58. *Hom. in Io.* 4. 3, PG 59, col. 50; cf. *Catena aurea*, 1:1c.
59. The movement called Manichaeism originated with Mani (Manichaeus),

have two contrary principles of nature. The Lord said against this error
(Dt 6:4): "Hear O Israel: The Lord our God is one Lord."

Since the Evangelist had said, *the Word was with God; and the
Word was God*, they could adduce this in support of their error by understanding the God with whom the Word is to be one [God], and
the Word to be another, having another, or contrary, will to the former; and this is against the law of the Gospel. And so to exclude this
he says, *He was in the beginning with God*, as if to say, according to
Hilary:[60] I say that the Word is God, not as if he has a distinct divinity,
but he is with God, that is, in the one same nature in which he is. Further, lest his statement, *and the Word was God*, be taken to mean that
the Word has an opposed will, he added that the Word was *in the beginning with God*, namely, the Father; not as divided from him or opposed, but having an identity of nature with him and a harmony of
will.[61] This union comes about by the sharing of the divine nature in
the three persons, and by the bond of the natural love of the Father
and the Son.

61. The Arians were able to draw out another error from the above.
They think that the Son is less than the Father because it says below (14:28): "The Father is greater than I." And they say the Father
is greater than the Son both as to eternity and as to divinity of nature. And so to exclude this the Evangelist added: *He was in the beginning with God*. For Arius[62] admits the first clause, *In the beginning
was the Word*, but he will not admit that *principium* should be taken
for the Father, but rather for the beginning of creatures. So he says
that the Word was in the beginning of creatures, and consequently is
in no sense coeternal with the Father. But this is excluded, according
to Chrysostom,[63] by this clause, *He was in the beginning*, not of creatures, but *in the beginning with God*, i.e., whenever God existed. For
the Father was never alone without the Son or Word, but *He*, that is,
the Word, was always *with God*.

62. Again, Arius admits that the Word was God, but nevertheless
inferior to the Father. This is excluded by what follows. For there are
two attributes proper to the great God which Arius attributed solely

---

c. 216–276, and spread from his home in Persia to both the East and the West
from the late third century onwards. The Manichaeans emphasized a cosmic du-
alism between the true God and the evil lord who fashioned the material world,
and taught the need to release the divine element in human beings through ascetical acts from this fallen, material world.

60. *De Trin.* 2. 16; PL 10, col. 62; cf. *Catena aurea*, 1:2.

61. See *ST* I, q. 42, a. 5.

62. Arius, a priest of Alexandria in the early fourth century, taught that the
Logos is not the eternal Son of God, but is a creature, made by the Father, and
not divine in the same sense that the Father is. The controversy over his teaching
resulted in his condemnation at the Council of Nicaea in 325.

63. *Hom. in Io.* 4. 1; PG 59, col. 47; cf. *Catena aurea*, 1:2.

to God the Father, that is, eternity and omnipotence. So in whomever these two attributes are found, he is the great God, than whom none is greater. But the Evangelist attributes these two to the Word. Therefore, the Word is the great God, and not inferior. He says the Word is eternal when he states, *He was in the beginning with God*, i.e., the Word was with God from eternity, and not only in the beginning of creatures (as Arius held), but with God, receiving being and divinity from him. Further, he attributes omnipotence to the Word when he adds, *Through him all things came into being.*[64] ωм η̣ ν ο + ' ̔ ι̣ Ṽ

63. Origen[65] gives a rather beautiful explanation of this clause, *He was in the beginning with God*, when he says that it is not separate from the first three, but is in a certain sense their epilogue. For the Evangelist, after he had indicated that truth was the Son's and was about to describe his power, in a way gathers together in a summary form, in this fourth clause, what he had said in the first three. For in saying *He*, he understands the third clause; by adding *was in the beginning*, he recalls the first clause; and by adding *with God*, he recalls the second, so that we do not think that the Word which was in the beginning is different than the Word which was God; but this Word which was God *was in the beginning with God*.

64. If one considers these four propositions well, he will find that they clearly destroy all the errors of the heretics and of the philosophers. For some heretics, as Ebion and Cerinthus, said that Christ did not exist before the Blessed Virgin, but took from her the beginning of his being and duration; for they held that he was a mere man, who had merited divinity by his good works. Photinus and Paul of Samosata,[66] following them, said the same thing. But the Evangelist excludes their errors saying, *In the beginning was the Word*, i.e., before all things, and in the Father from eternity. Thus he did not derive his beginning from the Virgin.[67]

Sabellius,[68] on the other hand, although he admitted that the God who took flesh did not receive his beginning from the Virgin, but existed from eternity, still said that the person of the Father, who existed

64. See *ST* I, q. 42, aa. 2, 4, 6.
65. *Comm. in Io.* II. 4, no. 34; PG 14, col. 116A; cf. *Catena aurea*, 1:2.
66. Photinus, bishop of Sirmium (died c. 376), was deposed for teaching that Jesus was a man inspired by God, not the pre-existant Logos become flesh. Paul of Samosata, bishop of Antioch (c. 260), was reported by Eusebius as also teaching that Jesus was an ordinary man inhabited by the Word of God, and who thus became the Son of God. Both Photinus and Paul represent an adoptionist Christology.
67. See *ST* III, q. 32, aa. 2–3; III, q. 35, aa. 2–4.
68. Sabellius (flourished in Rome, early third century) taught that the Father and Son were simply different modes of the one God, with no real distinction between them. He and others who taught this are known as Monarchian Modalists because they uphold the unity or monarchy of God by asserting that Father and Son are merely different economic modes of the activity of the one God.

from eternity, was not distinct from the person of the Son, who took flesh from the Virgin. He maintained that the Father and Son were the same person; and so he failed to distinguish the trinity of persons in the deity.[69] The Evangelist says against this error, *and the Word was with God*, i.e., the Son was with the Father, as one person with another.

Eunomius[70] declared that the Son is entirely unlike the Father. The Evangelist rejects this when he says, *and the word was God*. Finally, Arius said that the Son was less than the Father. The Evangelist excludes this by saying, *He was in the beginning with God*, as was explained above.

65. These words also exclude the errors of the philosophers. For some of the ancient philosophers, namely, the natural philosophers, maintained that the world did not come from any intellect or through some purpose, but by chance. Consequently, they did not place at the beginning as the cause of things a reason or intellect, but only matter in flux; for example, atoms, as Democritus thought, or other material principles of this kind as different philosophers maintained. Against these the Evangelist says, *In the beginning was the Word*, from whom, and not from chance, things derive their beginning.

Plato, however, thought that the Ideas of all the things that were made were subsistent, i.e., existing separately in their own natures; and material things exist by participating in these. For example, he thought men existed through the separated Idea of man, which he called Man *per se*. So lest you supposed, as did Plato, that this Idea through which all things were made be Ideas separated from God, the Evangelist adds, *and the Word was with God*.[71]

Other Platonists, as Chrysostom relates, maintained that God the Father was most eminent and first, but under him they placed a certain mind in which there were the likenesses and ideas of all things. So lest you think that the Word was with the Father in such a way as to be under him and less than he, the Evangelist adds, *and the Word was God*.

Aristotle,[72] however, thought that the ideas of all things are in God, and that in God, the intellect, the one understanding, and what is understood, are the same. Nevertheless, he thought that the world is coe-

---

69. See *ST* I, q. 27, a. 1.

70. Eunomius (c. 325–395) was the key representative of the later radical Arian party that asserted that the Son is entirely unlike the Father. He was the main opponent of the Cappadocian Fathers (Basil, Gregory of Nazianzus, and Gregory of Nyssa).

71. See *ST* I, q. 15.

72. See Aristotle, *Physics* VIII, for his explanation of eternal motion. For Aquinas's interpretation of Aristotle's view of God, see his *Commentary on Aristotle's Metaphysics*, especially nos. 2536–51 and 2600–63.

ternal with him. Against this the Evangelist says, *He*, the Word alone, *was in the beginning with God*, in such a way that *He* does not exclude another person, but only another coeternal nature.

66. Note the difference in what has been said between John and the other Evangelists: how he began his Gospel on a loftier plane than they. They announced Christ the Son of God born in time: "When Jesus was born in Bethlehem" (Mt 2:1); but John presents him existing from eternity: *In the beginning was the Word*. They show him suddenly appearing among men: "Now you dismiss your servant, O Lord, in peace, according to your word; because my eyes have seen your salvation" (Lk 2:29); but John says that he always existed with the Father: *and the Word was with God*. The others show him as a man: "They gave glory to God who had given such authority to men" (Mt 9:8); but John says that he is God: *and the Word was God*. The others say he lives with men: "While living in Galilee, Jesus said to them" (Mt 17:21); but John says that he has always been with the Father: *He was in the beginning with God*.

67. Note also how the Evangelist designedly uses the word *was* (*erat*) to show that the Word of God transcends all times: present, past and future. It is as though he were saying: He was beyond time: present, past and future, as the Gloss says.

LECTURE 2

3 All things were made through him, and without him nothing was made. What was made 4a in him was life.[73]

68. After the Evangelist has told of the existence and nature of the Divine Word, so far as it can be told by man, he then shows the might of his power. First, he shows his power with respect to all things that come into existence. Secondly, with respect to man. As to the first, he uses three clauses; and we will not distinguish these at present because they will be distinguished in different ways according to the different explanations given by the saints.

69. The first clause, *All things were made through him*, is used to show three things concerning the Word. First, according to Chrysostom,[74] to show the equality of the Word to the Father. For as stated earlier, the error of Arius was rejected by the Evangelist when he showed the coeternity of the Son with the Father by saying, "He was in the beginning with God." Here he excludes the same error when

---

73. St. Thomas quotes Jn 1:3 in *ST* I, q. 74, a. 3, obj. 1; III, q. 10, a. 2, ad 1; and Jn 1:3–4a in *ST* I, q. 18, a. 4, *sed contra*.
74. *Hom. in Io.* 5. 3; PG 59, col. 56; cf. *Catena aurea*, 1:3a.

he shows the omnipotence of the Son, saying, *All things were made through him*. For to be the principle of all the things that are made is proper to the great omnipotent God, as the Psalm (134:6) says, "Whatever the Lord wills he does, in heaven and on earth." Thus the Word, through whom all things were made, is God, great and coequal to the Father.[75]

70. Secondly, according to Hilary,[76] this clause is used to show the coeternity of the Word with the Father. For since someone might understand the earlier statement, "In the beginning was the Word," as referring to the beginning of creatures, i.e., that before there were any creatures there was a time in which the Word did not exist, the Evangelist rejects this by saying, *All things were made through him*. For if all things were made through the Word, then time was also. From this we can form the following argument: If all time was made through him, there was no time before him or with him, because before all these, he was. Therefore they [the Son and the Father] are eternally coeternal.[77]

71. Thirdly, according to Augustine,[78] this clause is used to show the consubstantiality of the Word with the Father. For if all things were made through the Word, the Word himself cannot be said to have been made; because, if made, he was made through some Word, since all things were made through the Word. Consequently, there would have been another Word through whom was made the Word of whom the Evangelist is speaking. This Word, through whom all things are made, we call the only begotten Son of God, because he is neither made nor is he a creature. And if he is not a creature, it is necessary to say that he is of the same substance with the Father, since every substance other than the divine essence is made. But a substance that is not a creature is God. And so the Word, through whom all things were made, is consubstantial with the Father, since he is neither made, nor is he a creature.

72. And so in saying *All things were made through him*, you have, according to Chrysostom, the equality of the Word with the Father; the coeternity of the Word with the Father, according to Hilary; and the consubstantiality of the Word with the Father, according to Augustine.

73. Here we must guard against three errors. First, the error of Valentinus.[79] He understood *All things were made through him* to mean

---

75. See *ST* I, q. 34, a. 3; I, q. 42, aa. 4, 6.
76. *De Trin.* 2. 17; PL 10, col. 62; cf. *Catena aurea*, 1:3a.
77. See *ST* I, q. 42, a. 2.
78. *Tract. in Io.* 1. 11; PL 35, col. 1384; *De Trin.* 1. 6, no. 9; PL 42, col. 825; cf. *Catena aurea*, 1:3a.
79. Valentinus (flourished in Rome c. 136) was probably the most influential

that the Word proffered to the Creator the cause of his creating the world; so that all things were made through the Word as if the Father's creating the world came from the Word. This leads to the position of those who said that God created the world because of some exterior cause; and this is contrary to Proverbs (16:4), "The Lord made all things for himself." The reason this is an error is that, as Origen says, if the Word had been a cause to the Creator by offering him the material for making things, he would not have said, *All things were made through him*, but on the contrary, that all things were made through the Creator by the Word.

74. Secondly, we must avoid the error of Origen.[80] He said that the Holy Spirit was included among all the things made through the Word; from which it follows that he is a creature. And this is what Origen thought. This is heretical and blasphemous, since the Holy Spirit has the same glory and substance and dignity as the Father and the Son, according to the words of Matthew (28:19), "Make disciples of all the nations, baptizing them in the name of the Father, and of the Son, and of the Holy Spirit." And, "There are three who give testimony in heaven, the Father, the Word, and the Holy Spirit; and these three are one" (1 Jn 5:7).[81] Thus when the Evangelist says, *All things were made through him*, one should not understand "all things" absolutely, but in the realm of creatures and of things made. As if to say: All things that were made, were made through him. Otherwise, if "all things" were taken absolutely, it would follow that the Father and the Holy Spirit were made through him; and this is blasphemous. Consequently, neither the Father nor anything substantial with the Father was made through the Word.

75. Thirdly, we must avoid other of Origen's[82] errors. For he said that all things were made through the Word as something is made by a greater through a lesser, as if the Son were inferior to, and an instrument of, the Father. But it is clear from many places in Scripture that the preposition "through" (*per*) does not signify inferiority in the thing which is its grammatical object, i.e., in the Son or Word. For the Apostle says, "God is faithful, through whom you were called into the fellowship of his Son" (1 Cor 1:9). If he "through" whom something is done has a superior, then the Father has a superior. But this is false. Therefore, the preposition "through" does not signify any inferiority in the Son when all things are said to have been made through him.[83]

---

of the early Gnostics. His theological system, known through the works of his disciples, was critiqued by Irenaeus, Tertullian, and Clement of Alexandria.

80. *Comm. in Io.* II. 10, no. 75; PG 14, col. 128A–B.
81. See *ST* I, q. 27, aa. 3–4.
82. *Comm. in Io.* II. 10, no. 72; PG 14, col. 125C.
83. See *ST* I, q. 45, a. 6.

76. To explain this point further, we should note that when something is said to be made through someone, the preposition "through" (*per*) denotes some sort of causality in its object with respect to an operation; but not always the same kind of causality. For since an operation, according to our manner of signifying, is considered to be medial between the one acting and the thing produced, the operation itself can be regarded in two ways. In one way, as issuing from the one operating, who is the cause of the action itself; in another way, as terminated in the thing produced. Accordingly, the preposition "through" sometimes signifies the cause of the operation insofar as it issues from the one operating; but sometimes as terminated in the thing which is produced. It signifies the cause of the operation as issuing from the one operating when the object of the preposition is either the efficient or formal cause why the one operating is operating. For example, we have a formal cause when fire is heating through heat; for heat is the formal cause of the fire's heating. We have a movent of efficient cause in cases where secondary agents act through primary agents; as when I say that the bailiff acts through the king, because the king is the efficient cause of the bailiff's acting. This is the way Valentinus understood that all things were made through the Word: as though the Word were the cause of the maker's production of all things. The preposition "through" implies the causality of the operation as terminated in the thing produced when what is signified through that causality is not the cause which operates, but the cause of the operation precisely as terminated in the thing produced. So when I say, "The carpenter is making a bench through [by means of] a hatchet," the hatchet is not the cause of the carpenter's operating; but we do say that it is the cause of the bench's being made by the one acting.

And so when it says that ***All things were made through him***, if the "through" denotes the efficient or movent cause, causing the Father to act, then in this sense the Father does nothing through the Son, but he does all things through himself, as has been said. But if the "through" denotes a formal cause, as when the Father operates through his wisdom, which is his essence, he operates through his wisdom as he operates through his essence. And because the wisdom and power of the Father are attributed to the Son, as when we say, "Christ, the power of God and the wisdom of God" (1 Cor 1:24), then by appropriation we say that the Father does all things through the Son, i.e., through his wisdom. And so Augustine[84] says that the phrase "from whom all things," is appropriated to the Father; "through whom all things," is appropriated to the Son; and "in whom all things," is appropriated to the Holy Spirit. But if the "through" denotes causality from the stand-

84. *De Trin.* 6. 10, no. 12; PL 42, col. 932.

point of the thing produced, then the statement, "The Father does all things through the Son," is not [mere] appropriation but proper to the Word, because the fact that he is a cause of creatures is had from someone else, namely the Father, from whom he has being.[85]

However, it does not follow from this that the Word is the instrument of the Father, although whatever is moved by another to effect something partakes of the nature of an instrument. For when I say that someone works through a power received from another, this can be understood in two ways. In one way, as meaning that the power of the giver and of the receiver is numerically one and the same power; and in this way the one operating through a power received from another is not inferior but equal to the one from whom he receives it. Therefore, since the same power which the Father has he gives to the Son, through which the Son works, when it is said that "the Father works through the Son," one should not on that account say that the Son is inferior to the Father or is his instrument.[86] This would be the case, rather, in those who receive from another not the same power, but another and created one. And so it is plain that neither the Holy Spirit nor the Son are causes of the Father's working, and that neither is the minister or instrument of the Father, as Origen[87] raved.

77. If we carefully consider the words, *All things were made through him*, we can clearly see that the Evangelist spoke with the utmost exactitude. For whoever makes something must preconceive it in his wisdom, which is the form and pattern of the thing made: as the form preconceived in the mind of an artisan is the pattern of the cabinet to be made. So, God makes nothing except through the conception of his intellect, which is an eternally conceived wisdom, that is, the Word of God, and the Son of God. Accordingly, it is impossible that he should make anything except through the Son. And so Augustine[88] says, in *The Trinity*, that the Word is the art full of the living patterns of all things. Thus it is clear that all things which the Father makes, he makes through him.

78. It should be remarked that, according to Chrysostom,[89] all the things which Moses enumerates, individually in God's production of things, saying, "And God said, 'Let there be light'" (Gen 1:3) and so forth, all these the Evangelist transcends and embraces in one phrase, saying, *All things were made through him*. The reason is that Moses wished to teach the emanation of creatures from God; hence he enumerated them one by one. But John, hastening toward loftier things,

85. See *ST* I, q. 33, a. 1.
86. See *ST* I, q. 42, a. 6.
87. *Comm. in Io.* II. 14, no. 104; PG 14, col. 140A. See also *ST* I, q. 34, a. 3.
88. *De Trin.* 6. 10, no. 11; PL 42, col. 931.
89. *Hom. in Io.* 5. 1; PG 59, col. 53; cf. *Catena aurea*, 1:3b.

intends in this book to lead us specifically to a knowledge of the Creator himself.

79. Then he says, *and without him nothing was made*. This is the second clause which some have distorted, as Augustine[90] says in his work, *The Nature of the Good*. Because of John's manner of speaking here, they believed that he was using "nothing" in an affirmative sense; as though nothing was something which was made without the Word. And so they claimed that this clause was added by the Evangelist in order to exclude something which was not made by the Word. They say that the Evangelist, having said that *All things were made through him*, added *and without him nothing was made*. It was as if to say: I say that all things were made through him in such a way that still something was made without him, that is, the "nothing."

80. Three heresies came from this. First, that of Valentinus. He affirmed, as Origen[91] says, a multitude of principles, and taught that from them came thirty eras. The first principles he postulates are two: The Deep, which he calls God the Father, and Silence. And from these proceed ten eras. But from the Deep and from Silence, he says, there are two other principles, Mind and Truth; and from these issued eight eras. Then from Mind and Truth, there are two other principles, Word and Life; and from these issued twelve eras; thus making a total of thirty. Finally, from the Word and Life there proceeded in time, the man Christ and the Church. In this way Valentinus affirmed many eras previous to the issuing forth of the Word. And so he said that because the Evangelist had stated that *all things were made through him*, then, lest anything think that those previous eras had been effected through the Word, he added, *and without him nothing was made*, i.e., all the preceding eras and all that had existed in them. All of these John calls "nothing," because they transcend human reason and cannot be grasped by the mind.

81. The second error to arise from this was that of Manichaeus, who affirmed two opposing principles: one is the source of incorruptible things, and the other of corruptible things. He said that after John had stated that *All things were made through him*, then, lest it be thought that the Word is the cause of corruptible things, he immediately added, *and without him nothing was made*, i.e., things subject to corruption, which are called "nothing" because their being consists in being continually transformed into nothing.

82. The third error is that of those who claim that by "nothing" we should understand the devil, according to Job (18:15), "May the companions of him who is not dwell in his house." And so they say that all

---

90. *De nat. boni* 25; PL 42, col. 559; cf. *Catena aurea*, 1:3b.
91. *Comm. in Io.* II, 14, nos. 100–101; PG 14, col. 137A–C; cf. *Catena aurea*, 1:3b.

things except the devil were made through the Word. In this way they explain, *without him nothing was made*, that is, the devil.

83. All these three errors, arising as they do from the same source namely, taking "nothing" in a positive sense, are excluded by the fact that "nothing" is not used here in an affirmative, but in a merely negative sense: the sense being that all things were made through the Word in such a way that there is nothing participating in existence that was not made through him.[92]

84. Perhaps someone will object and say that is was superfluous to add this clause, if it is to be understood negatively, on the ground that the Evangelist, in stating that *All things were made through him*, seems to have already said adequately enough that there is not something that was not made through the Word.

The answer to this is that, according to many expositors, this clause was added in many ways for a number of reasons. One of these reasons is, according to Chrysostom,[93] so that no one reading the Old Testament and finding only visible things listed by Moses in the creation of things, would think that these were the only things made through the Word. And so after he had said, *All things were made through him*, namely, those that Moses listed, the Evangelist then added, *and without him nothing was made*, as though he were saying: None of the things which exist, whether visible or invisible, was made without the Word.[94] Indeed, the Apostle also speaks in this way (Col 1:16), saying that all things, visible and invisible, were created in Christ; and here the Apostle makes specific mention of invisible things because Moses had made no express mention of them on account of the lack of erudition of that people who could not be raised above the things of sense.

Chrysostom[95] also gives another reason why this clause was added. For someone reading in the Gospels of the many signs and miracles worked by Christ, such as, "The blind see, the lame walk, lepers were cleansed" (Mt 11:5), might believe that in saying, *All things were made through him*, John meant that only the things mentioned in those Gospels, and nothing else, were made through him. So lest anyone suspect this, the Evangelist adds, *and without him nothing was made*. As if to say: Not only all the things contained in the Gospels were made through him, but none of the things that were made, was made without him. And so, according to Chrysostom, this clause is added to bring out his total causality, and serves, as it were, to complete his previous statement.

---

92. See *ST* I, q. 45, aa. 1–2.
93. *Hom. in Io.* 5. 1; PG 59, col. 53, 56; cf. *Catena aurea*, 1:3b.
94. See *ST* I, q. 44, a. 1.
95. *Hom. in Io.* 5. 1; PG 59, col. 57; cf. *Catena aurea*, 1:3b.

85. According to Hilary,[96] however, this clause is introduced to show that the Word has operative power from another. For since the Evangelist had said, *All things were made through him*, it might be supposed that the Father is excluded from all causality. For that reason he added, *and without him nothing was made.* As if to say: All things were made through him, but in such a way that the Father made all things with him. For "without him" is equivalent to saying, "not alone," so that the meaning is: It is not he alone through whom all things were made, but he is the other one without whom nothing was made. It is as if he said: *Without him*, with another working, i.e., with the Father, *nothing was made*, as it says, "I was with him forming all things" (Prv 8:30).

86. In a certain homily attributed to Origen,[97] and which begins, "The spiritual voice of the eagle," we find another rather beautiful exposition. It says there that the Greek has *choris* where the Latin has *sine* (without). Now *choris* is the same as "outside" or "outside of." It is as if he had said: *All things were made through him* in such a way that outside him *nothing was made*. And so he says this to show that all things are conserved through the Word and in the Word, as stated in Hebrews (1:3), "He sustains all things by his powerful word." Now there are certain things that do not need their producer except to bring them into existence, since after they have been produced they are able to subsist without any further activity on the part of the producer. For example, a house needs a builder if it is to come into existence, but it continues to exist without any further action on the part of the builder. So lest anyone suppose that all things were made through the Word in such a way that he is merely the cause of their production and not of their continuation in existence, the Evangelist added, *and without him nothing was made*, i.e., nothing was made outside of him, because he encompasses all things, preserving them.[98]

87. This clause is also explained by Augustine[99] and Origen[100] and several others in such a way that "nothing" indicates sin. Accordingly, because *All things were made through him* might be interpreted as including evil and sin, he added, *and without him nothing*, i.e., sin, *was made*. For just as art is not the principle or cause of the defects in its

---

96. *De Trin.* 2. 18; PL 10, col. 62; cf. *Catena aurea*, 1:3b.

97. This selection is from a sermon of John Scotus Erigena, *Hom. in prol. Evang. sec. Io.*; PL 122, col. 288A; cf. *Catena aurea* 1:3c. John Scotus Erigena (or Eriugena) (c. 810–877) was an Irish theologian at the palace school of Laon. He attempted the harmonization of Neoplatonic emanationism with the Christian view of creation. He is also credited with making available in Latin translation key works of Dionysius, Maximus the Confessor, and Gregory of Nyssa.

98. See *ST* I, q. 104, aa. 1–2.

99. *Tract. in Io.* 1. 13; PL 35, col. 1385.

100. *Comm. in Io.* II. 13, nos. 92–96; PG 14, col. 133C–36B.

products, but is through itself the cause of their perfection and form, so the Word, who is the art of the Father, full of living archetypes, is not the cause of any evil or disarrangement in things, particularly of the evil of sin, which carries the full notion of evil.[101] The *per se* cause of this evil is the will of the creature, either a man or an angel, freely declining from the end to which it is ordained by its nature. One who can act in virtue of his art but purposely violates it, is the cause of the defects occurring in his works, not by reason of his art, but by reason of his will. So in such cases, his art is not the source or cause of the defects, but his will is. Consequently, evil is a defect of the will and not of any art. And so to the extent that it is such [i.e., a defect], it is nothing.[102]

88. So then, this clause is added to show the universal causality of the Word, according to Chrysostom; his association with the Father, according to Hilary; the power of the Word in the preserving of things, according to Origen; and finally, the purity of his causality, because he is so the cause of good as not to be the cause of sin, according to Augustine, Origen, and a number of others.[103]

89. Then he says, *What was made in him was life*; and this is the third clause. Here we must avoid the false interpretation of Manichaeus, who was led by this to maintain that everything that exists is alive: for example, stones, wood, men, and anything else in the world. He understood the clause this way: *What was made in him*, comma, *was life*. But it was not life unless alive. Therefore, whatever was made in him is alive. He also claimed that *in him* is the same as saying "through him," since very often in Scripture "in him" and "through him" are interchangeable, as in "In him and through him all things were created" (Col 1:16). However, our present explanation shows that this interpretation is false.

90. There are, nevertheless, a number of ways to explain it without error. In that homily, "The spiritual voice,"[104] we find this explanation: *What was made in him*, i.e., through him, *was life*, not in each thing itself, but in its cause. For in the case of all things that are caused, it is always true that effects, whether produced by nature or by will, exist in their causes, not according to their respective existences but according to the power of the sun. Therefore, since the cause of all effects produced by God is a certain life and an art full of living archetypes, for this reason *What was made in him*, i.e., through him, *was life*, in its cause, i.e., in God.[105]

---

101. See *ST* I, q. 49, a. 2; I-II, q. 79, aa. 1–2.
102. See *ST* I, q. 48, a. 1.
103. See *ST* I, q. 34, a. 3, ad 5.
104. Erigena, *Hom. in prol. Evang. sec. Io.*; PL 122, col. 288B; cf. *Catena aurea*, 1:4a.
105. See *ST* I, q. 18, a. 4.

91. Augustine[106] reads this another way, as: **What was made**, comma, **in him was life**. For things can be considered in two ways: as they are in themselves, and as they are in the Word. If they are considered as they are in themselves, then it is not true that all things are life or even alive, but some lack life and some are alive. For example, the earth was made and metals were made, but none is life, none is living; animals and men were made, and these, considered in themselves, are not life, but merely living. Yet considered as they are in the Word, they are not merely living, but also life. For the archetypes which exist spiritually in the wisdom of God, and through which things were made by the Word, are life, just as a chest made by an artisan is in itself neither alive nor life, yet the exemplar of the chest in the artisan's mind prior to the existence of the chest is in some sense living, insofar as it has an intellectual existence in the mind of the artisan. Nevertheless it is not life, because it is neither in his essence nor is it his existence through the act of understanding of the artisan. But in God, his act of understanding is his life and his essence. And so whatever is in God is not only living, but is life itself, because whatever is in God is his essence. Hence the creature in God is the creating essence. Thus, if things are considered as they are in the Word, they are life.[107] This is explained in another place.

92. Origen,[108] commenting on John, gives another reading, thus: **That which was made in him**; and then, **was life**. Here we should note that some things are said of the Son of God as such; for example, that he is God, omnipotent, and the like. And some things are said of him in relation to ourselves; for example, we say he is Savior and Redeemer. Some things are said in both ways, such as wisdom and justice. Now in all things said absolutely and of the Son as such, it is not said that he was "made"; for example, we do not say that the Son was made God or omnipotent. But in things said in reference to us, or in both ways, the notion of being made can be used, as in, "God made him [Jesus Christ] our wisdom, our justice, our sanctification and redemption" (1 Cor 1:30). And so, although he was always wisdom and justice in himself, yet it can be said that he was newly made justice and wisdom for us.

And so Origen,[109] explaining it along these lines, says that although in himself the Son is life, yet he was made life for us by the fact that he gave us life, as is said, "Just as in Adam all die, so in Christ all will come to life" (1 Cor 15:22). And so he says "the Word that was made" life for us **in himself was life**, so that after a time he could become life

106. *Tract. in Io.* 1. 17; PL 35, col. 1387; cf. *Catena aurea*, 1:4a.
107. See *ST* I, q. 18, a. 4.
108. *Comm. in Io.* II. 16, no. 114; PG 14, col. 141D; cf. *Catena aurea*, 1:4a.
109. Ibid., II. 18, no. 128; PG 14, col. 148A; cf. *Catena aurea*, 1:4a.

for us; and so he immediately adds, *and that life was the light of men*.

93. Hilary[110] reads the clause differently, thus: *And without him was made nothing, which was made in him*, and later it says, *he was life*. For he says that when the Evangelist says *without him nothing was made*, one might be perplexed and ask whether there are still other things made by him that were not made through him, although not without him, but with respect to which he was associate with the maker; and this clause is added to correct the aforesaid error. Therefore lest this be so understood, when the Evangelist says, *All things were made through him*, he adds, *and without him nothing was made*, which was made, *in him*, that is, through him; and the reason for this is that *he was life*.

For it is plain that all things are said to have been made through the Word inasmuch as the Word, who proceeds from the Father, is God. But let us suppose that some father has a son who does not perfectly exercise the operations of a man, but reaches such a state gradually. In that case the father will do many things, not through the son, yet not without [having] him. Since, therefore, the Son of God has from all eternity the same life that the Father has—"Just as the Father possesses life in himself, so has he granted it to the Son to have life in himself" (below 5:26)—one cannot say that God the Father, although he made nothing without the Son, nevertheless made some things not through him, because he was life. For in living things which participate life, it can happen that imperfect life precedes perfect life; but in *per se* life, which does not participate life but is simply and absolutely life, there can be no imperfection at all. According, because the Word is *per se* life, there was never imperfect life in him, but always perfect life.[111] And so in such a way that nothing was made without him that was not also made in him, i.e., through him.

94. Chrysostom[112] has a different reading and punctuation, thus: *And without him was made nothing that was made*. The reason for this is that someone might believe that the Holy Spirit was made through the Word. So to exclude this, the Evangelist says, that *was made*, because the Holy Spirit is not something that is made. And afterward follows, *In him was life*, which is introduced for two reasons. First, to show that after the creation of all things his causality was indefectible not only with respect to the things already produced, but also with respect to things yet to be produced. As if to say: *In him was life*, by which he could not only produce all things, but which has an unfailing flow and a causality for producing things continually without undergoing any change, being a living fountain which is not diminished in spite of its continuous outflow; whereas collected water,

110. *De Trin.* 2. 20; PL 10, col. 63 B; cf. *Catena aurea*, 1:4a.
111. See *ST* I, q. 18, a. 3.
112. *Hom. in Io.* 5. 2; PG 59, col. 55–56; cf. *Catena aurea*, 1:4a.

that is not living [i.e., running] water, is diminished when it flows out, and is used up. So the Psalm (35:10) says, "With you is the fountain of life." The second reason is to show that things are governed by the Word. For since *In him was life*, this shows that he produced things by his intellect and will, not by a necessity of his nature, and that he governs the things he made. "The Word of God is living" (Heb 4:12).

Chrysostom is held in such esteem by the Greeks in his explanations that they admit no other where he expounded anything in Holy Scripture. For this reason, this passage in all the Greek works is found to be punctuated exactly as Chrysostom did, namely, *And without him was made nothing that was made.*

LECTURE 3

4b And that life was the light of men. 5 And the light shines in the darkness, and the darkness did not overcome it.

95. Above, the Evangelist described the power of the Word insofar as he brought all things into existence; here he describes his power as it is related to men, saying that this Word is a light to men. First, he introduces a certain light to us (v. 4b); secondly, the light's irradiation (v. 5a); thirdly, participation in the light (v. 5b). This whole section may be explained in two ways: first, according to the influx of natural knowledge; secondly, according to participation in grace.[113]

As to the first point he says, *And that life was the light of men.*

96. Here we should note first that, according to Augustine[114] and many others, light is more properly said of spiritual things than of sensible things. Ambrose,[115] however, thinks that brightness is said metaphorically of God. But this is not a great issue, for in whatever the name "light" is used, it implies a manifestation, whether that manifesting concerns intelligible or sensible things. If we compare sensible and intelligible manifestation, then, according to the nature of things, light is found first in spiritual things. But for us, who give names to things on the basis of their properties as known to us, light is discovered first in sensible things, because we first used this name to signify sensible light before intelligible light; although as to power, light belongs to spiritual things in a prior and truer way than to sensible things.

97. To clarify the statement, *And that life was the light of men*, we should remark that there are many grades of life.[116] For some things

113. See *ST* I-II, q. 109, a. 1.
114. *Tract. in Io.* 1. 18; PL 35, col. 1388; cf. *Catena aurea*, 1:4b. See also *ST* I, q. 67, a. 1.
115. See *ST* I, q. 67, a. 1, *sed contra*.
116. See *ST* I, q. 18, a. 1.

live, but do so without light, because they have no knowledge; for example, plants. Hence their life is not light. Other things both live and
know, but their knowledge, since it is on the sense level, is concerned
only with individual and material things, as in the case with the brutes.
So they have both life and a certain light. But they do not have the light
of men, who live, and know, not only truths, but also the very nature
of truth itself. Such are rational creatures, to whom not only this or
that are made manifest, but truth itself, which can be manifested and is
manifestive to all.

And so the Evangelist, speaking of the Word, not only says that he
is life but also *light*, lest anyone suppose he means life without knowledge. And he says that he is the *light of men*, lest anyone suppose he
meant only sensible knowledge, such as exists in the brutes.

98. But since he is also the light of angels, why did he say, *of men*?
Two answers have been given to this. Chrysostom[117] says that the
Evangelist intended in this Gospel to give us a knowledge of the Word
precisely as directed to the salvation of man, and therefore refers, in
keeping with his aim, more to men than to angels. Origen,[118] however, says that participation in this light pertains to men insofar as they
have a rational nature; accordingly, when the Evangelist says, *the light
of men*, he wants us to understand every rational nature.

99. We also see from this the perfection and dignity of this life, because it is intellectual or rational. For whereas all things that in some
way move themselves are called living, only those that perfectly move
themselves are said to have perfect life; and among lower creatures
only man moves himself, properly speaking, and perfectly. For although other things are moved by themselves by some inner principle, that inner principle is nevertheless not open to opposite alterna-
tives; hence they are not moved freely but from necessity. As a result,
those things that are moved by such a principle are more truly made to
act than act themselves. But man, since he is master of his act, moves
himself freely to all that he wills. Consequently, man has perfect life, as
does every intellectual nature.[119] And so the life of the Word, which is
the light of men, is perfect life.[120]

100. We find a fitting order in the above. For in the natural order
of things, existence is first; and the Evangelist implies this in his first
statement, *In the beginning was the Word*. Secondly, comes life; and
this is mentioned next, *In him was life*. Thirdly comes understanding;
and that is mentioned next; *And that life was the light of men*. And,

117. *Hom. in Io.* 5. 3; PG 59, col. 58; cf. *Catena aurea*, 1:5.
118. *Comm. in Io.* II. 22, nos. 141–43; PG 14, col. 152B–C; cf. *Catena aurea*, 1:4b.
119. See *ST* I, q. 83, a. 1; I, q. 105, a. 3.
120. See *ST* I, q. 19, a. 10.

according to Origen,[121] he fittingly attributes light to life because light
can be attributed to the living.

101. We should note that light can be related in two ways to what
is living: as an object and as something in which they participate, as
is clear in external sight. For the eyes know external light as an object, but if they are to see it, they must participate in an inner light by
which the eyes are adapted and disposed for seeing the external light.
And so his statement, *And that life was the light of men*, can be understood in two ways. First, that the *light of men* is taken as an object
that man alone can look upon, because the rational creature alone can
see it, since he alone is capable of the vision of God who "teaches us
more than the beasts of the earth, and enlightens us more than the
birds of the air" (Jb 35:11); for although other animals may know certain things that are true, nevertheless, man alone knows the nature itself of truth.

The *light of men* can also be taken as a light in which we participate. For we would never be able to look upon the Word and light itself except through a participation in it; and this participation is in man
and is the superior part of our soul, i.e., the intellectual light, about
which the Psalm (4:7) says, "The light of your countenance, O Lord,
is marked upon us," i.e., of your Son, who is your face, by whom you
are manifested.[122]

102. Having introduced a certain light, the Evangelist now considers
its irradiation, saying, *And the light shines in the darkness*. This can be
explained in two ways, according to the two meanings of "darkness."

First, we might take "darkness" as a natural defect, that of the created mind. For the mind is to that light of which the Evangelist speaks
here as air is to the light of the sun; because, although air is receptive of the light of the sun, considered in itself it is a darkness. According to this the meaning is: *the light*, i.e., that life which is the light of
men, *shines in the darkness*, i.e., in created souls and minds, by always
shedding its light on all. "On a man from whom the light is hidden"
(Jb 3:23).

And the darkness did not overcome it, i.e., enclose it [i.e., intellectu-
ally]. For to overcome something [*comprehendere*, to overcome, to comprehend, to seize or apprehend, and so forth], is to enclose and understand its boundaries. As Augustine says, to reach God with the mind is
a great happiness; but to overcome [comprehend] him is impossible.[123]
And so, *the darkness did not overcome it*. "Behold, God is great, exceeding our knowledge" (Jb 36:26); "Great in counsel, incomprehen-

121. *Comm. in Io.* II. 23, no. 153; PG 14, col. 156B.
122. See *ST* I, q. 79, a. 4; I, q. 84 a. 5; I, q. 93 a. 4; I-II, q. 19 a. 4.
123. See *ST* I, q. 12, a. 7.

sible in thought" as Jeremiah (32:19) says. This explanation is found in
that homily[124] which begins, "The spiritual voice of the eagle."

103. We can explain this passage in another way by taking "darkness" as Augustine[125] does, for the natural lack of wisdom in man,
which is called a darkness. "And I saw that wisdom excels folly as
much as light excels knowledge" (Ecc 2:13). Someone is without wisdom, therefore, because he lacks the light of divine wisdom. Consequently, just as the minds of the wise are lucid by reason of a participation in that divine light and wisdom, so by the lack of it they are
darkness. Now the fact that some are darkness is not due to a defect in
that light, since on its part it shines in the darkness and radiates upon
all. Rather, the foolish are without that light because *the darkness did
not overcome it*, i.e., they did not apprehend it, not being able to attain
a participation in it due to their foolishness; after having been lifted up,
they did not persevere. "From the savage," i.e., from the proud, "he
hides his light," i.e., the light of wisdom, "and shows his friend that
it belongs to him, and that he may approach it" (Jb 36:32); "They did
not know the way to wisdom, nor did they remember her paths" (Bar
3:23).

Although some minds are darkness, i.e., they lack savory and lucid
wisdom, nevertheless no man is in such darkness as to be completely
devoid of divine light, because whatever truth is known by anyone is
due to a participation in that light which shines in the darkness; for every truth, no matter by whom it is spoken, comes from the Holy Spirit.
Yet *the darkness*, i.e., men in darkness, *did not overcome it*, apprehend
it in truth. This is the way [i.e., with respect to the natural influx of
knowledge] that Origen and Augustine explain this clause.[126]

104. Starting from *And that life was the light of men*, we can explain this in another way, according to the influx of grace, since we are
illuminated by Christ.

After he had considered the creation of things through the Word,
the Evangelist considers here the restoration of the rational creature
through Christ, saying, *And that life*, of the Word, *was the light of men*,
i.e., of all men in general, and not only of the Jews. For the Son of God
assumed flesh and came into the world to illumine all men with grace
and truth. "I came into the world for this, to testify to the truth" (below
18:37); "As long as I am in the world I am the light of the world" (below 9:5). So he does not say, "the light of the Jews," because although
previously he had been known only in Judea, he later became known
to the world. "I have given you as a light to the nations, that you might
be my salvation to the ends of the earth" (Is 49:6).

---

124. Erigena, *Hom. in prol. Evang. sec. Io.*; PL 122, col. 288A; cf. *Catena aurea*, 1:5.
125. *Tract. in Io.* 1. 19; PL 34, col. 1388; cf. *Catena aurea*, 1:5.
126. See *ST* I-II, q. 85, a. 3; I-II, q. 94, a. 6.

It was fitting to join light and life by saying, *And that life was the light of men*, in order to show that these two have come to us through Christ: life, through a participation in grace, "Grace and truth have come through Jesus Christ" (below 1:17); and light, by a knowledge of truth and wisdom.[127]

105. According to this explanation, *the light shines in the darkness*, can be expounded in three ways, in the light of the three meanings of "darkness."

In one way, we can take "darkness" for punishment. For any sadness and suffering of heart can be called a darkness, just as any joy can be called a light. "When I sit in darkness and in suffering the Lord is my light," i.e., my joy and consolation (Mic 7:8). And so Origen[128] says: In this explanation, *the light shines in the darkness*, is Christ coming into the world, having a body capable of suffering and without sin, but "in the likeness of sinful flesh" (Rom 8:3). The light is in the flesh, that is, the flesh of Christ, which is called a darkness insofar as it has a likeness to sinful flesh.[129] As if to say: The light, i.e., the Word of God, veiled about by the darkness of the flesh, shines on the world: "I will cover the sun with a cloud" (Ex 32:7).

106. Secondly, we can take "darkness" to mean the devils, as in Ephesians (6:12), "Our struggle is not against flesh and blood; but against principalities and powers, against the rulers of the world of this darkness." Looked at this way he says, *the light*, i.e., the Son of God, *shines in the darkness*, i.e., has descended into the world where darkness, i.e., the devils, hold sway: "Now the prince of this world will be cast out" (below 12:31). *And the darkness*, i.e., the devils, *did not overcome it*, i.e., were unable to obscure him by their temptations, as is plain in Matthew (chap. 4).[130]

107. Thirdly, we can take "darkness" for the error or ignorance which filled the whole world before the coming of Christ: "You were at one time darkness" (Eph 5:8). And so he says that *the light*, i.e., the incarnate Word of God, *shines in the darkness*, i.e., upon the men of the world, who are blinded by the darkness or error and ignorance. "To enlighten those who sit in darkness and in the shadow of death" (Lk 1:79); "The people who were sitting in the darkness saw a great light" (Is 9:2).

And the darkness did not overcome it, i.e., did not overcome him. For in spite of the number of men darkened by sin, blinded by envy, shadowed over by pride, who have struggled against Christ (as is plain from the Gospel) by upbraiding him, heaping insults and calumnies

---

127. See *ST* I-II, q. 106, a. 1.
128. *Comm. in Io.* II. 26, nos. 163–66; PG 14, col. 160B–61A; cf. *Catena aurea*, 1:5.
129. See *ST* III, q. 14, a. 1.
130. Ibid.

upon him, and finally killing, nevertheless they **did not overcome it**, i.e., gain the victory of so obscuring him that his brightness would not shine throughout the whole world. Wisdom (7:30) says, "compared to light, she takes precedence, for night supplants it, but wisdom," that is, the incarnate Son of God, "is not overcome by wickedness," that is, of the Jews and of heretics, because it says, "She gave him the prize for his stern struggle that he might know that wisdom is mightier than all else" (Wis 10:12).

LECTURE 4

6 There was a man sent by God, whose name was John. 7 He came as a witness, that he might bear witness to the light, so that through him all men might believe. 8 He was not the light, but [he came] in order to bear witness to the light.

108. Above, the Evangelist considered the divinity of the Word; here he begins to consider the Incarnation of the Word. And he does two things concerning this: first, he treats of the witness to the incarnate Word, or the precursor; secondly, of the coming of the Word (1:9). As to the first, he does two things: first, he describes the precursor who comes to bear witness; secondly, he shows that he was incapable of the work of our salvation (1:8).

He describes the precursor in four ways. First, according to his nature, **There was a man**. Secondly, as to his authority, **sent by God**. Thirdly, as to his suitability for the office, **whose name was John**. Fourthly, as to the dignity of his office, **He came as a witness**.

109. We should note with respect to the first that, as soon as the Evangelist begins speaking of something temporal, he changes his manner of speech. When speaking above of eternal things, he used the word "was" (*erat*), which is the past imperfect tense; and this indicates that eternal things are without end. But now, when he is speaking of temporal things, he uses "was" (*fuit*, i.e., "has been"); this indicates temporal things as having taken place in the past and coming to an end there.

110. And so he says, **There was a man** (*Fuit homo*). This excludes at the very start the incorrect opinion of certain heretics who were in error on the condition or nature of John. They believed that John was an angel in nature, basing themselves on the words of the Lord, "I send my messenger [in Greek, *angelos*] before you, who will prepare your way" (Mt 11:10); and the same thing is found in Mark (1:2). But the Evangelist rejects this, saying, **There was a man** by nature, not an angel. "The nature of man is known, and that he cannot contend in judgment with one who is stronger than himself" (Ecc 6:10).

Now it is fitting that a man be sent to men, for men are more easily drawn to a man, since he is like themselves. So in Hebrews (7:28) it says, "The law appoints men who have weakness priests." God could have governed men through angels, but he preferred men so that we could be more instructed by their example. And so John was a man, and not an angel.

111. John is described by his authority when it says, **sent by God**. Indeed, although John was not an angel in nature, he was so by his office, because he was **sent by God**. For the distinctive office of angels is that they are sent by God and are messengers of God. "All are ministering spirits, sent to serve" (Heb 1:14). Hence it is that "angel" means "messenger."[131] And so men who are sent by God to announce something can be called angels. "Haggai the messenger of the Lord" (Hg 1:13).

If someone is to bear witness to God, it is necessary that he be sent by God. "How can they preach unless they are sent?" as is said in Romans (10:15). And since they are sent by God, they seek the things of Jesus Christ, not their own. "We do not preach ourselves, but Jesus Christ" (2 Cor 4:5). On the other hand, one who sends himself, and is not sent by God, seeks his own things or those of man, and not the things of Christ. And so he says here, **There was a man sent by God**, so that we would understand that John proclaimed something divine, not human.

112. Note that there are three ways in which we see men sent by God. First, by an inward inspiration. "And now the Lord God has sent me, and his spirit" (Is 48:16). As if to say: I have been sent by God through an inward inspiration of the spirit. Secondly, by an expressed and clear command, perceived by the bodily senses or the imagination. Isaiah was also sent in this way; and so he says, "And I heard the voice of the Lord saying, 'Whom shall I send, and who will go for us?' Then I said, 'Here I am! Send me'" (Is 6:8). Thirdly, by the order of a prelate, who acts in the place of God in this matter. "I have pardoned in the person of Christ for your sake" as it says in 2 Corinthians (2:10). This is why those who are sent by a prelate are sent by God, as Barnabas and Timothy were sent by the Apostle.

When it is said here, **There was a man sent by God**, we should understand that he was sent by God through an inward inspiration, or perhaps even by an outward command. "He who sent me to baptize with water had said to me: 'The man on whom you see the Spirit come down and rest is the one who is to baptize with the Holy Spirit'" (below 1:33).

113. We should not understand, **There was a man sent by God**, as some heretics did, who believed that from the very beginning human souls were created without bodies along with the angels, and that

131. See *ST* I, q. 112, a. 1.

one's soul is sent into the body when he is born, and that John was sent to life, i.e., his soul was sent to a body.[132] Rather, we should understand that he was sent by God to baptize and preach.

114. John's fitness is given when he says, *whose name was John.* One must be qualified for the office of bearing witness, because unless a witness is qualified for the office of bearing witness, then no matter in what way he is sent by another, his testimony is not acceptable. Now a man becomes qualified by the grace of God. "By the grace of God I am what I am" (1 Cor 15:10); "who has made us fit ministers of a new covenant" (2 Cor 3:6). So, the Evangelist appropriately implies the precursor's fitness from his name when he says, *whose name was John,* which is interpreted, "in whom is grace."

This name was not given to him meaninglessly, but by divine preordination and before he was born, as is clear from Luke (1:13), "You will name him John," as the angel said to Zechariah. Hence he can say what is said in Isaiah (49:1), "The Lord called me from the womb"; "He who will be, his name is already called" (Ecc 6:10). The Evangelist also indicates this from his manner of speaking, when he says *was,* as to God's preordination.

115. Then he is described by the dignity of his office. First, his office is mentioned. Secondly, the reason for his office, *to bear witness to the light.*

116. Now his office is to bear witness; hence he says, *He came as a witness.*

Here it should be remarked that God makes men, and everything else he makes, for himself. "The Lord made all things for himself" (Prv 16:4). Not, indeed, to add anything to himself, since he has no need of our good, but so that his goodness might be made manifest in all of the things made by him, in that "his eternal power and divinity are clearly seen, being understood through the things that are made" (Rom 1:20). Thus, each creature is made as a witness to God in so far as each creature is a certain witness of the divine goodness.[133] So, the vastness of creation is a witness to God's power and omnipotence; and its beauty is a witness to the divine wisdom. But certain men are ordained by God in a special way, so that they bear witness to God not only naturally by their existence, but also spiritually by their good works. Hence all holy men are witnesses to God inasmuch as God is glorified among men by their good works. "Let your light so shine before men, that they may see your good works, and glorify your Father who is in heaven" (Mt 5:16). But those who not only share in God's gifts in themselves by acting well through the grace of God, but also spread them to others by their teaching, influencing and encouraging others, are in a more

132. See *ST* I, q. 90, a. 4; I, q. 118, a. 3.
133. See *ST* I, q. 6, a. 4; I, q. 44, a. 4; I, q. 65, a. 2; I, q. 103, a. 2.

special way witnesses to God.[134] "Everyone who calls upon my name, I have created for my glory" (Is 43:7). And so John came as a witness in order to spread to others the gifts of God and to proclaim his praise.

117. This office of John, that of bearing witness, is very great, because no one can testify about something except in the manner in which he has shared in it. "We know of what we speak, and we bear witness of what we see" (below 3:11). Hence, to bear witness to divine truth indicates a knowledge of that truth. So Christ also had this office: "I have come into the world for this, to testify to the truth" (below 18:37). But Christ testifies in one way and John in another. Christ bears witness as the light who comprehends all things, indeed, as the existing light itself. John bears witness only as participating in that light. And so Christ gives testimony in a perfect manner and perfectly manifests the truth, while John and other holy men give testimony in so far as they have a share of divine truth. John's office, therefore, is great both because of his participation in the divine light and because of a likeness to Christ, who carried out this office. "I made him a witness to the peoples, a leader and a commander of the nations" (Is 55:4).[135]

118. The purpose of this office is given when he says, *that he might bear witness to the light.* Here we should understand that there are two reasons for bearing witness about something. One reason can be on the part of the thing with which the witness is concerned; for example, if there is some doubt or uncertainty about that thing. The other is on the part of those who hear it; if they are hard of heart and slow to believe. John came as a witness, not because of the thing about which he bore witness, for it was light. Hence he says, *bear witness to the light*, i.e., not to something obscure, but to something clear. He came, therefore, to bear witness on account of those to whom he testified, *so that through him* (i.e., John) *all men might believe.* For as light is not only visible in itself and of itself, but through it all else can be seen, so the Word of God is not only light in himself, but he makes known all things that are known. For since a thing is made known and understood through its form, and all forms exist through the Word, who is the art full of living forms, the Word is light not only in himself, but as making known all things; "all that appears is light" (Eph 5:13).

And so it was fitting for the Evangelist to call the Son "light," because he came as "a revealing light to the Gentiles" (Lk 2:32). Above, he called the Son of God the Word, by which the Father expresses himself and every creature. Now since he is, properly speaking, the light of men, and the Evangelist is considering him here as coming to

---

134. See *ST* I, q. 106, a. 4; I, q. 117, a. 1.
135. See *ST* III, q. 7, a. 8.

accomplish the salvation of man, he fittingly interrupts the use of the name "Word" when speaking of the Son, and says, "light."

119. But if that light is adequate of itself to make known all things, and not only itself, what need does it have of any witness? This was the objection of the Manichaeans, who wanted to destroy the Old Testament. Consequently, the saints gave many reasons, against their opinion, why Christ wanted to have the testimony of the prophets.

Origen[136] gives three reasons. The first is that God wanted to have certain witnesses, not because he needed their testimony, but to ennoble those whom he appointed witnesses. Thus we see in the order of the universe that God produces certain effects by means of intermediate causes, not because he himself is unable to produce them without these intermediaries, but he deigns to confer on them the dignity of causality because he wishes to ennoble these intermediate causes. Similarly, even though God could have enlightened all men by himself and lead them to a knowledge of himself, yet to preserve due order in things and to ennoble certain men, he willed that divine knowledge reach men through certain other men. "'You are my witnesses,' says the Lord" (Is 43:10).[137]

A second reason is that Christ was a light to the world through his miracles. Yet, because they were performed in time, they passed away with time and did not reach everyone. But the words of the prophets, preserved in Scripture, could reach not only those present, but could also reach those to come after. Hence the Lord willed that men come to a knowledge of the Word through the testimony of the prophets, in order that not only those present, but also men yet to come, might be enlightened about him. So it says expressly, *so that through him all men might believe*, i.e., not only those present, but also future generations.

The third reason is that not all men are in the same condition, and all are not led or disposed to a knowledge of the truth in the same way.[138] For some are brought to a knowledge of the truth by signs and miracles; others are brought more by wisdom. "The Jews require signs, and the Greeks seek wisdom" (1 Cor 1:22). And so the Lord, in order to show the path of salvation to all, willed both ways to be open, i.e., the way of signs and the way of wisdom, so that those who would not be brought to the path of salvation by the miracles of the Old and New Testaments, might be brought to a knowledge of the truth by the path of wisdom, as in the prophets and other books of Sacred Scripture.

A fourth reason, given by Chrysostom,[139] is that certain men of

---

136. *Comm. in Io.* II. 34, no. 199; PG 14, col. 173A; cf. *Catena aurea*, 1:6–8.
137. See *ST* III, q. 26, a. 1, ad 1.
138. See *ST* III, q. 55, a. 4.
139. *Hom. in Io.* 6; PG 59, col. 61; cf. *Catena aurea*, 1:6–8.

weak understanding are unable to grasp the truth and knowledge of God by themselves. And so the Lord chose to come down to them and to enlighten certain men before others about divine matters, so that these others might obtain from them in a human way the knowledge of divine things they could not reach by themselves. And so he says, *that through him all men might believe.* As if to say: *he came as a witness,* not for the sake of the light, but for the sake of men, *so that through him all men might believe.* And so it is plain that the testimonies of the prophets are fitting and proper, and should be received as something needed by us for the knowledge of the truth.

120. He says *believe,* because there are two ways of participating in the divine light. One is the perfect participation which is present in glory, "In your light, we shall see the light" (Ps 35:10). The other in imperfect and is acquired through faith, since *he came as a witness.* Of these two ways it is said, "Now we see through a mirror, in an obscure manner, but then we shall see face to face" (1 Cor 13:12). And in the same place we find, "Now I know in part, but then I shall know even as I am known." Among these two ways, the first is the way of participation through faith, because through it we are brought to vision. So in Isaiah (7:9) where our version has, "If you do not believe, you will not persist," another version has, "If you do not believe, you will not understand." "All of us, gazing on the Lord's glory with unveiled faces, are being transformed from glory to glory into his very image," which we have lost (2 Cor 3:18). "From the glory of faith to the glory of vision," as a Gloss says.[140]

And so he says, *that through him all men might believe,* not as though all would see him perfectly at once, but first they would believe through faith, and later enjoy him through vision in heaven.[141]

121. He says *through him,* to show that John is different from Christ. For Christ came so that all might believe in him. "He who believes in me, as Scripture says, 'Out of his heart shall flow rivers of living water'" (below 7:38). John, on the other hand, came *that all men might believe,* not in him, but in Christ *through him.*

One may object that not all have believed. So if John came that all might believe through him, he failed. I answer that both on the part of God, who sent John, and of John, who came, the method used is adequate to bring all to the truth. But on the part of those "who have fixed their eyes on the ground" (Ps 16:11), and refused to see the light, there was failure, because all did not believe.[142]

---

140. *Glossa Ordinaria;* PL 114, col. 556A. This text is also found in Peter Lombard, *Collect. in Epist. Pauli, In 2 Cor. 3.12–18;* PL 192, col. 28D.
141. See *ST* II-II, q. 2, a. 3; II-II, 5, a. 1.
142. See *ST* II-II, q. 10, a. 1.

122. Now although John, of whom so much has been said, even including that he was sent by God, is an eminent person, his coming is not sufficient to save men, because the salvation of man lies in participating in the light. If John had been the light, his coming would have sufficed to save men; but he was not the light. So he says, *he was not the light*. Consequently, a light was needed that would suffice to save men.

Or, we could look at it another way. John came to bear witness to the light. Now it is the custom that the one who testifies is of greater authority than the one for whom he bears witness. So, lest John be considered to have greater authority than Christ, the Evangelist says, *he was not the light, but he came in order to bear witness to the light*. For he bears witness not because he is greater, but because he is better known, even though he is not as great.

123. There is a difficulty about his saying, *he was not the light*. Conflicting with this is, "You were at one time darkness, but now you are light in the Lord" (Eph 5:8); and "You are the light of the world" (Mt 5:14). Therefore, John and the apostles and all good men are a light.

I answer that some say that John was not the light, because this belongs to God alone. But if "light" is taken without the article, then John and all holy men were made lights. The meaning is this: the Son of God is light by his very essence; but John and all the saints are light by participation.[143] So, because John participated in the true light, it was fitting that he bear witness to the light; for fire is better exhibited by something afire than by anything else, and color by something colored.

LECTURE 5

9 He [the Word] was the true light, which enlightens every man coming into this world. 10 He was in the world, and through him the world was made, and the world did not know him.[144]

124. Above, the Evangelist considered the precursor and his witness to the incarnate Word; in the present section he considers the incarnate Word himself. As to this he does three things. First, he shows why it was necessary for the Word to come. Secondly, the benefit we received from the coming of the Word (1:11). And thirdly, the way he came (1:14).

The necessity for the Word's coming is seen to be the lack of divine knowledge in the world. He points out this need for his coming when

---

143. See *ST* III, q. 23, a. 1, ad 2.
144. St. Thomas quotes Jn 1:9 in the *ST* I-II, q. 79, a. 3; III, q. 5, a. 4, obj. 2; III, q. 9, a. 1, ad 2; and Jn 1:10 in *ST* I, q. 47, a. 3, *sed contra*.

he says, "For this was I born, and I came into the world for this, to testify to the truth" (below 18:37). To indicate this lack of divine knowledge, the Evangelist does two things. First, he shows that this lack does not pertain to God or the Word. Secondly, that it does pertain to men (v. 10b).

He shows in three ways that there was no defect in God or in the Word that prevented men from knowing God and from being enlightened by the Word. First, from the efficacy of the divine light itself, because *He was the true light, which enlightens every man coming into this world.* Secondly, from the presence of the divine light, because *He was in the world.* Thirdly, from the obviousness of the light, because *through him the world was made.* So the lack of divine knowledge in the world was not due to the Word, because it is sufficient. First, he shows the nature of this efficiency, that is, *He was the true light.* Secondly, its very efficiency, *which enlightens every man.*

125. The divine Word is efficacious in enlightening because *He was the true light.* How the Word is light, and how he is the light of men need not be discussed again, because it was sufficiently explained above. What we must discuss at present is how he is the true light. To explain this, we should note that in Scripture the "true" is contrasted with three things. Sometimes it is contrasted with the false, as in "Put an end to lying, and let everyone speak the truth" (Eph 4:25). Sometimes it is contrasted with what is figurative, as in "The law was given through Moses; grace and truth have come through Jesus Christ" (below 1:17), because the truth of the figures contained in the law was fulfilled by Christ. Sometimes it is contrasted with what is something by participation, as in "that we may be in his true Son" (1 Jn 5:20), who is not his Son by participation.

Before the Word came there was in the world a certain light which the philosophers prided themselves on having; but this was a false light, because as is said, "They became stultified in their speculations, and their foolish hearts were darkened; claiming to be wise, they became fools" (Rom 1:21); "Every man is made foolish by his knowledge" (Jer 10:14). There was another light from the teaching of the law which the Jews boasted of having; but this was a symbolic light: "The law has a shadow of the good things to come, not the image itself of them" (Heb 10:1). There was also a certain light in the angels and in the holy men in so far as they knew God in a more special way by grace; but this was a participated light, "Upon whom does his light not shine?" (Jb 25:3), which is like saying, "Whoever shine, shine to the extent that they participate in his light, i.e., God's light."[145]

But the Word of God was not a false light, nor a symbolic light, nor

145. See *ST* I-II, q. 91, a. 4; I-II, q. 106, a. 3; I-II, q. 107, a. 2.

a participated light, but the true light, i.e., light by his essence. Therefore he says, *He was the true light.*

126. This excludes two errors. First, that of Photinus, who believed that Christ derived his beginning from the Virgin. So, lest anyone suppose this, the Evangelist, speaking of the Incarnation of the Word, says, *He was the true light*, i.e., eternally, not only before the Virgin, but before every creature. This also excludes the error of Arius and Origen; they said that Christ was not true God, but God by participation. If this were so, he could not be the true light, as the Evangelist says here, and as in "God is light" (1 Jn 1:5), i.e., not by participation, but *the true light.* So if the Word was the true light, it is plain that he is true God. Now it is clear how the divine Word is effective in causing divine knowledge.

127. The effectiveness or efficiency of the Word lies in the fact that he *enlightens every man coming into this world.* For everything which is what it is by participation is derived from that which is such by its essence; just as everything afire is so by participation in fire, which is fire by its very essence. Then since the Word is the true light by his very essence, then everything that shines must do so through him, insofar as it participates in him. And so he *enlightens every man coming into this world.*[146]

128. To understand this, we should know that "world" is taken in three ways in Scripture. Sometimes, from the point of view of its creation, as when the Evangelist says here, "through him the world was made" (v. 10). Sometimes, from the point of view of its perfection, which it reaches through Christ, as in "God was, in Christ, reconciling the world to himself" (2 Cor 5:19). And sometimes it is taken from the point of view of its perversity, as in "The whole world lies under the power of the evil one" (1 Jn 5:19).

On the other hand, "enlightenment" or "being enlightened" by the Word is taken in two ways. First, in relation to the light of natural knowledge, as in "The light of your countenance, O Lord, is marked upon us" (Ps 4:7). Secondly, as the light of grace, "Be enlightened, O Jerusalem" (Is 60:1).

129. With these two sets of distinctions in mind, it is easy to solve a difficulty which arises here. For when the Evangelist says, he *enlightens every man*, this seems to be false, because there are still many in darkness in the world. However, if we bear in mind these distinctions and take "world" from the standpoint of its creation, and "enlighten" as referring to the light of natural reason, the statement of the Evangelist is beyond reproach. For all men coming into this visible world are enlightened by the light of natural knowledge through participating in

146. See *ST* I, q. 89, a. 3, ad 1.

this true light, which is the source of all the light of natural knowledge participated in by men.

When the Evangelist speaks of *man coming into this world*, he does not mean that men had lived for a certain time outside the world and then came into the world, since this is contrary to the teaching of the Apostle in Romans (9:11), "When the children were not yet born nor had they done anything good or evil." Therefore, since they had done nothing before they were born, it is plain that the soul does not exist prior to its union with the body. He refers to *every man coming into this world*, to show that men are enlightened by God with respect to that according to which they came into the world, i.e., with respect to the intellect, which is something external [to the world]. For man is constituted of a twofold nature, bodily and intellectual. According to his bodily or sensible nature, man is enlightened by a bodily and sensible light; but according to his soul and intellectual nature, he is enlightened by an intellectual and spiritual light. Now man does not come into this world according to his bodily nature, but under this aspect, he is from the world. His intellectual nature is derived from a source external to the world, as has been said, i.e., from God through creation; as in "Until all flesh returns to its origin, and the spirit is directed to God, who made it" (Ecc 12:7).[147] For these reasons, when the Evangelist speaks of *every man coming into this world*, he is showing that this enlightenment refers to what is from without, that is, the intellect.

130. If we understand "enlightenment" with respect to the light of grace, then he *enlightens every man* may be explained in three ways. The first way is by Origin[148] in his homily, "The great eagle," and is this. "World" is understood from the point of view of its perfection, which man attains by his reconciliation through Christ. And so we have, he *enlightens every man coming*, by faith, *into this world*, i.e., this spiritual world, that is, the Church, which has been enlightened by the light of grace.[149]

Chrysostom[150] explains it another way. He takes "world" under the aspect of creation. Then the sense is: He *enlightens*, i.e., the Word does, in so far as it depends on him, because he fails no one, but rather "wants all men to be saved, and to come to the knowledge of the truth" (1 Tim 2:4); *every man coming*, i.e., who is born into this sensible world. If anyone is not enlightened, it is due to himself, because he turns from the light that enlightens.

147. See *ST* I, q. 118, a. 2.
148. Erigena, *Hom. in prol. Evang. sec. Io.*; PL 122, col. 293B; cf. *Catena aurea*, 1:9.
149. See *ST* I-II, q. 110, a. 1.
150. *Hom. in Io.* 8. 1, PG 59, col. 65; cf. *Catena aurea*, 1:9.

Augustine[151] explains it in a third way. For him, "every" has a restricted application, so that the sense is: He *enlightens every man coming into this world*, not every man universally, but every man who is enlightened, since no one is enlightened except by the Word. According to Augustine,[152] the Evangelist says, *coming into this world*, in order to give the reason why man needs to be enlightened, and he is taking "world" from the point of view of its perversity and defect. It is as though he were saying: Man needs to be enlightened because he is coming into this world which is darkened by perversity and defects and is full of ignorance. (This followed the spiritual world of the first man.) As Luke says (1:79), "To enlighten those who sit in darkness and in the shadow of death."

131. The above statement refutes the error of the Manichaeans, who think that men were created in the world from an opposing principle, i.e., the devil.[153] For if man were a creature of the devil when coming into this world, he would not be enlightened by God or by the Word, for "Christ came into the world to destroy the works of the devil" (1 Jn 3:8).

132. So it is clear, from the efficacy of the divine Word, that the lack of knowledge in men is not due to the Word, because he is effective in enlightening all, being *the true light, which enlightens every man coming into this world*.

But so you do not suppose this lack arose from the withdrawal or absence of the true light, the Evangelist rules this out adding, *He was in the world*. A comparable statement is found in "He is not far from any one of us," that is, God, "for in him we live, and move, and are" (Acts 17:28). It is as though the Evangelist were saying: The divine Word is effective and is at hand in order to enlighten us.

133. We should remark that something is said to be "in the world" in three ways. In one way, by being contained, as a thing in place exists in a place: "They are in the world" (below 17:11). In another way, as a part in a whole; for a part of the world is said to be in the world even though it is not in a place. For example, supernatural substances, although not in the world as in a place, are nevertheless in it as parts: "God . . . who made heaven and earth, the sea, and all things that are in them" (Ps 145:6). But the true light was not in the world in either of these ways, because that light is neither localized nor is it a part of the universe. Indeed, if we can speak this way, the entire universe is in a certain sense a part, since it participates in a partial way in his goodness.

Accordingly, the true light was in the world in a third way, i.e., as an efficient and preserving cause: "I fill heaven and earth" as said in

151. *Enchir.* 103. 27; PL 40, col. 280.
152. *Tract. in Io.* 2. 7; PL 35, col. 1392; cf. *Catena aurea*, 1:9.
153. See *ST* I, q. 45, a. 4.

Jeremiah (23:24). However, there is a difference between the way the Word acts and causes all things and the way in which other agents act. For other agents act as existing externally: since they do not act except by moving and altering a thing qualitatively in some way with respect to its exterior, they work from without. But God acts in all things from within, because he acts by creating. Now to create is to give existence (*esse*) to the thing created. So, since *esse* is innermost in each thing, God, who by acting gives *esse* acts in things from within. Hence God was in the world as one giving *esse* to the world.[154]

134. It is customary to say that God is in all things by his essence, presence and power.[155] To understand what this means, we should know that someone is said to be by his power in all things that are subject to his power; as a king is said to be in the entire kingdom subject to him, by his power. He is not there, however, by presence or essence. Someone is said to be by presence in all the things that are within his range of vision; as a king is said to be in his house by presence. And someone is said to be by essence in those things in which his substance is; as a king is in one determinate place.

Now we say that God is everywhere by his power, since all things are subject to his power: "If I ascend into heaven, you are there. . . . If I take my wings early in the morning, and dwell in the furthest part of the sea, even there your hand will lead me, and your right hand will hold me" (Ps 138:8–10). He is also everywhere by his presence, because "all things are bare and open to his eyes," as is said in Hebrews (4:13). He is present everywhere by his essence, because his essence is innermost in all things. For every agent, as acting, has to be immediately joined to its effect, because mover and moved must be together. Now God is the maker and preserver of all things, with respect to the *esse* of each. Hence, since the *esse* of a thing is innermost in that thing, it is plain that God, by his essence, through which he creates all things, is in all things.[156]

135. It should be noted that the Evangelist significantly uses the word "was," when he says, **He was in the world**, showing that from the beginning of creation he was always in the world, causing and preserving all things; because if God for even a moment were to withhold his power from the things he established, all would return to nothing and cease to be. Hence Origen[157] uses an apt example to show this, when he says that as a human vocal sound is to a human word conceived in the mind, so is the creature to the divine Word; for as our vocal sound is the effect of the work conceived in our mind, so the crea-

---

154. See *ST* I, q. 44, a. 1; I, q. 104, aa. 1–2.
155. See *ST* I, q. 8, aa. 1, 3.
156. See *ST* I, q. 8, a. 1; I, q. 105, a. 5.
157. Erigena, *Hom. in prol. Evang. sec. Io.*; PL 122, col. 293 C; cf. *Catena aurea*, 1:10.

ture is the effect of the Word conceived in the divine mind. "For he spoke, and they were created" (Ps 148:5). Hence, just as we notice that as soon as our inner word vanishes, the sensible vocal sound also ceases, so, if the power of the divine Word were withdrawn from things, all of them would immediately cease to be at that moment. And this is because he is "sustaining all things by his powerful word" (Heb 1:3).[158]

136. So it is plain that a lack of divine knowledge in minds is not due to the absence of the Word, because *He was in the world*; nor is it due to the invisibility or concealment of the Word, because he has produced a work in which his likeness is clearly reflected, that is, the world: "For from the greatness and beauty of creatures, their creator can be seen accordingly" (Wis 13:5), and "The invisible things of God are clearly seen, being understood through the things that are made" (Rom 1:20).[159] And so the Evangelist at once adds, *and through him the world was made*, in order that that light might be manifested in it. For as a work of art manifests the art of the artisan, so the whole world is nothing else than a certain representation of the divine wisdom conceived within the mind of the Father, "He poured her [wisdom] out upon all his works," as is said in Sirach (1:10).[160]

Now it is clear that the lack of divine knowledge is not due to the Word, because he is efficacious, being *the true light*; and he is at hand, since he *was in the world*; and he is knowable, since *through him the world was made*.

137. The Evangelist indicates the source of this lack when he says, *the world did not know him*. As if to say: It is not due to him, but to the world, who did not know him.

He says *him* in the singular, because earlier he had called the Word not only the "light of men," but also "God"; and so when he says *him*, he means God. Again, he uses "world" for man. For the angels knew him by their understanding, and the elements by their obeying him; but *the world*, i.e., man, who lives in the world, *did not know him*.

138. We attribute this lack of divine knowledge either to the nature of man or to his guilt. To his nature, indeed, because although all the aforesaid aids were given to man to lead him to the knowledge of God, human reason in itself lacks this knowledge. "Man beholds him from afar" (Jb 36:25), and immediately after, "God is great beyond our knowledge."[161] But if some have known him, this was not insofar as they were in the world, but above the world; and the kind for whom the world was not worthy, because *the world did not know him*. Hence

158. See *ST* I, q. 104, aa. 2–4.
159. See *ST* I, q. 2, a. 3.
160. See *ST* I, q. 15, a. 2, ad 2.
161. See *ST* I, q. 12, a. 12.

if they mentally perceived anything eternal, that was insofar as they were not of this world.[162]

But if this lack is attributed to man's guilt, then the phrase, *the world did not know him,* is a kind of reason why God was not known by man; in this sense *world* is taken for inordinate lovers of the world. It is as though it said, *The world did not know him,* because they were lovers of the world. For the love of the world, as Augustine[163] says, is what chiefly withdraws us from the knowledge of God, because "Love of the world makes one an enemy to God" (Jas 4:4); "The sensual man does not perceive the things that pertain to the Spirit of God" (1 Cor 2:14).

139. From this we can answer the question of the Gentiles who futilely ask this: If it is only recently that the Son of God is set before the world as the Savior of men, does it not seem that before that time he scorned human nature?[164] We should say to them that he did not scorn the world but was always in the world, and on his part is knowable by men; but it was due to their own fault that some have not known him, because they were lovers of the world.

140. We should also note that the Evangelist speaks of the Incarnation of the Word to show that the incarnate Word and that which "was in the beginning with God," and God, are the same. He repeats what he had said of him earlier. For above he had said he [the Word] "was the light of men"; here he says he was *the true light.* Above, he said that "all things were made through him"; here he says that *through him the world was made.* Earlier he had said, "without him nothing was made," i.e., according to one explanation, he conserves all things; here he says, *he was in the world,* creating and conserving the world and all things. There he had said, "the darkness did not overcome it"; here he says, *the world did not know him.* And so, all he says after *he was the true light,* is an explanation of what he had said before.

141. We can gather three reasons from the above why God willed to become incarnate.[165] One is because of the perversity of human nature which, because of its own malice, had been darkened by vices and the obscurity of its own ignorance.[166] And so he said before, *the darkness did not overcome it.* Therefore, God came in the flesh so that the darkness might apprehend the light, i.e., obtain a knowledge of it. "The people who walked in darkness saw a great light" (Is 9:2).

The second reason is that the testimony of the prophets was not enough. For the prophets came and John had come; but they were not able to give sufficient enlightenment, because *he was not the light.*

162. See *ST* I, q. 12, aa. 1 and 11; II-II, q. 175, a. 3.
163. See *Tract. in Io.* 2. 11; PL 35, col. 1393; cf. *Catena aurea,* 1:10. Cf. *ST* II-II, q. 163, a. 2.
164. See *ST* I-II, q. 106, a. 3.   165. See *ST* III, q. 1, a. 2.
166. See *ST* I-II, q. 85, a. 3.

And so, after the prophecies of the prophets and the coming of John, it was necessary that the light itself come and give the world a knowledge of itself. And this is what the Apostle says: "In past times, God spoke in many ways and degrees to our fathers through the prophets; in these days he has spoken to us in his Son" as we find in Hebrews (1:1). "We have the prophetic message, to which you do well to give attention, until the day dawns" (2 Pt 1:19).[167]

The third reason is because of the shortcomings of creatures. For creatures were not sufficient to lead to a knowledge of the Creator; hence he says, *through him the world was made, and the world did not know him.* Thus it was necessary that the Creator himself come into the world in the flesh, and be known through himself. And this is what the Apostle says: "Since in the wisdom of God the world did not know God by its wisdom, it pleased God to save those who believe by the foolishness of our preaching" (1 Cor 1:21).

LECTURE 6

11 He came unto his own, and his own did not receive him; 12 but whoever received him, he gave them power to become the sons of God, to all who believe in his name, 13 who are born not from blood, nor from the desires of the flesh nor from man's willing it, but from God.[168]

142. Having given the necessity for the Incarnation of the Word, the Evangelist then shows the advantage men gained from that Incarnation. First, he shows the coming of the light (v. 11); secondly, its reception by men (v. 11b); thirdly, the fruit brought by the coming of the light (v. 12).

143. He shows that the light which was present in the world and evident, i.e., disclosed by its effect, was nevertheless not known by the world. Hence, *he came unto his own,* in order to be known. The Evangelist says, *unto his own,* i.e., to things that were his own, which he had made. And he says this so that you do not think that when he says, *he came,* he means a local motion in the sense that he came as though ceasing to be where he previously was and newly beginning to be where he formerly had not been. He came where he already was. "I came forth from the Father, and have come into the world," as said below (16:28).

He came, I say, *unto his own,* i.e., to Judea, according to some, because it was in a special way his own. "In Judea God is known" (Ps

---

167. See *ST* III, q. 7, a. 8.
168. St. Thomas quotes Jn 1:12 in *ST* II-II, q. 104, a. 6, obj. 1; III, q. 23, a. 2; and Jn 1:13 in *ST* III, q. 27, a. 1, obj. 1.

75:1); "The vineyard of the Lord of hosts is the house of Israel" (Is 5:7). But it is better to say, *unto his own*, i.e., into the world created by him. "The earth is the Lord's" (Ps 23:1).

144. But if he was previously in the world, how could he come into the world? I answer that "coming to some place" is understood in two ways. First, that someone comes where he absolutely had not been before. Or, secondly, that someone begins to be in a new way where he was before. For example, a king, who up to a certain time was in a city of his kingdom by his power and later visits it in person, is said to have come where he previously was: for he comes by his substance where previously he was present only by his power. It was in this way that the Son of God came into the world and yet was in the world. For he was there, indeed, by his essence, power and presence, but he came by assuming flesh. He was there invisibly, and he came in order to be visible.[169]

145. Then when he says, *and his own did not receive him*, we have the reception given him by men, who reacted in different ways. For some did receive him, but these were not his own; hence he says, *his own did not receive him*. "His own" are men, because they were formed by him. "The Lord God formed man" (Gen 2:7); "Know that the Lord is God: he made us" (Ps 99:3). And he made them to his own image, "Let us make man to our image" (Gen 1:26).

But it is better to say, *his own*, i.e., the Jews, *did not receive him*, through faith by believing, and by showing honor to him. "I have come in the name of my Father, and you do not receive me" (below 5:43), and "I honor my Father and you have dishonored me" (below 8:49). Now the Jews are his own because they were chosen by him to be his special people. "The Lord chose you to be his special people" (Dt 26:18). They are his own because related according to the flesh, "from whom is Christ, according to the flesh," as said in Romans (9:3). They are also his own because enriched by his kindness, "I have reared and brought up sons" (Is 1:2). But although the Jews were his own, they did not receive him.

146. However, there were not lacking those who did receive him. Hence he adds, *but whoever received him*. The Evangelist uses this manner of speaking, saying, *but whoever*, to indicate that the deliverance would be more extensive than the promise, which had been made only to his own, i.e., to the Jews. "The Lord is our lawgiver, the Lord is our king; he will save us" (Is 33:22). But this deliverance was not only for his own, but for *whoever received him*, i.e., whoever believe in him. "For I say that Christ was a minister to the circumcised, for the sake of God's truth, to confirm the promises made to the fa-

169. See *ST* III, q. 2, a. 2.

thers" (Rom 15:8). The Gentiles, however, [are delivered] by his mercy, because they were received through his mercy.

147. He says, *whoever*, to show that God's grace is given without distinction to all who receive Christ. "The grace of the Holy Spirit has been poured out upon the Gentiles" (Acts 10:45). And not only to free men, but to slaves as well; not only to men, but to women also. "In Christ Jesus there is neither male nor female, Jew or Greek, the circumcised or uncircumcised" (Gal 3:28).

148. Then when he says, *he gave them power to become the sons of God*, we have the fruit of his coming. First, he mentions the grandeur of the fruit, for *he gave them power*. Secondly, he shows to whom it is given, *to all who believe*. Thirdly, he indicates the way it is given, *not from the blood*, and so forth.

149. The fruit of the coming of the Son of God is great, because by it men are made sons of God. "God sent his Son made from a woman . . . so that we might receive our adoption as sons" (Gal 4:4–5). And it was fitting that we, who are sons of God by the fact that we are made like the Son, should be reformed through the Son.[170]

150. So he says, *he gave them power to become the sons of God*. To understand this we should remark that men become sons of God by being made like God. Hence men are sons of God according to a three-fold likeness to God. First, by the infusion of grace; hence anyone having sanctifying grace is made a son of God. "You did not receive the spirit of slavery . . . but the spirit of adoption as sons," as said in Romans (8:15). "Because you are sons of God, God sent the Spirit of his Son into your hearts" (Gal 4:6).

Secondly, we are like God by the perfection of our actions, because one who acts justly is a son: "Love your enemies . . . so that you may be the children of your Father" (Mt 5:44).

Thirdly, we are made like God by the attainment of glory. The glory of the soul by the light of glory, "When he appears we shall be like him" (1 Jn 3:2); and the glory of the body, "He will reform our lowly body" (Phil 3:21). Of these two it is said in Romans (8:23), "We are waiting for our adoption as sons of God."

151. If we take the power to become the sons of God as referring to the perfection of our actions and the attainment of glory, the statement offers no difficulty. For then when he says, *he gave them power*, he is referring to the power of grace; and when a man possesses this, he can perform works of perfection and attain glory, since "The grace of God is eternal life" (Rom 6:23). According to this way we have, *he gave them*, to those who received him, *power*, i.e., the infusion of grace, *to become the sons of God*, by acting well and acquiring glory.[171]

170. See *ST* III, q. 3, a. 8.
171. See *ST* I-II, q. 110, a. 2.

152. But if this statement refers to the infusion of grace, then his saying, *he gave them power*, gives rise to a difficulty. And this is because it is not in our power to be made sons of God, since it is not in our power to possess grace. We can understand, *he gave them power*, as a power of nature; but this does not seem to be true since the infusion of grace is above our nature. Or we can understand it as the power of grace, and then to have grace is to have *power to become sons of God*. And in this sense he did not give them power to become sons of God, but to be sons of God.

153. The answer to this is that when grace is given to an adult, his justification requires an act of consent by a movement of his free will. So, because it is in the power of men to consent and not to consent, *he gave them power*. However, he gives this power of accepting grace in two ways: by preparing it, and by offering it to him. For just as one who writes a book and offers it to a man to read is said to give the power to read it, so Christ, through whom grace was produced (as will be said below), and who "accomplished salvation on the earth" (Ps 73:12), *gave* us *power to become the sons of God* by offering grace.[172]

154. Yet this is not sufficient since even free will, if it is to be moved to receive grace, needs the help of divine grace, not indeed habitual grace, but movent grace. For this reason, secondly, he gives power by moving the free will of man to consent to the reception of grace, as in "Convert us to yourself, O Lord," by moving our will to your love, "and we will be converted" (Lam 5:21). And in this sense we speak of an interior call, of which it is said, "Those whom he called," by inwardly moving the will to consent to grace, "he justified," by infusing grace (Rom 8:3).[173]

155. Since by this grace man has the power of maintaining himself in the divine sonship, one may read these words in another way. He gave them, i.e., those who received him, *power to become the sons of God*, i.e., the grace by which they are able to be maintained in the divine sonship. "Every one who is born from God does not sin, but the grace of God," through which we are reborn as children of God, "preserves him" (1 Jn 5:18).[174]

156. Thus, *he gave them power to become the sons of God*, through sanctifying grace, through the perfection of their actions, and through the attainment of glory; and he did this by preparing this grace, moving their wills, and preserving this grace.

157. Then when he says, *to all who believe in his name*, he shows those on whom the fruit of his coming is conferred. We can understand this in two ways: either as explaining what was said before, or as

---

172. See *ST* I-II, q. 113, a. 3.
173. See *ST* I-II, q. 111, a. 2.
174. See *ST* I-II, q. 109, a. 10; I-II, q. 111, a. 3; I-II, q. 114, a. 3.

qualifying it. We can regard it as explaining as the Evangelist had said, *whoever received him*, and now to show what it is to receive him, he adds by way of explanation, *who believe in his name*. It is as though he were saying: To receive him is to believe in him, because it is through faith that Christ dwells in your hearts, as in "that Christ may dwell in your hearts through faith" (Eph 3:17). Therefore, they *received him, who believe in his name*.[175]

158. Origen[176] regards this as a qualifying statement, in his homily, "The spiritual voice." In this sense, many receive Christ, declaring that they are Christians, but they are not sons of God, because they do not truly believe in his name; for they propose false dogmas about Christ by taking away something from his divinity or humanity, as in "Every spirit that denies Christ is not from God" (1 Jn 4:3). And so the Evangelist says, as though contracting his meaning, *he gave them*, i.e., those who receive him by faith, *power to become the sons of God*, to those, however, *who believe in his name*, i.e., who keep the name of Christ whole, in such a way as not to lessen anything of the divinity or humanity of Christ.

159. We can also refer this to formed faith, in the sense that *to all*, that is, *he gave power to become the sons of God, who believe in his name*, i.e., those who do the works of salvation through a faith formed by charity. For those who have only an unformed faith do not believe in his name because they do not work unto salvation.[177]

However, the first exposition, which is taken as explaining what preceded, is better.

160. Then when he says, *who are born not from blood*, he shows the way in which so great a fruit is conferred on men. For since he had said that the fruit of the light's coming is the power given to men to become the sons of God, then to forestall the supposition that they are born through a material generation he says, *not from blood*. And although the word "blood" (*sanguis*) has no plural in Latin, but does in Greek, the translator [from Greek into Latin] ignored a rule of grammar in order to teach the truth more perfectly. So he does not say, "from blood," in the Latin manner, but "from bloods" (*ex sanguinibus*). This indicates whatever is generated from blood, serving as the matter in carnal generation. According to the Philosopher,[178] "semen is a residue derived from useful nourishment in its final form." So "blood" indicates either the seed of the male or the menses of the female.

The cause moving to the carnal act is the will of those coming together, the man and the woman. For although the act of the genera-

---

175. See *ST* I-II, q. 113, a. 4.
176. Erigena, *Hom. in prol. Evang. sec. Io.*; PL 122, col. 294–95.
177. See *ST* II-II, q. 4, a. 4.
178. Aristotle, *On the Generation of Animals* I. 18; 726a26–28.

tive power as such is not subject to the will, the preliminaries to it are subject to the will. So he says, *nor from the desires of the flesh*, referring to the woman; *nor from man's willing it*, as from an efficient cause; *but from God*. It is as though he were saying: They became sons of God, nor carnally, but spiritually.

According to Augustine,[179] "flesh" is taken here for the woman, because as the flesh obeys the spirit, so woman should obey man. Adam (Gen 2:23) said of the woman, "This, at last, is bone of my bones." And note, according to Augustine, that just as the possessions of a household are wasted away if the woman rules and the man is subject, so a man is wasted away when the flesh rules the spirit. For this reason the Apostle says, "We are not debtors to the flesh, so that we should live according to the flesh" (Rom 8:12). Concerning the manner of his carnal generation, we read, "In the womb of my mother I was molded into flesh" (Wis 7:1).

161. Or, we might say that the moving force to carnal generation is twofold: the intellectual appetite on the one hand, that is, the will; and on the other hand, the sense appetite, which is concupiscence. So, to indicate the material cause he says, *not from blood*. To indicate the efficient cause, in respect to concupiscence, he says, *nor from the desires of the flesh* [*ex voluntate carnis*, literally, "from the will of the flesh"], even though the concupiscence of the flesh is improperly called a "will" in the sense of Galatians (5:17), "The flesh lusts against the spirit." Finally, to indicate the intellectual appetite he says, *nor from man's willing it*. So, the generation of the sons of God is not carnal but spiritual, because they were born *from God*. "Every one who is born from God conquers the world" (1 Jn 5:4).

162. Note, however, that this preposition *de* ("of," or "from"), always signifies a material cause as well as an efficient and even a consubstantial cause. Thus we say a blacksmith makes a knife *de ferro* ("from" iron), and a father generates his son *de seipso* ("from" himself), because something of his concurs somehow in begetting. But the preposition *a* ("by") always signifies a moving cause. The preposition *ex* ("from," or "by")—[in the sense of "out of" or "by reason of"]—is taken as something common, since it implies an efficient as well as a material cause, although not a consubstantial cause.

Consequently, since only the Son of God, who is the Word, is "of" (*de*) the substance of the Father and indeed is one substance with the Father, while the saints, who are adopted sons, are not of his substance, the Evangelist uses the preposition *ex*, saying of others that they are born *from God* (*ex Deo*), but of the natural Son, he says that he is born of the Father (*de Patre*).

179. *Tract. in Io.* 2. 14; PL 34, col. 1394; cf. *Catena aurea*, 1:11–13.

163. Note also that in the light of our last exposition of carnal generation, we can discern the difference between carnal and spiritual generation. For since the former is from blood, it is carnal; but the latter, because it is not from blood, is spiritual. "What is born from flesh is itself flesh; and what is born from Spirit is itself spirit" (below 3:6). Again, because material generation is from the desires of the flesh, i.e., from concupiscence, it is unclean and begets children who are sinners: "We were by nature children of wrath" as it says in Ephesians (2:3). Again, because the former is *from man's willing it*, that is, from man, it makes children of men; but the latter, because it is from God, makes children of God.[180]

164. But if he intends to refer his statement, *he gave them power*, to baptism, in virtue of which we are reborn as sons of God, we can detect in his words the order of baptism: that is, the first thing required is faith, as shown in the case of catechumens, who must first be instructed about the faith so that they may believe in his name; then through baptism they are reborn, not carnally from blood, but spiritually from God.[181]

LECTURE 7

14a And the Word was made flesh, and made his dwelling among us.[182]

165. Having explained the necessity for the Word's coming in the flesh as well as the benefits this conferred, the Evangelist now shows the way he came (v. 14a). He thus resumes the thread with his earlier statement, *he came unto his own*. As if to say: The Word of God came unto his own. But lest anyone suppose that he came by changing his location, he shows the manner in which he came, that is, by an Incarnation. For he came in the manner in which he was sent by the Father, by whom he was sent, i.e., he was made flesh. "God sent his Son made from a woman" (Gal 4:4). And Augustine says about this that "He was sent in the manner in which he was made."[183]

According to Chrysostom,[184] however, he is here continuing the

180. See *ST* I-II, q. 113, a. 9.
181. See *ST* III, q. 66, a.1; III, q. 68, a. 1
182. St. Thomas quotes Jn 1:14 in *ST* I-II, q. 108, a. 1; III, q. 1, a. 3, ad 1; III, q. 6, a. 3, obj. 3; III, q. 6, a. 6; III, q. 7, a. 7, obj. 1; III, q. 7, a. 9, *sed contra*; III, q. 7, a. 10, *sed contra*; III, q. 7, a. 12, *sed contra*; III, q. 8, a. 1; III, q. 10, a. 4; III, q. 15, a. 3, ad 1; III, q. 16, a. 6, *sed contra*; III, q. 23, a. 4, ad 2; III, q. 26, a. 2, ad 1; III, q. 27, a. 5, obj. 1; III, q. 34, a. 1; III, q. 49, a. 6, obj. 1; III, q. 59, a. 2, ad 1; III, q. 69, a. 5; III, q. 72, a. 1, ad 4.
183. See *ST* I, q. 43, a. 1, especially ad 2.
184. *Hom. in Io.* 11. 1; PG 59, col. 78–79; cf. *Catena aurea*, 1:14a.

earlier statement, *he gave them power to become the sons of God.* As if to say: If you wonder how he was able to give this power to men, i.e., that they become sons of God, the Evangelist answers: because *the Word was made flesh,* he made it possible for us to be made sons of God. "God sent his Son . . . so that we might receive our adoption as sons" (Gal 4:5).[185]

But according to Augustine,[186] he is continuing the earlier statement, *who are born from God.* For since it seemed a hard saying that men be born from God, then, as though arguing in support of this and to produce belief in the existence of the Word, the Evangelist adds something which seems less seemly, namely, that *the Word was made flesh.* As if to say: do not wonder if men are born from God, because *the Word was made flesh,* i.e., God became man.

166. It should be noted that this statement, *the Word was made flesh,* has been misinterpreted by some and made the occasion of error. For certain ones have presumed that the Word became flesh in the sense that he or something of him was turned into flesh, as when flour is made into bread, and air becomes fire. One of these was Eutyches,[187] who postulated a mixture of natures in Christ, saying that in him the nature of God and of man was the same. We can clearly see that this is false because, as was said above, "the Word was God." Now God is immutable, as is said, "I am the Lord, and I do not change" (Mal 3:6). Hence in no way can it be said that he was turned into another nature. Therefore, one must say in opposition to Eutyches, *the Word was made flesh,* i.e., the Word assumed flesh, but not in the sense that the Word himself is that flesh. It is as if we were to say: "The man became white," not that he is that whiteness, but that he assumed whiteness.

167. There were others who, although they believed that the Word was not changed into flesh but assumed it, nevertheless said that he assumed flesh without a soul; for if he had assumed flesh with a soul, the Evangelist would have said, "the Word was made flesh with a soul." This was the error of Arius, who said that there was no soul in Christ, but that the Word of God was there in place of a soul.

The falsity of this opinion is obvious, both because it is in conflict with Sacred Scripture, which often mentions the soul of Christ, as: "My soul is sad, even to the point of death" (Mt 26:38), and because certain affections of the soul are observed in Christ which can not pos-

185. See *ST* III, q. 23, a. 1.
186. *Tract. in Io.* 2. 15; PL 35, col. 1395; cf. *Catena aurea,* 1:14a.
187. Eutyches (c. 378–454), head of a monastery in Constantinople, taught that there was one nature of the Incarnate Word, such that the humanity of Christ was not the same as our humanity. In this he directly contradicted the teaching of Cyril of Alexandria (whose teaching he was seeking to defend), and his views were condemned by the Council of Chalcedon in 451. See *ST* III, q. 2, a. 1.

sibly exist in the Word of God or in flesh alone: "He began to be sorrowful and troubled" (Mt 26:37). Also, God cannot be the form of a body. Nor can an angel be united to a body as its form, since an angel, according to its very nature, is separated from body, whereas a soul is united to a body as its form. Consequently, the Word of God cannot be the form of a body.[188]

Furthermore, it is plain that flesh does not acquire the specific nature of flesh except through its soul. This is shown by the fact that when the soul has withdrawn from the body of a man or a cow, the flesh of the man or the cow is called flesh only in an equivocal sense. So if the Word did not assume flesh with a soul, it is obvious that he did not assume flesh. But *the Word was made flesh*; therefore, he assumed flesh with a soul.

168. And there were others who, influenced by this, said that the Word did indeed assume flesh with a soul, but this soul was only a sensitive soul, not an intellectual one; the Word took the place of the intellectual soul in Christ's body. This was the error of Apollinaris.[189] He followed Arius for a time, but later in the face of the [scriptural] authorities cited above, was forced to admit a soul in Christ which could be the subject of these emotions. But he said this soul lacked reason and intellect, and that in the man Christ their place was taken by the Word.

This too is obviously false, because it conflicts with the authority of Sacred Scripture in which certain things are said of Christ that cannot be found in his divinity, nor in a sensitive soul, nor in flesh alone; for example, that Christ marveled, as in Matthew (8:10). For to marvel or wonder is a state which arises in a rational and intellectual soul when a desire arises to know the hidden cause of an observed effect. Therefore, just as sadness compels one to place a sensitive element in the soul of Christ, against Arius, so marveling or amazement forces one to admit, against Apollinaris, an intellectual element in Christ.[190]

The same conclusion can be reached by reason. For as there is no flesh without a soul, so there is no human flesh without a human soul, which is an intellectual soul. So if the Word assumed flesh which was animated with a merely sensitive soul to the exclusion of a rational soul, he did not assume human flesh; consequently, one could not say: "God became man."

188. See *ST* I, q. 3, a. 8; III, q. 5, a. 3.
189. Apollinaris of Laodicea (c. 315–392) was a defender of the Nicene understanding of the Son, but he taught that the eternal Logos took the place of a rational soul in Christ, and as a consequence Christ did not have a human soul like ours. His views were condemned in Rome (377), in Antioch (379), and at the Council of Constantinople (381), as denying that Christ assumed our full humanity in order to redeem it. See *ST* III, q. 5, aa. 3 and 4.
190. See *ST* III, q. 5, a. 4.

Besides, the Word assumed human nature in order to repair it. Therefore, he repaired what he assumed. But if he did not assume a rational soul, he would not have repaired it. Consequently, no fruit would have accrued to us from the Incarnation of the Word; and this is false. Therefore, *the Word was made flesh*, i.e., assumed flesh which was animated by a rational soul.

169. But you may say: If the Word did assume flesh with such a soul, why did the Evangelist not mention "rational soul," instead of only "flesh," saying, *the Word was made flesh*? I answer that the Evangelist had four reasons for doing this.[191]

First, to show the truth of the Incarnation against the Manichaeans, who said that the Word did not assume true flesh, but only imaginary flesh, since it would not have been becoming for the Word of the good God to assume flesh, which they regarded as a creature of the devil. And so to exclude this the Evangelist made special mention of the flesh, just as Christ showed the truth of the resurrection to the disciples when they took him for a spirit, saying: "A spirit does not have flesh and bones, as you see that I have" (Lk 24:39).

Secondly, to show the greatness of God's kindness to us. For it is evident that the rational soul has a greater conformity to God than does flesh, and that it would have been a great sign of compassion if the Word had assumed a human soul, as being conformed to himself. But to assume flesh too, which is something far removed from the simplicity of his nature, was a sign of a much greater, indeed, of an incomprehensible compassion.[192] As the Apostle says (1 Tim 3:16): "Obviously great is the mystery of godliness which appeared in the flesh." And so to indicate this, the Evangelist mentioned only flesh.

Thirdly, to demonstrate the truth and uniqueness of the union in Christ. For God is indeed united to other holy men, but only with respect to their soul; so it is said: "She [wisdom] passes into holy souls, making them friends of God and prophets" (Wis 7:27). But that the Word of God is united to flesh is unique to Christ, according to the Psalmist: "I am alone until I pass" (Ps 140:10). "Gold cannot equal it" (Jb 28:17). So the Evangelist, wishing to show the uniqueness of the union in Christ, mentioned only the flesh, saying, *the Word was made flesh*.

Fourthly, to suggest its relevance to man's restoration. For man was weak because of the flesh. And thus the Evangelist, wishing to suggest that the coming of the Word was suited to the task of our restoration, made special mention of the flesh in order to show that the weak flesh was repaired by the flesh of the Word. And this is what the Apostle says: "The law was powerless because it was weakened by the flesh.

191. See *ST* III, q. 5, a. 3, ad 1.
192. See *ST* III, q. 5, a. 1.

God, sending his Son in the likeness of sinful flesh and in reparation for sin, condemned sin in his flesh" (Rom 8:3).[193]

170. A question arises as to why the Evangelist did not say that the Word assumed flesh, but rather that *the Word was made flesh*. I answer that he did this to exclude the error of Nestorius. He said that in Christ there were two persons and two sons, [one being the Son of God] the other being the son of the Virgin. Thus he did not admit that the Blessed Virgin was the mother of God.

But if this were so, it would mean that God did not become man, for one particular *suppositum* cannot be predicated of another. Accordingly, if the person or *suppositum* of the Word is different than the person or *suppositum* of the man, in Christ, then what the Evangelist says is not true, namely, *the Word was made flesh*. For a thing is made or becomes something in order to be it; if, then, the Word is not man, it could not be said that the Word became man. And so the Evangelist expressly said *was made*, and not "assumed," to show that the union of the Word to flesh is not such as was the "lifting up" of the prophets, who were not "taken up" into a unity of person, but for the prophetic act.[194] This union is such as would truly make God man and man God, i.e., that God would be man.

171. There were some, too, who, misunderstanding the manner of the Incarnation, did indeed admit that the aforesaid assumption was terminated at a oneness of person, acknowledging in God one person of God and man. But they said that in him there were hypostases, i.e., two *supposita*; one of a human nature, created and non-eternal, and the other of the divine nature, non-created and eternal. This is the first opinion presented in the *Sentences* (III, d6).

According to this opinion the proposition, "God was made man and man was made God," is not true. Consequently, this opinion was condemned as heretical by the Fifth Council,[195] where it is said: "If anyone shall assert one person and two hypostases in the Lord Jesus Christ, let him be anathema." And so the Evangelist, to exclude any assumption not terminated at a oneness of persons, says, *was made*.[196]

172. If you ask how the Word is man, it must be said that he is man in the way that anyone is man, namely, as having human nature. Not that the Word is human nature itself, but he is a divine *suppositum* united to a human nature. The statement, *the Word was made flesh*, does not indicate any change in the Word, but only in the nature newly assumed into the oneness of a divine person. *And the Word was made flesh* through a union to flesh. Now a union is a relation. And relations newly said of God with respect to creatures do not imply a

---

193. See *ST* III, q. 4, a. 6; III, q. 61, a. 1.
194. See *ST* III, q. 2, a. 8; III, q. 4, aa. 2–3; III, q. 23, a. 4.
195. The Second Council of Constantinople in 553.
196. See *ST* III, q. 2, aa. 2–4, 6.

change on the side of God, but on the side of the creature relating in a new way to God.[197]

173. Now follows, *and made his dwelling among us*. This is distinguished in two ways from what went before. The first consists in stating that above the Evangelist dealt with the Incarnation of the Word when he said, *the Word was made flesh*; but now he touches on the manner of the Incarnation, saying, *and made his dwelling among us*. For according to Chrysostom[198] and Hilary,[199] by the Evangelist saying *the Word was made flesh*, someone might think that he was converted into flesh and that there are not two distinct natures in Christ, but only one nature compounded from the human and divine natures. And so the Evangelist, excluding this, added, *and made his dwelling among us*, i.e., in our nature, yet so as to remain distinct in his own. For what is converted into something does not remain distinct in its nature from that into which it is converted.

Furthermore, something which is not distinct from another does not dwell in it, because to dwell implies a distinction between the dweller and that in which it dwells. But the Word dwelt in our nature; therefore, he is distinct in nature from it. And so, inasmuch as human nature was distinct from the nature of the Word in Christ, the former is called the dwelling place and temple of the divinity, according to John (2:21): "But he spoke of the temple of his body."[200]

174. Now although what is said here by these holy men is orthodox, care must be taken to avoid the reproach which some receive for this. For the early doctors and saints were so intent upon refuting the emerging errors concerning the faith that they seemed meanwhile to fall into the opposite ones. For example, Augustine, speaking against the Manichaeans, who destroyed the freedom of the will, disputed in such terms that he seemed to have fallen into the heresy of Pelagius. Along these lines, John the Evangelist added, *and made his dwelling among us*, so that we would not think there was a mingling or transformation of natures in Christ because he had said, *the Word was made flesh*.

Nestorius misunderstood this phrase, *and made his dwelling among us*, and said that the Son of God was united to man in such a way that there was not one person of God and of man. For he held that the Word was united to human nature only by an indwelling through grace. From this, however, it follows that the Son of God is not man.[201]

175. To clarify this we should know that we can consider two things in Christ: his nature and person. In Christ there is a distinction in na-

197. See *ST* III, q. 2, a. 7.
198. *Hom. in Io.* 11. 2; PG 59, col. 80; cf. *Catena aurea*, 1:14a.
199. *De Trin.* 10. 22; PL 10, col. 359–360; cf. *Catena aurea*, 1:14a.
200. See *ST* III, q. 2, a. 1.
201. See *ST* III, q. 2, a. 6.

ture, but not in person, which is one and the same in the two natures, since the human nature in Christ was assumed into a oneness of person.[202] Therefore, the indwelling which the saints speak of must be referred to the nature, so as to say, he *made his dwelling among us,* i.e., the nature of the Word inhabited our nature; not according to the hypostasis or person, which is the same for both natures in Christ.

176. The blasphemy of Nestorius is further refuted by the authority of the Sacred Scripture. For the Apostle calls the union of God and man an emptying, saying of the Son of God: "He, being in the form of God . . . emptied himself, taking the form of a servant" (Phil 2:6). Clearly, God is not said to empty himself insofar as he dwells in the rational creature by grace, because then the Father and the Holy Spirit would be emptying themselves, since they too are said to dwell in man through grace: For Christ, speaking of himself and of the Father says, "We will come to him and make our home with him" (below 14:23); and of the Holy Spirit the Apostle says: "The Spirit of God dwells in us" (1 Cor 3:16).[203]

Furthermore, if Christ was not God as to his person, he would have been most presumptuous to say: "I and the Father are one" (below 10:30), and "Before Abraham came to be, I am," as is said below (8:58). Now "I" refers to the person of the speaker. And the one who was speaking was a man, who, as one with the Father, existed before Abraham.

177. However, another connection [besides that given in 173] with what went before is possible, by saying that above he dealt with the Incarnation of the Word, but that now he is treating the manner of life of the incarnate Word, saying, he *made his dwelling among us,* i.e., he lived on familiar terms with us apostles. Peter alludes to this when he says, "During all the time that the Lord Jesus came and went among us" (Acts 1:21). "Afterwards, he was seen on earth" (Bar 3:38).

178. The Evangelist added this for two reasons. First, to show the marvelous likeness of the Word to men, among whom he lived in such a way as to seem one of them. For he not only willed to be like men in nature, but also in living with them on close terms without sin, in order to draw to himself men won over by the charm of his way of life.[204]

Secondly, to show the truthfulness of his [the Evangelist's] statements. For the Evangelist had already said many great things about the Word, and was yet to mention more wonderful things about him; and so that his testimony would be more credible he took as a proof of his truthfulness the fact that he had lived with Christ, saying, he *made*

202. See *ST* III, q. 2, a. 2.
203. See *ST* III, q. 43, a. 6.
204. See *ST* III, q. 40, aa. 1–2.

his dwelling among us. As if to say: I can well bear witness to him, because I lived on close terms with him. "We tell you . . . what we have heard, what we have seen with our eyes" (1 Jn 1:1); "God raised him up on the third day, and granted that he be seen, not by all the people, but by witnesses preordained by God," that is, "to us who ate and drank with him" (Acts 10:40).

LECTURE 8

14b And we have seen his glory, the glory as of the Only Begotten of the Father, full of grace and truth.

179. Having set forth the Incarnation of the Word, the Evangelist then begins to give the evidence for the incarnate Word. He does two things about this. First, he shows the ways in which the incarnate Word was made known. Secondly, he clarifies each way, below (1:16). Now the incarnate Word was made known to the apostles in two ways: first of all, they obtained knowledge of him by what they saw; secondly, by what they heard of the testimony of John the Baptist. So first, he states what they saw about the Word; secondly, what they heard from John (v. 15).

He states three things about the Word. First, the manifestation of his glory; hence he says, *we have seen the glory.* Secondly, the uniqueness of his glory, when he adds, *as of the Only Begotten.* Thirdly, the precise nature of this glory, because *full of grace and truth.*

180. *And we have seen his glory,* can be connected in three ways with what went before. First, it can be taken as an argument for his having said, *the Word was made flesh.* As if to say: I hold and know that the Word of God was incarnate because I and the other apostles *have seen his glory.* "We know of what we speak, and we bear witness of what we see" (below 3:11). "We tell you . . . what we have heard, what we have seen with our eyes" (1 Jn 1:1).

181. Secondly, according to Chrysostom,[205] the connection is made by taking this statement as expressing many benefits. As if to say: The Incarnation of the Word not only conferred on us the benefit of becoming sons of God, but also the good of seeing his glory. For dull and feeble eyes cannot see the light of the sun; but they can see it when it shines in a cloud or on some opaque body. Now before the Incarnation of the Word, human minds were incapable of seeing the divine light in itself, the light which enlightens every rational nature. And so, in order that it might be more easily seen and contemplated by us, he covered it with the cloud of our flesh: "They looked towards the desert,

205. *Hom. in Io.* 12. 1; PG 59, col. 81; cf. *Catena aurea,* 1:14b.

and saw the glory of the Lord in a cloud" (Ex 16:10), i.e., the Word of God in the flesh.[206]

182. According to Augustine,[207] however, the connection refers to the gift of grace. For the failure of the spiritual eyes of men to contemplate the divine light is due not only to their natural limitations but also to the defects incurred by sin: "Fire," that is, of concupiscence, "fell on them, and they did not see the sun," of justice (Ps 57:9). Hence in order that the divine light might be seen by us, he healed our eyes, making an eye salve of his flesh, so that with the salve of his flesh the Word might heal our eyes, weakened by the concupiscence of the flesh. And this is why just after saying, *the Word was made flesh*, he says, *we have seen his glory*. To indicate this the Lord made clay from his saliva and spread the clay upon the eyes of the man born blind (below 9:6). For clay is from the earth, but saliva comes from the head. Similarly, in the person of Christ, his human nature was assumed from the earth; but the incarnate Word is from the head, i.e., from God the Father. So, when this clay was spread on the eyes of men, *we saw his glory*.

183. This is the glory of the Word Moses longed to see, saying, "Show me your glory" (Ex 32:18). But he did not deserve to see it; indeed, he was answered by the Lord: "You shall see my back" (Ex 33:23), i.e., shadows and figures. But the apostles saw his brightness: "All of us, gazing on the Lord's glory with unveiled faces, are being transformed from glory to glory into his very image" (2 Cor 3:18). For Moses and the other prophets saw in an obscure manner and in figures the glory of the Word that was to be manifested to the world at the end of their times; hence the Apostle says: "Now we see through a mirror, in an obscure manner, but then face to face" in 1 Corinthians (13:12); and below (12:41), "Isaiah said this when he saw his glory." But the apostles saw the very brilliance of the Word through his bodily presence: "All of us, gazing on the Lord's glory," and so forth (2 Cor 3:18); "Blessed are the eyes which see what you see. For many kings and prophets desired to see what you see, and did not see it" (Lk 10:23).[208]

184. Then when he says, *the glory as of the Only Begotten*, he shows the uniqueness of his glory. For since it is written of certain men that they were in glory, as of Moses it says that "his face shone" (Ex 34:29), or was "horned," according to another text, someone might say that from the fact that they saw him [Jesus] in glory, it should not be said that the Word of God was made flesh. But the Evangelist excludes this when he says, *the glory as of the Only Begotten of the Father*. As if to say: His glory is not like the glory of an angel, or of Moses, or Elijah, or

206. See *ST* III, q. 1, a. 1.
207. *Tract. in Io.* 2. 16; PL 35, col. 1395; cf. *Catena aurea*, 1:14b.
208. See *ST* I-II, q. 101, a. 2; III, q. 25, a. 1.

Elisha, or anything like that; but *the glory as of the Only Begotten*; for as it is said, "He [Jesus] was counted worthy of more glory than Moses" (Heb 3:3); "Who among the sons of God is like God?" (Ps 88:7).

185. The word *as*, according to Gregory,[209] is used to express the fact. But according to Chrysostom,[210] it expresses the manner of the fact: as if someone were to see a king approaching in great glory and being asked by another to describe the king he saw, he could, if he wanted to be brief, express the grandeur of his glory in one word, and say that he approached "as" a king, i.e., as became a king. So too, here, the Evangelist, as though asked by someone to describe the glory of the Word which he had seen, and being unable to fully express it, said that it was "as" of the Only Begotten of the Father, i.e., such as became the Only Begotten of God.

186. The uniqueness of the glory of the Word is brought out in four ways. First, in the testimony which the Father gave to the Son. For John was one of the three who had seen Christ transfigured on the mountain and heard the voice of the Father saying: "This is my beloved Son, with whom I am well pleased" (Mt 17:5). Of this glory it is said, "He received honor and glory from God the Father . . . 'This is my beloved Son'" (2 Pt 1:17).[211]

Secondly, it is brought out by the service of the angels. For prior to the Incarnation of Christ, men were subject to the angels. But after it, angels ministered, as subjects, to Christ. "Angels came and ministered to him" (Mt 4:11).[212]

Thirdly, it is brought out by the submission of nature. For all nature obeyed Christ and heeded his slightest command, as something established by him, because "All things were made through him" (above 1:3). This is something granted neither to angels nor to any creature, but to the incarnate Word alone. And this is what we read, "What kind of man is this, for the winds and the sea obey him?" (Mt 8:27).[213]

Fourthly, we see it in the way he taught and acted. For Moses and the other prophets gave commands to men and taught them not on their own authority, but on the authority of God. So they said: "The Lord says this"; and "The Lord spoke to Moses." But Christ speaks as the Lord, and as one having power, i.e., by reason of his own power. Hence he says, "I say to you" (Mt 5:22). This is the reason why, at the end of the Sermon on the Mount, it is said that he taught as one "having authority" (Mt 7:29). Furthermore, other holy men worked mira-

209. *Mor.* 18. 6; PL 76, col. 43–44; cf. *Catena aurea*, 1:14.
210. *Hom. in Io.* 12. 1; PG 59, col. 81–82; cf. *Catena aurea*, 1:14.
211. See *ST* III, q. 45, aa. 2, 4.
212. See *ST* I, q. 113, a. 4, ad 1; III, q. 8, a. 4; III, q. 22, a. 1, ad 1; III, q. 26, a. 1, ad 2.
213. See *ST* III, q. 44, a. 4, ad 3.

cles, but not by their own power. But Christ worked them by his own power. In these ways, then, the glory of the Word is unique.[214]

187. Note that sometimes in Scripture we call Christ the Only Begotten, as here, and below (1:18): "It is the Only Begotten Son, who is in the bosom of the Father, who has made him known." At other times we call him the First-born: "When he brings the First-born into the world, he says, 'Let all the angels of God adore him'" (Heb 1:6). The reason for this is that just as it belongs to the whole Blessed Trinity to be God, so it belongs to the Word of God to be God Begotten. Sometimes, too, he is called God according to what he is in himself; and in this way he alone is uniquely God by his own essence. It is in this way that we say there is but one God: "Hear, O Israel: the Lord your God is one" (Dt 6:4). At times, we even apply the name of deity to others, insofar as a certain likeness of the divinity is given to men; in this sense we speak of many gods: "Indeed, there are many gods and many lords" (1 Cor 8:5).

Along these lines, if we consider what is proper to the Son as Begotten, and consider the way in which this sonship is attributed to him, that is, through nature, we say that he is the Only Begotten of God: because, since he alone is naturally begotten by the Father, the Begotten of the Father is one only. But if we consider the Son, insofar as sonship is conferred on others through a likeness to him, then there are many sons of God through participation. And because they are called sons of God by a likeness to him, he is called the First-born of all. "Those whom he foreknew, he predestined to become conformed to the image of his Son, so that he might be the First-born of many brothers" (Rom 8:29).

So, Christ is called the Only Begotten of God by nature; but he is called the First-born insofar as from his natural sonship, by means of a certain likeness and participation, a sonship is granted to many.[215]

188. Then when he says, **full of grace and truth**, he determines the glory of the Word. As if to say: His glory is such that he is full of grace and divinity. Now these words can be applied to Christ in three ways.

First, from the point of view of union. For grace is given to someone so that he might be united to God through it. So he who is most perfectly united to God is full of grace. Now some are joined to God by participating in the natural likeness: "Let us make man to our image and likeness" (Gen 1:26). Some are joined by faith: "That Christ may dwell in your hearts through faith" (Eph 3:17). And others are united by charity, because "He who abides in love abides in God" (1 Jn 4:16). But all these ways are partial: because one is not perfectly united to God by participating a natural likeness; nor is God seen as he is

214. See *ST* III, q. 42, a. 1; III, q. 43, a. 3.
215. See *ST* III, q. 4, a. 1; III, q. 23, a. 1.

by faith; nor is he loved to the extent that he is lovable by charity—for since he is the infinite Good, his lovableness is infinite, and the love of no creature is able to love this infinitely. And so these unions are not full.

But in Christ, in whom human nature is united to the divinity in the unity of a *suppositum*, we find a full and perfect union with God. The reason for this is that this union was such that all the acts not only of his divine but also of his human nature were acts of the *suppositum* [or person]. So he was **full of grace** insofar as he did not receive any special gratuitous gift from God, but that he should be God himself. "He gave him," i.e., God the Father gave to the Son, "a name which is above every name" (Phil 2:9). "He was foreordained to be the Son of God in power" (Rom 1:4). He was also **full of truth**, because the human nature in Christ attained to the divine truth itself, that is, that this man should be the divine Truth itself. In other men we find many participated truths, insofar as the First Truth gleams back into their minds through many likenesses; but Christ is Truth itself. Thus it is said: "In whom all the treasures of wisdom are hidden" (Col 2:3).[216]

189. Secondly, these words can be applied in relation to the perfection of his soul. Then he is said to be **full of grace and truth** inasmuch as in his soul there was the fullness of all graces without measure: "God does not bestow the Spirit in fractions," as we read below (3:34). Yet it was given in fractions to all rational creatures, both angels and men. For according to Augustine, just as there is one sense common to all the parts of the body, namely, the sense of touch, while all the senses are found in the head, so in Christ, who is the head of every rational creature (and in a special way of the saints who are united to him by faith and charity), all virtues and graces and gifts are found superabundantly; but in others, i.e., the saints, we find participations of the graces and gifts, although there is a gift common to all the saints, and that is charity. We read about this fullness of Christ's grace: "there shall come forth a shoot out of the root of Jesse, and a flower shall spring up out of his root. And the spirit of the Lord shall rest upon him: The spirit of wisdom and of understanding, the spirit of counsel and of fortitude, the spirit of knowledge and of piety" (Is 11:1).[217]

Further, Christ was also **full of truth** because his precious and blessed soul knew every truth, human and divine, from the instant of his conception. And so Peter said to him, "You know all things" (below 21:17). And the Psalm (88:25) says: "My truth," i.e., the knowledge of every truth, "and my mercy," i.e., the fullness of all graces, "shall be with him."[218]

216. See *ST* III, q. 6, a. 6; III, q. 7, a. 13.
217. See *ST* III, q. 9, aa. 1–3; III, q. 10, a. 2; III, q. 11, a. 1.
218. See *ST* III, qq. 9–12.

190. In a third way these words can be explained in relation to his dignity as head, i.e., inasmuch as Christ is the head of the Church. In this way it is his prerogative to communicate grace to others, both by producing virtue in the minds of men through the inpouring of grace and by meriting, through his teaching and works and the sufferings of his death, superabundant grace for an infinite number of worlds, if there were such. Therefore, he is *full of grace* insofar as he conferred perfect justice upon us. We could not acquire this perfect justice through the law, which was infirm and could make no one just or bring anyone to perfection. As we read: "The law was powerless because it was weakened by the flesh. God, sending his son in the likeness of sinful flesh and in reparation for sin, condemned sin in his flesh" (Rom 8:3).[219]

Again, he was *full of truth* insofar as he fulfilled the figures of the Old Law and the promises made to the fathers. "Christ was a minister to the circumcised to confirm the promises made to the fathers" (Rom 15:8); "All the promises of God are fulfilled in him" (2 Cor 1:20).[220]

Further, he is said to be *full of grace* because his teaching and manner of life were most gracious. "Grace is poured out upon your lips" (Ps 44:3). And so it is said, "All the people came to him early in the morning," i.e., in the morning they were eager to come (Lk 21:38). He was *full of truth*, because he did not teach in enigmas and figures, nor gloss over the vices of men, but preached the truth to all, openly and without deception. As it says below: "Now you are speaking plainly" (16:29).[221]

LECTURE 9

15 John bore witness to him, and he cried out saying: "This is the one of whom I said: 'He who comes after me, ranks ahead of me, because he existed before me.'"

191. Having given the evidence by which the Word was made known to the apostles by sight, the Evangelist then presents the evidence by which the Word was made known to persons other than the apostles by their hearing the testimony of John. He does three things about this. First, the witness is presented. Secondly, his manner of testifying is indicated. Thirdly, his testimony is given.

192. So he says: We indeed have seen his glory, the glory as of the Only Begotten of the Father. But we are not believed, perhaps because

219. See *ST* III, q. 8, aa. 1, 6; III, q. 22, a. 4; III, q. 48, a. 1; III, q. 49, a. 1.
220. See *ST* III, q. 47, a. 2, ad 1.
221. See *ST* III, q. 42, a. 3.

we are held in suspicion. So let his witness come forth, that is, John the Baptist, who bears witness to Christ. He is a faithful witness who will not lie: "A faithful witness will not lie" (Prv 14:5); "You sent [messengers] to John; and he bore witness to the truth" (below 5:33). John gives his testimony here and fulfills his office with perseverance because he came as a witness. As Proverbs (12:19) says, "Truthful lips endure forever."

193. Then when he says, *John bore witness to him, and he cried out*, he describes the way he bore witness, that is, it was with a cry. So he says, *he cried out*, i.e., freely without fear. "Cry out loud voice. . . . Say to the cities of Judah: Here is your God" (Is 40:9). He cried out ardently and with great fervor, because it is said, "His word burned like a torch" (Sir 48:1); "Seraphim cried one to another" (Is 6:3), which is expressive of a more interior eagerness of spirit. The use of a cry shows that the statements of the witness are not made to a few in figurative language or secretly, but that a truth is being declared openly and publicly, and told not to a few but to many. "Cry out, and do not stop" (Is 58:1).

194. Then he adds his testimony. And he does two things. First, he shows that his testimony was continuous. Secondly, he describes the person to whom he bore witness.

195. The testimony of the Baptist was continuous because he bore witness to him not only once but many times, and even before Christ had come to him. And so he says, *This is the one of whom I said*, i.e., before I saw him in the flesh I bore witness to him. "And you, child, shall be called the prophet of the Most High" (Lk 1:76). He pointed him out both as present and when about to come. And his testimony is certain because he not only predicted that he would come, but pointed him out when he was present, saying, *Look! There is the Lamb of God*. This implies that Christ was physically present to John; for he had often come to John before being baptized.

196. Then he describes the one to whom he bore witness, saying, *He who comes after me, ranks ahead of me*. Here we should note that John does not at once preach to his disciples that Christ is the Son of God, but he draws them little by little to higher things: first, by preferring Christ to himself, even though John had such a great reputation and authority as to be considered the Christ or one of the great prophets. Now he compares Christ to himself: first, with regard to the order of their preaching; secondly, as to the order of dignity; and thirdly, as to the time of their existence.

197. With respect to the order of their preaching, John preceded Christ as a servant precedes his master, and as a soldier his king, or as the morning star the sun: "See, I am sending my messenger, and he will prepare the way before me" (Mal 3:1), So, *He comes after me*, in being known to men, through my preaching. Observe that *comes* is in the present tense, because in Greek the present participle is used.

Now John preceded Christ for two reasons. First, according to Chrysostom,[222] because John was a blood relation of Christ according to the flesh: "your relative, Elizabeth" (Lk 1:36). Therefore, had he borne witness to Christ after knowing him, his testimony might have been open to question; accordingly, John came preaching before he was acquainted with Christ, in order that his testimony might have more force. Hence he says, "And I did not know him! And yet it was to reveal him to Israel that I came baptizing with water" (below 1:31).

Secondly, John preceded Christ because in things that pass into act from potency, the imperfect is naturally prior to the perfect; hence it is said in 1 Corinthians (15:46): "The spiritual is not first, but the animal." Accordingly, the perfect doctrine of Christ should have been preceded by the less perfect teaching of John, which was in a certain manner midway between the doctrine of the law and the prophets (which announced the coming of Christ from afar), and the doctrine of Christ, which was clear and plainly made Christ known.

198. He [John] compares him to himself with respect to dignity when he says, he *ranks ahead of me* [*ante me factus est*, literally, he "was made before me"]. It should be noted that it is from this text that the Arians took occasion for their error. For they said that "He who comes after me," is to be understood of Christ as to the flesh he assumed, but what follows, "was made before me," can only be understood of the Word of God, who existed before the flesh; and for this reason Christ as the Word was made, and was not coeternal with the Father.

According to Chrysostom,[223] however, this exposition is stupid, because if it were true, the Baptist would not have said, he "was made before me, because he existed before me," since no one is unaware that if he was before him, he was made before him. He rather would have said the opposite: "He was before me, because he was made before me." And so, according to Chrysostom, these words should be taken as referring to his [Christ's] dignity, that is, he was preferred to me and placed ahead of me. It is as though he said: Although Jesus came to preach after me, he was made more worthy than I both in eminence of authority and in the repute of men: "Gold will not be equal to it" (Jb 28:17). Or alternatively: he is preferred *ahead of me*, that is, before my eyes, as the Gloss[224] says and as the Greek text reads. As if to say: Before my eyes, i.e., in my sight, because he came into my view and was recognized.

199. He compares him to himself with respect to their duration, saying, *because he existed before me*. As if to say: He was God from all eternity, I am a frail man of time. And therefore, even though I came

222. *Hom. in Io.* 13. 2; PG 59, col. 88; cf. *Catena aurea,* 1:15.
223. Ibid. 13. 3; PG 59, col. 89; cf. *Catena aurea,* 1:15.
224. *Glossa ordinaria;* PL 114, col. 357.

to preach ahead of him, yet it was fitting that he rank before me in the reputation and opinion of men, because he preceded all things by his eternity: "Jesus Christ is the same yesterday, today, and forever" (Heb 13:8). "Before Abraham came to be, I am," as we read below (8:58).

If we understand this passage as saying that he "was made before me," it can be explained as referring to the order of time according to the flesh. For in the instant of his conception Christ was perfect God and perfect man, having a rational soul perfected by the virtues, and a body possessed of all its distinctive features, except that it lacked perfect size: "A woman shall enclose a man," i.e., a perfect man (Jer 31:22).[225] Now it is evident that Christ was conceived as a perfect man before John was born; consequently he says that he "was made before me," because he was a perfect man before I came forth from the womb.

LECTURE 10

16 Of his fullness we have all received—indeed, grace upon grace; 17 because, while the law was given through Moses, grace and truth have come through Jesus Christ.[226]

200. He follows with, **Of his fullness we have all received.** These words and those that follow to (v. 19), "This is the testimony of John," are taken in two ways. According to Origen,[227] these are the words of John the Baptist and are added by him to support what he had said previously. It is as though he said: Truly, *he existed before me*, because *of his fullness*, i.e., of his grace, not only I but *all*, including the prophets and patriarchs, *have received*, because all had the grace they possessed by faith in the incarnate Word. According to this explanation, John the Baptist began weaving the story of the Incarnation at, "John bore witness to him" (v. 15).

But according to Augustine[228] and Chrysostom,[229] the words from "John bore witness to him" (v. 15), are those of John the Evangelist. And they are connected with the previous words, "full of grace and

225. See *ST* III, q. 34, aa. 1–2, 4.
226. St. Thomas quotes Jn 1:16 in *ST* I-II, q. 108, a. 1; II-II, q. 176, a. 1, obj. 3; III, q. 1, a. 6; III, q. 2, a. 11, ad. 2; III, q. 7, a. 1; III, q. 8, a. 1; III, q. 8, a. 5, *sed contra*; III, q. 19, a. 4, obj. 2; III, q. 24, a. 3; III, q. 27, a. 5, ad 1; III, q. 39, a. 6, obj. 4; III, q. 53, a. 3, obj. 3; III, q. 64, a. 4, obj. 3; III, q. 69, aa. 4 and 5; and Jn 1:17 in *ST* I, q. 75, a. 1, ad 1; I-II, q. 98, a. 1; I-II, q. 98, a. 3, obj. 2; I-II, q. 112, a. 1, obj. 1; II-II, q. 12, a. 2, obj. 3; III, q. 2, a. 11; III, q. 27, a. 5; III, q. 38, a. 3; III, q. 61, a. 4, obj. 1; III, q. 79, a. 1.
227. *Comm. in Io.* VI. 6, no. 33; PG 14, col. 209A–B; cf. *Catena aurea*, 1:16, 17.
228. *Tract. in Io.* 3. 8; PL 35, col. 1399.
229. *Hom. in Io.* 14. 1; PG 59, col. 92; cf. *Catena aurea*, 1:16, 17.

truth," as though he were saying: Above, the Evangelist gave the evidence for the Word which was learned through sight and by hearing; but here he explains each. First, how he was made known to the apostles through sight, which was tantamount to receiving the evidence from Christ. Secondly, how John bore witness to him, at "This is the testimony of John" (v. 19). As to the first he does two things. First, he shows that Christ is the origin, as a fountain, of every spiritual grace. Secondly, he shows that grace is dispensed to us through him and from him.

201. He says first of all: We know from our own experience that we have seen him full of grace and truth, because *of his fullness we have all received*. Now one fullness is that of sufficiency, by which one is able to perform acts that are meritorious and excellent, as in the case of Stephen. Again, there is a fullness of superabundance, by which the Blessed Virgin excels all the saints because of the eminence and abundance of her merits. Further, there is a fullness of efficiency and overflow, which belongs only to the man Christ as the author of grace. For although the Blessed Virgin super-abounds her grace into us, it is never as authoress of grace. But grace flowed over from her soul into her body: for through the grace of the Holy Spirit, not only was the mind of the Virgin perfectly united to God by love, but her womb was supernaturally impregnated by the Holy Spirit. And so after Gabriel said, "Hail, full of grace," he refers at once to the fullness of her womb, adding, "the Lord is with you" (Lk 1:28).[230] And so the Evangelist, in order to show this unique fullness of efficiency and overflow in Christ, said, *Of his fullness we have all received*, i.e., all the apostles and patriarchs and prophets and just men who have existed, do now exist, and will exist, and even all the angels.[231]

202. Note that the preposition *de* [of, from] sometimes signifies efficiency, i.e., an originative cause, as when it is said that a ray is or proceeds "from" the sun. In this way it signifies the efficiency of grace in Christ, i.e., authorship, because the fullness of grace in Christ is the cause of all graces that are in intellectual creatures. "Come to me, all you who desire me, and be filled with my fruits," that is to say, share in the fullness of those fruits which come from me (Sir 24:26).

But sometimes this preposition *de* signifies consubstantiality, as when it is said that the Son is "of" the Father [*de Patre*]. In this usage, the fullness of Christ is the Holy Spirit, who proceeds from him, consubstantial with him in nature, in power and in majesty. For although the habitual gifts in the soul of Christ are other than those in us, nevertheless it is one and the same Holy Spirit who is in him and who fills all those to be sanctified. "One and the same Spirit produces all these"

---

230. See *ST* III, q. 25, a. 5; III, q. 27, aa. 1, 5.
231. See *ST* III, q. 8, aa. 1, 4; III, q. 26, a. 1.

(1 Cor 12:11); "I will pour out my Spirit upon all flesh" (Jl 2:28); "If anyone does not have the Spirit of Christ, he does not belong to him" (Rom 8:9). For the unity of the Holy Spirit produces unity in the Church: "The Spirit of the Lord filled the whole world" (Wis 1:7).[232]

In a third way, the preposition *de* [of, from] can signify a portion, as when we say "take 'from' this bread or wine [*de hoc pane, vel vino*]," i.e., take a portion and not the whole. Taken in this way it signifies that those who take a part derive it from the fullness. For he [Christ] received all the gifts of the Holy Spirit without measure, according to a perfect fullness; but we participate through him some portion of his fullness; and this is according to the measure which God grants to each. "Grace has been given to each of us according to the degree to which Christ gives it" (Eph 4:7).[233]

203. Then when he says, **grace upon grace**, he shows the distribution of graces into us through Christ. Here he does two things. First, he shows that we receive grace from Christ, as its author. Secondly, that we receive wisdom from him (1:18). As to the first he does two things. First he shows that we have received of his fullness. Secondly, our need to receive it.

204. First, he says that we have received of the fullness of Christ what is described as **grace upon grace**. In the light of what is said, we are forced to understand that of his fullness we have received grace, and that upon that grace we have received another. Accordingly, we must see what that first grace is upon which we have received a second one, and also what that second grace is.

According to Chrysostom,[234] the first grace, which was received by the whole human race, was the grace of the Old Testament received in the law. And this was indeed a great grace: "I will give you a good gift" (Prv 4:2). For it was a great benefit for idolatrous men to receive precepts from God, and a true knowledge of the one true God.[235] "What is the advantage of being a Jew, or the benefit of circumcision? It is great in every way. First indeed, because the words of God were entrusted to them" (Rom 3:1). Upon that grace, then, which was first, we have received a second far better. "He will follow grace with grace" (Zec 4:7).

But was not the first grace sufficient? I answer that it was not, because the law gives only a knowledge of sin, but does not take it away. "The law brought nothing to perfection" (Heb 7:19). Hence it was necessary that another grace come that would take away sin and reconcile one with God.[236]

---

232. See *ST* I, q. 43, a. 6; III, q. 8, a. 1, ad 1.
233. See *ST* III, q. 7, a. 10.
234. *Hom. in Io.* 14. 1; PG 59, col. 92–93; cf. *Catena aurea*, 1:16, 17.
235. See *ST* I-II, q. 98, a. 1.
236. See *ST* I-II, q. 91, a. 5.

205. And so he says, *because, while the law was given through Moses, grace and truth have come through Jesus Christ*. Here the Evangelist ranks Christ above Moses the lawgiver, whom the Baptist ranked above himself. Now Moses was regarded as the greatest of the prophets: "There did not arise again in Israel a prophet like Moses" (Dt 34:10).[237] But he ranks Christ above Moses in excellence and in dignity of works, *because the law was given through Moses*; and between these two, the One excels the other as the reality excels the symbol and the truth the shadow: "The law had a shadow of the good things to come" (Heb 10:1). Further, Christ excels him in the way he works, because the law was given by Moses as by one proclaiming it, but not originating it; for "The Lord alone is our lawgiver" (Is 33:22).[238] But *grace and truth have come through Jesus Christ*, as through the Lord and Author of truth and grace, as was explained above.

206. According to Augustine,[239] however, the first grace is justifying and prevenient grace, which is not given to us because of our works: "If it is by grace, it is not now by works" (Rom 11:6). Upon that grace, then, which is imperfect, we have received another grace which is perfect, i.e., the grace of eternal life. And although eternal life is in some way acquired by merits, nevertheless, because the principle of meriting in everyone is prevenient grace, eternal life is called a grace: "The grace of God is eternal life" (Rom 6:23). To be brief, whatever grace is added to prevenient grace, the whole is called *grace upon grace*.[240]

The need for this second grace arises from the insufficiency of the law, which showed what was to be done and what avoided; but it gave no help to fulfill what was commanded. Indeed, what seemed to have been directed to life was the occasion for producing death. Hence the Apostle says that the law was a minister of death: "If the ministry that condemned had glory, the ministry that justifies has much more glory" (2 Cor 3:9). Also, it promised the help of grace but did not fulfill, because "The law brought nothing to perfection" (Heb 7:19). Again, it prefigured the truth of the new grace by its sacrifices and ceremonies; indeed, its very rites proclaimed that it was a figure. Hence it was necessary that Christ come, who by his own death would destroy other deaths and grant the help of new grace, in order that we might both fulfill his precepts with ease and joy, and die to our sins and our old way of life: "Our old self was crucified with him" (Rom 6:6), and in order that the truth of the figures contained in the law might be revealed and the promises made to the fathers be fulfilled.[241]

This can be explained in another way: *truth has come through Je-*

---

237. See *ST* II-II, q. 174, a. 4.
238. See *ST* I-II, q. 98, a. 3; I-II, q. 101, a. 2.
239. *Tract. in Io.* 3. 9; PL 35, col. 1400; cf. *Catena aurea*, 1:16, 17.
240. See *ST* I-II, q. 111, a. 3.
241. See *ST* I-II, q. 101, a. 2.

sus Christ as to the wisdom and truth which was hidden for centuries, and which he openly taught when he came into the world: "I came into the world for this, to testify to the truth," as we read below (18:37).

207. But if Christ is the Truth, as it says below (14:6), how did truth come [i.e., come to be, be made] through him, because nothing can make itself? I answer that by his essence he is the uncreated Truth, which is eternal and not made, but is begotten of the Father; but all created truths were made through him, and these are certain participations and reflections of the first Truth, which shines out in those souls who are holy.

LECTURE 11

18 No one has ever seen God; it is the Only Begotten Son, who is in the bosom of the Father, who has made him known.[242]

208. Above, the Evangelist showed how the apostles received grace from Christ as its author; here he shows how they received it from him as a teacher. About this he does three things. First, he shows the need for this teaching. Secondly, the competency of the teacher. Thirdly, the teaching itself.

209. The need for this teaching arose from the lack of wisdom among men, which the Evangelist implies by alluding to the ignorance concerning God which prevailed among men, saying: *No one has ever seen God.* And he does this fittingly, for wisdom consists properly in the knowledge of God and of divine things. Hence Augustine[243] says that wisdom is the knowledge of divine things, as science is the knowledge of human things.

210. But this statement of the Evangelist, *No one has ever seen God,* seems to contradict many passages of divine Scripture. For it is said in Isaiah (6:1): "I saw the Lord seated on a high and lofty throne." And about the same is found in 2 Samuel (6:2). Again in Matthew (5:8), the Lord says: "Blessed are the pure in heart, for they shall see God." If someone were to answer this last statement by saying that it is true that in the past no one has seen God, but will see him in the future, as the Lord promises, the Apostle would exclude this, saying, "He dwells in unapproachable light, whom no man has seen or can see" (1 Tim 6:16).

Because the Apostle says, "no man has seen," someone might say that if he cannot be seen by men, then at least he can be seen by an-

---

242. St. Thomas quotes Jn 1:18 in *ST* I, q. 12, a. 1, obj. 1; I, q. 33, a. 3, ad 2; I, q. 41, a. 3; I, q. 88, a. 3, *sed contra*.

243. *De Trin.* 12. 15, no. 25; PL 42, col. 1012. See also *ST* I-II, q. 57, a. 2.

gels; especially since God says, "Their angels in heaven always see the face of my Father" (Mt 18:10). But it cannot be taken in this way either, because it is said, "The sons of the resurrection will be like the angels of God in heaven" (Mt 22:30). If, therefore, the angels see God in heaven, then it is plain that the sons of the resurrection also see him: "When he appears we shall be like him, and we shall see him as he is" (1 Jn 3:2).[244]

211. How then are we to understand what the Evangelist says: *No one has ever seen God*? To understand it we must know that God is said to be seen in three ways. First, through a created substitute presented to the bodily sight; as Abraham is believed to have seen God when he saw three [men] and adored one (Gen 18:1–21). He adored one because he recognized the mystery of the Trinity in the three, whom he first thought to be men, and later believed to be angels. In a second way, through a representation in the imagination; and in this way Isaiah saw the Lord seated on a high and lofty throne. Many visions of this sort are recorded in the Scriptures. In a third way, he is seen through an intelligible species abstracted from material things, and in this way he is seen by those who, considering the greatness of creatures, see with their intellect the greatness of the Creator, as it is said: "From the greatness and beauty of creatures, their Creator can be seen accordingly" (Wis 13:5); "The invisible things of God are clearly seen, being understood through the things that are made," as found in Romans (1:20). In another way, God is seen through a certain spiritual light infused by God into spiritual minds during contemplation; and this is the way Jacob saw God face to face, as it says in Genesis (32:30).[245] According to Gregory, this vision came about through his lofty contemplation.

But the vision of the divine essence is not attained by any of the above visions: for no created species, whether it be that by which an external sense is informed, or by which the imagination is informed or by which the intellect is informed, is representative of the divine essence as it is. Now man knows as to its essence only what the species he has in his intellect represents as it is. Therefore, the vision of the divine essence is not attained through any species.[246]

The reason why no created species can represent the divine essence is plain: for nothing finite can represent the infinite as it is; but every created species is finite; therefore [it cannot represent the infinite as it is]. Further, God is his own *esse*; and therefore his wisdom and greatness and anything else are the same. But all those cannot be repre-

244. See *ST* I, q. 12, a. 1; I-II, q. 69, a. 2, obj. 3; II-II, q. 1, a. 2, ad 3; III, q. 45, a. 4.
245. See *ST* I, q. 12, a. 11.
246. See *ST* I, q. 12, aa. 1–4.

sented through one created thing. Therefore, the knowledge by which God is seen through creatures is not a knowledge of his essence, but a knowledge that is dark and mirrored, and from afar. "Everyone sees him," in one of the above ways, "from afar" (Jb 36:25), because we do not know what God is by all these acts of knowing, but what he is not, or that he is. Hence Dionysius[247] says, in his *Mystical Theology*, that the perfect way in which God is known in this present life is by taking away all creatures and every thing understood by us.[248]

212. There have been some who said that the divine essence will never by seen by any created intellect, and that it is seen neither by the angels nor by the blessed. But this statement is shown to be false and heretical in three ways. First, because it is contrary to the authority of divine Scripture: "We shall see him as he is" (1 Jn 3:2); "This is eternal life, that they know you, the only true God, and Jesus Christ whom you have sent" (below 17:3). Secondly, because the brightness of God is the same as his substance: for he does not give forth light by participating in light, but through himself. And thirdly, because it is impossible for anyone to attain perfect happiness except in the vision of the divine essence. This is because the natural desire of the intellect is to understand and know the causes of all the effects that it knows; but this desire cannot be fulfilled unless it understands and knows the first universal cause of all things, which is a cause that is not composed of cause and effect, as second causes are. Therefore, to take away the possibility of the vision of the divine essence by man is to take away happiness itself. Therefore, in order for the created intellect to be happy, it is necessary that the divine essence be seen. "Blessed are the pure in heart, for they shall see God" (Mt 5:8).[249]

213. Three things should be noted about the vision of the divine essence. First, it will never be seen with a bodily eye, either by sense or imagination, since only sensate bodily things are perceived by the senses, and God is not bodily: "God is spirit" (below 4:24). Secondly, that as long as the human intellect is in the body it cannot see God, because it is weighed down by the body so that it cannot attain the summit of contemplation. So it is that the more a soul is free of passions and is purged from affections for earthly things, the higher it rises in the contemplation of truth and tastes how sweet the Lord is. Now the highest degree of contemplation is to see God through his essence; and so as long as a man lives in a body which is necessarily subject to many passions, he cannot see God through his essence. "Man will not see me and live" (Ex 33:20). Therefore, if the human intellect is to see the

247. *De myst. theol.* 1. 2; PG 3, col. 1000B; see also *De div. nom* 13. 3; PG 3, col. 981 A–B, and *De coel. hier.* 2. 3; PG 3, col. 141A. See *ST* I, qq. 12–13.
248. See *ST* I, q. 13, a. 2.
249. See *ST* I, q. 12, a. 1.

divine essence it must wholly depart from the body: either by death, as the Apostle says, "We would prefer to be absent from the body and present with the Lord" (2 Cor 5:8); or by being wholly abstracted by rapture from the senses of the body, as is mentioned of Paul in 2 Corinthians (12:3).[250]

Thirdly, no created intellect (however abstracted, either by death, or separated from the body) which does not see the divine essence, can comprehend it in any way. And so it is commonly said that although the whole divine essence is seen by the blessed, since it is most simple and has no parts, yet it is not wholly seen, because this would be to comprehend it. For "wholly" implies a certain mode. But any mode of God is the divine essence. Hence one who does not see him wholly does not comprehend him. For one is properly said to comprehend a thing through knowledge when he knows that thing to the extent that it is knowable in itself; otherwise, although he may know it, he does not comprehend it. For example, one who knows this proposition, "A triangle has three angles equal to two right angles," by a dialectical syllogism, does not know it as well as it is knowable in itself; thus he does not know it wholly. But one who knows this by a demonstrative syllogism does know it wholly. For each thing is knowable to the extent that it has being and truth; while one is a knower according to his amount of cognitive power. Now a created intellectual substance is finite; hence it knows in a finite way. And since God is infinite in power and being, and as a consequence is infinitely knowable, he cannot be known by any created intellect to the degree that he is knowable. And thus he remains incomprehensible to every created intellect. "Behold, God is great, exceeding our knowledge" (Jb 36:26). He alone contemplates himself comprehensively, because his power to know is as great as his entity in being. "O most mighty, great, powerful, your name is Lord of hosts, great in counsel, incomprehensible in thought" (Jer 32:18).[251]

214. Using the above explanations, we can understand, *No one has ever seen God.* First, *No one,* i.e., no man, has seen God, that is, the divine essence, with the eye of the body or of the imagination. Secondly, *No one,* living in this mortal life, has seen the divine essence in itself. Thirdly, *No one,* man or angel, has seen God by a vision of comprehension. So when it is said that certain ones have seen God with their eyes or while living in the body, he is not seen through his essence, but through a creature acting as a substitute, as was said.

And thus it was necessary for us to receive wisdom, because *No one has ever seen God.*

---

250. See *ST* I, q. 12, aa. 3–4; II-II, q. 175, aa. 3–6.
251. See *ST* I, q. 12, a. 7.

215. The Evangelist mentions the competent teacher of this wisdom when he adds, *it is the Only Begotten Son, who is in the bosom of the Father.* He shows the competence of this teacher in three ways: by a natural likeness, by a singular excellence, and by a most perfect consubstantiality.

216. By natural likeness, because a son is naturally like his father. Wherefore it also follows that one is called a son of God insofar as he shares in the likeness of his natural son; and one knows him insofar as he has a likeness to him, since knowledge is attained through assimilation [or "likeness to"]. Hence 1 John (3:2) says, "Now we are sons of God," and he immediately adds, "when he comes, we will be like him, and we will see him as he is." Therefore, when the Evangelist says *Son,* he implies a likeness as well as an aptitude for knowing God.

217. Because this teacher knows God in a more special way than other sons do, the Evangelist suggests this by his singular excellence, saying, *the Only Begotten.* As if to say: He knows God more than other sons do. Hence, because he is the natural Son, having the same nature and knowledge as the Father, he is called *the Only Begotten.* "The Lord said to me: 'You are my Son'" (Ps 2:7).

218. Although he may know in a unique way, he would be lacking the ability to teach if he were not to know wholly. Hence he adds a third point, namely, his consubstantiality to the Father, when he says, *who is in the bosom of the Father.* "Bosom" is not to be taken here as referring to men in their garments, but it indicates the secret things of the Father. For what we carry in our bosom we do in secret. The secret things of the Father refer to his unsurpassed power and knowledge, since the divine essence is infinite. Therefore, in that bosom, i.e., in the most secret things of the paternal nature and essence, which transcends all the power of the creature, is *the Only Begotten Son*; and so he is consubstantial with the Father.

What the Evangelist signifies by "bosom," David expressed by "womb," saying: "From the womb, before the daystar," i.e., from the inmost secret things of my essence, incomprehensible to every created intellect, "I begot you" (Ps 109:3), consubstantial with me, and of the same nature and power, and virtue and knowledge. "What man knows the things of a man except the spirit of the man that is in him? So also, no one knows the things of God except the Spirit of God" (1 Cor 2:11). Therefore, he comprehends the divine essence, which is his own.[252]

219. But the soul of Christ, which knows God, does not comprehend him, because this is attributed only to the Only Begotten Son who is in the bosom of the Father.[253] So the Lord also says: "No one

---

252. See *ST* I, q. 27, a. 1.
253. See *ST* III, q. 10, a. 1.

knows the Father except the Son, and any to whom the Son wishes to reveal him" (Mt 11:27); we should understand this as referring to the knowledge of comprehension, about which the Evangelist seems to be speaking here. For no one comprehends the divine essence except the Father, the Son, and the Holy Spirit. And so we have shown the competence of the teacher.

220. We should note that the phrase, *who is in the bosom of the Father*, rejects the error of those who say that the Father is invisible, but the Son is visible, though he was not seen in the Old Testament. For from the fact that he is among the hidden things of the Father, it is plain that he is naturally invisible, as is the Father. So it is said of him: "Truly, you are a hidden God" (Is 45:15). And so Scripture mentions the incomprehensibility of the Son: "No one knows the Son except the Father, and no one knows the Father except the Son" (Mt 11:27), "What is the name of his son, if you know?" as we read in Proverbs (30:4).

221. Then the Evangelist indicates the way in which this teaching is handed down, saying that it is the Only Begotten Son *who has made him known*. For in the past, the Only Begotten Son revealed knowledge of God through the prophets, who made him known to the extent that they shared in the eternal Word. Hence they said things like, "The Word of the Lord came to me." But now the Only Begotten Son *has made him known* to the faithful: "It is I who spoke; here I am" (Is 52:6); "God, who in many and varied ways, spoke to the fathers in past times through the prophets, has spoken to us in these days in his Son" (Heb 1:1).

And this teaching surpasses all other teachings in dignity, authority and usefulness, because it was handed on immediately by the Only Begotten Son, who is the first Wisdom. "It was first announced by the Lord, and confirmed to us by those who heard him" (Heb 2:3).

222. But what did he make known except the one God? And even Moses did this: "Hear, O Israel: the Lord your God is one" (Dt 6:4). What did this add to Moses? It added the mystery of the Trinity, and many other things that neither Moses nor any of the prophets made known.[254]

LECTURE 12

19 This is the testimony of John, when the Jews sent priests and Levites from Jerusalem to him, to ask him: "Who are you?" 20 He declared openly, and did not deny, and stated clearly, "I am not the Messiah." 21 And they questioned him, "Who then? Are you Elijah?" And

254. See *ST* II-II, q. 2, a. 8.

*he said, "I am not. "Are you the Prophet?" And he responded "No."
22 They therefore said to him, "Who are you? We must take back an
answer to those who sent us. What have you to say about yourself?"
23 He said, quoting the prophet Isaiah, "I am 'a voice that cries in the
wilderness: Make a straight way for the Lord'" [Is 40:3].*[255]

223. Above, the Evangelist showed how Christ was made known to
the apostles through the testimony of John; here he develops this testimony more fully. First, he presents John's testimony to the people.
Secondly, the testimony he gave of Christ to his own disciples (below
1:35). If we carefully consider what was said, we discover a twofold
testimony of John to Christ: one which he gave to Christ in his presence, the other in his absence. For he would not have said, "It is he"
(below 1:30), unless he had given testimony in Christ's presence; and
he would not have said, "of whom I said," unless he gave testimony
to him in his absence. So first, the Evangelist develops the testimony
John gave to Christ in his absence; secondly, that he gave in his presence (v. 29).

Now these two testimonies differ, because the first was given when
he was questioned; the other was spontaneous. So in the first instance,
we are given not only his testimony, but also the questions. First, he
was asked about himself; secondly, about his office (v. 24). First we are
shown how John stated that he was not what he really was not; secondly, that he did not deny what he was.

224. As to the first, there are three questions and three answers,
as is plain from the text. In the first question there is great respect for
John shown by the Jews. They had sent certain ones to him to ask
about his testimony. The greatness of their respect is gathered from
four facts. First, from the dignity of those who sent the questioners;
for they were not sent by Galileans, but by those who were first in
rank among the people of Israel, namely, Judeans, of the tribe of Judah, who lived about Jerusalem. It was from Judah that God chose the
princes of the people.

Secondly, from the preeminence of the place, that is, from Jerusalem, which is the city of the priesthood, the city dedicated to divine
worship: "You people claim that Jerusalem is the place where men
must worship God" (below 4:20); "They will worship him with sacrifices and offerings" (Is 19:21).[256] Thirdly, from the authority of the
messengers, who were religious and from among the holier of the people, namely, priests and Levites; "You will be called the priests of the
Lord" (Is 61:6).

Fourthly, from the fact that they sent them so that John might bear
witness to himself, indicating that they put such trust in his words as

to believe John even when giving testimony about himself. Hence he says they were sent to ask him, *Who are you?* They did not do this to Christ, in fact they said to him: "You are bearing witness to yourself; Your testimony is not true" (below 8:13).

225. Then when he says, *He declared openly, and did not deny*, John's answer is given. The Evangelist twice mentioned that John spoke forth to show his humility; for although he was held in such high esteem among the Jews that they believed he might be the Messiah, he, on his part, usurped no honor that was not due him; indeed, he stated clearly, *I am not the Messiah*.

226. What of the statement, *He declared openly, and did not deny*? For it seems that he did deny, because he said that he was not the Messiah. It must be answered that he did not deny the truth, for he said he was not the Messiah; otherwise he would have denied the truth. "A very great iniquity, and a denial of the most high God" (Jb 31:28). Thus he did not deny the truth, because however great he might have been considered, he did not become proud, usurping for himself the honor of another. He stated clearly, *I am not the Messiah*; because in truth he was not. "He was not the light," as was said above (1:8).

227. Why did John answer, *I am not the Messiah*, since those who had been sent did not ask if he was the Messiah, but who he himself was? I answer that John directed his answer more to the mind of the questioners than to their question. And we can understand this in two ways. According to Origen,[257] the priests and Levites came to John with a good intention. For they knew from the Scriptures, and particularly from the prophecy of Daniel, that the time for the coming of the Messiah had arrived. So, seeing John's holiness, they suspected that he might be the Messiah. So they sent to John, wishing to learn by their question, *Who are you?* whether John would admit that he was the Messiah. And so he directs his answer to their thoughts: *I am not the Messiah*.

Chrysostom,[258] however, says that they questioned him as a stratagem. For John was related to priests, being the son of a chief priest, and he was holy. Yet, he bore witness to Christ, whose family seemed lowly; for that reason they even said, "Is not this the son of the carpenter?"; and they did not know him. So, preferring to have John as their master, not Christ, they sent to him, intending to entice him by flattery and persuade him to take this honor for himself, and to state that he was the Messiah. But John, seeing their evil intent, said, *I am not the Messiah*.

257. *Comm. in Io.* VI. 8, nos. 50–51; PG 14, col. 213D–216A; cf. *Catena Aurea*, 1:19–23.
258. *Hom. in Io.* 16. 1; PG 59, col. 103; cf. *Catena aurea*, 1:19–23.

228. The second question is stated when they ask him, **Who then? Are you Elijah?** Here we should note that just as the Jews awaited the Lord who was to come, so too they waited for Elijah, who would precede the Messiah: "I will send you Elijah, the prophet" (Mal 4:5). And so those who were sent, seeing that John did not say that he was the Messiah, pressed him that at least he state if he were Elijah. And this is what they ask: **Who then? Are you Elijah?**

229. There are certain heretics who say that souls migrate from one body to another. And this belief was current among the Jews of that time. For this reason they believed that the soul of Elijah was in John's body, because of the similarity of John's actions to those of Elijah. And they say that these messengers asked John whether he was Elijah, i.e., whether the soul of Elijah was in John. They support this with Christ's statement, "He is Elijah who is to come," as is found in Matthew (11:14). But John's answer conflicts with their opinion, as he says, **I am not**, i.e., Elijah.

They counter this by saying that John answered in ignorance, not knowing whether his soul was the soul of Elijah. But Origen[259] says in answer to this that it seems most unreasonable that John, a prophet enlightened by the Spirit, and telling such things about the Only Begotten Son of God, should be ignorant of himself, and not know whether his soul had been in Elijah.

230. So this was not the reason John was asked, **Are you Elijah?** Rather it was because they took it from Scripture (2 Kings 2:11) that Elijah did not die, but had been carried alive by a whirlwind into heaven. Accordingly, they believed that he had suddenly appeared among them.

But against this opinion is the fact that John was born from parents who were known, and his birth had been known to everyone. So it says in Luke (1:66) that all said, "What do you think this child will be?" One might say to this that it is not incredible that they should regard John in the manner described. For a similar situation in found in Matthew (14:1): for Herod thought that Christ was John, whom he had beheaded, even though Christ had been preaching and was known for some time before John had been beheaded. And so from a similar stupidity and madness the Jews asked John whether he was Elijah.

231. Why does John say, **I am not** Elijah, while Christ said, "He is Elijah" (Mt 11:14). The angel gives us the answer: "He will go before him in the spirit and power of Elijah" (Lk 1:17), i.e., in his works. Thus he was not Elijah in person, but in spirit and power, i.e., because he showed a similarity to Elijah in his works.

259. *Comm. in Io.* VI. 13, nos. 74–75; PG 14, col. 224A; cf. *Catena aurea*, 1:19–23.

232. This likeness can be found in three matters. First, in their office: because as Elijah will precede the second coming of Christ, so John preceded the first. Thus the angel said, "He will go before him." Secondly, in their manner of living. For Elijah lived in desert places, ate little food and wore coarse clothing, as recorded in 1 and 2 Kings. John, also, lived in the desert, his food was locusts and wild honey, and he wore clothing of camel's hair. Thirdly, in their zeal. For Elijah was filled with zeal, thus it was said, "I have been very zealous for the Lord" (1 Kgs 19:10). So, also, John died because of his zeal for the truth, as is clear from Matthew (14:6).

233. Then when he says, *Are you the Prophet?* the third question is presented. Here there is a difficulty, for since it is said in Luke (1:76), "And you, child, shall be called the prophet of the Most High," why does John, when asked if he is a prophet, answer that he is not a prophet?

There are three ways of answering this. One is that John is not just a prophet, but more than a prophet. For the other prophets only predicted future things from afar: "If there is a delay, wait for it" (Hab 2:3). But John proclaimed that the Messiah was present, pointing him out with his finger: "Look, there is the Lamb of God," as it says below (1:36). And so the Lord says that he is more than a prophet (Mt 11:9).[260]

Again, in another way, according to Origen,[261] because through a misunderstanding the Jews associated three great personages with the coming of Christ: Christ himself, Elijah, and some other person, the greatest of the prophets, about whom Deuteronomy (18:15) says: "The Lord your God will raise up a prophet for you." And although this greatest of the prophets is in fact none other than Christ, according to the Jews he is someone other than Christ. And so they do not ask simply whether he is a prophet, but whether he is that "greatest of the prophets." And this is clear from the order of their questions. For they first ask whether he is the Messiah; secondly, whether he is Elijah; thirdly, whether he is that prophet. Accordingly, in Greek, the article is used here as signifying *the* prophet, as it were, antonomastically.

In a third way, because the Pharisees were indignant at John for assuming the office of baptizing outside the order of the law and their tradition. For the Old Testament mentions three persons to whom this office could belong. First, to the Messiah, since "I will pour clean water upon you, and you will be cleansed" (Ez 36:25), are words considered as spoken by the person of the Messiah. Secondly, to Elijah, of whom it says in 2 Kings that he divided the water of the Jordan, and crossing over, was taken up. Finally, to Elisha, who made Naaman the

260. See *ST* II-II, q. 174, a. 6, especially ad 3.
261. *Comm. in Io.* VI. 15, no. 90; PG 14, col. 228C; cf. *Catena aurea*, 1:19–23.

Syrian wash seven times in the Jordan so as to be cured of leprosy, as mentioned in 2 Kings (chap. 5). And so when the Jews saw that John was baptizing, they believed that he was one of those three: the Messiah, or Elijah, or Elisha. Accordingly, when they ask here, *Are you the Prophet?* they are asking whether he is Elisha, who is called "prophet" in a special way because of the many miracles he had performed; hence he himself says, "Let him come to me, so that he may know that there is a prophet in Israel" (2 Kgs 5:8). And to this John answers, *No, I am not Elisha.*

234. Then he shows how he declared who he was. First, the question of the messengers is given; secondly, his answer (v. 23).

235. They said, *Who are you?* We must take back an answer to those who sent us. As if to say: We were sent to learn who you are; so tell us, What have you to say about yourself?

Notice John's devotion. He has already fulfilled what the Apostle says, "It is not I who now live, but Christ lives in me" (Gal 2:20). And so he does not answer, "I am the son of Zechariah," or this or that, but only the way in which he followed Christ.

236. So he says, *I am a voice that cries in the wilderness.* And he says that he is a voice because from the point of view of origin, a voice comes after the [mental, interior] word, but before the knowledge it causes. For we know a [mental, interior] word conceived in the heart by means of the voice which speaks it, since it is its sign. But God the Father sent the precursor John, who came to be in time, in order to make known his Word, which was conceived from eternity. And so he fittingly says, *I am a voice.*

237. The addition, *that cries,* can be understood in two ways: as referring to John, crying and preaching in the wilderness; or to Christ crying in him, according to, "Do you want proof that Christ is speaking in me" (2 Cor 13:3).

Now he cries for four reasons. First of all, a cry implies a showing; and so he cries in order to show that Christ is clearly speaking in John and in himself: "Now on the last, the great day of the feast, Jesus stood and cried out, saying, 'If any one thirsts, let him come to me and drink'" (below 7:37). But he did not cry out in the prophets because prophecies were given in enigmas and figures; so it is said that he was "wrapped in dark rain-clouds" (Ps 17:12). Secondly, because a cry is made to those who are at a distance; and the Jews were far from God. Thus it was necessary that he cry: "You have taken my friends and neighbors away from me" (Ps 87:19). He cries, in the third place, because they were deaf: "Who is deaf, but my servant?" (Is 42:19). He cries, fourthly, because he speaks with indignation, for they deserved God's wrath: "He will speak to them in his anger" (Ps 2:5).

238. Note that he cries *in the wilderness,* because "The word of the Lord came to John, the son of Zechariah, in the desert," as we read in

Luke (3:2). There can be both a literal and a mystical reason for this. The literal reason is that by living in the desert he would be immune from all sin, and so be more worthy to bear witness to Christ, and his testimony would be more credible to men because of his life.

The mystical reason is twofold. For the wilderness or desert designates paganism, according to Isaiah (54:1): "She who is deserted has more children than she who has a husband." Accordingly, in order to show that God's teaching would from now on not be in Jerusalem alone, but also among the pagans, he cried *in the wilderness*. "The kingdom of God will be taken away from you, and given to a people that will produce its fruits" (Mt 21:43). Again, the desert can indicate Judea, which was already deserted: "Your house will be left to you, deserted" (Mt 23:38). And so he cried in the desert, *in the wilderness*, i.e., in Judea, to indicate that the people to whom he was preaching had already been deserted by God: "In a desert land, where there is no way or water, so I have come to your sanctuary" (Ps 62:3).

239. Why does he cry, *Make a straight way for the Lord*? Because this is the task for which he was sent. "And you, child, will be called the prophet of the Most High, for you will go before the face of the Lord to prepare his way" (Lk 1:76). The way, prepared and straight, for receiving the Lord is the way of justice, according to Isaiah (26:7): "The way of the just is straight." For the way of the just is straight when the whole man is subject to God, i.e., the intellect through faith, the will through love, and actions through obedience, are all subject to God.[262]

And this was spoken, i.e., predicted, by *the prophet Isaiah*. As if to say: I am the one in whom these things are fulfilled.

LECTURE 13

24 *Now these men had been sent from the Pharisees,* 25 *and they put this further question to him: "Why then do you baptize, if you are not the Messiah, nor Elijah, nor the Prophet?"* 26 *John replied,* "*I baptize with water. But there is one standing in your midst whom you do not recognize*—27 *the one who is to come after me, who ranks ahead of me*—*the strap of whose sandal I am not worthy to unfasten.*" 28 *This happened at Bethany, on the far side of the Jordan, where John was baptizing.*

240. Above, we saw John bear witness to Christ as he was being questioned on matters concerning himself; here, on matters concerning his office. Four things are set forth: first, those who question him;

262. See *ST* I, q. 95, a. 1.

secondly, their questions; thirdly, his answer, in which he bore witness; and fourthly, the place where all this happened.

241. His interrogators were Pharisees. Hence he says, *Now these men had been sent from the Pharisees.* According to Origen,[263] what is being said from this point on describes a different testimony given by John; and further, those who were sent from the Pharisees are not the same as those priests and Levites sent by the generality of the Jews, but others who were specifically sent by the Pharisees. And according to this it says: *Now these men had been sent,* not by the Jews, as the priests and Levites had been, but were others, *from the Pharisees.* So he says about this that because the priests and Levites were educated and respectful, they ask John humbly and respectfully whether he is the Messiah, or Elijah, or the Prophet. But these others, who were from the Pharisees, according to their name "separated" and importunate, used disdainful language. Thus they asked him, *Why then do you baptize, if you are not the Messiah, nor Elijah, nor the Prophet?*

But according to others, such as Gregory,[264] Chrysostom,[265] and Augustine,[266] these Pharisees are the same priests and Levites who had been sent by the Jews. For there was among the Jews a certain sect which was separated from the others by reason of its external cult; and for this reason its members were called Pharisees, i.e., "divided." In this sect there were some priests and Levites, and some of the people. And so, in order that the delegates [to John] might possess a greater authority, they sent priests and Levites, who were Pharisees, thus furnishing them with the dignity of a priestly caste and with religious authority.

242. The Evangelist adds, *these men had been sent from the Pharisees,* to disclose, first, the reason why they asked about John's baptizing, which was not why they were sent. It is as though he were saying: They were sent to ask John who he was. But they asked, *Why do you baptize?* because they were from the Pharisees, whose religion was being challenged. Secondly, as Gregory says, in order to show with what intention they asked John, "Who are you?" (1:19). For the Pharisees, more than all the others, showed themselves crafty and insulting to Christ. Thus they said of him: "He casts out devils by Beelzebub, the prince of devils" (Mt 12:24). Further, they consulted with the Herodians on how to trap Jesus in his speech (Mt 22:15). And so in saying that these men had been sent from the Pharisees, he shows that they were disrespectful and were questioning him out of envy.

243. Their questions concerned his office of baptizing. Hence he says that they asked him, *Why then do you baptize?* Here we should

263. *Comm. in Io.* VI. 22, no. 120; PG 14, col. 240A–B; cf. *Catena aurea,* 1:24–28.
264. *XL hom. in Evang.* I, Hom. 7. 3; PL 76, col. 1100D.
265. *Hom. in Io.* 16. 2; PG 59, col. 104; cf. *Catena aurea,* 1:24–28.
266. *Tract. in Io.* 4. 8; PL 35, col. 1409.

note that they are asking not to learn, but to obstruct. For since they saw many people coming to John because of the new rite of baptism, foreign both to the rite of the Pharisees and of the law, they became envious of John and tried all they could to hinder his baptism. But being unable to contain themselves any longer, they reveal their envy and say, *Why then do you baptize if you are not the Messiah, nor Elijah, nor the Prophet?* As if to say: You should not baptize, since you deny that you are any of those three persons in whom baptism was prefigured, as was said above. In other words, *if you are not the Messiah*, who will possess the fountain by which sins are washed away, *nor Elijah, nor the Prophet*, i.e., Elisha, who made a dry passageway through the Jordan (2 Kgs 2:8), how do you dare baptize? They are like envious persons who hinder the progress of souls, "who say to the seers, 'See no visions'" (Is 30:10).

244. His answer is true: and so he says that John answered, *I baptize with water*. As if to say: You should not be disturbed, if I, who am not the Messiah, nor Elijah, nor the Prophet, baptize; because my baptism is not completive but imperfect. For the perfection of baptism requires the washing of the body and of the soul; and the body, by its nature, is indeed washed by water, but the soul is washed by the Spirit alone. So, *I baptize with water*, i.e., I wash the body with something bodily; but another will come who will baptize perfectly, namely, with water and with the Holy Spirit; God and man, who will wash the body with water and the spirit with the Spirit, in such a way that the sanctification of the spirit will be distributed throughout the body. "For John indeed baptized with water but you will be baptized with the Holy Spirit not many days from now" (Acts 1:5).[267]

245. Then he bears witness to Christ. First, in relation to the Jews. Secondly, in relation to himself (v. 27).

246. He relates him to the Jews when he says, *But there is one standing in your midst.* As if to say: I have done an incomplete work, but there is another who will complete my work, and he is *standing in your midst*.

This is explained in a number of ways. First, according to Gregory,[268] Chrysostom[269] and Augustine,[270] it refers to the ordinary way Christ lived among men, because according to his human nature he appeared to be like other men: "He, being in the form of God . . . emptied himself, taking the form of a servant" (Phil 2:6). And according to this he says, *there is one standing in your midst*, i.e., in many ways he lived as one of you: "I am in your midst" (Lk 22:27), *whom you do not recognize*, i.e., you cannot grasp the fact that God was made man.

267. See *ST* III, q. 38, a. 3.
268. *XL hom. in Evang.* I, *Hom.* 7. 3; PL 76, col. 1101A.
269. *Hom. in Io.* 16. 3; PG 59, col. 104; cf. *Catena aurea*, 1:24–28.
270. *Tract. in Io.* 4. 9; PL 35, col. 1409.

Likewise, you do not recognize how great he is according to the divine nature which is concealed in him: "God is great, and exceeds our knowledge" (Jb 36:26). And so, as Augustine[271] says, "The lantern was lighted," namely, John, "so that Christ might be found." "I have prepared a lamp for my anointed" (Ps 131:17).

It is explained differently by Origen:[272] and in two ways. First, as referring to the divinity of Christ: and according to this, *there is one standing*, namely, Christ, *in your midst*, that is, in the midst of all things; because he, as Word, has filled all from the beginning of creation: "I fill heaven and earth" (Jer 23:24). *Whom you do not recognize*, because, as was said above (1:10), "He was in the world . . . and the world did not know him."

It is explained another way as referring to his causality of human wisdom. *But there is one standing in your midst*, i.e., he shines in everyone's understanding; because whatever light and whatever wisdom exists in men has come to them from participating in the Word.[273] And he says, *in your midst*, because in the midst of man's body lies the heart, to which is attributed a certain wisdom and understanding; hence, although the intellect has no bodily organ, yet because the heart is our chief organ, it is the custom to take it for the intellect. So he is said to stand among men because of this likeness, insofar as he "enlightens every man coming into this world" (1:9). Whom you do not recognize, because, as was said above (1:5), "The light shines in the darkness, and the darkness did not overcome it."

In a fourth way, it is explained as referring to the prophetic foretelling of the Messiah. In this sense the answer is directed chiefly to the Pharisees, who continually searched the writings of the Old Testament in which the Messiah was foretold; and yet they did not recognize him. And according to this it says, *there is one standing in your midst*, i.e., in the Sacred Scriptures which you are always considering: "Search the Scriptures" (below 5:39); whom you do not recognize, because your heart is hardened by unbelief, and your eyes blinded, so that you do not recognize as present the person you believe is to come.

247. Then John compares Christ to himself. First, he states the superiority of Christ as compared to himself. Secondly, he shows the greatness of this superiority.

248. He shows the superiority of Christ in comparison to himself both in preaching and in dignity. Now, as to the order of preaching, John was the first to become known. Thus he says, *the one who is to come after me*, to preach, to baptize and to die; because as was said in Luke (1:76): "You will go before the face of the Lord to prepare his way." John preceded Christ as the imperfect the perfect, and as the dis-

271. *Tract. in Io.* 4. 9; PL 35, col. 1409; cf. *Catena aurea*, 1:24–28.
272. *Comm. in Io.* VI. 38, no. 188; PG 14, col. 264C; cf. *Catena aurea*, 1:24–28.
273. See *ST* I, q. 79, a. 4.

position the form; for as is said, "The spiritual is not first but the animal" (1 Cor 15:46). For the entire life of John was a preparation for Christ; so he said above, that he was "a voice that cries in the wilderness."[274]

But Christ preceded John and all of us as the perfect precedes the imperfect and the exemplar precedes the copy: "If any one wishes to come after me, let him deny himself, and take up his cross, and follow me" (Mt 16:24); "Christ suffered for us, leaving you an example" (1 Pt 2:21).

Then he compares Christ to himself as to dignity, saying, *who ranks ahead of me*, i.e., he has been placed above me and is above me in dignity, because as he says (below 3:30), "He must increase, and I must decrease."

249. He touches on the greatness of his superiority when he says, *the strap of whose sandal I am not worthy to unfasten*. As if to say: You must not suppose that he ranks ahead of me in dignity in the way that one man is placed ahead of another, rather he is ranked so far above me that I am nothing in comparison to him. And this is clear from the fact that it is *the strap of whose sandal I am not worthy to unfasten*, which is the least service that can be done for men. It is clear from this that John had made great progress in the knowledge of God, so far that from the consideration of God's infinite greatness, he completely lowered himself and said that he himself was nothing.[275] So did Abraham, when he recognized God, and said (Gen 18:27), "I will speak to my Lord, although I am but dust and ashes." And so also did Job, saying, "Now I see you, and so I reprove myself, and do penance in dust and ashes" (Jb 42:5). Isaiah also said, after he had seen the glory of God, "Before him all the nations are as if they are not" (Is 40:17). And this is the literal explanation.

250. This is also explained mystically. Gregory[276] explains it so that the sandal, made from the hides of dead animals, indicates our mortal human nature, which Christ assumed: "I will stretch out my sandal to Edom" (Ps 59:10). The strap of Christ's sandal is the union of his divinity and humanity, which neither John nor anyone can unfasten or fully investigate, since it is this which made God man and made man God. And so he says, *the strap of whose sandal I am not worthy to unfasten*, i.e., to explain the mystery of the Incarnation perfectly and fully. For John and other preachers unfasten the strap of Christ's sandal in some way, although imperfectly.

It is explained in another way by recalling that it was ordered in the

274. See *ST* III, q. 38, a. 2, ad 2.
275. See *ST* II-II, q. 161, a. 6, ad 1.
276. *XL. hom. in Evang.* I, *Hom.* 7. 3; PL 76, col. 1101C–D; cf. *Catena aurea*, 1:24–28.

Old Law that when a man died without children, his brother was obligated to marry the wife of the dead man and raise up children from her as his brother's. And if he refused to marry her, then a close relative of the dead man, if willing to marry her, was to remove the sandals of the dead man as a sign of this willingness and marry her; and his home was then to be called the home of the man whose sandals were removed (Dt 15:5). And so according to this he says, *the strap of whose sandal I am not worthy to unfasten*, i.e., I am not worthy to have the bride, that is, the Church, to which Christ has a right. As if to say: I am not worthy to be called the bridegroom of the Church, which is consecrated to Christ in the baptism of the Spirit; but I baptize only in water.[277] As it says below (3:29): "It is the groom who has the bride."

251. The place where these events happened is mentioned when he says, *This happened at Bethany, on the far side of the Jordan*. A question arises on this: Since Bethany is on the Mount of Olives, which is near Jerusalem, as is said in John (11:1) and also in Matthew (26:6), how can he say that these things happened beyond the Jordan, which is quite far from Jerusalem? Origen[278] and Chrysostom[279] answer that it should be called Bethabora, not Bethany, which is a village on the far side of the Jordan; and that the reading "Bethany" is due to a copyist's error. However, since both the Greek and Latin versions have Bethany, one should rather say that there are two places called Bethany: one is near Jerusalem on the side of the Mount of Olives, and the other is on the far side of the Jordan where John was baptizing.

252. The fact that he mentions the place has both a literal and a mystical reason. The literal reason, according to Chrysostom,[280] is that John wrote this Gospel for certain ones, perhaps still alive, who would recall the time and who saw the place where these things happened. And so, to lead us to a greater certitude, he makes them witnesses of the things they had seen.

The mystical reason is that these places are appropriate for baptism. For in saying "Bethany," which is interpreted as "house of obedience," he indicates that one must come to be baptized through obedience to the faith. "To bring all the nations to have obedience to the faith" (Rom 1:5). But if the name of the place is "Bethabora," which is interpreted as "house of preparation," it signifies that a man is prepared for eternal life through baptism.

There is also a mystery in the fact that this happened on the far side of the Jordan. For "Jordan" is interpreted as "the descent of them"; and

---

277. See *ST* III, q. 38.
278. *Comm. in Io.* VI. 40, nos. 204–7; PG 14, col. 269A–C.
279. *Hom. in Io.* 17. 1; PG 59, col. 107; cf. *Catena aurea*, 1:24–28.
280. Ibid.

according to Origen[281] it signifies Christ, who descended from heaven, as he himself says that he descended from heaven to do the will of his Father (below 6:38).

Further, the river Jordan aptly signifies baptism. For it is the border line between those who received their inheritance from Moses on one side of the Jordan, and those who received it from Joshua on the other side. Thus baptism is a kind of border between Jews and Gentiles, who journey to this place to wash themselves by coming to Christ so that they might put off the debasement of sin. For just as the Jews had to cross the Jordan to enter the promised land, so one must pass through baptism to enter into the heavenly land. And he says, *on the far of the Jordan*, to show that John preached the baptism of repentance even to those who transgressed the law and sinners; and so the Lord also says, "I did not come to call the righteous, but sinners" (Mt 9:13).

LECTURE 14

29 The next day John saw Jesus coming toward him and he said, "Look! There is the Lamb of God who takes away the sins of the world. 30 It is he of whom I said: 'After me is to come a man, who ranks ahead of me, because he existed before me.' 31 And I did not know him! And yet it was to reveal him to Israel that I came baptizing with water." 32 John gave this testimony also: "I saw the Spirit coming down on him from heaven like a dove, and resting on him. 33 And I did not know him, but he who sent me to baptize with water had said to me: 'The man on whom you see the Spirit come down and rest is the one who is to baptize with the Holy Spirit.' 34 Now I have seen for myself and have given testimony that he is the Son of God."[282]

253. Above, John had given testimony to Christ when he was questioned. Here, he gives testimony to him on his own initiative. First, he gives the testimony; secondly, he confirms it (v. 32). As to the first: first, the circumstances of the testimony are given; and secondly, the testimony itself is given (v. 29); thirdly, suspicion is removed from the witness (v. 31).

281. *Comm. in Io.* VI. 42, nos. 217–18; PG 14, col. 273A; cf. *Catena aurea,* 1:24–28.
282. St. Thomas quotes Jn 1:29 in *ST* I-II, q. 82, a. 2, *sed contra*; I-II, q. 103, a. 2; III, q. 1, a. 4, *sed contra*; III, q. 22, a. 3, ad 3; III, q. 28, a. 1; III, q. 31, a. 8; III, q. 37, a. 3, obj. 4; Jn 1:31 in *ST* III, q. 36, a. 4, ad 3; III, q. 38, a. 1; III, q. 38, a. 5, obj. 1; III, q. 64, a. 4, *sed contra*; Jn 1:33 in *ST* I, q. 36, a. 2, ad 4; I-II, q. 68, a. 3, obj. 1; III, q. 38, a. 2, *sed contra*; III, q. 64, a. 3, obj. 1; III, q. 64, a. 5, *sed contra*; III, q, 66, a. 5, obj, 1; III, q. 67, a. 4; III, q. 66, a. 9, ad 2; and Jn 1:34 in *ST* II-II, q. 2, a. 7, ad 2.

254. The circumstances are first described as to the time. Hence he says, *The next day*. This gives credit to John for his steadfastness, because he bore witness to Christ not for just one day or once, but on many days and frequently: "Every day I will bless you" (Ps 144:2). His progress, too, is cited, because one day should not be just like the day before, but the succeeding day should be different, i.e., better: "They will go from strength to strength" (Ps 83:8).

Another circumstance mentioned is his manner of testifying, because *John saw Jesus*. This shows his certitude, for testimony based on sight is most certain. The last circumstance he mentions is about the one to whom he bore witness. Hence he says that he saw *Jesus coming toward him*, i.e., from Galilee, as it says, "Jesus came from Galilee" (Mt 3:13). We should not understand this as referring to the time when he came to be baptized, of which Matthew is here speaking, but of another time, i.e., a time when he came to John after he had already been baptized and was staying near the Jordan. Otherwise, he would not have said, "'The man on whom you see the Spirit come down and rest is the one who is to baptize with the Holy Spirit.' Now I have seen" (v. 33). Therefore, he had already seen him and the Spirit come down as a dove upon him.

255. One reason why Christ now came to John was to confirm the testimony of John. For John had spoken of Christ as "the one who is to come after me" (v. 27). But since Christ was now present, some might not understand who it was that was to come. So Christ came to John to be pointed out by him, with John saying, *Look! There is the Lamb of God*. Another reason Christ came was to correct an error. For some might believe that the first time Christ came, i.e., to be baptized, he came to John to be cleansed from his sins.[283] So, in order to preclude this, Christ came to him even after his baptism. Accordingly, John clearly says, *There is the Lamb of God who takes away the sins of the world*. He committed no sin, but came to take away sin. He also came to give us an example of humility, because as it is said, "The greater you are the more humble you should be in all matters" (Sir 3:20).

Note that after the conception of Christ, when his mother, the Virgin, went in haste to the mountainous country to visit John's mother, Elizabeth, that John, still in his mother's womb and unable to speak, leaped in her womb as though performing a religious dance out of reverence for Christ. And as then, so even now; for when Christ comes to John out of humility, John offers his testimony and reverence and breaks out saying, *Look! There is the Lamb of God*.

256. With these words John gives his testimony showing the power of Christ. Then Christ's dignity is shown (v. 30). He shows the pow-

283. See *ST* III, q. 39, a. 2.

er of Christ in two ways: first, by means of a symbol; secondly, by explaining it (v. 29).

257. As to the first, we should note, as Origen[284] says, that it was customary in the Old Law for five animals to be offered in the temple: three land animals, namely, the heifer, goat and sheep (although the sheep might be a ram, a sheep or a lamb) and two birds, namely, the turtle-dove and the dove. All of these prefigured the true sacrifice, which is Christ, who "gave himself for us as an offering to God," as is said in Ephesians (5:2).

Why then did the Baptist, when giving witness to Christ, specifically call him a Lamb? The reason for this is that, as stated in Numbers (28:3), although there were other sacrifices in the temple, at other times, yet each day there was a time in which a lamb was offered every morning, and another was offered in the evening. This never varied, but was regarded as the principal offering, and the other offerings were in the form of additions. And so the lamb, which was the principal sacrifice, signified Christ who is the principle sacrifice.[285] For although all the saints who suffered for the faith of Christ contribute something to the salvation of the faithful, they do this only inasmuch as they are immolated upon the oblation of the Lamb, they being, as it were, an oblation added to the principal sacrifice. The lamb is offered in the morning and in the evening because it is through Christ that the way is opened to the contemplation and enjoyment of the intelligible things of God, and this pertains to "morning knowledge"; and we are instructed how to use earthly things without staining ourselves, and this pertains to "evening knowledge."[286] And so he says, **Look! There is the Lamb of God**, i.e., the one signified by the lamb.

He says, **of God**, because there are two natures in Christ, a human nature and a divine nature. And it is due to the power of the divinity that this sacrifice has the power to cleanse and sanctify us from our sins, inasmuch as "God was, in Christ, reconciling the world to himself" (2 Cor 5:19).[287] Or, he is called **the Lamb of God**, because offered by God, i.e., by Christ himself, who is God; just as we call what a man offers the offering of the man. Or, he is called **the Lamb of God**, that is, of the Father, because the Father provided man with an oblation to offer that satisfied for sins, which man could not have through himself. So when Isaac asked Abraham, "Where is the victim for the holocaust?" he answered, "God himself will provide a victim for the holocaust" (Gen 22:7); "God did not spare his own Son, but delivered him up for all of us" (Rom 8:32).

284. *Comm. in Io.* VI. 51, nos. 266–67; PG 14, col. 289B–C; cf. *Catena aurea* 1:29–31.

285. See *ST* III, q. 73, a. 6.   286. See *ST* I, q. 58, aa. 6–7.

287. See *ST* III, q. 48, a. 6.

258. Christ is called a *Lamb*, first, because of his purity: "Your lamb will be without blemish" (Ex 12:5); "You were not redeemed by perishable gold or silver" (1 Pt 1:18). Secondly, because of his gentleness: "Like a lamb before the shearer, he will not open his mouth" (Is 53:7). Thirdly, because of his fruit; both with respect to what we put on: "Lambs will be your clothing" (Prv 27:26), "Put on the Lord Jesus Christ" (Rom 13:14); and with respect to food: "My flesh is for the life of the world" (below 6:52). And so Isaiah said (16:1); "Send forth, O Lord, the lamb, the ruler of the earth."

259. Then when he says, *who takes away the sins of the world*, he explains the symbol he used. In the law, sin could not be taken away either by a lamb or by any other sacrifice, because as is said in Hebrews (10:4), "It is impossible that sins be taken away by the blood of bulls and goats." This blood *takes away*, i.e., removes, *the sins of the world*. "Take away all iniquity" (Hos 14:3). Or, *takes away*, i.e., he takes upon himself *the sins of the* whole *world*, as is said, "He bore our sins in his own body" (1 Pt 2:24); "It was our infirmities that he bore, our sufferings that he endured," as we read in Isaiah (53:4).[288]

However, according to a Gloss,[289] he says *sin*, and not "sins," in order to show in a universal way that he has taken away every kind of sin: "He is the offering for our sins" (1 Jn 2:2); or because he died for one sin, that is, original sin: "Sin entered into this world through one man" (Rom 5:12).

260. Above, the Baptist bore witness to the power of Christ; now he bears witness to his dignity, comparing Christ to himself in three respects. First, with respect to their office and order of preaching. So he says, *It is he*, pointing him out, that is, the Lamb, *of whom I said*, i.e., in his absence, *After me is to come a man*, to preach and baptize, who in birth came after me.

Christ is called a man by reason of his perfect age, because when he began to teach, after his baptism, he had already reached a perfect age: "Jesus was now about thirty years of age" (Lk 3:23).[290] He is also called a man because of the perfection of all the virtues that were in him: "Seven women," i.e., the virtues, "will take hold of one man" (Is 4:1), the perfect Christ; "Look, a man! His name is the Orient" (Zec 6:12), because he is the origin of all the virtues found in others. He is also called a man because of his espousal, since he is the spouse of the Church: "You will call me 'my husband'" (Hos 2:16); "I espoused you to one husband" (2 Cor 11:2).

261. Secondly, he compares himself to Christ with respect to dignity when he says, *who ranks ahead of me*. As if to say: Although he

288. See *ST* III, q. 49, a. 1.
289. In the *Catena aurea* for Jn 1:29–31, the first comment noted here by Aquinas is attributed to Theophylact, and the second to the Gloss.
290. See *ST* III, q. 39, a. 3.

comes to preach after me, yet he ranks before me in dignity. "See, he comes, leaping upon the mountains, skipping over the hills" (Sg 2:8). One such hill was John the Baptist, who was passed over by Christ, because as is said below (3:30), "He must increase, and I must decrease."

262. Thirdly, he compares himself to Christ with respect to duration, saying, *because he existed before me*. As if to say: It is not strange if he ranks ahead of me in dignity; because although he is after me in time, he is before me in eternity, *because he existed before me*.

This statement refutes a twofold error. First, that of Arius, for John does not say that "he was made before me," as though he were a creature, but *he existed before me*, from eternity, before every creature: "The Lord brought me forth before all the hills," as is said in Proverbs (8:25). The second error refuted is that of Paul of Samosata: for John said, *he existed before me*, in order to show that he did not take his beginning from Mary. For if he had taken the beginning of his existence from the Virgin, he would not have existed before the precursor, who, in the order of human generation, preceded Christ by six months.

263. Next (v. 31), he precludes an erroneous conjecture from his testimony. For someone might say that John bore witness to Christ because of his affection for him, coming from a special friendship. And so, excluding this, John says, *And I did not know him!*; for John had lived in the desert from boyhood. And although many miracles happened during the birth of Christ, such as the Magi and the star and so on, they were not known to John: both because he was an infant at the time, and because, after withdrawing to the desert, he had no association with Christ. In the interim between his birth and baptism, Christ did not perform any miracles, but led a life similar to any other person, and his power remained unknown to all.

264. It is clear that he worked no miracles in the interim until he was thirty years old from what is said below (2:11): "This beginning of signs Jesus worked in Cana of Galilee." This shows the error of the book, *The Infancy of the Savior*.[291] The reason he performed no miracles during this period was that if his life had not been like that of other infants, the mystery of the circumcision and Incarnation might have been regarded as pure fancy. Accordingly, he postponed showing his knowledge and power to another time, corresponding to the age when other men reach the fullness of their knowledge and power. About this we read, "And Jesus increased in grace and wisdom" (Lk 2:52); not that he acquired a power and wisdom that he previously lacked, for in this respect he was perfect from the instant of his conception,[292] but

291. See *ST* III, q. 43, a. 3.
292. See *ST* III, q. 7, a. 12; III, q. 12, a. 2.

because his power and wisdom were becoming known to men: "Indeed, you are a hidden God" (Is 45:15).

265. The reason why John did not know him was that he had so far seen no signs, and no one else had known Christ through signs. Hence he adds: *It was to reveal him to Israel that I came baptizing with water.* As if to say: My entire ministry is to reveal: "He was not the light, but he came in order to bear witness to the light," as was said above (1:8).

266. He says, *I came baptizing with water*, to distinguish his baptism from that of Christ. For Christ baptized not just in water, but in the Spirit, conferring grace; and so the baptism of John was merely a sign, and not causative.

John's baptism made Christ known in three ways. First, by the preaching of John. For although John could have prepared the way for the Lord and led the people to Christ without baptizing, yet because of the novelty of the service many more came to him than would have come if his preaching were done without baptism. Secondly, John's baptism was useful because of Christ's humility, which he showed by willing to be baptized by John: "Christ came to John, to be baptized by him" (Mt 3:13). This example of humility he gives us here is that no one, however great, should disdain to receive the sacraments from any person ordained for this purpose. Thirdly, because it was during Christ's baptism by John that the power of the Father was present in the voice, and the Holy Spirit was present in the dove, by which the power and dignity of Christ were all the more shown: "And the voice of the Father was heard: 'This is my beloved Son'" (Lk 3:22).[293]

267. Then when he says, *John gave this testimony also*, he confirms by the authority of God the great things he testified to about Christ, that Christ alone would take away the sins of the whole world. As to this he does three things. First, he presents a vision. Secondly, he tells us the meaning of the vision (v. 33). Thirdly, he shows what he learned from this vision (v. 34).

268. He presents the vision when he says, *I saw the Spirit coming down on him from heaven.* When this actually happened John the Evangelist does not tell us, but Matthew and Luke say that it took place when Christ was being baptized by John.[294] And it was indeed fitting for the Holy Spirit to be present at this baptism and to the person being baptized. It was appropriate for the one baptized, for as the Son, existing by the Father, manifests the Father, "Father, I have manifested your name" (below 17:6), so the Holy Spirit, existing by the Son, manifests the Son, "He will glorify me, because he will receive from me"

293. See *ST* I q. 43, a. 7; III, q. 38, a. 1.
294. See *ST* III, q. 39, a. 6.

(below 16:14). It was appropriate for this baptism because the baptism of Christ begins and consecrates our baptism. Now our baptism is consecrated by invoking the whole Trinity: "Baptizing them in the name of the Father, and of the Son, and of the Holy Spirit" (Mt 28:19).[295] Thus, the ones we invoke in our baptism were present at the baptism of Christ: the Father in the voice, the Holy Spirit in the dove, and the Son in his human nature.

269. He says, *coming down*, because descent, since it has two termini, the start, which is from above, and the end, which is below, suits baptism in both respects. For there is a twofold spirit: one of the world and the other of God. The spirit of the world is the love of the world, which is not from above; rather, it comes up to man from below and makes him descend. But the Spirit of God, i.e., the love of God, comes down to man from above and makes him ascend: "We have not received the spirit of this world, but the Spirit of God," as is said in 1 Corinthians (2:12). And so, because that Spirit is from above, he says, *coming down*.

Similarly, because it is impossible for the creature to receive God's goodness in the fullness in which it is present in God, the communication of this goodness to us is in a way a certain coming down: "Every perfect gift is from above, coming down from the Father of lights" (Jas 1:17).

270. The Evangelist, in describing the manner of the vision and of the coming down, says that the Holy Spirit did not appear in the spirit, i.e., in his nature, but in the form of a dove, saying, that he came like a dove. The reason for this is that the Holy Spirit cannot be seen in his nature, as is said, "The Spirit blows where it wills, and you hear its sound, but you do not know where it comes from or where it goes" (below 3:8), and because a spirit does not come down but goes up, "The spirit lifted me up" (Ez 8:3).

It was appropriate that the Son of God, who was made visible through flesh, should be made known by the Holy Spirit in the visible form of a dove. However, the Holy Spirit did not assume the dove into a unity of person, as the Son of God assumed human nature.[296] The reason for this is that the Son did not appear as a manifester but as a Savior. And so, according to Pope Leo,[297] it was appropriate that he be God and man: God, in order to provide a remedy; and man, in order to offer an example. But the Holy Spirit appeared only to make known, and for this it was sufficient merely to assume a visible form which was suitable for this purpose.

271. As to whether this dove was a real animal and whether it existed prior to its appearance, it seems reasonable to say that it was a

295. See *ST* III, q. 66, aa. 5–6.
296. See *ST* I, q. 43, a. 7; III, q. 39, a. 6.
297. *Serm.* 21. 2; PL 54, col. 192 B.

real dove.[298] For the Holy Spirit came to manifest Christ, who, being the Truth, ought to have been manifested only by the truth. As to the other part of the question, it would seem that the dove did not exist prior to its appearance, but was formed at the time by the divine power, without any parental union, as the body of Christ was conceived by the power of the Holy Spirit, and not from a man's seed. Yet it was a real dove, for as Augustine[299] says in his work, *The Christian Combat*: "It was not difficult for the omnipotent God, who produced the entire universe of creatures from nothing, to form a real body for the dove without the aid of other doves, just as it was not difficult to form the true body of Christ in the womb of the Blessed Virgin without natural semen."

Cyprian,[300] in his *The Unity of the Church*, says: "It is said that the Holy Spirit appeared in the form of a dove because the dove is a simple harmless animal, not bitter with gall, not savage with its bites, not fierce with rending talons; it loves the dwellings of men, is able to live together in one nest, together it raises its young, they remain together when they fly, spend their life in mutual association, signify the concord of peace with the kiss of their bill, and fulfill the law of harmony in all things."

272. Many reasons are given why the Holy Spirit appeared as a dove rather than in some other form. First, because of its simplicity, for the dove is simple: "Be wise as serpents, and simple as doves" (Mt 10:16). And the Holy Spirit, because he inclines souls to gaze on one thing, that is, God, makes them simple; and so he appeared in the form of a dove. Further, according to Augustine,[301] the Holy Spirit also appeared in the form of fire over the heads of the assembled apostles. This was done because some are simple, but lukewarm; while others are fervent but guileful. And so in order that those sanctified by the Spirit may have no guile, the Spirit is shown in the form of a dove; and in order that their simplicity may not grow tepid, the Spirit is shown in fire.

A dove was used, secondly, because of the unity of charity; for the dove is much aglow with love: "One is my dove" (Sg 6.9). So, in order to show the unity of the Church, the Holy Spirit appears in the form of a dove. Nor should it disturb you that when the Holy Spirit rested on each of the disciples, there appeared separate tongues of fire; for although the Spirit appears to be different according to the different functions of his gifts, he nevertheless unites us through charity. And so, because of the first he appeared in separate tongues of fire, as is said, "There are different kinds of gifts" (1 Cor 12:4); but he appears in the form of a dove because of the second.

298. See *ST* III, q. 39, a. 7.
299. *De agon. chris.* 22; PL 40, col. 303; cf. *Catena aurea*, 1:32–34.
300. *De unit. Eccl.* 9, PL 4, col. 522B.
301. *Tract. in Io.* 6. 3; PL 35, col. 1426; cf. *Catena aurea*, 1:32–34.

A dove was used, thirdly, because of its groaning, for the dove has a groaning chant; so also the Holy Spirit "pleads for us with indescribable groanings" (Rom 8:26); "Her maidens, groaning like doves" (Nah 2:7). Fourthly, because of the dove's fertility, for the dove is a very prolific animal. And so in order to signify the fecundity of spiritual grace in the Church, the Holy Spirit appeared in the form of a dove. This is why the Lord commanded an offering of two doves (Lv 5:7).

A dove was used, fifthly, because of its cautiousness. For it rests upon watery brooks, and gazing into them can see the hawk flying overhead and so save itself: "His eyes are like doves beside brooks of water" (Sg 5:12). And so, because our refuge and defense is found in baptism, the Holy Spirit appropriately appeared in the form of a dove.

The dove also corresponds to a figure in the Old Testament. For as the dove bearing the green olive branch was a sign of God's mercy to those who survived the waters of the deluge, so too in baptism, the Holy Spirit, coming in the form of a dove, is a sign of the divine mercy which takes away the sins of those baptized and confers grace.

273. He says that the Holy Spirit was *resting on him*. If the Holy Spirit does not rest on someone, it is due to two causes. One is sin. For all men except Christ are either suffering from the wound of mortal sin, which banishes the Holy Spirit, or are darkened with the stain of venial sin, which hinders some of the works of the Holy Spirit. But in Christ there was neither mortal nor venial sin; so, the Holy Spirit in him was never disquieted, but was *resting on him*.

The other reason concerns charismatic graces, for the other saints do not always possess their power. For example, the power to work miracles is not always present in the saints, nor is the spirit of prophecy always in the prophets. But Christ always possessed the power to accomplish any work of the virtues and the graces.[302] So to indicate this, he says, *resting on him*. Hence this was the characteristic sign for recognizing Christ, as the Gloss says. "The Spirit of the Lord will rest on him" (Is 11:2), which we should understand of Christ as man, according to which he is less than the Father and the Holy Spirit.

274. Then when he says, *I did not know him*, he teaches us how this vision should be understood. For certain heretics, as the Ebionites, said that Christ was neither the Christ nor the Son of God from the time he was born, but only began to be the Son of God and the Christ when he was anointed with the oil of the Holy Spirit at his baptism. But this is false, because at the very hour of his birth the angel said to the shepherds: "This day a Savior has been born for you in the city of David, Christ the Lord" (Lk 2:11). Therefore, so that we do not believe that the Holy Spirit descended upon Christ in his baptism as though to receive the Spirit anew for his sanctification, the Baptist gives the rea-

302. See *ST* III, q. 7, aa. 2, 7.

son for the Spirit's coming down. He says that the Spirit descended not for the benefit of Christ, but for our benefit, that is, so that the grace of Christ might be made known to us. And so he says, *And I did not know him! And yet it was to reveal him to Israel that I came baptizing with water.*

275. There is a problem here. For he says, *he who sent me to baptize.* If he is saying that the Father sent him, it is true. Also, if he is saying that the Son sent him, it is even more clear, since it is said that both the Father and the Son sent him, because John is not one of those referred to in Jeremiah (23:21), "I did not send the prophets, yet they ran." But if the Son did send him, how can he then say, *I did not know him?* If it is said that although he knew Christ according to his divinity, yet he did not know him according to his humanity until after he saw the Spirit coming down upon him, one might counter that the Holy Spirit descended upon Christ when he was being baptized, and John had already known Christ before he was baptized, otherwise he would not have said: "I ought to be baptized by you, and you come to me?" (Mt 3:14).

So we must say that this problem can be resolved in three ways. In one way, according to Chrysostom,[303] so that the meaning is to know familiarly; the sense being that *I did not know him,* i.e., in a familiar way. And if the objection is raised that John says, "I ought to be baptized by you," it can be answered that two different times are being discussed: so that *I did not know him,* refers to a time long before baptism, when he was not yet familiar with Christ; but when he says, "I ought to be baptized by you," he is referring to the time when Christ was being baptized, when he was now familiar with Christ because of his frequent visits. In another way, according to Jerome,[304] it could be said that Christ was the Son of God and the Savior of the world, and that John did in fact know this; but it was not through the baptism that he knew that he was the Savior of the world. And so to remedy this ignorance he adds, he *is the one who is to baptize with the Holy Spirit.* But it is better to say with Augustine[305] that John knew certain things and was ignorant of others. Explaining what he did not know, he adds that the power of baptizing, which Christ could have shared with his faithful followers, would be reserved for himself alone. And this is what he says, *he who sent me to baptize with water . . . is the one,* exclusively and solely, *who is to baptize with the Holy Spirit,* i.e., he and no one else, because this power he reserved for himself alone.

276. We should note that a threefold power of Christ is found in baptism. One is the power of efficiency, by which he interiorly cleans-

---

303. *Hom. in Io.* 17. 2; PG 59, col. 110; cf. *Catena aurea,* 1:32–34.
304. *Expos. in quat. Evang., In Evang. sec. Ioan.,* PL 30, col. 578.
305. *Tract. in Io.* 5. 8; PL 35, col. 1417, 1418; cf. *Catena aurea,* 1:32–34.

es the soul from the stain of sin. Christ has this power as God, but not as man, and it cannot be communicated to any other. Another is the power of ministry, which he does share with the faithful: "Baptizing them in the name of the Father, and of the Son, and of the Holy Spirit" (Mt 28:19).[306] Therefore priests have the power to baptize as ministers. Christ too, as man, is called a minister, as the Apostle says. But he is also the head of all the ministers of the Church.

Because of this he alone has the power of excellence in the sacraments. And this excellence shows itself in four things. First, in the institution of the sacraments, because no mere man or even the entire Church could institute sacraments, or change the sacraments, or dispense with the sacraments. For by their institution the sacraments give invisible grace, which only God can give. Therefore, only one who is true God can institute sacraments.[307] The second lies in the efficacy of Christ's merits, for the sacraments have their power from the merit of Christ's passion: "All of us who have been baptized into Christ Jesus, have been baptized into his death" (Rom 6:3).[308] The third is that Christ can confer the effect of baptism without the sacrament; and this is peculiar to Christ.[309] Fourthly, because at one time baptism was conferred in the name of Christ, although this is no longer done.[310]

Now he did not communicate these four things to anyone; although he could have communicated some of them, for example, that baptism be conferred in the name of Peter or of someone else, and perhaps one of the remaining three. But this was not done lest schisms arise in the Church by men putting their trust in those in whose name they were baptized.[311]

And so John, in stating that the Holy Spirit came down upon Christ, teaches that it is Christ alone who baptizes interiorly by his own power.

277. One might also say that when John said, "I ought to be baptized by you," he recognized Christ through an interior revelation, but that when he saw the Holy Spirit coming down upon him, he knew him through an exterior sign. And so he mentions both of these ways of knowing. The first when he says, *he who sent me to baptize with water had said to me*, i.e., revealed something in an interior way. The second when he adds, *The man on whom you see the Spirit come down and rest is the one who is to baptize with the Holy Spirit*.

278. Then he shows what the Baptist understood from this vision, that is, that Christ is the Son of God. And this is what he says, *Now I have seen for myself*, that is, the Spirit coming down on him, *and have given testimony that he*, that is, Christ, *is the Son of God*, that is, the true and natural Son. For there were adopted sons of the Fa-

306. See *ST* III, q. 64, aa. 1, 3, 4.   307. See *ST* III, q. 64, a. 2.
308. See *ST* III, q. 62, a. 5.   309. See *ST* III, q. 64, a. 3.
310. See *ST* III, q. 66, a. 6.   311. See *ST* III, q. 64, a. 4.

ther who had a likeness to the natural Son of God: "Conformed to the image of his Son" (Rom 8:29). So he who baptizes in the Holy Spirit, through whom we are adopted as sons, ought to fashion sons of God. "You did not receive the spirit of slavery . . . but the spirit of adoption" (Rom 8:15). Therefore, because Christ is the one who baptizes in the Holy Spirit, the Baptist correctly concludes that he is the true and pure Son of God: "that we may be in his true Son" (1 Jn 5:20).

279. But if there were others who saw the Holy Spirit coming down upon Christ, why did they not also believe? I answer that they had not been so disposed for this.[312] Or perhaps, this vision was seen only by the Baptist.

LECTURE 15

35 On the following day John was standing there again with two of his disciples. 36 And seeing Jesus walking by, he said, "Look! There is the Lamb of God." 37 Hearing this, the two disciples followed Jesus. 38 Jesus turned around, and seeing them following him said, "What are you looking for?" They replied, "Rabbi (which means Teacher), where do you live?" 39 "Come and see," he replied. They went and saw where he lived, and they stayed with him the rest of that day. It was about the tenth hour. 40 One of the two who had followed him after hearing John was Simon Peter's brother, Andrew. 41 The first thing he did was to look for his brother Simon, and say to him, "We have found the Messiah" (which means the Christ), 42 and he brought him to Jesus. Looking at him intently Jesus said, "You are Simon, son of John; you are to be called Cephas" (which is translated Peter).[313]

280. Above, the Evangelist presented the Baptist's testimony to the people; here he presents his testimony to John's disciples. First, his testimony is given; secondly, the fruit of this testimony (v. 37). As to the first he does three things: first, the one giving the testimony is described; secondly, his way of testifying is given (v. 36); and thirdly, his testimony itself, *Look! There is the Lamb of God.*

281. The witness is described when he says, *On the following day John was standing there again with two of his disciples.* In saying *standing*, three things are noted about John. First, his manner of teaching, which was different from that of Christ and his disciples. For Christ went about teaching; hence it is said: "Jesus traveled over all Galilee" (Mt 4:23). The apostles also traveled the world teaching: "Go to the whole world, and preach the good news to every creature" (Mk 16:15).

312. See *ST* I-II, q. 112, a. 2; III, q. 55, a. 4.
313. St. Thomas refers to Jn 1:39 in *ST* III, q. 43, a. 3, obj. 3.

But John taught in one place; hence he says, *standing*, that is, in one place, on the far side of the Jordan. And John spoke of Christ to all who came to him.

The reason why Christ and his disciples taught going about is that the preaching of Christ was made credible by miracles, and so they went to various places in order that the miracles and powers of Christ might be made known.[314] But the preaching of John was not confirmed by miracles, so that it is written, "John performed no sign" (below 10:41), but by the merit and sanctity of his life. And so he was *standing* in one place so that various people might stream to Christ by his holiness. Furthermore, if John had gone from place to place to announce Christ without performing any miracles; his testimony would have been quite unbelievable, since it would seem to be inopportune and he would seem to be forcing himself upon the people.

Secondly, John's perseverance in the truth is noted, because John was not a reed shaken by the wind, but was firm in the faith; "Let him who thinks that he stands, take heed so he will not fall" (1 Cor 10:12), "I will stand my watch" (Hab 2:1).

Thirdly, and allegorically, it is noted that to stand is, in an allegorical sense, the same as to fail or cease: "The oil stood," i.e., failed (2 Kgs 4:6). So when Christ came John was standing, because when the truth comes the figure ceases. John stands because the law passes away.

282. The manner of his testifying is presented as being certain, because based on sight. So he says, *seeing Jesus walking by*. Here it should be remarked that the prophets bore witness to Christ: "All the prophets bear witness to him" (Acts 10:43). So did the apostles as they traveled the world: "You will be my witnesses in Jerusalem and in all of Judea and Samaria, and to the remotest parts of the world" (Acts 1:8). However, their testimony was not about a person then visible or present, but on one who was absent. In the case of the prophets about one who was to come; in the case of the apostles, about one who was now gone. But John bore witness when Christ was present and seen by him; and so he says, *seeing Jesus*, with the eyes of his body and of his mind: "Look on the face of your Christ" (Ps 83:10); "They will see eye to eye" (Is 52:8).

He says, *walking*, to point out the mystery of the Incarnation, in which the Word of God assumed a changeable nature: "I came forth from the Father, and have come into the world," as it says below (16:28).

283. Then he gives John's testimony in saying, *Look! There is the Lamb of God*. He says this not just to point out the power of Christ, but also in admiration of it: "His name will be called Wonderful" (Is 9:6).

314. See *ST* III, q. 43, a. 1.

And this Lamb did possess truly wonderful power, because being slain, it killed the lion—that lion, I say, of which it says: "Your enemy, the devil, goes about like a roaring lion, seeking whom he can devour" (1 Pt 5:8). And so this Lamb, victorious and glorious, deserved to be called a lion: "Look! The Lion of the tribe of Judah has conquered" (Rev 5:5).

The testimony he bears is brief, **Look! There is the Lamb of God**. It is brief both because the disciples before whom he testified had already been sufficiently instructed about Christ from the things they had heard from John, and also because this is sufficient for John's intention, whose only aim was to lead them to Christ. Yet he does not say, "Go to him," so that the disciples would not seem to be doing Christ a favor by following him. But he does praise the grace of Christ so that they would regard it as of benefit to themselves if they followed Christ. And so he says, **Look! There is the Lamb of God**, i.e., here is the One in whom is found the grace and the power which cleanses from sin: for the lamb was offered for sins, as we have said.

284. The fruit of his testimony is given when he says, **Hearing this, the two disciples followed Jesus**. First, the fruit resulting from the testimony of John and his disciples is given. Secondly, the fruit resulting from the preaching of Christ (v. 43). In relation to the first: first, the fruit arising from John's testimony is given; secondly, the fruit coming from the preaching of one of his disciples (v. 40). With respect to the first he does two things. First, he shows the very beginning of the fruit coming from John's testimony. Secondly, its consummation as accomplished by Christ (v. 38).

285. He says, **Hearing this**, John saying, "Look! There is the Lamb of God," **the two disciples**, who were with him, **followed Jesus**, literally, going with him. First, the fact that it is John who speaks while Christ is silent, and that disciples gather to Christ through the words of John, all this points out a mystery. For Christ is the groom of the Church, and John, the friend and groomsman of the groom. Now the function of the groomsman is to present the bride to the groom, and verbally make known the agreements; the role of the groom is to be silent, from modesty, and to make arrangements for his new bride as he wills. Thus, the disciples are presented by John to Christ and espoused in faith. John speaks, Christ is silent; yet after Christ accepts them, he carefully instructs them.

We can note, secondly, that no one was converted when John praised the dignity of Christ, saying, he "ranks ahead of me," and "I am not worthy to unfasten the strap of his sandal." But the disciples followed Christ when John revealed Christ's humility and about the mystery of the Incarnation; and this is because we are more moved by Christ's humility and the sufferings he endured for us. So it is said: "Your name is like oil poured out," i.e., mercy, by which you have obtained salvation for all; and the text immediately follows with, "young maidens have greatly loved you" (Sg 1:2).

We can note, thirdly, that the words of a preacher are like seed falling on different kinds of ground: on one they bear fruit, and on another they do not. So too, John, when he preaches, does not convert all his disciples to Christ, but only two, those who were well disposed.[315] The others are envious of Christ, and they even question him, as mentioned in Matthew (9:14).

Fourthly, we may note that John's disciples, after hearing his witness to Christ, did not at once thrust themselves forward to speak with him hastily; rather, seriously and with a certain modesty, they tried to speak to Christ alone and in a private place: "There is a time and fitness for everything" (Ecc 8:6).

286. The consummation of this fruit is now set forth (v. 38), for what John began is completed by Christ, since "the law brought nothing to perfection" (Heb 7:19). And Christ does two things. First, he questions the disciples who were following him. Secondly, he teaches them (v. 39). As to the first we have: first, the question of Christ is given; secondly, the answer of the disciples.

287. He says, *Jesus turned around, and seeing them following him said*. According to the literal sense we should understand that Christ was walking in front of them, and these two disciples, following him, did not see his face at all; and so Christ turns to them to bolster their confidence. This lets us know that Christ gives confidence and hope to all who begin to follow him with a pure heart: "She goes to meet those who desire her" (Wis 6:14). Now Jesus turns to us in order that we may see him; this will happen in that blessed vision when he will show us his face, as is said: "Show us your face, and we will be saved" (Ps 79:4). For as long as we are in this world we see his back, because it is through his effects that we acquire a knowledge of him; so it is said, "You will see my back" (Ex 33:23). Again, he turns to give us the riches of his mercy. This is requested in Psalm 89 (13): "Turn to us, O Lord." For as long as Christ withholds the help of his mercy he seems to be turned away from us. And so Jesus turned to the disciples of John who were following him in order to show them his face and to pour his grace upon them.

288. Christ examines them specifically about their intention. For all who follow Christ do not have the same intention: some follow him for the sake of temporal goods, and others for spiritual goods. And so the Lord asks their intention, saying, *What are you looking for?*; not in order to learn their intention, but so that, after they showed a proper intention, he might make them more intimate friends and show that they are worthy to hear him.

---

315. See *ST* I-II, q. 112, a. 2; II-II, q. 45, a. 2; III, q. 55, a. 4.

289. It may be remarked that these are the first words which Christ speaks in this Gospel. And this is appropriate, because the first thing that God asks of a man is a proper intention. And, according to Origen,[316] after the six words that John had spoken, Christ spoke the seventh. The first words spoken by John were when, bearing witness to Christ, he cried out, saying, "This is the one of whom I said." The second is when he said, "I am not worthy to unfasten the strap of his sandal." The third is, "I baptize with water. But there is one standing in your midst whom you do not recognize." The fourth is, "Look! There is the Lamb of God." The fifth, "I saw the Spirit coming down on him from heaven like a dove." The sixth, when he says here, "Look! There is the Lamb of God." But it is Christ who speaks the seventh words so that we may understand, in a mystical sense, that rest, which is signified by the seventh day, will come to us through Christ, and that in him is found the fullness of the seven gifts of the Holy Spirit.[317]

290. The disciples answer; and although there was one question, they gave two answers. First, why they are following Christ, namely, to learn; thus they call him Teacher, **Rabbi (which means Teacher)**. As if to say: We ask you to teach us. For they already knew what is stated in Matthew (23:10): "You have one Teacher, the Christ." The second answer is what they want in following him, that is, **Where do you live?** And literally, it can be said that in truth they were looking for the home of Christ. For because of the great and wonderful things they had heard about him from John, they were not satisfied with questioning him only once and in a superficial way, but wanted to do so frequently and seriously. And so they wanted to know where his home was so that they might visit him often, according to the advice of the wise man: "If you see a man of understanding, go to him early" (Sir 6:36), and "Happy is the man who hears me, who watches daily at my gates" (Prv 8:34).

In the allegorical sense, God's home is in heaven, according to the Psalm (122:1): "I have lifted up my eyes to you, who live in heaven." So they asked where Christ was living because our purpose in following him should be that Christ leads us to heaven, i.e., to heavenly glory.

Finally, in the moral sense, they ask, **Where do you live?** as though desiring to learn what qualities men should possess in order to be worthy to have Christ dwell in them. Concerning this dwelling Ephesians (2:22) says: "You are being built into a dwelling place for God." And the Song (1:6) says: "Show me, you whom my soul loves, where you graze your flock, where you rest at midday."

291. Then when he says, **Come and see**, Christ's instruction of the disciples is given. First we have the instruction of the disciples by

316. *Comm. in Io.* II. 35–36, nos. 212–219; PG 14, col. 177B–180B; cf. *Catena aurea*, 1:37–40.
317. See *ST* III, q. 7, a. 5.

Christ; secondly, their obedience is cited; and thirdly, the time is given.

292. First he says, *Come and see*, that is, where I live. There is a difficulty here: for since the Lord says, "The Son of Man does not have any place to lay his head" (Mt 8:20), why does he tell them to *Come and see* where he lives? I answer, according to Chrysostom[318] that when the Lord says, "The Son of Man does not have any place to lay his head," he showed that he had no home of his own, but not that he did not remain in someone else's home. And such was the home he invited them to see, saying, *Come and see*.

In the mystical sense, he says, *Come and see*, because the dwelling of God, whether of glory or grace, cannot be known except by experience: for it cannot be explained in words: "I will give him a white stone upon which is written a new name, which no one knows but he who receives it" (Rev 2:17). And so he says, *Come and see*: *Come*, by believing and working; *and see*, by experiencing and understanding.

293. It should be noted that we can attain to this knowledge in four ways. First, by doing good works; so he says, *Come*: "When shall I come and appear before the face of God" (Ps 41:3). Secondly, by the rest or stillness of the mind: "Be still and see" (Ps 45:11). Thirdly, by tasting the divine sweetness: "Taste and see that the Lord is sweet" (Ps 33:9). Fourthly, by acts of devotion: "Let us lift up our hearts and hands in prayer" (Lam 3:41). And so the Lord says: "It is I myself. Feel and see" (Lk 24:39).[319]

294. Next the obedience of the disciples is mentioned; for immediately *they went and saw*, because by coming they saw him, and seeing they did not leave him. Thus it says, *and they stayed with him the rest of that day*, for as stated below (6:45): "Every one who hears the Father, and has learned, comes to me." For those who leave Christ have not yet seen him as they should. But those who have seen him by perfectly believing *stayed with him the rest of that day*; hearing and seeing that blessed day, they spent a blessed night: "Happy are your men, and happy are your servants, who always stand before you" (1 Kgs 8:10). And as Augustine[320] says: "Let us also build a dwelling in our heart and fashion a home where he may come and teach us."

And he says, *that day*, because there can be no night where the light of Christ is present, where there is the Sun of justice.

295. The time is given when he says, *It was about the tenth hour*. The Evangelist mentions this in order that, considering the literal sense, he might give credit to Christ and the disciples. For the tenth hour is near the end of the day. And this praises Christ who was so

318. *Hom. in Io.* 18. 3; PG 59, col. 118; cf. *Catena aurea*, 1:37–40.
319. See *ST* II-II, q. 82, a. 3; II-II, q. 180, a. 7.
320. *Tract. in Io.* 7. 9; PL 35, col. 1441; cf. *Catena aurea*, 1:37–40.

eager to teach that not even the lateness of the hour induced him to postpone teaching them; but he taught them at the tenth hour. "In the morning sow your seed, and in the evening do not let your hands be idle" (Ecc 11:6).

296. The moderation of the disciples is also praised, because even at the tenth hour, when men usually have eaten and are less self-possessed for receiving wisdom, they were both self-possessed and prepared to hear wisdom and were not hindered because of food or wine. But this is not unexpected, for they had been disciples of John, whose drink was water and whose food was the locust and wild honey.

297. According to Augustine,[321] however, the tenth hour signifies the law, which was given in ten precepts. And so the disciples came to Christ at the tenth hour and remained with him to be taught so that the law might be fulfilled by Christ, since it could not be fulfilled by the Jews. And so at that hour he is called Rabbi, that is, Teacher.

298. Then (v. 40), he sets forth the fruit produced by the disciple of John who was converted to Christ. First, the disciple is described; secondly, the fruit begun by him (v. 41); thirdly, the consummation of this fruit by Christ (v. 42).

299. The disciple is described by name when he says, **Andrew**, i.e., "manly". "Act manfully, and let your heart be strong," as it says in Psalm 30 (v. 25). He mentions his name in order to show his privilege: he was not only the first to be perfectly converted to Christ, but he also preached Christ. So, as Stephen was the first martyr after Christ, so Andrew was the first Christian.

He is described, secondly, by his relationship, that is, as **Simon Peter's brother**, for he was the younger. And this is mentioned to commend him, for although younger in age, he became first in faith.

He is described, thirdly, by his discipleship, because he was **one of the two who had followed him**. His name is mentioned in order to show that Andrew's privilege was remarkable. For the name of the other disciple is not mentioned: either because it was John the Evangelist himself, who through humility followed the practice in his Gospel of not mentioning his own name when he was involved in some event, or, according to Chrysostom,[322] because the other one was not a notable person, nor had he done anything great, and so there was no need to mention his name. Luke does the same in his Gospel (10:1), where he does not mention the names of the seventy-two disciples sent out by the Lord, because they were not the outstanding and important persons that the apostles were. Or, according to Alcuin,[323] this

---

321. Ibid. 7. 10; PL 35, col. 1442; cf. *Catena aurea*, 1:37–40.
322. *Hom. in Io.* 18. 3; PG 59, col. 117; cf. *Catena aurea*, 1:37–40.
323. *Comm. in S. Ioannis Evang.* 1; PL 100, col. 761; cf. *Catena aurea*, 1:37–40.

other disciple was Philip: for the Evangelist, after discussing Andrew, begins at once with Philip, saying: "On the following day Jesus wanted to go to Galilee, and coming upon Philip" (below 1:43).

He is commended, fourthly, for the zeal of his devotion; hence he says that Andrew *followed him*, i.e., Jesus: "My foot has followed in his steps" (Jb 23:11).

300. The fruit begun by Andrew is mentioned when he says, *The first thing he did was to look for his brother Simon*. He first mentions the one for whom he bore fruit, that is, his brother, in order to mark the perfection of his conversion. For as Peter says, in the *Itinerary of Clement*,[324] the evident sign of a perfect conversion of anyone is that, once converted, the closer one is to him the more he tries to convert him to Christ. And so Andrew, being now perfectly converted, does not keep the treasure he found to himself, but hurries and quickly runs to his brother to share with him the good things he has received.[325] And so he says the *first thing he*, that is, Andrew, *did was to look for his brother Simon*, so that related in blood he might make him related in faith: "A brother that is helped by his brother is like a strong city" (Prv 18:19); "Let him who hears say, 'Come'" (Rev 22:17).

301. Secondly, he mentions the words spoken by Andrew, *We have found the Messiah (which means the Christ)*. Here, according to Chrysostom,[326] he is tacitly answering a certain question: namely, that if someone were to ask what they had been instructed about by Christ, they would have the ready answer that through the testimony of the Scriptures he instructed him in such a way that he knew he was the Christ. And so he says, *We have found the Messiah*. He implies by this that he had previously sought him by desire for a long time: "Happy is the man who finds wisdom" (Prv 3:13).

"Messiah," which is Hebrew, is translated as "Christos" in Greek, and in Latin as "Unctus" (anointed), because he was anointed in a special way with invisible oil, the oil of the Holy Spirit. So Andrew explicitly designates him by this title: "Your God has anointed you with the oil of gladness above your fellows" (Ps 44:8), i.e., above all the saints. For all the saints are anointed with that oil, but Christ was singularly anointed and is singularly holy. So, as Chrysostom[327] says, he does not simply call him "Messiah," but *the Messiah*.

---

324. This apocryphal life of St. Clement of Rome is part of a longer work, the *Clementine Recognitions*, that recounts the history of Clement's life, his relationship with the Apostle Peter, and their struggles against Simon Magus. The origin of the *Recognitions* is obscure, but it is often dated to the early third century. It was translated into Latin by Rufinus of Aquileia (d. 410).

325. See *ST* II-II, q. 4, a. 2, ad 1.

326. *Hom. in Io.* 19. 1; PG 59, col. 121; cf. *Catena aurea*, 1:41–42.

327. Ibid. 19. 1, 2.

302. Thirdly, he mentions the fruit he produced, because *he brought him*, that is, Peter, *to Jesus*. This gives recognition to Peter's obedience, for he came at once, without delay.[328] And consider the devotion of Andrew: for he brought him to Jesus and not to himself (for he knew that he himself was weak); and so he leads him to Christ to be instructed by him. This shows us that the efforts and the aim of preachers should not be to win for themselves the fruits of their preaching, i.e., to turn them to their own private benefit and honor, but to bring them to Jesus, i.e., to refer them to his glory and honor. "What we preach is not ourselves, but Jesus Christ," as is said in 2 Corinthians (4:5).

303. The consummation of this fruit is given when he says, *Looking at him intently Jesus said*. Here Christ, wishing to raise him up to faith in his divinity, begins to perform works of divinity, making known things that are hidden. First of all, things which are hidden in the present: so *looking at him*, i.e., as soon as Jesus saw him, he considered him by the power of his divinity and called him by name, saying, *You are Simon*. This is not surprising, for as it is said: "Man sees the appearances, but the Lord sees the heart" (1 Sm 16:7). This name is appropriate for the mystery. For "Simon" means "obedient," to indicate that obedience is necessary for one who has been converted to Christ through faith: "He gives the Holy Spirit to all who obey him" (Acts 5:32).

304. Secondly, he reveals things hidden in the past. Hence he says, *son of John*, because that was the name of Simon's father; or he says, "son of Jonah," as we find in Matthew (16:17), "Simon Bar-Jonah." And each name is appropriate to this mystery. For "John" means "grace," to indicate that it is through grace that men come to the faith of Christ: "You are saved by his grace" (Eph 2:5). And "Jonah" means "dove," to indicate that it is by the Holy Spirit, who has been given to us, that we are made strong in our love for God: "The love of God is poured out into our hearts by the Holy Spirit" (Rom 5:5).

305. Thirdly, he reveals things hidden in the future. So he says, *you are to be called Cephas (which is translated Peter)*, and in Greek, "head." And this is appropriate to this mystery, which is that he who was to be the head of the others and the vicar of Christ should remain firm. As Matthew (16:18) says: "You are Peter, and upon this rock I will build my church."

306. There is a question here about the literal meaning. First, why did Christ give Simon a name at the beginning of his conversion, rather than will that he have this name from the time of his birth? Two different answers have been given for this. The first, according to Chrys-

328. See *ST* II-II, q. 104, a. 3.

ostom,[329] is that divinely given names indicate a certain eminence in spiritual grace. Now when God confers a special grace upon anyone, the name indicating that grace is given at one's birth: as in the case of John the Baptist, who was named before he was born, because he had been sanctified in his mother's womb. But sometimes a special grace is given during the course of one's life: then such names are divinely given at that time and not at birth: as in the case of Abraham and Sarah, whose names were changed when they received the promise that their posterity would multiply. Likewise, Peter is named in a divine way when he is called to the faith of Christ and to the grace of apostleship, and particularly because he was appointed Prince of the apostles of the entire Church—which was not done with the other apostles.

But, according to Augustine,[330] if he had been called Cephas from birth, this mystery would not have been apparent. And so the Lord willed that he should have one name at birth, so that by changing his name the mystery of the Church, which was built on his confession of faith, would be apparent. Now "Peter" (*Petrus*) is derived from "rock" (*petra*). But the rock was Christ. Thus, the name "Peter" signifies the Church, which was built upon that solid and immovable rock which is Christ.[331]

307. The second question is whether this name was given to Peter at this time, or at the time mentioned by Matthew (16:18). Augustine[332] answers that this name was given to Simon at this time; and at the event reported by Matthew the Lord is not giving this name but reminding him of the name that was given, so that Christ is using this name as already given. But others think that this name was given when the Lord said, "You are Peter, and upon this rock I will build my church" (Mt 16:18); and in this passage in the Gospel of John, Christ is not giving this name, but foretelling what will be given later.

308. The third question is about the calling of Peter and Andrew: for here it says that they were called near the Jordan, because they were John's disciples; but in Matthew (4:18) it says that Christ called them by the Sea of Galilee. The answer to this is that there was a triple calling of the apostles. The first was a call to knowledge or friendship and faith—and this is the one recorded here. The second consisted in the diction of their office: "From now on you will be catching men" (Lk 5:10). The third call was to their apostleship, which is mentioned by Matthew (4:18). This was the perfect call because after this they were not to return to their own pursuits.

329. *Hom. in Io.* 19. 2; PG 59, col. 122; cf. *Catena aurea*, 1:41–42.
330. *Tract. in Io.* 7. 14; PL 35, col. 1444; cf. *Catena aurea*, 1:41–42.
331. See *ST* III, q. 8, a. 6.
332. *De cons. Evang.* 2. 17, no. 34; PL 34, col. 1094; cf. *Catena aurea*, 1:41–42.

LECTURE 16

43 On the following day Jesus wanted to go to Galilee, and coming upon Philip, he said, "Follow me." 44 Now Philip came from Bethsaida, the same town as Andrew and Peter. 45 Philip sought out Nathanael, and said to him, "We have found the one Moses spoke of in the law—the prophets too—Jesus, son of Joseph, from Nazareth." 46 "From Nazareth!" Nathanael replied, "What good can come from that place?" Philip said, "Come and see." 47 When Jesus saw Nathanael coming toward him, he said of him: "Here is a true Israelite, in whom there is no guile." 48 Nathanael asked him, "How do you know me?" Jesus replied and said, "Before Philip called you, I saw you when you were sitting under the fig tree." 49 "Rabbi," said Nathanael, "you are the Son of God; you are the King of Israel." 50 Jesus responded and said, "You believed just because I said to you that I saw you sitting under the fig tree! You will see greater things than this." 51 He went on to say, "Amen, amen, I say to you, you will see the heavens opened and the angels of God ascending and descending on the Son of Man."

309. After having shown the fruit produced by John's preaching and that of his disciples, the Evangelist now shows the fruit obtained from the preaching of Christ. First, he deals with the conversion of one disciple as the result of Christ's preaching. Secondly, the conversion of others due to the preaching of the disciple just converted to Christ (v. 45). As to the first he does three things: first, the occasion when the disciple is called is given; secondly, his calling is described; thirdly, his situation.

310. The occasion of his calling was the departure of Jesus from Judea. So he says, **On the following day Jesus wanted to go to Galilee, and coming upon Philip**. There are three reasons why Jesus left for Galilee, two of which are literal. One of these is that after being baptized by John and desiring to shed honor on the Baptist, he left Judea for Galilee so that his presence would not obscure and lessen John's teaching authority (while he still retained that state); and this teaches us to show honor to one another, as is said in Romans (12:10).[333]

The second reason is that there are no distinguished persons in Galilee: "No prophet is to rise from Galilee" (below 7:52). And so, to show the greatness of his power, Christ wished to go there and choose there the princes of the earth, who are greater than the prophets: "He has turned the desert into pools of water," as we read in Psalm 106 (v. 35).

The third reason is mystical: for "Galilee" means "passage." So Christ desired to go from Judea into Galilee in order to indicate that

333. See *ST* III, q. 38, a. 5.

"on the following day," i.e., on the day of grace, that is, the day of the Good News, he would pass from Judea into Galilee, i.e., to save the Gentiles: "Is he going to go to those who are dispersed among the Gentiles, and teach the Gentiles?" (below 7:35).

311. A disciple's vocation is to follow: hence he says that after Christ found Philip he said, *Follow me.* Note that sometimes man finds God, but without knowing it, as it were: "He who finds me will find life, and will have salvation from the Lord" (Prv 8:35). And at other times God finds the man, in order to bestow honor and greatness upon him: "I have found David, my servant" (Ps 88:21). Christ found Philip in this way, that is, to call him to the faith and to grace. And so he says at once, *Follow me.*

312. There is a question here: Why did not Jesus call his disciples at the very beginning? Chrysostom answers that he did not wish to call anyone before someone clung to him spontaneously because of John's preaching, for men are drawn by example more than by words.

313. One might also ask why Philip followed Christ immediately after only a word, while Andrew followed Christ after hearing about him from John, and Peter after hearing from Andrew.

Three answers can be given. One is that Philip had already been instructed by John: for according to one of the explanations given above, Philip was that other disciple who followed Christ along with Andrew. Another is that Christ's voice had power not only to act on one's hearing from without, but also on the heart from within: "My words are like fire" (Jer 23:29). For the voice of Christ was spoken not only to the exterior, but it enkindled the interior of the faithful to love him. The third answer is that Philip had perhaps already been instructed about Christ by Andrew and Peter, since they were from the same town. In fact, this is what the Evangelist seems to imply by adding, *Now Philip came from Bethsaida, the same town as Andrew and Peter.*

314. This gives us the situation of the disciples he called: for they were from Bethsaida. And this is appropriate to this mystery. For "Bethsaida" means "house of hunters," to show the attitude of Philip, Peter and Andrew at that time, and because it was fitting to call, from the house of hunters, hunters who were to capture souls for life: "I will send my hunters" (Jer 16:16).

315. Now the fruit produced by the disciple who was converted to Christ is given. First, the beginning of the fruit, coming from this disciple. Secondly, its consummation by Christ (v. 47). As to the first, he does three things: first, the statement of Philip is given; secondly, Nathanael's response; and thirdly, Philip's ensuing advice.

316. As to the first, note that just as Andrew, after having been perfectly converted, was eager to lead his brother to Christ, so too Philip with regard to his brother, Nathanael. And so he says that Philip found Nathanael, whom he probably looked for as Andrew did for Peter; and

this was a sign of a perfect conversion. The word "Nathanael" means "gift of God"; and it is God's gift if anyone is converted to Christ.

He tells him that all the prophecies and the law have been fulfilled, and that the desires of their holy forefathers are not in vain, but have been guaranteed, and that what God has promised was now accomplished. *We have found the one Moses spoke of in the law—the prophets too—Jesus.* We understand by this that Nathanael was fairly learned in the law, and that Philip, now having learned about Christ wished to lead Nathanael to Christ through the things he himself knew, that is, from the law and the prophets. So he says, *the one Moses spoke of in the law.* For Moses wrote of Christ: "if you believed Moses, you would perhaps believe me, for he wrote of me" (below 5:46). The prophets too wrote of Christ: "All the prophets bear witness to him" (Acts 10:43).

317. Note that Philip says three things about Christ that are in agreement with the law and the prophets. First, the name: for he says, *We have found Jesus.* And this agrees with the prophets: "I will send them a Savior" (Is 19:20); "I will rejoice in God, my Jesus" (Hab 3:18).

Secondly, the family from which Christ took his human origin, when he says, *son of Joseph*, i.e., who was of the house and family of David. And although Jesus did not derive his origin from him, yet he did derive it from the Virgin, who was of the same line as Joseph. He calls him the *son of Joseph*, because Jesus was considered to be the son of the one to whom his mother was married. So it is said: "the son of Joseph (as was supposed)" (Lk 3:23). Nor is it strange that Philip called him the son of Joseph, since his own mother, who was aware of his divine Incarnation, called him his son: "Your father and I have been looking for you in sorrow" (Lk 2:48). Indeed, if one is called the son of another because he is supported by him, this is more reason why Joseph should be called the father of Jesus, even though he was not so according to the flesh: for he not only supported him, but was the husband of his virgin mother. However, Philip calls him the son of Joseph (not as though he was born from the union of Joseph and the Virgin) because he knew that Christ would be born from the line of David; and this was the house and family of Joseph, to whom Mary was married. And this also is in agreement with the prophets: "I will raise up a just branch for David" (Jer 23:5).[334]

Thirdly, he mentions his native land, saying, *from Nazareth*; not because he had been born there, but because he was brought up there; but he had been born in Bethlehem. Philip omits to mention Bethlehem but not Nazareth because, while the birth of Christ was not known to many, the place where he was brought up was. And this also agrees with the prophets: "A shoot will arise from the root of Jesse,

334. See *ST* III, q. 31, a. 2.

and a flower (or Nazarene, according to another version) will rise up from his roots" (Is 11:1).

318. Then when he says, *Nathanael replied*, the answer of Nathanael is given. His answer can be interpreted as an assertion or as a question: and in either way it is suitable to Philip's affirmation. If it is taken as an assertion, as Augustine[335] does, the meaning is: "Some good can come from Nazareth." In other words, from a city with that name it is possible that there come forth to us some very excellent grace or some outstanding teacher to preach to us about the flower of the virtues and the purity of sanctity; for "Nazareth" means "flower." We can understand from this that Nathanael, being quite learned in the law and a student of the Scriptures, knew that the Savior was expected to come from Nazareth—something that was not so clear even to the Scribes and Pharisees. And so when Philip said, *We have found Jesus from Nazareth*, his hopes were lifted and he answered: "Indeed, some good can come from Nazareth."

But if we take his answer as a question, as Chrysostom[336] does, then the sense is: *From Nazareth! What good can come from that place?* As if to say: Everything else you say seems credible, because his name and his lineage are consistent with the prophecies; but your statement that he is *from Nazareth* does not seem possible. For Nathanael understood from the Scriptures that the Christ was to come from Bethlehem, according to: "And you, Bethlehem, land of Judah, are not the least among the princes of Judah: for out of you a ruler will come forth, who will rule my people Israel," as we read in Matthew (2:6). And so, not finding Philip's statement in agreement with the prophecy, he prudently and moderately inquires about its truth, *What good can come from that place?*

319. Then Philip's advice is given, *Come and see*. And this advice suits either interpretation of Nathanael's answer. To the assertive interpretation it is as though he says: You say that something good can come from Nazareth, but I say that the good I state to you is of such a nature and so marvelous that I am unable to express it in words, so *Come and see*. To the interpretation that makes it a question, it is as though he says: You wonder and say: *What good can come from that place?*, thinking that this is impossible according to the Scriptures. But if you are willing to experience what I experienced, you will understand that what I say is true, so *Come and see*.

Then, not discouraged by his questions, Philip brings Nathanael to Christ. He knew that he would no longer argue with him if he tasted the words and teaching of Christ. And in this, Philip was imitat-

---

335. *Tract. in Io.* 7. 16; col. 1445; cf. *Catena aurea*, 1:43–46; see also *Enarr. in Ps.* 65. 4; PL 36, col. 788–89.
336. *Hom. in Io.* 20. 1; PG 59, col. 125; cf. *Catena aurea*, 1:43–46.

ing Christ who earlier answered those who had asked about the place where he lived: "Come and see." "Come to him, and be enlightened" (Ps 33:6).

320. Then when he says, *When Jesus saw Nathanael,* the consummation of this fruit by Christ is described. We should note that there are two ways in which men are converted to Christ: some by miracles they have seen and things experienced in themselves or in others; others are converted through internal insights, through prophecy and the foreknowledge of what is hidden in the future.[337] The second way is more efficacious than the first: for devils and certain men who receive their help can simulate marvels; but to predict the future can only be done by divine power. "Tell us what is to come, and we will say that you are gods" (Is 41:23); "Prophecies are for those who believe." And so our Lord draws Nathanael to the faith not by miracles but by making known things which are hidden. And so he says of him, *Here is a true Israelite, in whom there is no guile.*

321. Christ mentions three hidden matters: things hidden in the present, in the heart; past facts; and future heavenly matters. To know these three things is not a human but a divine achievement.

He mentions things hidden in the present when he says, *Here is a true Israelite, in whom there is no guile.* Here we have, first, the prior revelation of Christ; secondly, Nathanael's question, *How do you know me?*

322. First he says, *When Jesus saw Nathanael coming toward him.* As if to say: Before Nathanael reached him, Jesus said, *Here is a true Israelite.* He said this about him before he came to him, because had he said it after he came, Nathanael might have believed that Jesus had heard it from Philip.

Christ said, *Here is a true Israelite, in whom there is no guile.* Now "Israel" has two meanings. One of these, as the Gloss says, is "most righteous." "Do not fear, my most righteous servant, whom I have chosen" (Is 44:2). Its second meaning is "the man who sees God." And according to each meaning Nathanael is a true Israelite. For since one in whom there is no guile is called righteous, Nathanael is said to be *a true Israelite, in whom there is no guile.* As if to say: You truly represent your race because you are righteous and without guile. Further, because man sees God through cleanness of heart and simplicity, Christ said, *a true Israelite,* i.e., you are a man who truly sees God because you are simple and without guile.

Further, he said, *in whom there is no guile,* so that we do not think that it was with malice that Nathanael asked: *What good can come from that place?*

337. See *ST* III, q. 44, a. 3.

323. Augustine[338] has a different explanation of this passage. It is clear that all are born under sin. Now those who have sin in their hearts but outwardly pretend to be just are called guileful. But a sinner who admits that he is a sinner is not guileful. So Christ said, *Here is a true Israelite, in whom there is no guile*, not because Nathanael was without sin, or because he had no need of a physician, for no one is born in such a way as not to need a physician; but he was praised by Christ because he admitted his sins.

324. Then when he says, *How do you know me?*, we have Nathanael's question. For Nathanael, in wonder at the divine power in this revelation of what is hidden, because this can only be from God— "The heart is depraved and inscrutable, and who is able to know it? I the Lord search the heart and probe the loins" (Jer 17:9); "Man sees the appearances, but the Lord sees the heart" (1 Sm 16:7)—asks, *How do you know me?* Here we can recognize Nathanael's humility, because, although he had been praised, he did not become elated, but held this praise of himself suspect. "My people, who call you blessed, they are deceiving you" (Is 3:12).

325. Then he touches on matters in the past, saying, *Before Philip called you, I saw you when you were sitting under the fig tree.* First we have the statement of Christ; secondly, the confession of Nathanael.

326. As to the first, we should note that Nathanael might have had two misgivings about Christ. One, that Christ said this in order to win his friendship by flattery; the other, that Christ had learned what he knew from others. So, to remove Nathanael's suspicions and raise him to higher things, Christ reveals certain hidden matters that no one could know except in a divine way, that is, things that related only to Nathanael. He refers to these when he says, *Before Philip called you, I saw you when you were sitting under the fig tree.* In the literal sense this means that Nathanael was under a fig tree when he was called by Philip—which Christ knew by divine power, for "The eyes of the Lord are far brighter than the sun" (Sir 23:28).

In the mystical sense, the fig tree signifies sin: both because we find a fig tree, bearing only leaves but no fruit, being cursed, as a symbol of sin (Mt 21:19); and because Adam and Eve, after they had sinned, made clothes from fig leaves. So he says here, *when you were sitting under the fig tree*, i.e., under the shadow of sin, before you were called to grace, *I saw you*, with the eye of mercy; for God's predestination looks upon the predestined, who are living under sin, with an eye of pity, for as Ephesians (1:4) says, "He chose us before the foundation of the world." And he speaks of this eye here: I saw you, by predestining you from eternity.[339]

338. *Tract. in Io.* 7. 18; col. 1446; cf. *Catena aurea*, 1:47–51.
339. See *ST* I, q. 23, a. 4; I-II, q. 112, a. 1.

Or, the meaning is, according to Gregory,[340] *I saw you when you were sitting under the fig tree*, i.e., under the shadow of the law. "The law has only a shadow of the good things to come" (Heb 10:1).

327. Hearing this, Nathanael is immediately converted, and, seeing the power of the divinity in Christ, breaks out in words of conversion and praise, saying, **Rabbi, you are the Son of God**. Here he considers three things about Christ. First, the fullness of his knowledge, when he says, **Rabbi**, which is translated as Teacher. As if to say: You are perfect in knowledge. For he had already realized what is said in Matthew (23:10); "You have one Teacher, the Christ."[341] Secondly, the excellence of his singular grace, when he says, **you are the Son of God**. For it is due to grace alone that one becomes a son of God by adoption. And it is also through grace that one is a son of God through union, and this is exclusive to the man Christ, because that man is the son of God not due to any preceding merit, but through the grace of union.[342] Thirdly, he considers the greatness of his power when he says, **you are the King of Israel**, i.e., awaited by Israel as its king and defender: "His power is everlasting (Dn 7:14)."[343]

328. A question comes up at this point, according to Chrysostom.[344] For since Peter, who after many miracles and much teaching, confessed what Nathanael confesses here about Christ, that is, **you are the Son of God**, merited a blessing, as the Lord said: "Blessed are you, Simon Bar-Jona" (Mt 16:17), why not the same for Nathanael, who said the same thing before seeing any miracles or receiving any teaching? Chrysostom answers that the reason for this is that even though Nathanael and Peter spoke the same words, the meaning of the two was not the same. For Peter acknowledged that Christ was the true Son of God by nature, i.e., he was man, and yet truly God; but Nathanael acknowledged that Christ was the Son of God by means of adoption, in the sense of, "I said: You are gods, and all of you the sons of the Most High" (Ps 81:6).[345] This is clear from what Nathanael said next: for if he had understood that Christ was the Son of God by nature, he would not have said, **you are the King of Israel**, but "of the whole world." It is also clear from the fact that Christ added nothing to the faith of Peter, since it was perfect, but stated that he would build the Church on that profession. But he raises Nathanael to greater things, since the greater part of his profession was deficient; to greater things, i.e., to a knowledge of his divinity.

340. *Mor.* 18. 38; PL 76, col. 70C–D; cf. *Catena aurea*, 1:47–51.
341. See *ST* III, q. 9, a. 2.
342. See *ST* III, q. 2, aa. 10, 12; q. 6, a. 6.
343. See *ST* III, q. 13, a. 1.
344. *Hom. in Io.* 21. 1; PG 59, col. 127–128; cf. *Catena aurea*, 1:47–51.
345. See *ST* III, q. 23, a. 4.

329. And so he said, *You will see greater things than this*. Here we have, thirdly, an allusion to the future. As if to say: Because I have revealed the past to you, you believe that I am the Son of God only by adoption, and the King of Israel; but I will bring you to greater knowledge, so that you may believe that I am the natural Son of God, and the King of all ages. And accordingly he says, *Amen, amen, I say to you, you will see the heavens opened and the angels of God ascending and descending on the Son of Man*. By this, according to Chrysostom,[346] the Lord wishes to prove that he is the true Son of God, and God. For the peculiar task of angels is to minister and be subject: "Bless the Lord, all of you, his angels, his ministers, who do his will" (Ps 102:20). So when you see angels minister to me, you will be certain that I am the true Son of God. "When he leads his First-Begotten into the world, he says: 'Let all the angels of God adore him'" (Heb 1:6).[347]

330. When did the apostles see this? They saw it, I say, during the Passion, when an angel stood by to comfort Christ (Lk 22:13); again, at the resurrection, when the apostles found two angels who were standing over the tomb. Again, at the ascension, when the angels said to the apostles: "Men of Galilee, why are you standing here looking up to heaven? This Jesus, who has been taken from you into heaven, will come in the same way as you have seen him going into heaven" (Acts 1:11).[348]

331. Because Christ spoke the truth about the past, it was easier for Nathanael to believe what he foretells about the future, saying, *you will see*. For one who has revealed the truth about things hidden in the past, has an evident argument that what he is saying about the future is true. He says, *the angels of God ascending and descending on the Son of Man*, because, in his mortal flesh, he was a little less than the angels; and from this point of view, angels ascend and descend upon him. But insofar as he is the Son of God, he is above the angels, as was said.

332. According to Augustine,[349] Christ is here revealing his divinity in a beautiful way. For it is recorded that Jacob dreamed of a ladder, standing on the ground, with "the angels of God ascending and descending on it" (Gen 28:16). Then Jacob arose and poured oil on a stone and said, "Truly, the Lord is in this place" (Gen 28:16). Now that stone is Christ whom the builders rejected; and the invisible oil of the Holy Spirit was poured on him. He is set up as a pillar, because he was to be the foundation of the Church: "No one can lay another foundation except that which has been laid" (1 Cor 3:11). The angels are ascending and descending inasmuch as they are ministering and serv-

---

346. *Hom. in Io.* 21. 1; PG 59, col. 129; cf. *Catena aurea*, 1:47–51.
347. See *ST* III, q. 8, a. 4.
348. See *ST* III, q. 55, a. 2; III, q. 57.
349. *Serm. supposit.* 11. 2; PL 39, col. 1761; cf. *Catena aurea*, 1:47–51.

ing before him. So he said, *Amen, amen, I say to you, you will see the heavens opened*, and so forth, as if to say: Because you are truly an Israelite, give heed to what Israel saw, so that you may believe that I am the one signified by the stone anointed by Jacob, for you also will see angels ascending and descending upon him [viz. Jesus].

333. Or, the angels are, according to Augustine,[350] the preachers of Christ: "Go, swift angels, to a nation rent and torn to pieces," as it says in Isaiah (18:2). They ascend through contemplation, just as Paul had ascended even to the third heaven (2 Cor 12:2); and they descend by instructing their neighbor. *On the Son of Man*, i.e., for the honor of Christ, because "what we preach is not ourselves, but Jesus Christ" (2 Cor 4:5). In order that they might ascend and descend, the heavens were opened, because heavenly graces must be given to preachers if they are to ascend and descend. "The heavens broke at the presence of God" (Ps 67:9); "I saw the heavens open" (Rev 4:1).[351]

334. Now the reason why Nathanael was not chosen to be an apostle after such a profession of faith is that Christ did not want the conversion of the world to the faith to be attributed to human wisdom, but solely to the power of God. And so he did not choose Nathanael as an apostle, since he was very learned in the law; he rather chose simple and uneducated men. "Not many of you are learned," and "God chose the simple of the world" (1 Cor 1:26).

350. *Tract. in Io.* 7. 23; col. 1449; cf. *Serm. supposit.* 11. 5; PL 39, col. 1762; cf. *Catena aurea*, 1:47–51.
351. See *ST* I, q. 117, a. 1.

CHAPTER 2

LECTURE 1

1 On the third day there was a wedding at Cana in Galilee, and the mother of Jesus was there. 2 Jesus and his disciples were also invited to the feast. 3 When the wine ran out, the mother of Jesus said to him, "They have no more wine." 4 Jesus then said to her, "Woman, what does that have to do with me and you? My time has not yet come." 5 His mother said to the servants, "Do whatever he tells you." 6 Now there were six stone water jars near by for purifications according to Jewish customs, each holding two or three metretes. 7 Jesus said to them, "Fill those jars with water." And they filled them to the top. 8 Then Jesus said to them, "Now pour out a drink and take it to the head waiter." They did as he instructed them. 9 Now when the head waiter tasted the water made wine, and not knowing where it came from (although the servants knew, since they had drawn the water), he called the groom over 10 and said to him, "People usually serve the choice wines first, and when the guests have had their fill, then they bring out inferior wine; but you have saved the best wine until now." 11 This beginning of signs Jesus worked in Cana of Galilee; and Jesus revealed his glory, and his disciples believed in him.[1]

335. Above, the Evangelist showed the dignity of the incarnate Word and gave various evidence for it. Now he begins to relate the effects and actions by which the divinity of the incarnate Word was made known to the world. First, he tells the things Christ did, while living in the world, that show his divinity. Secondly, he tells how Christ showed his divinity while dying; and this from chapter twelve on.

As to the first he does two things. First, he shows the divinity of Christ in relation to the power he had over nature. Secondly, in relation to the effects of grace; and this from chapter three on. Christ's power over nature is pointed out to us by the fact that he changed a nature. And this change was accomplished by Christ as a sign: first, to his disciples, to strengthen them; secondly, to the people, to lead them to believe (2:12). This transformation of a nature, in order to strengthen the disciples, was accomplished at a marriage, when he turned wa-

---

1. St. Thomas quotes Jn 2:1–11 in *ST* II-II, q. 176, a. 1, obj. 1; Jn 2:3 in *ST* III, q. 27, a. 4, obj. 3; Jn 2:4 in *ST* III, q. 46, a. 9, *sed contra*; Jn 2:10 in *ST* III, q. 44, a. 3, ad. 2; and Jn 2:11 in *ST* III, q. 36, a. 4, ad 3; III, q. 43, a. 3, *sed contra*.

ter into wine. First, the marriage is described. Secondly, those present. Thirdly, the miracle performed by Christ.

336. In describing the marriage, the time is first mentioned. Hence he says, *On the third day there was a wedding*, i.e., after the calling of the disciples mentioned earlier. For, after being made known by the testimony of John, Christ also wanted to make himself known. Secondly, the place is mentioned; hence he says, *at Cana in Galilee*. Galilee is a province, and Cana a small village located in that province.

337. As far as the literal meaning is concerned, we should note that there are two opinions about the time of Christ's preaching. Some say that there were two and a half years from Christ's baptism until his death. According to them, the events at this wedding took place in the same year that Christ was baptized. However, both the teaching and practice of the Church are opposed to this. For three miracles are commemorated on the feast of the Epiphany: the adoration of the Magi, which took place in the first year of the Lord's birth; secondly, the baptism of Christ, which implies that he was baptized on the same day thirty years later; thirdly, this marriage, which took place on the same day one year later. It follows from this that at least one year elapsed between his baptism and this marriage. In that year the only things recorded to have been done by the Lord are found in the sixth chapter of Matthew: the fasting in the desert, and the temptation by the devil; and what John tells us in this Gospel of the testimony by the Baptist and the conversion of the disciples. After this wedding, Christ began to preach publicly and to perform miracles up to the time of his passion, so that he preached publicly for two and one half years.

338. In the mystical sense, marriage signifies the union of Christ with his Church, because as the Apostle says: "This is a great mystery: I am speaking of Christ and his Church" (Eph 5:32). And this marriage was begun in the womb of the Virgin, when God the Father united a human nature to his Son in a Unity of person.[2] So, the chamber of this union was the womb of the Virgin: "He established a chamber for the sun" (Ps 18:6). Of this marriage it is said: "The kingdom of heaven is like a king who married his son" (Mt 22:2), that is, when God the Father joined a human nature to his Word in the womb of the Virgin. It was made public when the Church was joined to him by faith: "I will bind you to myself in faith" (Hos 2:20). We read of this marriage: "Blessed are they who are called to the marriage supper of the Lamb" (Rv 19:9). It will be consummated when the bride, i.e., the Church, is led into the resting place of the groom, i.e., into the glory of heaven.

The fact that this marriage took place *on the third day* is not without its own mystery. For the first day is the time of the law of nature; the second day is the time of the written law; but the third day is the time

2. See *ST* III, q. 30, a. 1.

of grace, when the incarnate Lord celebrated the marriage: "He will revive us after two days; on the third day he will raise us up" (Hos 6:3).
The place too is appropriate. For "Cana" means "zeal," and "Galilee" means "passage." So this marriage was celebrated in the zeal of a
passage, to suggest that those persons are most worthy of union with
Christ who, burning with the zeal of a conscientious devotion, pass
over from the state of guilt to the grace of the Church. "Pass over to
me, all who desire me" (Sir 24:26). And they pass from death to life,
i.e., from the state of mortality and misery to the state of immortality
and glory: "I make all things new" (Rv 21:5).

339. Then the persons invited are described. Mention is made of
three: the mother of Jesus, Jesus himself, and the disciples.

340. The mother of Jesus is mentioned when he says, **the mother
of Jesus was there.** She is mentioned first to indicate that Jesus was
still unknown and not invited to the wedding as a famous person,
but merely as one acquaintance among others; for as they invited the
mother, so also her son. Or, perhaps his mother is invited first because
they were uncertain whether Jesus would come to a wedding if invited, because of the unusual piety they noticed in him and because they
had not seen him at other social gatherings. So I think that they first
asked his mother whether Jesus should be invited. That is why the
Evangelist expressly said first that his mother was at the wedding, and
that later Jesus was invited.

341. And this is what comes next: **Jesus was invited.** Christ decided
to attend this wedding, first of all, to give us an example of humility.
For he did not look to his own dignity, but "just as he condescended
to accept the form of a servant, so he did not hesitate to come to the
marriage of servants," as Chrysostom[3] says. And as Augustine[4] says:
"Let man blush to be proud, for God became humble." For among his
other acts of humility, the Son of the Virgin came to a marriage, which
he had already instituted in paradise when he was with his Father. Of
this example it is said: "Learn from me, for I am gentle and humble of
heart" (Mt 11:29).

He came, secondly, to reject the error of those who condemn marriage, for as Bede[5] says: "If there were sin in a holy marriage bed and
in a marriage carried out with due purity, the Lord would not have
come to the marriage." But because he did come, he implies that the
baseness of those who denounce marriage deserves to be condemned.
"If she marries, it is not a sin" (1 Cor 7:36).[6]

342. The disciples are mentioned when he says, **and his disciples.**

3. *Hom. in Io.* 21. 1; PG 59, col. 129; cf. *Catena aurea,* 2:1–4.
4. *Serm. supposit.* 92. 1; PL 39, col. 1922; cf. *Catena aurea,* 2:1–4.
5. *Hom. XIII in dom. sec. post Epiphan.*; PL 94, col. 68B; cf. *Catena aurea,* 2:1–4.
6. See *ST* III, q. 29, a. 2.

343. In its mystical meaning, the mother of Jesus, the Blessed Virgin, is present in spiritual marriages as the one who arranges the marriage, because it is through her intercession that one is joined to Christ through grace: "In me is every hope of life and of strength" (Sir 24:25).[7] Christ is present as the true groom of the soul, as is said below (3:29): "It is the groom who has the bride." The disciples are the groomsmen uniting the Church to Christ, the one of whom it is said: "I betrothed you to one husband, to present you as a chaste virgin to Christ" (2 Cor 11:2).

344. At this physical marriage some role in the miracle belongs to the mother of Christ, some to Christ, and some to the disciples. When he says, *When the wine ran out*, he indicates the part of each. The role of Christ's mother was to superintend the miracle; the role of Christ to perform it; and the disciples were to bear witness to it. As to the first, Christ's mother assumed the role of a mediatrix.[8] Hence she does two things. First, she intercedes, with her Son. In the second place, she instructs the servants. As to the first, two things are mentioned. First, his mother's intercession; secondly, the answer of her Son.

345. In Mary's intercession, note first her kindness and mercy. For it is a quality of mercy to regard another's distress as one's own, because to be merciful is to have a heart distressed at the distress of another: "Who is weak, and I am not weak?" (2 Cor 11:29). And so because the Blessed Virgin was full of mercy, she desired to relieve the distress of others. So he says, *When the wine ran out, the mother of Jesus said to him*.

Note, secondly, her reverence for Christ: for because of the reverence we have for God it is sufficient for us merely to express our needs: "Lord, all my desires are known by you" (Ps 37:10). But it is not our business to wonder about the way in which God will help us, for as it is said: "We do not know what we should pray for as we ought" (Rom 8:26). And so his mother merely told him of their need, saying, *They have no more wine*.

Thirdly, note the Virgin's concern and care. For she did not wait until they were in extreme need, but *When the wine ran out*, that is, immediately. This is similar to what is said of God: "A helper in times of trouble" (Ps 9:10).

346. Chrysostom[9] asks: Why did Mary never encourage Christ to perform any miracles before this time? For she had been told of his power by the angel, whose work had been confirmed by the many things she had seen happening in his regard, all of which she remembered, thinking them over in her heart (Lk 2:51). The reason is that be-

7. See *ST* II-II, q. 83, a. 11; III, q. 25, a. 5.
8. See *ST* III, q. 26, a. 1.
9. *Hom. in Io.* 21. 2; PG 59, col. 130; cf. *Catena aurea*, 2:1–4.

fore this time he lived like any other person. So, because the time was not appropriate, she put off asking him. But now, after John's witness to him and after the conversion of his disciples, she trustingly prompted Christ to perform miracles. In this she was true to the symbol of the synagogue, which is the mother of Christ: for it was customary for the Jews to require miracles: "The Jews require signs" (1 Cor 1:22).

347. She says to him, *They have no more wine.* Here we should note that before the Incarnation of Christ three wines were running out: the wine of justice, of wisdom, and of charity or grace. Wine stings, and in this respect it is a symbol of justice. The Samaritan poured wine and oil into the wounds of the injured man, that is, he mingled the severity of justice with the sweetness of mercy. "You have made us drink the wine of sorrow" (Ps 59:5). But wine also delights the heart, "Wine cheers the heart of man" (Ps 103:15). And in this respect wine is a symbol of wisdom, the meditation of which is enjoyable in the highest degree: "Her companionship has no bitterness" (Wis 8:16). Further, wine intoxicates: "Drink, friends, and be intoxicated, my dearly beloved" (Sg 5:1). And in this respect wine is a symbol of charity: "I have drunk my wine with my milk" (Sg 5:1).[10] It is also a symbol of charity because of charity's fervor: "Wine makes the virgins flourish" (Zec 9:17).

The wine of justice was indeed running out in the Old Law, in which justice was imperfect. But Christ brought it to perfection: "Unless your justice is greater than that of the scribes and of the Pharisees, you will not enter into the kingdom of heaven" (Mt 5:20). The wine of wisdom was also running out, for it was hidden and symbolic, because as it says in 1 Corinthians (10:11): "All these things happened to them in symbol." But Christ plainly brought wisdom to light: "He was teaching them as one having authority" (Mt 7:29). The wine of charity was also running out, because they had received a spirit of serving only in fear. But Christ converted the water of fear into the wine of charity when he gave "the Spirit of adoption as sons, by which we cry: 'Abba, Father'" (Rom 8:15), and when "the charity of God was poured out into our hearts," as Romans (5:5) says.[11]

348. Then when he says, *Jesus said to her,* the answer of Christ is given. This answer has been the occasion for three heresies.

349. The Manicheans claim that Christ had only an imaginary body, not a real one. Valentinus maintained that Christ assumed a celestial body and that, as far as his body was concerned, Christ was not related to the Virgin at all. The source of this error was that he understood, *Woman, what does that have to do with me and you?* as if it meant: "I have received nothing from you." But this is contrary to the authority of Sacred Scripture. For the Apostle says: "God sent his Son, made

10. See *ST* III, q. 79, a. 1, ad 2.
11. See *ST* II-II, q. 19, a. 2.

from a woman" (Gal 4:4). Now Christ could not be said to have been made from her, unless he had taken something from her.[12] Further, Augustine[13] argues against them: "How do you know that our Lord said, *What does that have to do with me and you?* You reply that it is because John says so. But he also says that the Virgin was the mother of Christ. So, if you believe the Evangelist when he states that Jesus said this to his mother, you should also believe him when he says, *and the mother of Jesus was there.*"

350. Then there was Ebion who said that Christ was conceived from a man's seed, and Helvidius,[14] who said that the Virgin did not remain a virgin after childbirth. They were deceived by the fact that he said, *Woman*, which seems to imply the loss of virginity. But this is false, for in Sacred Scripture the word "woman" sometimes refers merely to the female sex, as it does in "made from a woman" (Gal 4:4). This is obvious also by the fact that Adam, speaking to God about Eve, said: "The woman whom you gave me as a companion, gave me fruit from the tree, and I ate it" (Gn 3:12); for Eve was still a virgin in Paradise, where Adam had not known her. Hence the fact that the mother of Christ is here called "woman" in this Gospel does not imply a loss of virginity, but refers to her sex.[15]

351. The Priscillianists,[16] however, erred by misunderstanding the words of Christ, *My time has not yet come.* They claimed that all things happen by fate, and that the actions of men, including those of Christ, are subject to predetermined times. And that is why, according to them, Christ said, *My time has not yet come.*

But this is false for any man. For since man has free choice, and this is because he has reason and will, both of which are spiritual, then obviously, as far as choice is concerned, man, so far from being subject to bodies, is really their master.[17] For spiritual things are superior to material things, so much so that the Philosopher says that the wise man is master of the stars. Further, their heresy is even less true of Christ, who is the Lord and Creator of the stars. Thus when he says, *My time has not yet come*, he is referring to the time of his passion, which was fixed for him, not by necessity, according to divine providence.[18] What

12. See *ST* III, q. 31, aa. 4–5.

13. *Tract. in Io.* 8. 7; PL 35, col. 1454; cf. *Catena aurea*, 2:1–4.

14. Helvidius (late fourth century), a disciple of the Arian Auxentius, was reputed to have denied the virginity of Mary.

15. See *ST* III, q. 28, aa. 2–3.

16. The Priscillianist sect, founded by the Spaniard Priscillian (c. 370s), was a strongly ascetical movement that practiced liturgical irregularities and accepted apocryphal works beyond the New Testament canon. They were accused of Manichaean errors, though it is unclear how widely the sect adopted cosmic speculation and a dualist framework.

17. See *ST* I, q. 115, a. 4; I-II, q. 9, a. 5.

18. See *ST* III, q. 46, a. 9.

is said in Sirach (33:7) is also contrary to their opinion: "Why is one day better than another?" And the answer is: "They have been differentiated by the knowledge of the Lord," i.e., they were differentiated from one another not by chance, but by God's providence.[19]

352. Since we have eliminated the above opinions, let us look for the reason why our Lord answered, *Woman, what does that have to do with me and you?* For Augustine,[20] Christ has two natures, the divine and the human. And although the same Christ exists in each, nevertheless things appropriate to him according to his human nature are distinct from what is appropriate to him according to his divine nature.[21] Now to perform miracles is appropriate to him according to his divine nature, which he received from the Father; while to suffer is according to his human nature, which he received from his mother. So when his mother requests this miracle, he answers, *Woman, what does that have to do with me and you?* as if saying: I did not receive from you that in me which enables me to perform miracles, but that which enables me to suffer, i.e., that which makes it appropriate for me to suffer, i.e., I have received a human nature from you. And so I will recognize you when this weakness hangs on the cross. And so he continues with, *My time has not yet come.* As if to say: I will recognize you as my mother when the time of my passion arrives. And so it was that on the cross he entrusted his mother to the disciple.

353. Chrysostom[22] explains this differently. He says that the Blessed Virgin, burning with zeal for the honor of her Son, wanted Christ to perform miracles at once, before it was opportune; but that Christ, being much wiser than his mother, restrained her. For he was unwilling to perform the miracle before the need for it was known; otherwise, it would have been less appreciated and less credible. And so he says, *Woman, what does that have to do with me and you?* As if to say: Why bother me? *My time has not yet come,* i.e., I am not yet known to those present. Nor do they know that the wine ran out; and they must first know this, because when they know their need they will have a greater appreciation of the benefit they will receive.

354. Now although his mother was refused, she did not lose hope in her Son's mercy. So she instructs the servants, *Do whatever he tells you,* in which, indeed, consists the perfection of all justice. For perfect justice consists in obeying Christ in all things: "We will do all that the Lord commanded us" (Ex 29:35). *Do whatever he tells you,* is fittingly said of God alone, for man can err now and then. Hence in matters that are against God, we are not held to obey men: "We ought to obey

19. See *ST* I, q. 22, aa. 2–3; I, q. 116, a. 1.
20. *Serm. de symb. ad catechum.* 5. 14; PL 40, col. 644; cf. *Catena Aurea,* 2:1–4. See also *Tract. in Io.* 8. 9; PL 35, col. 1455–1456; cf. *Catena Aurea,* 2:1–4.
21. See *ST* III, q. 16, aa. 4–5.
22. *Hom. in Io.* 22. 1; PG 59, col. 134; cf. *Catena aurea,* 2:1–4.

God rather than men" (Acts 5:29). We ought to obey God, who does not err and cannot be deceived, in all things.[23]

355. Now Christ's completion of the miracle is set forth.[24] First, the vessels in which the miracle was performed are described. Secondly, the matter of the miracle is stated (v. 7). Thirdly, we have how the miracle was made known and approved (v. 8).

356. The miracle was performed in six vessels; *Now there were six stone water jars near by*. Here we should note, that as mentioned in Mark (7:2), the Jews observed many bodily washings and the cleansing of their cups and dishes. So, because they were in Palestine where there was a shortage of water, they had vessels in which they kept the purest water to be used for washing themselves and their utensils. Hence he says, *there were six stone water jars near by*, i.e., vessels for holding water, *for purifications according to Jewish customs*, i.e., to use for purification, *each holding two or three metretes* of liquid, that is, two or three measures; for the Greek "metrete" is the same as the Latin "mensura."

These jars were standing there, as Chrysostom[25] says, in order to eliminate any suspicion about the miracle: both on account of their cleanliness, lest anyone suspect that the water had acquired the taste of wine from the dregs of wine previously stored in them, for these jars were standing there *for purifications according to Jewish customs*, and so had to be very pure; and also on account of the capacity of the jars, so that it would be abundantly clear that the water in such jars could be changed into wine only by divine power.

357. In the mystical sense, the six water jars signify the six eras of the Old Testament during which the hearts of men were prepared and made receptive of God's Scriptures, and put forward as an example for our lives.

The term *metretes*, according to Augustine,[26] refers to the Trinity of persons. And they are described as *two or three* because at times in Scripture three persons in the Trinity are distinctly mentioned: "Baptizing them in the name of the Father, and of the Son, and of the Holy Spirit" (Mt 28:19), and at other times only two, the Father and the Son, in whom the Holy Spirit, who is the union of the two, is implied: "If anyone loves me, he will keep my word, and my Father will love him, and we will come to him" (below 14:23). Or they are described as two on account of the two states of mankind from which the Church arose, that is, Jews and Gentiles. Or three on account of the three sons of Noah, from whom the human race arose after the deluge.

23. See *ST* II-II, q. 104, a. 4; II-II, q. 186, a. 5.
24. See *ST* III, q. 43, a. 3.
25. *Hom. in Io.* 22. 2; PG 59, col. 135; cf. *Catena aurea*, 2:5–11.
26. *Tract. in Io.* 9. 7; PL 35, col. 1461.

358. Then when he says that Jesus instructed them, *Fill those jars with water*, he gives the material of the miracle. Here we might ask why this miracle was performed with already existing material, and not from nothing. There are three reasons for this. The first reason is literal, and is given by Chrysostom:[27] to make something from nothing is much greater and more marvelous than to make something from material already existing; but it is not so evident and believable to many. And so, wishing to make what he did more believable, Christ made wine from water, thus condescending to man's capacity.

Another reason was to refute wrong dogmas. For there are some (as the Marcionists[28] and Manicheans) who said that the founder of the world was someone other than God, and that all visible things were established by such a one, that is, the devil. And so the Lord performed many miracles using created and visible substances in order to show that these substances are good and were created by God.[29]

The third reason is mystical. Christ made the wine from water, and not from nothing, in order to show that he was not laying down an entirely new doctrine and rejecting the old, but was fulfilling the old: "I have not come to destroy the law, but to fulfill it" (Mt 5:17). In other words, what was prefigured and promised in the Old Law, was disclosed and revealed by Christ: "Then he opened their minds so they could understand the Scriptures"' (Lk 24:45).

Finally, he had the servants fill the jars with water so that he might have witnesses to what he did; so it is said, *the servants knew, since they had drawn the water.*

359. Then, the miracle is made known. For as soon as the jars were filled, the water was turned into wine. So the Lord reveals the miracle at once, saying: *Now pour out a drink and take it to the head waiter.* First, we have the command of Christ selecting who is to test the wine; secondly, the judgment of the head waiter who tasted it.

360. *Then Jesus said to them*, i.e., to the servants, *Now pour out a drink*, that is, of wine, from the jars, *and take it to the head waiter (architriclinus)*. Here we should note that a *triclinium is* a place where there are three rows of tables, and it is called a *triclinium* from its three rows of dining couches: for *cline* in Greek means couch. For the ancients were accustomed to eat reclining on couches, as Maximus Valerius recounts.[30] This is the reason why the Scriptures speak of lying next to

27. *Hom. in Io.* 22. 2; PG 59, col. 135; cf. *Catena aurea*, 2:5–11.
28. Marcion flourished in Rome, c. 140, and founded a network of Christian communities gathered around his teaching. He taught a gospel of love to the exclusion of law, and so rejected the Old Testament entirely, accepting as inspired Scripture only ten epistles of St. Paul and an edited version of the Gospel of Luke. He rejected the material world as a creation of the evil god of the Old Testament and taught a docetic view of Christ.
29. See *ST* III, q. 44, a. 4.
30. Valerius Maximus, c. 20 BC–c. AD 50, was a notable Latin author and col-

and lying down. Thus the *architriclinus* was the first and chief among those dining. Or, according to Chrysostom,[31] the *architriclinus* was the one in charge of the whole banquet. And because he had been busy and had not tasted anything, the Lord wanted him, and not the guests, to be the judge of what had been done, so some could not detract from the miracle by saying the guests were drunk and, their senses dulled, could not tell wine from water. For Augustine, the *architriclinus* was the chief guest, as was mentioned; and Christ wanted to have the opinion of this person in high position so it would be more acceptable.

361. In the mystical sense, those who pour out the water are preachers: "With joy you will draw water from the springs of the Savior" (Is 12:3). And the *architriclinus* is someone skilled in the law, as Nicodemus, Gamaliel or Paul. So, when the word of the Gospel, which was hidden under the letter of the law, is entrusted to such persons, it is as though wine made from water is poured out for the *architriclinus*, who, when he tastes it, gives his assent to the faith of Christ.

362. Then the judgment of the one examining the wine is given. First, he inquires into the truth of the fact; secondly, he gives his opinion.

He says, **Now when the head waiter tasted the water made wine, and not knowing where it came from,** because he did not know that the water had miraculously been made wine by Christ, **although the servants knew,** the reason being, since they had drawn the water, he **called the groom** over, in order to learn the truth and give his opinion of the wine. Hence he adds: **People usually serve the choice wines first, and when the guests have had their fill, then they bring out inferior wine.**

Here we should consider, according to Chrysostom,[32] that everything is most perfect in the miracles of Christ. Thus, he restored most complete health to Peter's mother-in-law, so that she arose at once and waited on them, as we read in Mark (1:30) and Matthew (8:14). Again, he restored the paralytic to health so perfectly that he also arose immediately, took up his mat, and went home, as we read below (5:9). And this is also evident in this miracle, because Christ did not make mediocre wine from the water, but the very best possible. And so the head waiter says, **People usually serve the choice wines first, and when the guests have had their fill, then they bring out inferior wine,** because they drink less, and because good wine consumed in quantity along with a quantity of food causes greater discomfort. It is as though he were saying: Where did this very good wine come from which, contrary to custom, you saved until now?

lector of historical anecdotes. His nine books of memorable deeds and sayings *(Factorum ac dictorum memorabilium libri IX)* were popular and widely quoted.
31. *Hom. in Io.* 22. 2; PG 59, col. 135; cf. *Catena aurea,* 2:5–11.
32. Ibid., 22. 3; PG 59, col. 136; cf. *Catena aurea,* 2:5–11.

363. This is appropriate to a mystery. For in the mystical sense, he serves good wine first who, with an intent to deceive others, does not first mention the error he intends, but other things that entice his hearers, so that he can disclose his evil plans after they have been intoxicated and enticed to consent. We read of such wine: "It goes down pleasantly, but finally it will bite like a serpent" (Prv 23:31). Again, he serves good wine first who begins to live in a saintly and spiritual manner at the start of his conversion, but later sinks into a carnal life: "Are you so foolish as, having begun in the Spirit, to end in the flesh?" (Gal 3:3).

Christ, however, does not serve the good wine first, for at the very outset he proposes things that are bitter and hard: "Narrow is the way that leads to life" (Mt 7:14). Yet the more progress a person makes in his faith and teaching, the more pleasant it becomes and he becomes aware of a greater sweetness: "I will lead you by the path of justice, and when you walk you will not be hindered" (Prv 4:11).[33] Likewise, all those who desire to live conscientiously in Christ suffer bitterness and troubles in this world: "You will weep and mourn" (below 16:20). But later they will experience delights and joys. So he goes on: "but your sorrow will be turned into joy." "I consider that the sufferings of this present time are not worthy to be compared with the glory to come, which will be revealed in us," as is said in Romans (8:18).[34]

364. Then when he says, **This beginning of signs Jesus worked in Cana of Galilee**, he gives the disciples' acknowledgment of the miracle. We can see from this the falsity of the *History of the Infancy of the Savior*, which recounts many miracles worked by Christ as a boy.[35] For if these accounts were true, the Evangelist would not have said, **This beginning of signs Jesus worked**. We have already given the reason why Christ worked no miracles during his childhood, that is, lest men regard them as illusions.

It was for the reason given above, then, that Jesus performed this miracle of turning water into wine at Cana of Galilee; and this was the first of the signs he did. And Jesus revealed his glory, i.e., the power by which he is glorious: "The Lord of hosts, he is the King of glory" (Ps 23:10).

365. And his disciples believed in him. But how did they believe? For they already were his disciples and had believed before this. I answer that sometimes a thing is described not according to what it is at the time, but according to what it will be. For example, we say that the apostle Paul was born at Tarsus, in Cilicia; not that an actual apostle was born there, but a future one was. Similarly, it says here that his

---

33. See *ST* I-II, q. 69, a. 3.
34. See *ST* III, q. 45, a. 1.
35. *The Arabic Gospel of the History of the Infancy of the Savior*, probably fifth century, is one of several early apocryphal accounts of Christ's childhood that ascribe legendary miracles to the infant Jesus.

disciples believed in him, i.e., those who would be his disciples. Or, one might answer that previously they had believed in him as a good man, preaching what was right and just; but now they believed in him as God.

LECTURE 2

12 After this he went down to Capernaum together with his mother, his brethren and his disciples; but they did not remain there many days. 13 The Jewish Passover was near at hand, and Jesus went up to Jerusalem. 14 In the temple precincts he came upon merchants selling oxen, sheep and doves, and moneychangers seated at tables. 15 And when he had made a kind of whip from cords, he drove everyone, including sheep and oxen, out of the temple, swept away the gold of the moneychangers, and knocked over their tables. 16 To those selling doves he said, "Get out of here! And stop making my Father's house into a marketplace." 17 His disciples then remembered that it is written: "Zeal for your house consumes me."[36]

366. Above, the Evangelist presented the sign Christ worked in order to confirm his disciples; and this sign pertained to his power to change nature. Now he deals with the sign of his resurrection; a sign pertaining to the same power, but proposed by Christ to convert the people.

The Evangelist does two things as to this miracle. First, he mentions its occasion. Secondly, the prediction of the miracle (v. 18). As to the first he does two things. First, he describes the place. Secondly, he tells of the incident which was the occasion for proposing this miracle (v. 14). Now the place where this happened was Jerusalem. And so the Evangelist recounts step by step how the Lord had come to Jerusalem. First, then, he shows how he went down to Capernaum. Secondly, how he then went up to Jerusalem. As to the first he does three things. First, he mentions the place to which he went down. Secondly, he describes his company. Thirdly, he mentions the length of his stay.

367. The place to which Christ went down was Capernaum; and so he says, *After this*, i.e., the miracle of the wine, *he went down to Capernaum*. Now as far as the historical truth is concerned, this seems to conflict with Matthew's account that the Lord went down to Capernaum after John had been thrown into prison (Mt 4:12), while the entire series of events the Evangelist refers to here took place before John's imprisonment.

I answer that in order to settle this question we should bear in mind

---

36. St. Thomas quotes Jn 2:12 in *ST* III, q. 28, a. 3, obj. 5; Jn 2:16 in *ST* II-II, q. 84, a. 3, *sed contra*; and Jn 2:17 in *ST* I-II, q. 28, a. 4; III, q. 15, a. 9, *sed contra*.

what is learned from the *Ecclesiastical History*,[37] that is, that the other Evangelists, Matthew, Mark and Luke, began their account of the public life of Christ from the time that John was thrown into prison. Thus Matthew (4:12), after describing the baptism, fast and temptation of Christ, began at once to weave his story after John's imprisonment, saying: "When Jesus heard that John had been arrested. And Mark (1:14) says the same: "After John had been arrested, Jesus came into Galilee." John, who outlived the other three Evangelists, approved the accuracy and truth of their accounts when they came to his notice. Yet he saw that certain things had been left unsaid, namely, things which the Lord had done in the very first days of his preaching before John's imprisonment. And so, at the request of the faithful, John, after he began his own Gospel in a loftier manner, recorded events that took place during the first year in which Christ was baptized before John's imprisonment, as is plain from the order of the events in his Gospel. According to this, then, the Evangelists are not in disagreement. Rather, the Lord went down to Capernaum twice: once before John's imprisonment (which is the one dealt with here), and once after his imprisonment, which is dealt with in Matthew (4:13) and Luke (4:31).

368. Now "Capernaum" means "very pretty village," and signifies this world, which has its beauty from the order and disposition of divine wisdom: "The beauty of the land is mine" (Ps 49:2). So the Lord went down to Capernaum, i.e., this world, with his mother and brethren and disciples. For in heaven the Lord has a Father without a mother; and on earth a mother without a father. Thus, he significantly mentions only his mother. In heaven he does not have brothers either, but is "the Only Begotten Son, who is in the bosom of the Father" (above 1:18). But on earth he is "the Firstborn of many brothers" (Rom 8:29). And on earth he has disciples, to whom he can teach the mysteries of the divinity, which were not known to men before: "In these days he has spoken to us in his Son" as we read in Hebrews (1:1).

Or, "Capernaum" means "the field of consolation"; and this signifies every man who bears good fruit: "The odor of my son is like the odor of a fruitful field" (Gn 27:27). Such a person is called a field of consolation because the Lord is consoled and rejoices in his achievement: "God will rejoice over you" (Is 62:5), and because the angels rejoice over his good: "There is joy in the angels of God over one repentant sinner" (Lk 15:10).

369. His companions were, first of all, his mother. So he says, **with his mother**, for because she had come to the wedding and had brought about the miracle, the Lord accompanied her back to the village of Nazareth. Nazareth was a village in Galilee, whose chief town was Capernaum.

37. Eusebius, *HE* 3. 24; PG 20, col. 266–267; cf. *Catena aurea*, 2:12–13.

370. Secondly, his companions were his brethren; and so he says, **his brethren** *(fratres,* brothers, brethren). We must avoid two errors here. First, that of Helvidius, who said that the Blessed Virgin had other sons after Christ: and he called these the brothers of the Lord. This is heretical, because our faith maintains that just as the mother of Christ was a virgin before giving birth, so in giving birth and after giving birth, she remained a virgin.[38] We must also avoid the error of those who say that Joseph fathered sons with another wife, and that these are called the brothers of the Lord; for the Church does not admit this.

Jerome refutes this opinion: for on the cross the Lord entrusted his virgin mother to the care of his virgin disciple. Therefore, since Joseph was the special guardian of the Virgin, and of the Savior too, in his childhood, one may believe that he was a virgin. Consequently, it is a reasonable interpretation to say that the brothers of the Lord were those related to his virgin mother in some degree of consanguinity, or even to Joseph, who was the reputed father. And this conforms to the custom of Scripture which generally refers to relatives as brothers. Thus we read: "Let us not quarrel, for we are brothers" (Gn 13:8), as Abram said to Lot, who was his nephew. And note that he distinguishes between relatives and disciples, because not all of Christ's relatives were his disciples; hence we read: "Even his brethren did not believe in him" (below 7:5).

371. Thirdly, his disciples were his companions; hence he says, **and his disciples**. But who were his disciples? For it seems, according to Matthew, that the first ones to be converted to Christ were Peter and Andrew, John and James; but they were called after John's imprisonment, as is clear from Matthew (4:18). Thus it does not seem that they went down to Capernaum with Christ, as it says here, since this was before John's imprisonment.

There are two answers to this. One is from Augustine,[39] in his *De consensu Evangelistarum*, namely, that Matthew does not follow the historical, order, but in summarizing what he omitted, relates events that occurred before John's imprisonment as though they happened after. So, without any suggestion of a time lapse he says, "As Jesus was walking by the Sea of Galilee, he saw two brothers" (Mt 4:18), without adding "after this" or "at that time." The other answer, also by Augustine, is that in the Gospel not only the twelve whom the Lord chose and named apostles are called disciples of the Lord (Lk 6:13), but also all who believed in him and were instructed for the kingdom of heaven by his teaching. Therefore, it is possible that although those twelve did not yet follow him, others who adhered to him are called disciples here. But the first answer is better.

38. See *ST* III, q. 28, a. 3.
39. *De cons. Evang.* 2. 17, no. 39; PL 34, col. 1096; cf. *Catena aurea,* 2:12–13.

372. His stay there was short; hence he says, **but they did not remain there many days**. The reason for this was that the citizens of Capernaum were not eager to accept the teachings of Christ, being very corrupt, so that in Matthew (11:23) the Lord rebukes them for not doing penance in spite of the miracles done there and of Christ's teaching: "And you Capernaum, will you be lifted up to heaven? You will go down to hell. For if the mighty works that were done in you had been performed in Sodom, it would have stood until this day." But although they were evil, he went there to accompany his mother, and to stay there for a few days for her consolation and honor.

373. As for its mystical sense, this signifies that some cannot remain long with the many words spoken by Christ; a few of these words are enough for them, to enlighten them, because of the weakness of their understanding. Hence as Origen[40] said, Christ reveals few things to such persons, according to "I have many things to tell you, but you cannot bear them now" (Jn 16:12).

374. Then when he says, **The Jewish Passover was near at hand**, he mentions the place to which he went up. And concerning this he does two things. First, the occasion is given. Secondly, the going up.

375. Now the occasion for his going up was the Jewish Passover. For in Exodus (13:17) it is commanded that every male be presented to the Lord three times a year; and one of these times was the Jewish Passover. So, since the Lord came to teach everyone by his example of humility and perfection, he wished to observe the law as long as it was in force. For he did not come to destroy the law, but to fulfill it (Mt 5:17).[41] And so, because the Passover of the Jews was at hand, he went up to Jerusalem. So we, after his example, should carefully observe the divine precepts. For if the Son of God fulfilled the decrees of a law he himself had given, and celebrated the great feasts, with what zeal for good works ought we both to prepare for them and observe them?

376. It should be noted that in John's Gospel mention is made of the Passover in three passages: here, and in (6:4), when he worked the miracle of the loaves, where it is said: "Now the Jewish Passover was near at hand", and again in (13:1), where it says: "Before the feast day of the Passover." So, according to this Gospel, we understand that after the miracle of the wine Christ preached for two years plus the interval between his baptism and this Passover. For what he did here occurred near the Passover, as it says here, and then a year later, near the time of another Passover, he performed the miracle of the loaves, and in the same year John was beheaded. Thus John was beheaded near the time of the Passover, because we read in Matthew (14:13) that imme-

40. *Comm. in Io.* X, 9, no. 41; PG 14, col. 320D; cf. *Catena aurea*, 2:12–13.
41. See *ST* III, q. 40, a. 4.

diately after John was beheaded Christ withdrew to the desert, where he worked the miracle of the loaves; and this miracle took place near Passover time, as stated below (6:4). Nevertheless, the feast of this beheading of John is celebrated on the day his head was found. It was later, during another Passover, that Christ suffered.

So, according to the opinion of those who say that the miracle worked at the wedding and the events being discussed here occurred in the same year in which Christ was baptized, there was an interval, of two and one half years between Christ's baptism and his passion. So, according to them, the Evangelist says, *The Jewish Passover was near at hand*, in order to show that Christ had been baptized just a few days before.

But the Church holds the opposite. For we believe that Christ worked the miracle of the wine on the first anniversary of the day of his baptism; then a year later, near Passover time, John was beheaded; and then there was another year between the Passover near which John was beheaded and the Passover during which Christ suffered. So between the baptism of Christ and the miracle of the wine there had to be another Passover which the Evangelist does not mention. And so, according to what the Church holds, Christ preached for three and one half years.

377. He says, *the Jewish Passover*, not as though the people of other nations celebrated a Passover, but for two reasons. One, because when people celebrate a feast in a holy and pure way, it is said that they celebrate it for the Lord; but when they celebrate it in neither of those ways, they do not celebrate it for the Lord, but for themselves: "My soul hates your new moons and your feasts" (Is 1:14). It is as though he said: Those who celebrate for themselves and not for me, do not please me: "When you fasted, did you fast for me?" (Zec 7:5), as if to say: You did not do it for me, but for yourselves. And so because these Jews were corrupt and celebrated their Passover in an unbecoming manner, the Evangelist does not say, "the Passover of the Lord," but *the Jewish Passover* was at hand.

Or, he says this to differentiate it from our Passover. For the Passover of the Jews was symbolic, being celebrated by the immolation of a lamb which was a symbol. But our Passover is true, in which we recall the true passing [passion] of the Immaculate Lamb: "Christ, our Passover, has been sacrificed" (1 Cor 5:7).[42]

378. The journey was to Jerusalem, and so he says, *and Jesus went up to Jerusalem*. Note here that according to the historical order, Jesus went up to Jerusalem near the time of the Passover and expelled the merchants from the temple on two occasions. The first, before John's imprisonment, is the one the Evangelist mentions here, the other is

42. See *ST* I-II, q. 101, a. 2; III, q. 73, a. 6.

mentioned by Matthew (21:13) as occurring when the Passover and the hour of his passion were at hand. For the Lord frequently repeated works that were similar. For example, the two cases of giving sight to the blind: one in Matthew (9:28) and another in Mark (10:46). In like manner he twice cast merchants from the temple.

379. In the mystical sense, *Jesus went up to Jerusalem*, which is translated as the "vision of peace," and signifies eternal happiness. It is to here that Jesus ascended, and he took his own with him. There is no lack of mystery in the fact that he went down to Capernaum and later went up to Jerusalem. For if he did not first go down, he would not have been suited to go up, because, as it is said: "He who descended is the same as he who ascended" (Eph 4:10). Further, no mention is made of the disciples in the ascent to Jerusalem, because the ascent of the disciples comes from the ascent of Christ: "No one has gone up to heaven except the one who came down from heaven, the Son of Man, who lives in heaven" (below 3:13).

380. Then when he says, *In the temple precincts he came upon merchants selling oxen, sheep and doves*, the Evangelist sets down what moved Christ to propose the sign of the resurrection. He does three things with this. First, he exposes the faulty behavior of the Jews. Secondly, he discloses Christ's remedy (v. 15). Thirdly, he gives the announcement of the prophecy (v. 22).

381. With respect to the first, we should note that the devil plots against the things of God and strives to destroy them. Now among the means by which he destroys holy things, the chief is avarice; hence it is said: "The shepherds have no understanding. All have turned aside to their own way; everyone after his own gain, from the first one to the last" (Is 56:11).[43] And the devil has done this from the earliest times. For the priests of the Old Testament, who had been established to care for divine matters, gave free rein to avarice. God commanded, in the law, that animals should be sacrificed to the Lord on certain feasts. And in order to fulfill this command, those who lived nearby brought the animals with them. But those who came a long distance were unable to bring animals from their own homes. And so because offerings of this kind resulted in profit for the priests, and so animals to offer would not be lacking to those who came from a distance, the priests themselves saw to it that animals were sold in the temple. And so they had them shown for sale in the temple, i.e., in the atrium of the temple. And this is what he says: *In the temple precincts he came upon merchants selling oxen, sheep and doves*.

Mention is first made of two land animals, which according to the law could be offered to the Lord: the ox and the sheep. The third land

---

43. See *ST* I, q. 114, a. 3; I-II, q. 77, a. 1; I-II, q. 80, aa. 1–4.

animal offered, the goat, is implied when he says "sheep", similarly, the turtle-dove is included when he says "doves."

382. It sometimes happened that some came to the temple not only without animals, but also without money to buy them. And so the priests found another avenue for their avarice; they set up moneychangers who would lend money to those who came without it. And although they would not accept a usurious gain, because this was forbidden in the law, nevertheless in place of this they accepted certain "collibia," i.e., trifles and small gifts. So this also was turned to the profit of the priests. And this is what he says, *moneychangers seated at tables*, i.e., in the temple, ready to lend money.

383. This can be understood mystically in three ways. First of all, the merchants signify those who sell or buy the things of the Church: for the oxen, sheep and doves signify the spiritual goods of the Church and the things connected with them. These goods have been consecrated and authenticated by the teachings of the apostles and doctors, signified by the oxen: "When there is an abundant harvest the strength of the ox is evident" (Prv 14:4); and by the blood of the martyrs, who are signified by the sheep: so it is said for them: "We are regarded as sheep for the slaughter" (Rom 8:36); and by the gifts of the Holy Spirit, signified by the doves, for as stated above, the Holy Spirit appeared in the form of a dove. Therefore, those who presume to sell the spiritual goods of the Church and the goods connected with them are selling the teachings of the apostles, the blood of the martyrs, and the gifts of the Holy Spirit.[44]

Secondly, it happens that certain prelates or heads of churches sell these oxen, sheep and doves, not overtly by simony, but covertly by negligence; that is, when they are so eager for and occupied with temporal gain that they neglect the spiritual welfare of their subjects. And this is the way they sell the oxen, sheep and doves, i.e., the three classes of people subject to them. First of all, they sell the preachers and laborers, who are signified by the oxen: "Happy are you who sow beside all the streams, letting the ox and the donkey range free" (Is 32:20); because prelates ought to arrange the oxen, i.e., teachers and wise men, with the donkeys, i.e., the simple and uneducated. They also sell those in the active life, and those occupied with ministering, signified by the sheep: "My sheep hear my voice" (below 10:27); and as is said in 2 Samuel (24:17): "But these, who are the sheep, what have they done?" They also sell the contemplatives, signified by the doves: "Who will give me wings like a dove, and I will fly?" (Ps 54:7).[45]

Thirdly, by the temple of God we can understand the spiritual soul,

44. See *ST* II-II, q. 100, aa. 1–3.
45. See *ST* II-II, q. 185, a. 3.

as it says: "The temple of God is holy, and that is what you are" (1 Cor 3:17). Thus a man sells oxen, sheep and doves in the temple when he harbors bestial movements in his soul, for which he sells himself to the devil. For oxen, which are used for cultivating the earth, signify earthly desires; sheep, which are stupid animals, signify man's obstinacy, and the doves signify man's instability. It is God who drives these things out of men's hearts.

384. The Lord's remedy is at once set forth (v. 15). Here the Lord's remedy consisted in action and in words, in order to instruct those who have charge of the Church that they must correct their subjects in deed and in word.[46] And he does two things with respect to this. First, he gives the remedy Christ applied by his action. Secondly, the remedy he applied by word (v. 16).

385. As to the first he does three things. First, he drives the men out. Secondly, the oxen and sheep. Thirdly, he sweeps away the money.

He drives the men out with a whip; and this is what he says, **when he had made a kind of whip from cords**. This is something that could be done only by divine power. For as Origen[47] says, the divine power of Jesus was as able, when he willed, to quench the swelling anger of men as to still the storms of minds: "The Lord brings to nought the thoughts of men" (Ps 32:10). He makes the whip from cords because, as Augustine[48] says, it is from our own sins that he forms the matter with which he punishes us: for a series of sins, in which sins are added to sins, is called a cord: "He is bound fast by the cords of his own sins" (Prv 5:22); "Woe to you who haul wickedness with cords" (Is 5:18). Then, just as he drove the merchants from the temple, so he swept away the gold of the moneychangers and knocked over their tables.

386. And mark well that if he expelled from the temple things that seemed somehow licit, in the sense that they were ordained to the worship of God, how much more if he comes upon unlawful things? The reason he cast them out was because in this matter the priests did not intend God's glory, but their own profit. Hence it is said: "It is for yourselves that you placed guardians of my service in my sanctuary" (Ez 44:8)

Further, our Lord showed zeal for the things of the law so that he might by this answer the chief priests and the priests who were later to bring a charge against him on this very point. Again, by casting things of this kind out of the temple he let it be understood that the time was coming in which the sacrifices of the law were due to cease, and the true worship of God transferred to the Gentiles: "The kingdom of God will be taken away from you" (Mt 21:43).[49] Also, this shows us the

46. See ST II-II, q. 185, a. 1; III, q. 42, a. 2.
47. Comm. in Io. X, 25, no. 147; PG 14, col. 352B; cf. Catena aurea, 2:14–17.
48. Tract. in Io. 10. 5; PL 35, col. 1469; cf. Catena aurea, 2:14–17.
49. See ST I-II, q. 103, a. 3.

condemnation of those who sell spiritual things: "May your money perish together with you" (Acts 8:20).

387. Then when he says, **To those selling doves he said**, he records the treatment which the Lord applied by word. Here it should be noted that those who engage in simony should, of course, first be expelled from the Church. But because as long as they are alive, they can change themselves by free will and by the help of God return to the state of grace, they should not be given up as hopeless. If, however, they are not converted, then they are not merely to be expelled, but handed over to those to whom it is said: "Bind him hand and foot, and cast him into outer darkness" (Mt 22:13).[50] And so the Lord, attending to this, first warns them, and then gives the reason for his warning, saying, **stop making my Father's house into a marketplace**.

388. He warns those selling the doves by reproaching them, for they signify those who sell the gifts of the Holy Spirit, i.e., those who engage in simony.

389. He gives his reason for this when he says, **stop making my Father's house into a marketplace**. "Take away your evil from my sight" (Is 1:16). Note that Matthew (21:13) says: "Do not make my house a den of thieves," while here he says, **a marketplace**. Now the Lord does this because, as a good physician, he begins first with the gentler things; later on, he would propose harsher things. Now the action recorded here was the first of the two; hence in the beginning he does not call them thieves but merchants. But because they did not stop such business out of obstinacy, the Lord, when driving them out the second time (as mentioned in Mark 11:15), rebukes them more severely, calling robbery what he had first called business.

He says, **my Father's house**, to exclude the error of Manicheus, who said that while the God of the New Testament was the Father of Christ, the God of the Old Testament was not. But if this were true, then since the temple was the house of the Old Testament, Christ would not have referred to the temple as **my Father's house**.[51]

390. Why were the Jews not disturbed here when he called God his Father, for as is said below (5:18), this is why they persecuted him? I answer that God is the Father of certain men through adoption; for example, he is the Father of the just in this way. This was not a new idea for the Jews: "You will call me Father, and you will not cease to walk after me" (Jer 3:19). However, by nature he is the Father of Christ alone: "The Lord said to me: 'You are my Son'" (Ps 2:7), i.e., the true and natural Son. It is this that was unheard of among the Jews.[52] And so the Jews persecuted him because he called himself the true Son of God: "the Jews tried all the harder to kill him, because he not only

50. See *ST* II-II, q. 100, a. 6.
51. See *ST* I-II, q. 98, aa. 1–2.
52. See *ST* I, q. 33, a. 3; III, q. 23, aa. 1, 4.

broke the Sabbath rest, but even called God his own Father, making himself equal to God" (below 5:18). But when he called God his Father on this occasion, they said it was by adoption.

391. That the house of God shall not be made a marketplace is taken from Zechariah (4:21): "On that day there will no longer be any merchants in the house of the Lord of hosts": and from the Psalm (70:10), where one version has the reading: "Because I was not part of the marketplace, I will enter into the strength of the Lord."

392. Then when he says, **His disciples then remembered**, he sets down a prophecy which was written in Psalm 68 (v. 10): "Zeal for your house consumes me." Here we should remark that zeal, properly speaking, signifies an intensity of love, whereby the one who loves intensely does not tolerate anything which is repugnant to his love. So it is that men who love their wives intensely and cannot endure their being in the company of other men, as this conflicts with their own love, are called "zelotypes." Thus, properly speaking, one is said to have zeal for God who cannot patiently endure anything contrary to the honor of God, whom he loves above all else: "I have been very zealous for the Lord God of hosts" (1 Kgs 19:10).[53] Now we should love the house of the Lord, according to the Psalm (25:8): "O Lord, I have loved the beauty of your house." Indeed, we should love it so much that our zeal consumes us, so that if we notice anything amiss being done, we should try to eliminate it, no matter how dear to us are those who are doing it; nor should we fear any evils that we might have to endure as a result. So the Gloss[54] says: "Good zeal is a fervor of spirit, by which, scorning the fear of death, one is on fire for the defense of the truth. He is consumed by it who takes steps to correct any perversity he sees; and if he cannot, he tolerates it with sadness."

LECTURE 3

18 At this the Jews responded and said, "What sign can you show us authorizing you to do these things?" 19 Jesus replied, "Destroy this temple, and in three days I will raise it up again." 20 The Jews then retorted, "This temple took forty-six years to build, and you are going to raise it up again in three days!" 21 He was speaking, however, of the temple of his body. 22 When, therefore, he had risen from the dead, his disciples recalled that he had said this; they then believed the Scriptures and the statement Jesus had made. 23 While he was in Jerusalem

53. See *ST* II-II, q. 26, a. 3.
54. In the *Catena aurea* for Jn. 2:14–17, the first half of this quotation is ascribed to Alcuin: see *Comm. in S. Ioannis Evang.* 2. 1; PL 100, col. 775D; and the second half to Augustine: see *Tract. in Io.* 10. 9; PL 35, col. 1471–72.

during the Passover feast, many people, seeing the signs he was work-
ing, believed in his name. 24 But Jesus did not trust himself to them,
for he knew all men, 25 and he did not need anyone to give him tes-
timony about men. He was well aware of what was in man's heart.[55]

393. Having set forth the occasion for showing the sign, the Evangelist then states the sign which would be given. First, he gives the sign.
Secondly, he mentions the fruit of the signs Christ performed (v. 23).
As to the first he does three things. First, the request for the sign is giv-
en. Secondly, the sign itself (v. 19). Thirdly, the way the sign was understood (v. 20).

394. The Jews ask for a sign; and this is what he says: **What sign**
can you show us authorizing you to do these things?

395. Here we should note that when Jesus drove the merchants out
of the temple, two things could be considered in Christ: his rectitude
and zeal, which pertain to virtue; and his power or authority. It was
not appropriate to require a sign from Christ concerning the virtue and
zeal with which he did the above action, since everyone may lawfully act according to virtue. But he could be required to give a sign concerning his authority for driving them out of the temple, since it is not
lawful for anyone to do this unless he has the authority.

And so the Jews, not questioning his zeal and virtue, ask for a sign
of his authority; and so they say, **What sign can you show us autho-**
rizing you to do these things? i.e., Why do you drive us out with such
power and authority, for this does not seem to be your office? They say
the same thing in Matthew (21:23): "By what authority are you doing
these things?"

396. The reason they ask for a sign is that it was the usual thing
for Jews to require a sign, seeing that they were called to the law by
signs: "There did not arise again in Israel a prophet like Moses, whom
the Lord knew face to face, with all his signs and wonders," as is said
in Deuteronomy (34:10), and "The Jews require signs," as we find in
1 Corinthians (1:22). Hence David complains for the Jews saying: "We
have not seen our signs" (Ps 73:9). However, they asked him for a sign
not in order to believe, but in the hope that he would not be able to
provide the sign, and then they could obstruct and restrain him. And
so, because they asked in an evil manner, he did not give them an evident sign, but a sign clothed in a symbol, a sign concerning the resurrection.

397. Hence he says, **Jesus replied**, and he gives the sign for which
they asked. He gives them the sign of his future resurrection because
this shows most strikingly the power of his divinity. For it is not within
the power of mere man to raise himself from the dead. Christ alone,

55. St. Thomas quotes Jn 2:20 in *ST* III, q. 33, a. 1, obj. 1; and Jn 2:21 in *ST* III,
q. 32, a. 1, obj. 3.

who was free among the dead, did this by the power of his divinity.[56] He shows them a similar sign in Matthew (12:30): "An evil and adulterous generation asks for a sign. And a sign will not be given it, except the sign of Jonah the prophet." And although he gave a hidden and symbolic sign on both occasions, the first was stated more clearly, and the second more obscurely.

398. We should note that before the Incarnation, God gave a sign of the Incarnation to come: "The Lord himself will give you a sign. A virgin will conceive, and give birth to a son" (Is 7:14). And in like manner, before the resurrection he gave a sign of the resurrection to come. And he did this because it is especially by these two events that the power of the divinity in Christ is evidenced. For nothing more marvelous could be done than that God become man and that Christ's humanity should become a partaker of divine immortality after his resurrection: "Christ, rising from the dead, will not die again . . . his life is life with God" (Rom 6:9), i.e., in a likeness to God.[57]

399. We should note the words Christ used in giving this sign. For Christ calls his body a temple, because a temple is something in which God dwells, according to "The Lord is in his holy temple" (Ps 10:5). And so a holy soul, in which God dwells, is also called a temple of God: "The temple of God is holy, and that is what you are" (1 Cor 3:17). Therefore, because the divinity dwells in the body of Christ, the body of Christ is the temple of God, not only according to the soul but also according to the body: "In him all the fullness of the divinity dwells bodily" (Col 2:9). God dwells in us by grace, i.e., according to an act of the intellect and will, neither of which is an act of the body, but of the soul alone. But he dwells in Christ according to a union in the person; and this union includes not only the soul, but the body as well. And so the very body of Christ is God's temple.

400. But Nestorius, using this text in support of his error, claims that the Word of God was joined to human nature only by an indwelling, from which it follows that the person of God is distinct from that of man in Christ. Therefore it is important to insist that God's indwelling in Christ refers to the nature, since in Christ human nature is distinct from the divine, and not to the person, which in the case of Christ is the same for both God and man, that is, the person of the Word, as was said above.[58]

401. Therefore, granting this, the Lord does two things with respect to this sign. First, he foretells his future death. Secondly, his resurrection.

402. Christ foretells his own death when he says, **Destroy this temple.** For Christ died and was killed by others: "And they will kill him"

---

56. See *ST* III, q. 53, a. 4.   57. See *ST* III, q. 2, a. 9.
58. See *ST* III, q. 2, aa. 1–2, 6.

(Mt 17:22), yet with him willing it: because as is said: "He was offered because it was his own will" (Is 53:7). And so he says, **Destroy this temple**, i.e., my body. He does not say, "it will be destroyed," lest you suppose he killed himself. He says, **Destroy**, which is not a command but a prediction and a permission. A prediction, so that the sense is, **Destroy this temple**, i.e., you will destroy. And a permission, so that the sense is, **Destroy this temple**, i.e., do with my body what you will, I submit it to you. As he said to Judas: "What you are going to do, do quickly" (below 13:27), not as commanding him, but as abandoning himself to his decision.

He says **Destroy**, because the death of Christ is the dissolution of his body, but in a way different from that of other men. For the bodies of other men are destroyed by death even to the point of the body's returning to dust and ashes. But such a dissolution did not take place in Christ, for as it is said: "You will not allow your Holy One to see corruption" (Ps 15:10). Nevertheless, death did bring a dissolution to Christ, because his soul was separated from his body as a form from matter, and because his blood was separated from his body, and because his body was pierced with nails and a lance.[59]

403. He foretells his resurrection when he says, **and in three days I will raise it up again**, that is, his body; i.e., I will raise it from the dead. He does not say, "I will be raised up," or "The Father will raise it up," but **I will raise it up**, to show that he would rise from the dead by his own power. Yet we do not deny that the Father raised him from the dead, because as it is said: "Who raised Jesus from the dead" (Rom 8:11); and "O Lord, have pity on me, and raise me up" (Ps 40:11). And so God the Father raised Christ from the dead, and Christ arose by his own power: "I have slept and have taken my rest, and I have risen, because the Lord has taken me" (Ps 3:6). There is no contradiction in this, because the power of both is the same; hence "whatever the Father does, the Son does likewise" (below 5:19). For if the Father raised him up, so too did the Son: "Although he was crucified through weakness, he lives through the power of God" (2 Cor 13:4).[60]

404. He says, **and in three days**, and not "after three days," because he did not remain in the tomb for three complete days; but, as Augustine says, he is employing synecdoche, in which a part is taken for the whole.

Origen,[61] however, assigns a mystical reason for this expression, and says: The true body of Christ is the temple of God, and this body symbolizes the mystical body, i.e., the Church: "You are the body of Christ" (1 Cor 12:27). And as the divinity dwells in the body of Christ

59. See *ST* III, q. 50, aa. 1–3.
60. See *ST* III, q. 53, a. 4.
61. *Comm. in Io.* X, 35, no. 228; PG 14, col. 369D. See *ST* III, q. 8, a. 3.

through the grace of union, so too he dwells in the Church through the grace of adoption. Although that body may seem to be destroyed mystically by the adversities of persecutions with which it is afflicted, nevertheless it is raised up in "three days," namely, in the "day" of the law of nature, the "day" of the written law, and the "day" of the law of grace: because in those days a part of that body was destroyed, while another still lived. And so he says, in three days, because the spiritual resurrection of this body is accomplished in three days. But after those three days we will be perfectly risen, not only as to the first resurrection, but also as to the second: "Happy are they who share in the second [sic] resurrection" (Rv 20:6).[62]

405. Then when he says, **The Jews then retorted**, we have the interpretation of the sign he gave. First, the false interpretation of the Jews. Secondly, its true understanding by the apostles (v. 21).

406. The interpretation of the Jews was false, because they believed that Christ was saying this of the material temple in which he then was; consequently, they answer according to this interpretation and say: **This temple took forty-six years to build**, i.e., this material temple in which we are standing, **and you are going to raise it up again in three days!**

407. There is a literal objection against this. For the temple in Jerusalem was built by Solomon, and it is recorded in 2 Chronicles (6:1) that it was completed by Solomon in seven years. How then can it be said that this temple took forty-six years to build? I answer that according to some this is not to be understood of the very first temple, which was completed by Solomon in seven years: for that temple built by Solomon was destroyed by Nebuchadnezzar. But it is to be understood of the temple rebuilt under Zerubbabel, after they returned from captivity, as recorded in the book of Ezra (5:2). However, this rebuilding was so hindered and delayed by the frequent attacks of their enemies on all sides, that the temple was not finished until forty-six years had passed.

408. Or it could be said, according to Origen,[63] that they were speaking of Solomon's temple: and it did take forty-six years to build if the time be reckoned from the day when David first spoke of building a temple and discussed it with Nathan the prophet, as we find in 2 Samuel (7:2), until its final completion under Solomon. For from that first day onward David began preparing the material and the things necessary for building the temple. Accordingly, if the time in question is carefully calculated, it will come to forty-six years.

409. But although the Jews referred their interpretation to the material temple, nevertheless, according to Augustine,[64] it can be referred

---

62. See also *ST* III, q. 56, a. 1.
63. *Comm. in Io.* X, 38, no. 255; PG 14, col. 377B; cf. *Catena aurea*, 2:18–22.
64. *De div. quaest. 83*, q. 56; PL 40, col. 39; cf. *Catena aurea*, 2:18–22.

to the temple of Christ's body. As he says in *The Book of Eighty-three Questions*, the conception and formation of the human body is completed in forty-five days in the following manner: "During the first six days, the conception of a human body has a likeness to milk; during the next nine days it is converted into blood; then in the next twelve days, it is hardened into flesh; then the remaining eighteen days, it is formed into a perfect outlining of all the members. But if we add six, nine, twelve and eighteen, we get forty-five; and if we add 'one' for the sacrament of unity, we get forty-six."

410. However a question arises about this: because this process of formation does not seem to have taken place in Christ, who was formed and animated at the very instant of conception.[65] But one may answer that although in the formation of Christ's body there was something unique, in that Christ's body was perfect at that instant as to the outlining of its members, it was not perfect as to the quantity due the body; and so he remained in the Virgin's womb until he attained the due quantity.

However, let us take the above numbers and select six, which was the first, and forty-six, which was the last, and let us multiply one by the other. The result is two hundred seventy-six. Now if we assemble these days into months, allotting thirty days to a month, we get nine months and six days. Thus it was correct to say that it took forty-six years to build the temple, which signifies the body of Christ; the suggestion being that there were as many years in building the temple as there were days in perfecting the body of Christ. For from March twenty-five, when Christ was conceived, and (as is believed) when he suffered, to December twenty-five, there are this number of days, namely, two hundred seventy-six, a number that is the result of multiplying forty-six by six.

411. Augustine[66] (as is plain from the Gloss) has another mystical interpretation of this number. For he says that if one adds the letters in the name "Adam," using for each the number it represented for the Greeks, the result is forty-six. For in Greek, A represents the number one, since it is the first letter of the alphabet. And according to this order, D is four. Adding to the sum of these another one for the second A and forty for the letter M, we have forty-six. This signifies that the body of Christ was derived from the body of Adam.

Again, according to the Greeks, the name "Adam" is composed of the first letters of the names of the four directions of the world: namely, Anathole, which is the east; Disis, which is the west; Arctos, which is the north; and Mensembria, the south. This signifies that Christ derived his flesh from Adam in order to gather his elect from the four parts of the world: "He will gather his elect from the four winds" (Mt 24:31).

65. See *ST* III, q. 33, aa. 1–2.
66. *Tract. in Io.* 10. 12; PL 35, col. 1473–74; cf. *Catena aurea*, 2:18–22.

412. Then, the true interpretation of this sign as understood by the apostles is given (v. 21). First, the way they understood it is given. Secondly, the time when they understood it (v. 22).

413. He says therefore: The Jews said this out of ignorance. But Christ did not understand it in their way; in fact, he meant the temple of his body, and this is what he says: He was speaking, however, of the temple of his body. We have already explained why the body of Christ could be called a temple.

Apollinarius misunderstood this and said that the body of Christ was inanimate matter because the temple was inanimate. He was mistaken in this for when it is said that the body of Christ is a temple, one is speaking metaphorically. And in this way of speaking a likeness does not exist in all respects, but only in some respect, namely, as to indwelling, which is referred to the nature, as was explained. Further, this is evident from the authority of Sacred Scripture, when Christ himself said: "I have the power to lay down my life," as we read below (10:18).

414. The time when the apostles acquired this true understanding is then shown by the Evangelist when he says, **When, therefore, he had risen from the dead, his disciples recalled that he had said this.** Prior to the resurrection it was difficult to understand this. First, because this statement asserted that the true divinity was in the body of Christ; otherwise it could not be called a temple. And to understand this at that time was above human ability. Secondly, because in this statement mention is made of the passion and resurrection, when he says, **I will raise it up again**; and this is something none of the disciples had heard mentioned before. Consequently, when Christ spoke of his resurrection and passion to the apostles, Peter was scandalized when he heard it, saying, "God forbid, Lord" (Mt 16:22). But after the resurrection, when they now clearly understood that Christ was God, through what he had shown in regard to his passion and resurrection, and when they had learned of the mystery of his resurrection, **his disciples recalled that he had said this** of his body, and **they then believed the Scriptures**, i.e., the prophets: "He will revive us after two days; on the third day he will raise us up" (Hos 6:3), and "Jonah was in the belly of the fish three days and three nights" (Jon 2:1). So it is that on the very day of the resurrection he opened their understanding so that they might understand the Scriptures **and the statement Jesus had made**, namely, **Destroy this temple, and in three days I will raise it up again.**[67]

415. In the anagogical sense, according to Origen,[68] we understand by this that in the final resurrection of nature we will be disciples of Christ, when in the great resurrection the entire body of Jesus, that is, his Church, will be made certain of the things we now hold through

67. See *ST* III, q. 55, a. 6.
68. *Comm. in Io.* X, 43, nos. 299–306; PG 14, col. 392B–393B; cf. *Catena aurea*, 2:18–22.

faith in a dark manner. Then we shall receive the fulfillment of faith, seeing in actual fact what we now observe through a mirror.

416. Then (v. 23) he sets forth the fruit which resulted from the signs, namely, the conversion of certain believers. Concerning this he does three things. First, he mentions those who believed on account of the miracles. Secondly, he shows the attitude of Christ to them (v. 24). Thirdly, he gives the reason for this (v. 25).

417. The fruit which developed from the signs of Jesus was abundant, because many believed and were converted to him; and this is what he says, *While he was in Jerusalem during the Passover feast, many people, seeing the signs he was working, believed in his name*, i.e., in him.

418. Note that they believed in two ways: some on account of the miracles they saw, and some on account of the revelation and prophecy of hidden things. Now those who believe on account of doctrine are more commendable, because they are more spiritual than those who believe on account of signs, which are grosser and on the level of sense. Those who were converted are shown to be more on the level of sense by the fact that they did not believe on account of the doctrine, as the disciples did, but *seeing the signs he was working*: "Prophecies are for those who believe" (1 Cor 14:22).[69]

419. One might ask which signs worked by Jesus they saw, for we do not read of any sign worked by him in Jerusalem at that time. According to Origen,[70] there are two answers to this. First, Jesus did work many miracles there at that time, which are not recorded here; for the Evangelist purposely omitted many of Christ's miracles, since he worked so many that they could not easily be recorded: "Jesus did many other signs, and if every one was written, the world itself, I think, would not be able to contain the books that would be written" (below 21:25). And the Evangelist expressly shows this when he says, *seeing the signs he was working*, without mentioning them, because it was not the intention of the Evangelist to record all the signs of Jesus, but as many as were needed to instruct the Church of the faithful. The second answer is that among the miracles the greatest could be the sign in which Jesus by himself drove from the temple a crowd of men with a whip of small cords.

420. The attitude of Jesus to those who believed in him is shown when he says, *But Jesus did not trust himself to them*, i.e., those who had believed in him. What is this, men entrust themselves to God, and Jesus himself does not entrust himself to them? Could they kill him against his will? Some will say that he did not trust himself to them because he knew that their belief was not genuine. But if this were

69. See *ST* III, q. 43, a. 1.
70. *Comm. in Io.* X, 46, nos. 319–20; PG 14, col. 397A–B; cf. *Catena aurea*, 2:23–25.

true, the Evangelist would surely not have said that many believed in his name, and yet he did not trust himself to them. According to Chrysostom,[71] the reason is that they did believe in him, but imperfectly because they were not yet able to attain to the profound mysteries of Christ, and so Jesus did not trust himself to them, i.e., he did not yet reveal his secret mysteries to them; for there were many things he would not reveal even to the apostles: "I still have many things to say to you, but you cannot bear them now" (below 16:12), and "I could not speak to you as spiritual persons, but as sensual" (1 Cor 3:1). And so it is significant that in order to show that they believed imperfectly, the Evangelist does not say that they believed "in him," because they did not yet believe in his divinity, but he says, *in his name*, i.e., they believed what was said about him, nominally, i.e., that he was just, or something of that sort.

Or, according to Augustine,[72] these people represent the catechumens in the Church, who, although they believe in the name of Christ, Jesus does not trust himself to them, because the Church does not give them the body of Christ. For just as no priest except one ordained in the priesthood can consecrate that body, so no one but a baptized person may receive it.[73]

421. The reason Jesus did not trust himself to them arises from his perfect knowledge; hence he says, *for he knew all men*. For although one must ordinarily presume good of everyone, yet after the truth about certain people is known, one should act according to their condition. Now because nothing in man was unknown to Christ and since he knew that they believed imperfectly, he did not trust himself to them.

422. The universal knowledge of Christ is then described: for he knew not only those who were on close terms with him, but strangers too. And therefore he says, *for he knew all men*; and this by the power of his divinity: "The eyes of the Lord are far brighter than the sun" (Sir 23:28). Now a man, although he may know other people, cannot have a sure knowledge of them, because he sees only what appears; consequently, he must rely on the testimony of others. But Christ knows with the greatest certainty, because he beholds the heart; and so *he did not need anyone to give testimony about men*. In fact, he is the one who gives testimony: "Look, my witness is in heaven" (Jb 16:20)

His knowledge was perfect, because it extended not only to what was exterior, but even to the interior; thus he says, *He was well aware of what was in man's heart*, i.e., the secrets of the heart: "Hell and destruction are open to the Lord: how much more the hearts of the children of men" (Prv 15:11).[74]

71. *Hom. in Io.* 24. 1; PG 59, col. 143; cf. *Catena aurea*, 2:23–25.
72. *Tract. in Io.* 11. 3; PL 35, col. 1476; cf. *Catena aurea*, 2:23–25.
73. See *ST* III, q. 63, a. 6; III, q. 82, a. 1.
74. See *ST* III, q. 10, a. 2; III, q. 11, a. 1.

CHAPTER 3

LECTURE 1

1 There was a certain Pharisee named Nicodemus, a member of the Sanhedrin. 2 He came to Jesus at night and said to him, "Rabbi, we know that you are a teacher come from God, for no one could perform the signs you perform, unless he had God with him." 3 Jesus responded and said to him, "Amen, amen, I say to you, unless one is born again, he cannot see the kingdom of God." 4 Nicodemus said to him, "How can a man be born again when he is already an old man? Is it possible for him to return to his mother's womb and be born all over again?" 5 Jesus replied, "Amen, amen, I say to you, unless one is born again of water and the Holy Spirit, he cannot enter the kingdom of God. 6 What is born of flesh is itself flesh; and what is born of Spirit is itself spirit."[1]

423. Above, the Evangelist showed Christ's power in relation to changes affecting nature; here he shows it in relation to our reformation by grace, which is his principal subject. Reformation by grace comes about through spiritual generation and by the conferring of benefits on those regenerated. First, then, he treats of spiritual generation. Secondly, of the spiritual benefits divinely conferred on the regenerated, and this in chapter five.

As to the first he does two things. First, he treats of spiritual regeneration in relation to the Jews. Secondly, of the spreading of the fruits of this regeneration even to foreign peoples, and this in chapter four. Concerning the first he does two things. First, he explains spiritual regeneration with words. Secondly, he completes it with deeds (3:22).

As to the first he does three things. First, he shows the need for a spiritual regeneration. Secondly, its quality (3:4). Thirdly, its mode and nature (3:9). As to the first he does two things. First, he mentions the occasion for showing this need. Secondly, the need itself for this regeneration (3:3).

The occasion was presented by Nicodemus; hence he says, *There*

---

1. St. Thomas quotes Jn 3:1 in *ST* III, q. 51, a. 2, obj. 1; Jn 3:3 in *ST* I-II, q. 87, a. 5, obj. 2; Jn 3:4 in *ST* III, q. 66, a. 9; III, q. 67, a. 4, obj. 3; III, q. 80, a. 10, ad 1; and Jn 3:5 in *ST* I, q. 74, a. 3, ad 4; I-II, q. 112, a. 1, ad 2; III, q. 38, a. 6; III, q. 39, a. 4; III, q. 60, a. 5, *sed contra*; III, q. 66, a. 2, ad 3; III, q. 66, a. 3, *sed contra*; III, q. 66, a. 7, obj. 2; III, q. 66, a. 9; III, q. 66, obj. 10, ad 1; III, q. 68, a. 1, *sed contra*; III, q. 68, a. 2, obj. 1; III, q. 68, a. 9; III, q. 80, a. 1, obj. 1; III, q. 84, a. 7, ad 3.

was a certain Pharisee named Nicodemus. And he describes him as to his person, from the time, and from his statements.

424. He describes his person in three ways. First, as to his religion, because he was a Pharisee; hence he says, *There was a certain Pharisee*. For there were two sects among the Jews: the Pharisees and the Sadducees. The Pharisees were closer to us in their beliefs, for they believed in the resurrection, and admitted the existence of spiritual creatures. The Sadducees, on the other hand, disagree more with us, for they believed neither in the resurrection to come nor in the existence of spirits. The former were called Pharisees, as being separated from the others. And because their opinion was the more credible and nearer to the truth, it was easier for Nicodemus to be converted to Christ. "I lived as a Pharisee, according to the strictest sect of our religion" (Acts 26:5).

425. As to his name he says, *named Nicodemus*, which means "victor," or "the victory of the people." This signifies those who overcame the world through faith by being converted to Christ from Judaism. "This is the victory that overcomes the world, our faith" (1 Jn 5:4).

426. Thirdly, as to his rank he says, a *member of the Sanhedrin*. For although our Lord did not choose the wise or powerful or those of high birth at the beginning, lest the power of the faith be attributed to human wisdom and power—"Not many of you are learned in the worldly sense, not many powerful, not many of high birth. But God chose the simple ones of the world" (1 Cor 1:26)—still he willed to convert some of the wise and powerful to himself at the very beginning. And he did this so that his doctrine would not be held in contempt, as being accepted exclusively by the lowly and uneducated, and so that the number of believers would not be attributed to the rusticity and ignorance of the converts rather than to the power of the faith. However, he did not will that a large number of those converted to him be powerful and of high birth, lest, as has been said, it should be ascribed to human power and wisdom. And so it says, "many of those in authority believed in him" (below 12:42), among whom was this Nicodemus. "The rulers of the people have come together" (Ps 46:10).

427. Then he describes him as to the time, saying, he came to Jesus at night. In regard to this, it might be noted that in Scripture the quality of the time is mentioned as to certain persons in order to indicate their knowledge or the condition of their actions. Here an obscure time is mentioned, *at night*. For the night is obscure and suited to the state of mind of Nicodemus, who did not come to Jesus free of care and anxiety, but in fear; for he was one of those of whom it is said that they "believed in him; but they did not admit it because of the Pharisees, so that they would not be expelled from the synagogue" (below 12:42). For their love was not perfect, so it continues, "For they loved the glory of men more than the glory of God."

Further, night was appropriate to his ignorance and the imperfect understanding he had of Christ: "The night has passed, and day is at hand. So let us cast off the works of darkness" (Rom 13:12); "They have not known or understood; they are walking in darkness" (Ps 81:5).

428. Then he is described from his statements, when he says that Nicodemus said to Jesus: *Rabbi, we know that you are a teacher come from God.* Here he affirms Christ's office as teacher when he says, *Rabbi*, and his power of acting, saying, *for no one could perform the signs you perform, unless he had God with him.* And in both remarks he says what is true, but he does not affirm enough.

He is right in calling Jesus *Rabbi*, i.e., Teacher, because, "You call me Teacher and Lord; and you do well, for so I am," as we read below (13:13). For Nicodemus had read what was written in Joel (2:23): "Children of Zion, rejoice, and be joyful in the Lord your God, because he has given you a teacher of justice." But he says too little, because he says that Jesus came as a teacher from God, but is silent on whether he is God. For to come as a teacher from God is common to all good prelates: "I will give you shepherds after my own heart, and they will feed you with knowledge and doctrine," as it says in Jeremiah (3:15). Therefore, this is not unique to Christ even though Christ taught in a manner unlike other men. For some teachers teach only from without, but Christ also instructs within, because "He was the true light, which enlightens every man" (above 1:9); thus he alone gives wisdom: "I will give you an eloquence and a wisdom" (Lk 21:15), and this is something that no mere man can say.[2]

429. He affirms his power because of the signs he saw. As if to say: I believe that you have come as a teacher from God, *for no one could perform the signs you perform.* And he is speaking the truth, because the signs which Christ did cannot be worked except by God, and because God was with him: "he who sent me is with me" (below 8:29). But he says too little, because he believed that Christ did not perform these signs through his own power, but as relying on the power of another; as though God were not with him by a unity of essence but merely by an infusion of grace. But this is false, because Christ performed these signs not by an exterior power but by his own; for the power of God and of Christ is one and the same.[3] It is similar to what the woman says to Elijah: "Because of this I know that you are a man of God" (1 Kgs 17:24).

430. Then when he says that Jesus answered, *Amen, amen, I say to you,* he sets down the necessity for spiritual regeneration, because of the ignorance of Nicodemus. And so he says, *Amen, amen.* Here we should note that this word, *amen*, is a Hebrew word frequently employed by Christ; hence out of reverence for him no Greek or Latin

2. See *ST* III, q. 42, a. 4.
3. See *ST* III, q. 43, a. 2.

translator wanted to translate it. Sometimes it means the same as "true" or "truly"; and sometimes the same as "so be it." Thus in the Psalms 71 (v. 19), 88 (v. 53), and 105 (v. 47), where we have, "So be it, so be it," the Hebrew has "Amen, amen." But John is the only Evangelist who duplicates or makes a twin use of this word. The reason for this is that the other Evangelists are concerned mainly with matters pertaining to the humanity of Christ, which, since they are easier to believe, need less reinforcement; but John deals chiefly with things pertaining to the divinity of Christ, and these, since they are hidden and remote from men's knowledge and experience, require greater formal declaration.

431. Next we should point out that at first glance this answer of Christ seems to be entirely foreign to Nicodemus' statement. For what connection is there between Nicodemus' statement, *Rabbi, we know that you are a teacher come from God*, and the Lord's reply, *unless one is born again, he cannot see the kingdom of God*.

But we should note, as has already been stated, that Nicodemus, having an imperfect opinion about Christ, affirmed that he was a teacher and performed these signs as a mere man. And so the Lord wishes to show Nicodemus how he might arrive at a deeper understanding of him. And as a matter of fact, the Lord might have done so with an argument, but because this might have resulted in a quarrel—the opposite of which was prophesied about him: "He will not quarrel" (Is 42:2)—he wished to lead him to a true understanding with gentleness. As if to say: It is not strange that you regard me as a mere man, because one cannot know these secrets of the divinity unless he has achieved a spiritual regeneration. And this is what he says: unless one is born again, he cannot see the kingdom of God.

432. Here we should point out that since vision is an act of life, then according to the diverse kinds of life there will be diversity of vision. For there is a sentient life which some living things share in common, and this life has a sentient vision or knowledge. And there is also a spiritual life, by which man is made like God and other holy spirits; and this life enjoys a spiritual vision. Now spiritual things cannot be seen by the sentient: "The sensual man does not perceive those things that pertain to the Spirit of God" (1 Cor 2:14), but they are perceived by the spiritual vision: "No one knows the things of God but the Spirit of God" (1 Cor 2:11).[4] So the apostle says: "You did not receive the spirit of slavery, putting you in fear again, but the spirit of adoption" (Rom 8:15). And we receive this spirit through a spiritual regeneration: "He saved us by the cleansing of regeneration in the Holy Spirit" (Ti 3:3). Therefore, if spiritual vision comes only through the Holy Spirit, and if the Holy Spirit is given through a cleansing of spiritual regeneration, then it is only by a cleansing of regeneration that we can

4. See *ST* II-II, q. 1, a. 4.

see the kingdom of God. Thus he says, *unless one is born again of water and the Holy Spirit, he cannot enter the kingdom of God.* As if to say: It is not surprising if you do not see the kingdom of God, because no one can see it unless he receives the Holy Spirit, through whom one is reborn a son of God.[5]

433. It is not only the royal throne that pertains to a kingdom, but also the things needed for governing the kingdom, such as the royal dignity, royal favors, and the way of justice by which the kingdom is consolidated. Hence he says, *he cannot see the kingdom of God,* i.e., the glory and dignity of God, i.e., the mysteries of eternal salvation which are seen through the justice of faith: "The kingdom of God is not food and drink" (Rom 14:17).

Now in the Old Law there was a spiritual regeneration; but it was imperfect and symbolic: "All were baptized into Moses, in the cloud and in the sea" (1 Cor 10:2), i.e., they received baptism in symbol.[6] Accordingly, they did see the mysteries of the kingdom of God, but only symbolically: "seeing from afar" (Heb 11:13). But in the New Law there is an evident spiritual regeneration, although imperfect, because we are renewed only inwardly by grace, but not outwardly by incorruption: "Although our outward nature is wasting away, yet our inward nature is being renewed day by day" (2 Cor 4:16).[7] And so we do see the kingdom of God and the mysteries of eternal salvation, but imperfectly, for as it says, "Now we see in a mirror, in an obscure manner" (1 Cor 13:12). But there is perfect regeneration in heaven, because we will be renewed both inwardly and outwardly. And therefore we shall see the kingdom of God in a most perfect way: "But then we will see face to face," as is said in 1 Corinthians (13:12), and "When he appears we will be like him, because we will see him as he is" (1 Jn 3:2).[8]

434. It is clear, therefore, that just as one does not have bodily vision unless he is born, so one cannot have spiritual vision unless he is reborn. And according to the threefold regeneration, there is a threefold kind of vision.

435. Note that the Greek reading is not "again," but *anōthen,* i.e., "from above," which Jerome translated as "again," in order to suggest addition. And this is the way Jerome understood the saying, *unless one is born again.*[9] It is as if he were saying: Unless one is reborn once more through a fraternal generation.

5. See *ST* I-II, q. 113, a. 2; II-II, q. 6, a. 1.
6. See *ST* I-II, q. 101, a. 2; III, q. 62, a. 6; III, q. 70, a. 4.
7. See *ST* III, q. 69, a. 3.
8. See *ST* I-II, q. 106, a. 4.
9. Thomas is referring to Jerome's translation of the Latin Vulgate text for Jn 3:3, in which Jerome has selected the Latin term *denuo* ("again") rather than *desuper* ("from above") to translate the Greek term, *anōthen.* In fact, *anōthen* can mean either "again" or "from above," and Jesus appears to be intentionally playing off of this equivocation in his conversation with Nicodemus.

Chrysostom,[10] however, says that to be "born from above" is peculiar to the Son of God, because he alone is born from above: "The one who came from above is above all things" (below 3:31). And Christ is said to be born from above both as to time (if we may speak thus), because he was begotten from eternity: "Before the daystar I begot you" (Ps 109:3), and as to the principle of his generation, because he proceeds from the heavenly Father: "I came down from heaven not to do my own will, but the will of him who sent me" (below 6:38). Therefore, because our regeneration is in the likeness of the Son of God, inasmuch as "Those whom he foreknew he predestined to become conformed to the image of his Son" (Rom 8:29), and because that generation is from above, our generation also is from above: both as to the time, because of our eternal predestination, "He chose us in him before the foundation of the world" (Eph 1:4), and as to its being a gift of God, as we read below (6:44), "No one can come to me unless the Father, who sent me, draws him"; and "You have been saved by the grace of God" (Eph 2:5).[11]

436. Then when he says, **Nicodemus said to him**, he gives the manner of and the reason for this spiritual regeneration. First, the doubt of Nicodemus is set forth. Secondly, Christ's response (v. 5).

437. As to the first we should note that as stated in 1 Corinthians (2:14): "The sensual man does not perceive those things that pertain to the Spirit of God." And so because Nicodemus was yet carnal and sensual, he was unable to grasp, except in a carnal manner, the things that were said to him. Consequently, what the Lord said to him about spiritual regeneration, he understood of carnal generation. And this is what he says: **How can a man be born again when he is already an old man?**

We should note here, according to Chrysostom,[12] that Nicodemus wanted to object to what was said by the Savior. But his objection is foolish, because Christ was speaking of spiritual regeneration, and he is objecting in terms of carnal regeneration. In like manner, all the reasons brought forth to attack the things of faith are foolish, since they are not according to the meaning of Sacred Scripture.

438. Nicodemus objected to the Lord's statement that a man must be born again according to the two ways in which this seemed impossible. In one way, on account of the irreversibility of human life; for a man cannot return to infancy from old age. Hence we read, "I am walking on a path," namely, this present life, "by which I will not return" (Jb 16:23). And it is from this point of view that he says, **How can a man be born again when he is already an old man?** As if to say:

10. *Hom. in Io.* 26. 1; PG 59, col. 154; cf. *Catena aurea*, 3:1–3.
11. See *ST* I, q. 23, aa. 1, 4; III, q. 24, aa. 3–4.
12. *Hom. in Io.* 25. 1; PG 59, col. 149; cf. *Catena aurea*, 3:4–8.

Shall he become a child once more so that he can be reborn? "He will not return again to his home, and his place will not know him any more" (Jb 7:10). In the second way, regeneration seemed impossible because of the mode of carnal generation. For in the beginning, when a man is generated, he is small in size, so that his mother's womb can contain him; but later, after he is born, he continues to grow and reaches such a size that he cannot be contained within his mother's womb. And so Nicodemus says, *Is it possible for him to return to his mother's womb and be born all over again?* As if to say: He cannot, because the womb cannot contain him.

439. But this does not apply to spiritual generation. For no matter how spiritually old a man might become through sin, according to the Psalm (31:3): "Because I kept silent, all my bones grew old," he can, with the help of divine grace, become new, according to the Psalm (102:5): "Your youth will be renewed like the eagle's." And no matter how enormous he is, he can enter the spiritual womb of the Church by the sacrament of baptism. And it is clear what that spiritual womb is; otherwise it would never have been said: "From the womb, before the daystar, I begot you" (Ps 109:3). Yet there is a sense in which his objection applies. For just as a man, once he is born according to nature, cannot be reborn, so once he is born in a spiritual way through baptism, he cannot be reborn, because he cannot be baptized again: "One Lord, one faith, one baptism," as we read in Ephesians (4:5).[13]

440. Then we have the answer of Christ. Concerning this he does three things. First, he answers the arguments of Nicodemus by showing the nature of regeneration. Secondly, he explains this answer with a reason (v. 6). Thirdly, he explains it with an example.

441. He answers the objections by showing that he is speaking of a spiritual regeneration, not a carnal one. And this is what he says: *unless one is born again of water and the Holy Spirit, he cannot enter the kingdom of God.* As if to say: You are thinking of a carnal generation, but I am speaking of a spiritual generation.

Note that above he had said, *he cannot see the kingdom of God*, while here he says, *he cannot enter the kingdom of God*, which is the same thing. For no one can see the things of the kingdom of God unless he enters it; and to the extent that he enters, he sees. "I will give him a white stone upon which is written a new name, which no one knows but he who receives it" (Rev 5:5).

442. Now there is a reason why spiritual generation comes from the Spirit. It is necessary that the one generated be generated in the likeness of the one generating; but we are regenerated as sons of God, in the likeness of his true Son. Therefore, it is necessary that our spiritual regeneration come about through that by which we are made like

13. See *ST* III, q. 66, a. 9.

the true Son and this comes about by our having his Spirit: "If any one does not have the Spirit of Christ, he is not his" (Rom 8:9); "By this we know that we abide in him, and he in us: because he has given us of his Spirit" (1 Jn 4:13). Thus spiritual regeneration must come from the Holy Spirit. "You did not receive the spirit of slavery, putting you in fear again, but the spirit of adoption" (Rom 8:15); "It is the Spirit that gives life" (below 6:63).[14]

443. Water, too, is necessary for this regeneration, and for three reasons. First, because of the condition of human nature.[15] For man consists of soul and body, and if the Spirit alone were involved in his regeneration, this would indicate that only the spiritual part of man is regenerated. Hence in order that the flesh also be regenerated, it is necessary that, in addition to the Spirit through whom the soul is regenerated, something bodily be involved, through which the body is regenerated; and this is water.

Secondly, water is necessary for the sake of human knowledge. For, as Dionysius[16] says, divine wisdom so disposes all things that it provides for each thing according to its nature. Now it is natural for man to know; and so it is fitting that spiritual things be conferred on men in such a way that he may know them: "so that we may know what God has given us" (1 Cor 2:12). But the natural manner of this knowledge is that man know spiritual things by means of sensible things, since all our knowledge begins in sense knowledge.[17] Therefore, in order that we might understand what is spiritual in our regeneration, it was fitting that there be in it something sensible and material, that is, water, through which we understand that just as water washes and cleanses the exterior in a bodily way, so through baptism a man is washed and cleansed inwardly in a spiritual way.

Thirdly, water was necessary so that there might be a correspondence of causes for the cause of our regeneration is the incarnate Word: "He gave them power to become the sons of God," as we saw above (1:12). Therefore it was fitting that in the sacraments, which have their efficacy from the power of the incarnate Word, there be something corresponding to the Word, and something corresponding to the flesh, or body.[18] And spiritually speaking, this is water when the sacrament is baptism, so that through it we may be conformed to the death of Christ, since we are submerged in it during baptism as Christ was in the womb of the earth for three days: "We are buried with him by baptism" (Rom 6:4).

14. See *ST* III, q. 66, aa. 1 and 11.
15. See *ST* III, q. 60, a. 1; III, q. 61, a. 1; III, q. 66, a. 3.
16. See *De div. nom.* 4. 33; PG 3, col. 812. Thomas also refers to this Dionysian principle in the *ST*, III, q. 61, a. 1.
17. See *ST* III, q. 1, a. 1; III, q. 60, a. 4.
18. See *ST* III, q. 62, a. 5.

Further, this mystery was suggested in the first production of things, when the Spirit of God hovered over the waters (Gn 1:2). But a greater power was conferred on water by contact with the most pure flesh of Christ; because in the beginning water brought forth crawling creatures with living souls, but since Christ was baptized in the Jordan, water has yielded spiritual souls.[19]

444. It is clear that the Holy Spirit is God, since he says, **unless one is born again of water and the Holy Spirit** (ex aqua et Spiritu Sancto). For above (1:13) he says: "who are born not from blood, nor from the desires of the flesh, nor from man's willing it, but from God (ex Deo)." From this we can form the following argument: He from whom men are spiritually reborn is God; but men are spiritually reborn through the Holy Spirit, as it is stated here; therefore, the Holy Spirit is God.[20]

445. Two questions arise here. First, if no one enters the kingdom of God unless he is born again of water, and if the fathers of old were not born again of water (for they were not baptized), then they have not entered the kingdom of God. Secondly, since baptism is of three kinds, that is, of water, of desire, and of blood, and many have been baptized in the latter two ways (who we say have entered the kingdom of God immediately, even though they were not born again of water), it does not seem to be true to say that **unless one is born again of water and the Holy Spirit, he cannot enter the kingdom of God.**

The answer to the first is that rebirth or regeneration from water and the Holy Spirit takes place in two ways: in truth and in symbol. Now the fathers of old, although they were not reborn with a true rebirth, were nevertheless reborn with a symbolic rebirth, because they always had a sense perceptible sign in which true rebirth was prefigured. So according to this, thus reborn, they did enter the kingdom of God, after the ransom was paid.[21]

The answer to the second is that those who are reborn by a baptism of blood and fire, although they do not have regeneration in deed, they do have it in desire.[22] Otherwise neither would the baptism of blood mean anything nor could there be a baptism of the Spirit. Consequently, in order that man may enter the kingdom of heaven, it is necessary that there be a baptism of water in deed, as in the case of all baptized persons, or in desire, as in the case of the martyrs and catechumens, who are prevented by death from fulfilling their desire, or in symbol, as in the case of the fathers of old.

446. It might be remarked that it was from this statement, **unless one is born again of water and the Holy Spirit**, that the Pelagians de-

19. See ST III, q. 66, a. 2.
20. See ST I, q. 38, a. 1.
21. See ST I-II, q. 102, a. 4; I-II, q. 107, a. 3; III, q. 49, a. 5; III, q. 52, a. 5; III, q. 70, a. 4.
22. See ST III, q. 66, a. 11.

rived their error that children are baptized not in order to be cleansed from sin, since they have none, but in order to be able to enter the kingdom of God. But this is false, because as Augustine[23] says in his book, *The Baptism of Children*, it is not fitting for an image of God, namely, man, to be excluded from the kingdom of God except for some obstacle, which can be nothing but sin. Therefore, there must be some sin, namely, original sin, in children who are excluded from the kingdom.

447. Then when he says, **What is born of flesh is itself flesh**, he proves by reason that it is necessary to be born of water and the Holy Spirit. And the reasoning is this: No one can reach the kingdom unless he is made spiritual; but no one is made spiritual except by the Holy Spirit; therefore, no one can enter the kingdom of God unless he is born again of the Holy Spirit.[24]

So he says, **what is born of flesh** (*ex carne*) **is itself flesh**, i.e., birth according to the flesh makes one be born into the life of the flesh: "The first man was from the earth, earthly" (1 Cor 15:47); **and what is born of Spirit** (*ex Spiritu*), i.e., from the power of the Holy Spirit, **is itself spirit**, i.e., spiritual.

448. Note, however, that this preposition *ex* (from, of, by) sometimes designates a material cause, as when I say: "A knife is made of (*ex*) iron"; sometimes it designates an efficient cause, as when I say: "The house was built by (*ex*) a carpenter." Accordingly, the phrase, **what is born of** (*ex*) **flesh is itself flesh**, can be understood according to either efficient or material causality. As efficient cause, indeed, because a power existing in flesh is productive of generation; and as material cause, because some carnal element in animals makes up the animal generated. But nothing is said to be made out of spirit (*ex spiritu*) in a material sense, since spirit is unchangeable, whereas matter is the subject of change; but it is said in the sense of efficient causality.

According to this, we can discern a threefold generation. One is materially and effectively from (*ex*) the flesh, and is common to all who exist according to the flesh. Another is according to the Spirit effectively, and according to it we are reborn as sons of God through the grace of the Holy Spirit, and are made spiritual.[25] The third is midway, that is, only materially from the flesh but effectively from the Holy Spirit. And this is true in the singular case of Christ: because he was born deriving his flesh materially from the flesh of his mother, but effectively from the Holy Spirit: "What she has conceived is of the Holy Spirit" (Mt 1:20).[26] Therefore, he was born holy: "The Holy Spirit will come

23. *De bapt. parv.* 30; PL 44, col. 142; cf. *Catena aurea*, 3:4–8. See *ST* III, q. 68, a. 9.

24. See *ST* I-II, q. 113, a. 2.   25. See *ST* III, q. 23, a. 1.

26. See *ST* III, q. 32, aa. 2–3.

upon you, and the power of the Most High will overshadow you. And so the Holy One who will be born from you, will be called the Son of God" (Lk 1:35).

LECTURE 2

7 "Do not be surprised that I said to you, you must be born again. 8 The wind blows where it wills, and you hear its sound, but you do not know where it comes from or where it goes. So it is with everyone who is born of the Spirit." 9 "How can all this happen?" asked Nicodemus. 10 Jesus replied: "You are a teacher in Israel and you do not know these things? 11 "Amen, amen I say to you, that we know of what we speak, and we bear witness of what we see; but you do not accept our testimony. 12 If I spoke of earthly things, and you did not believe me, how will you believe if I tell you of heavenly things? 13 No one has gone up to heaven except the One who came down from heaven, the Son of Man, who lives in heaven. 14 Just as Moses lifted up the serpent in the desert, so must the Son of Man be lifted up, 15 so that everyone who believes in him may not be lost, but have eternal life."[27]

449. Above, in his instruction on spiritual generation, the Lord presented a reason; here he gives an example. For we are led to see that Nicodemus was troubled when he heard that *what is born of Spirit is itself spirit*. And so the Lord says to him, *Do not be surprised that I said to you, you must be born again*.

Here we should note that there are two kinds of surprise or astonishment. One is the astonishment of devotion in the sense that someone, considering the great things of God, sees that they are incomprehensible to him; and so he is full of astonishment: "The Lord on high is wonderful" (Ps 92:4), "Your testimonies are wonderful" (Ps 118:129). Men are to be encouraged, not discouraged, to this kind of astonishment.[28] The other is the astonishment of disbelief, when someone does not believe what is said. So Matthew (13:54) says: "They were astonished," and further on adds that "They did not accept him." It is from this kind of astonishment that the Lord diverts Nicodemus when he proposes an example and says: *The wind* (*spiritus*, wind, spirit) *blows where it wills*. In the literal sense, the same words can be explained in two ways.

27. St. Thomas refers to Jn 3:8 in *ST* II-II, q. 24, a. 3, *sed contra*; Jn 3:13 in *ST* III, q. 5, a. 2, ad 1; III, q. 39, a. 5, obj. 1; III, q. 55, a. 6; III, q. 57, a. 2, obj. 2; and Jn 3:14 in *ST* III, q. 18, a. 2, obj. 2; III, q. 46, a. 1, *sed contra*; III, q. 46, a. 4; III, q. 46, a. 9, obj. 2.
28. See *ST* II-II, q. 82, a. 3.

450. In the first way, according to Chrysostom,[29] *spiritus* is taken for the wind, as in Psalm 148 (v. 8): "The winds of the storm that fulfill his word." According to this interpretation, he says four things about the wind. First, the power of the wind, when he says, **the wind blows where it wills.** And if you say that the wind has no will, one may answer that "will" is taken for a natural appetite, which is nothing more than a natural inclination, about which it is said: "He created the weight of the wind" (Jb 28:25). Secondly, he tells the evidence for the wind, when he says, **and you hear its sound,** where "sound" (*vox*, voice, sound) refers to the sound the wind makes when it strikes a body. Of this we read: "The sound (*vox*) of your thunder was in the whirlwind" (Ps 76:19).

Thirdly, he mentions the origin of the wind, which is unknown; so he says, **but you do not know where it comes from,** i.e., from where it starts: "He brings forth the winds out of his storehouse" (Ps 134:7). Fourthly, he mentions the wind's destination, which is also unknown; so he says, **or where it goes** you do not know, i.e., where it remains.

And he applies this similarity to the subject under discussion, saying, **So it is with everyone who is born of the Spirit.** As if to say: If the wind, which is corporeal, has an origin which is hidden and a course that is unknown, why are you surprised if you cannot understand the course of spiritual regeneration.

451. Augustine[30] objects to this explanation and says that the Lord was not speaking here about the wind, for we know where each of the winds comes from and where it goes. For "Auster" comes from the south and goes to the north; "Boreas" comes from the north and goes to the south. Why, then, does the Lord say of this wind, you do not know where it comes from or where it goes?

One may answer that there are two ways in which the source of the wind might be unknown. In one way, in general: in this way it is possible to know where it comes from, i.e., from which direction of the world, for example that Auster comes from the south, and where it goes, that is, to the north. In another way, in particular: and in this sense it is not known where the wind comes from, i.e., at which precise place it originated, or where it goes, i.e., exactly where it stops. And almost all the Greek doctors agree with this exposition of Chrysostom.

452. In another way, *spiritus* is taken for the Holy Spirit. And according to this, he mentions four things about the Holy Spirit. First, his power, saying, **The Spirit blows where it wills,** because it is by the free use of his power that he breathes where he wills and when he wills, by instructing hearts: "One and the same Spirit does all these things,

---

29. *Hom. in Io.* 26. 2; PG 59, col. 154–155; cf. *Catena aurea*, 3:4–8.
30. *Tract. in Io.* 12. 7; PL 35, col. 1488; cf. *Catena aurea*, 3:4–8.

distributing to each as he wills" (1 Cor 12:11).[31] This refutes the error of Macedonius who thought that the Holy Spirit was the minister of the Father and the Son. But then he would not be breathing where he willed, but where he was commanded.

453. Secondly, he mentions the evidence for the Holy Spirit, when he says, *and you hear its voice*: "Today, if you hear his voice, do not harden your hearts" (Ps 94:8).

Chrysostom[32] objects to this and says that this cannot pertain to the Holy Spirit. For the Lord was speaking to Nicodemus, who was still an unbeliever, and thus not fit to hear the voice of the Holy Spirit. We may answer to this, with Augustine,[33] that there is a twofold voice of the Holy Spirit. One is that by which he speaks inwardly in man's heart; and only believers and the saints hear this voice, about which the Psalm (84:9) says: "I will hear what the Lord God says within me." The other voice is that by which the Holy Spirit speaks in the Scriptures or through those who preach, according to Matthew (10:20): "For it is not you who speak, but the Holy Spirit who is speaking through you." And this voice is heard by unbelievers and sinners.

454. Thirdly, he refers to the origin of the Holy Spirit, which is hidden; thus he says, *but you do not know where it comes from*, although you may hear its voice. And this is because the Holy Spirit comes from the Father and the Son: "When the Paraclete comes, whom I will send you from the Father, the Spirit of truth, who proceeds from the Father" (below 15:26).[34] But the Father and the Son "dwell in inaccessible light, whom no man has seen or is able to see" (1 Tim 6:16).

455. Fourthly, he gives the destination of the Holy Spirit, which is also hidden: and so he says, you do not know *where it goes*, because the Spirit leads one to a hidden end, that is, eternal happiness. Thus it says in Ephesians (1:14) that the Holy Spirit is "the pledge of our inheritance." And again, "The eye has not seen, nor has the ear heard, nor has the heart of man conceived, what God has prepared for those who love him" (1 Cor 2:9).

Or, *you do not know where it comes from*, i.e., how the Spirit enters into a person, *or where it goes*, i.e., to what perfection he may lead him: "If he comes toward me, I will not see him" (Jb 9:11).

456. *So it is with everyone who is born of the Spirit*, i.e., they are like the Holy Spirit. And no wonder: for as he had said before, "What is born of Spirit is itself spirit," because the qualities of the Holy Spirit are present in the spiritual man, just as the qualities of fire are present in burning coal.

---

31. See *ST* I, q. 36, a. 1.
32. *Hom. in Io.* 26. 2; PG 59, col. 155; cf. *Catena aurea*, 3:4–8.
33. See *Quaest. ex Novo Test.*, q. 59; PL 35, col. 2254–55.
34. See *ST* I, q. 36, a. 2.

Therefore, the above four qualities of the Holy Spirit are found in one who has been born of the Holy Spirit. First of all, he has freedom: "Where the Spirit of the Lord is, there is freedom" (2 Cor 3:17), for the Holy Spirit leads us to what is right: "Your good Spirit will lead me to the right path" (Ps 142:10); and he frees us from the slavery of sin and of the law: "The law of the Spirit, of life in Christ, has set me free" (Rom 8:2). Secondly, we get an indication of him through the sound of his words; and when we hear them we know his spirituality, for it is out of the abundance of the heart that the mouth speaks.

Thirdly, he has an origin and an end that are hidden, because no one can judge one who is spiritual: "The spiritual man judges all things, and he himself is judged by no one" (1 Cor 2:15). Or, we do not know where such a person comes from, i.e., the source of his spiritual birth, which is baptismal grace; or where he goes, i.e., of what he is made worthy, that is, of eternal life, which remains concealed from us.

457. Then the cause and reason for spiritual regeneration are set forth. First, a question is asked by Nicodemus; secondly, the Lord's answer is given (v. 10).

458. It is apparent from the first that Nicodemus, as yet dull, and remaining a Jew on the level of sense, was unable to understand the mysteries of Christ in spite of the examples and explanations that were given. And so he says, *How can all this happen?*

There are two reasons why one may question about something. Some question because of disbelief, as did Zechariah, saying: "How will I know this? For I am an old man, and my wife is advanced in age" (Lk 1:18); "He confounds those who search into mysteries" (Is 40:23). Others, on the other hand, question because of a desire to know, as the Blessed Virgin did when she said to the angel: "How shall this be, since I do not know man?" (Lk 1:34). It is the latter who are instructed. And so, because Nicodemus asked from a desire to learn, he deserved to be instructed.

459. And this is what follows: Jesus replied. First the Lord chides him for his slowness. Secondly, he answers his question (v. 13).

460. He chides him for his slowness, basing himself on three things. First, the condition of the person to whom he is speaking, when he says, *You are a teacher in Israel.* And here the Lord did not chide him to insult him. Rather, because Nicodemus, presuming on his own knowledge, was still relying on his status as a teacher, the Lord wished to make him a temple of the Holy Spirit by humbling him: "For whom will I have regard? For he who is humble and of contrite spirit" (Is 66:2). And he says, *You are a teacher*, because it is tolerable if a simple person cannot grasp profound truths, but in a teacher, it deserves rebuke. And so he says, You are a teacher, i.e., of the letter that kills (2 Cor 3:6), *and you do not know these things?* i.e., spiritual things.

"For although you ought to be teachers by now, you yourselves need
to be taught again" (Heb 5:12).

461. You might say that the Lord would have rebuked Nicodemus
justly if he had spoken to him about matters of the Old Law and he
did not understand them; but he spoke to him about the New Law. I
answer that the things which the Lord says of spiritual generation are
contained in the Old Law, although under a figure, as is said in 1 Corinthians (10:2): "All were baptized into Moses, in the cloud and in the
sea." And the prophets also said this: "I will pour clean water upon
you, and you will be cleansed from all your uncleanness" (Ez 36:25).[35]

462. Secondly, he rebukes him for his slowness on account of the
character of the person who is speaking. For it is tolerable if one does
not acquiesce to the statements of an ignorant person; but it is reprehensible to reject the statements of a man who is wise and who possesses great authority. And so he says, *Amen, amen I say to you, that
we know of what we speak, and we bear witness of what we see.* For a
qualified witness must base his testimony on hearing or sight: "What
we have seen and heard" (1 Jn 1:3). And so the Lord mentions both:
we know of what we speak, and we bear witness, of what we see. Indeed, the Lord as man knows all things: "Lord, you know all things"
(below 21:17); "The Lord, whose knowledge is holy, knows clearly"
(2 Mc 6:30). Further, he sees all things by his divine knowledge: "I
speak of what I have seen with my Father," as we read below (8:38).[36]

He speaks in the plural, *we know, we see,* in order to suggest the
mystery of the Trinity: "The Father, who dwells in me, he does the
works" (below 14:10). Or, we know, i.e., I, and others who have been
made spiritual, because "No one knows the Father but the Son, and he
to whom the Son wishes to reveal him" (Mt 11:27).

But you do not accept our testimony, so approved, so solid. "And his
testimony no one accepts" (below 3:32).

463. Thirdly, he rebukes him for his slowness because of the quality of the things under discussion. For it is not unusual when someone
does not grasp difficult matters, but it is inexcusable not to grasp easy
things. So he says, *If I spoke of earthly things, and you did not believe,
how will you believe if I tell you of heavenly things?* As if to say: If you
do not grasp these easy things, how will you be able to understand the
progress of the Holy Spirit? "What is on earth we find difficult, and
who will search out the things in heaven," as is said in Wisdom (9:16).

464. But one might object that the above does not show that the
Lord spoke of earthly things to Nicodemus. I answer, according to
Chrysostom,[37] that the Lord's statement, *If I spoke of earthly things,* re-

35. See *ST* I-II, q. 101, a. 2.
36. See *ST* III, q. 9, a. 1.
37. *Hom. in Io.* 27. 1; PG 59, col. 157.

fers to the example of the wind. For the wind, being something which is generable and corruptible, is regarded as an earthly thing. Or one might say, again according to Chrysostom,[38] that the spiritual generation which is given in baptism is heavenly as to its source, which sanctifies and regenerates; but it is earthly as to its subject, for the one regenerated, man, is of the earth.

Or one might answer, according to Augustine,[39] that we must understand this in reference to what Christ said earlier: "Destroy this temple," which is earthly, because he said this about the temple of his body, which he had taken from the earth.

If I spoke of earthly things, and you did not believe, how will you believe if I tell you of heavenly things? As if to say: If you do not believe in a spiritual generation occurring in time, how will you believe in the eternal generation of the Son? Or, if you do not believe what I tell you about the power of my body, how will you believe what I tell you about the power of my divinity and about the power of the Holy Spirit?

465. *Jesus replied.* Here he answers the question. First, he lays down the causes of spiritual regeneration. Secondly, he explains what he says (3:16). Now there are two causes of spiritual regeneration, namely, the mystery of the Incarnation of Christ, and his passion. So first, he treats of the Incarnation; secondly, of the passion (3:14).

466. Here we should consider, first of all, how this answer of Christ is an adequate reply to the question of Nicodemus. For above, when the Lord was speaking of the Spirit, he said: *you do not know where it comes from or where it goes.* We understand by this that spiritual regeneration has a hidden source and a hidden end. Now the things in heaven are hidden from us: "Who will search out the things in heaven?" (Wis 9:16). Therefore, the sense of Nicodemus' question, *How can all this happen?* is this: How can something come from the secret things of heaven or go to the secret things of heaven? So before answering, the Lord expressed this interpretation of the question, saying, *how will you believe if I tell you of heavenly things?*

And immediately he begins to show whose prerogative it is to ascend into heaven, namely, anyone who came down from heaven, according to the statement of Ephesians (4:10): "He who descended is he who ascended." This is verified even in natural things, namely, that each body tends to a place according to its origin or nature. And so in this way it can come about that someone, through the Spirit, may go to a place which carnal persons do not know, i.e., by ascending into heaven, if this is done through the power of one who descended from heaven: because he descended in order that, in ascending, he might open

38. Ibid; cf. *Catena aurea*, 3:9–12.
39. *Tract in Io.* 12. 7; PL 35, col. 1488; cf. *Catena aurea*, 3:9–12.

a way for us: "He ascends, opening the way before them" (Mic 2:13).

467. Some have fallen into error because of his saying, *the One who came down from heaven, the Son of Man*. For since Son of Man designates human nature, which is composed of soul and body, then because he says that the Son descended from heaven, Valentinus wanted to maintain that he even took his body from heaven and thus passed through the Virgin without receiving anything from her, as water passes through a pipe; so that his body was neither of an earthly substance nor taken from the Virgin. But this is contrary to the statement of the Apostle, writing to the Romans (1:3): "who was made from the seed of David according to the flesh."[40]

On the other hand, Origen[41] said that he descended from heaven as to his soul, which, he says, had been created along with the angels from the very beginning, and that later this soul descended from heaven and took flesh from the Virgin. But this also conflicts with the Catholic faith, which teaches that souls do not exist before their bodies.

468. Therefore, we should not understand that the Son of Man descended from heaven according to his human nature, but only according to his divine nature. For since in Christ there is one suppositum, or hypostasis, or person of the two natures, the divine and human natures, then no matter from which of these two natures this suppositum is named, divine and human things can be attributed to him. For we can say that the Son of Man created the stars and that the Son of God was crucified. But the Son of God was crucified, not according to his divine nature, but according to his human nature; and the Son of Man created the stars according to his divine nature. And so in things that are said of Christ, the distinction is not to be taken with respect to that about which they are said, because divine and human things are said of God and man indifferently; but a distinction must be made with respect to that according to which they are said, because divine things are said of Christ according to his divine nature, but human things according to his human nature. Thus, to descend from heaven is said of the Son of Man, not according to his human nature, but according to his divine nature, according to which it was appropriate to him to have been from heaven before the Incarnation, as is said, "Heaven belongs to the Lord" (Ps 113:24).[42]

469. He is said to have come down, but not by local motion, because then he would not have remained in heaven; for nothing which moves locally remains in the place from which it comes down. And so to exclude local motion, he adds, *who lives in heaven*. As if to say: He descended from heaven in such a way as yet to be in heaven. For he came

40. See *ST* III, q. 31, a. 1.
41. See Origen, *Comm. in Io.* XX. 4, no. 17; PG 14, col. 580B–C.
42. See *ST* III, q. 16, aa. 4–5, 11.

down from heaven without ceasing to be above, yet assuming a nature which is from below. And because he is not enclosed or held fast by his body which exists on earth, he was, according to his divinity, in heaven and everywhere. And therefore to indicate that he is said to have come down in this way, because he assumed a [human] nature, he said, *the Son of Man* came down, i.e., insofar as he became Son of Man.[43]

470. Or it can be said, as Hilary[44] does, that he came down from heaven as to his body: not that the material of Christ's body came down from heaven, but that the power which formed it was from heaven.

471. But why does he say, *No one has gone up to heaven except the Son of Man, who lives in heaven?* For have not Paul and Peter and the other saints gone up, according to 2 Corinthians (5:1): "We have a house in the heavens." I answer that no one goes up into heaven except Christ and his members, i.e., those believers who are just. Accordingly, the Son of God came down from heaven in order that, by making us his members, he might prepare us to ascend into heaven: now, indeed, in hope, but later in reality. "He has raised us up, and has given us a place in heaven in Christ Jesus" (Eph 2:6).[45]

472. Here he mentions the mystery of the passion, in virtue of which baptism has its efficacy: "We who have been baptized into Christ Jesus, have been baptized into his death" (Rom 6:3).[46] And with regard to this he does three things. First, he gives a symbol for the passion. Secondly, the manner of the passion. Thirdly, the fruit of the passion.

473. He takes the symbol from the Old Law, in order to adapt to the understanding of Nicodemus; so he says, *Just as Moses lifted up the serpent in the desert.* This refers to Numbers (21:5) when the Lord, faced with the Jewish people saying, "We are sick of this useless food," sent serpents to punish them; and when the people came to Moses and he interceded with the Lord, the Lord commanded that for a remedy they make a serpent of bronze; and this was to serve both as a remedy against those serpents and as a symbol of the Lord's passion. Hence it says that this bronze serpent was lifted up as a sign (Nm 21:9).

Now it is characteristic of serpents that they are poisonous, but not so the serpent of bronze, although it was a symbol of a poisonous serpent. So, too, Christ did not have sin, which is also a poison: "Sin, when it is fully developed, brings forth death" (Jas 1:15); but he had the likeness of sin: "God sent his own Son, in the likeness of sinful flesh" (Rom 8:3).[47] And thus Christ had the effect of the serpent against the insurgence of inflamed concupiscences.

43. See *ST* III, q. 5, a. 2, ad 1.
44. *De Trin.* X. 16; PL 10, col 355A; cf. *Catena aurea*, 3:13.
45. See *ST* III, q. 57, a. 6.
46. See *ST* III, q. 62, a. 5; III, q. 66, a. 2.
47. See *ST* III, q. 14, a. 1; III, q. 15, a. 1.

474. He shows the manner of the passion when he says, *so must the Son of Man be lifted up*: and this refers to the lifting up of the cross. So below (12:34) when it says, "The Son of Man must be lifted up," it also has, "He said this to indicate the manner of his death."

He willed to die lifted up, first of all, to cleanse the heavens: for since he had cleansed the things on earth by the sanctity of his life, the things of the air were left to be cleansed by his death: "through him he should reconcile all things to himself, whether on earth or in the heavens, making peace through his blood" (Col 1:20). Secondly, to triumph over the demons who prepare for war in the air: "the prince of the power of the air" (Eph 2:2). Thirdly, he wished to die lifted up to draw our hearts to himself: "I, if I am lifted up from the earth, will draw all to myself" (below 12:32). And fourthly, because in the death of the cross he was lifted up in the sense that there he triumphed over his enemies; so it is not called a death, but a lifting up: "He will drink from the stream on the way, therefore he will lift up his head" (Ps 109:7). Fifthly, he willed to die lifted up because the cross was the reason for his being lifted up, i.e., exalted: "He became obedient to the Father even to death, the death of the cross; on account of which God has exalted him" (Phil 2:8).[48]

475. Now the fruit of Christ's passion is eternal life; hence he says, *so that everyone who believes in him*, performing good works, *may not be lost, but have eternal life*. And this fruit corresponds to the fruit of the symbolic serpent. For whoever looked upon the serpent of bronze was freed from poison and his life was preserved. But he who looks upon the lifted up Son of Man, and believes in the crucified Christ, he is freed from poison and sin: "Whoever believes in me will never die" (below 11:26), and is preserved for eternal life. "These things are written that You may believe . . . and that believing you may have life in his name" (below 20:31).[49]

LECTURE 3

16 *"For God so loved the world that he gave his Only Begotten Son, so that whoever believes in him should not perish, but have eternal life. 17 God did not send his Son into the world to judge the world, but that the world might be saved through him. 18 Whoever believes in him is not judged; but whoever does not believe is already judged, since he does not believe in the name of the Only Begotten Son of God. 19 The judgment of condemnation is this: the light came into the world,*

48. See *ST* III, q. 46, a. 4.
49. See *ST* III, q. 49, a. 5.

and men loved darkness more than the light, because their deeds were evil. 20 Everyone who practices evil hates the light, and does not approach the light for fear that his deeds might be exposed. 21 But everyone who practices the truth comes to the light, to make clear that his deeds are done in God."[50]

476. Above, the Lord assigned as the cause of spiritual regeneration the coming down of the Son and the lifting up of the Son of Man; and he set forth its fruit, which is eternal life. But this fruit seemed unbelievable to men laboring under the necessity of dying. And so now the Lord explains this. First, he proves the greatness of the fruit from the greatness of God's love. Secondly, he rejects a certain reply (v. 17).

477. Here we should note that the cause of all our good is the Lord and divine love.[51] For to love is, properly speaking, to will good to someone. Therefore, since the will of God is the cause of things, good comes to us because God loves us. And God's love is the cause of the good of nature: "You love everything which exists" (Wis 11:25). It is also the cause of the good which is grace: "I have loved You with an everlasting love, and so I have drawn you" i.e., through grace (Jer 31:3). But it is because of his great love that he gives us the good of glory. So he shows us here, from four standpoints, that this love of God is the greatest.

First, from the person of the one loving, because it is God who loves, and immeasurably.[52] So he says, **For God so loved**: "He has loved the people; all the holy ones are in his hand" (Dt 33:3). Secondly, from the condition of the one who is loved, because it is man, a bodily creature of the world, i.e., existing in sin: "God shows his love for us, because while we were still his enemies, we were reconciled to God by the death of his Son" (Rom 5:8). Thus he says, **the world**. Thirdly, from the greatness of his gifts, for love is shown by a gift; as Gregory[53] says: "The proof of love is given by action." But God has given us the greatest of gifts, his Only Begotten Son: and so he says, **that he gave his Only Begotten Son**. "God did not spare his own Son, but delivered him up for all of us" (Rom 8:32).[54]

He says his Son, i.e., his natural Son, consubstantial, not an adopted son, i.e., not those sons of which the Psalmist says: "I said: You are gods" (Ps 81:6). This shows that the opinion of Arius is false: for if the

50. St. Thomas quotes Jn 3:16 in *ST* I, q. 38, a. 2, ad 1; III, q. 4, a. 5, obj. 2; Jn 3:21 in *ST* I, q. 17, a. 1; I-II, q. 102, a. 3; III, q. 1, a. 2, *sed contra*; III, q. 32, a. 1; III, q. 49, a. 4, obj. 2; Jn 3:17 in *ST* III, q. 44, a. 3; Jn 3:19 in *ST* III, q. 1, a. 4; and Jn 3:20 in *ST* I-II, q. 18, a. 1, *sed contra*.
51. See *ST* I, q. 6, a. 4; I, q. 20, a. 2.
52. See *ST* I, q. 20, a. 3.
53. *XL hom. in Evang.*, II, *Hom*. 30. 1; PL 76, col. 1220.
54. See *ST* III, q. 47, a. 3.

Son of God were a creature, as he said, the immensity of God's love through the taking on of infinite goodness, which no creature can receive, could not have been revealed in him. He further says *Only Begotten*, to show that God does not have a love divided among many sons, but all of it is for that Son whom he gave to prove the immensity of his love: "For the Father loves the Son, and shows him everything that he does" (below 5:20).[55]

Fourthly, from the greatness of its fruit, because through him we have eternal life. Hence he says, *so that whoever believes in him should not perish, but have eternal life*, which he obtained for us through the death of the cross.[56]

478. But did God give his Son with the intention that he should die on the cross? He did indeed give him for the death of the cross inasmuch as he gave him the will to suffer on it. And he did this in two ways. First, because as the Son of God he willed from eternity to assume flesh and to suffer for us; and this will he had from the Father. Secondly, because the will to suffer was infused into the soul of Christ by God.[57]

479. Note that above, when the Lord was speaking about the coming down which belongs to Christ according to his divinity, he called him the Son of God; and this because of the one suppositum of the two natures, as was explained above. And so divine things can be said about the suppositum of the human nature, and human things can be said about the suppositum of the divine nature, but not with reference to the same nature. Rather, divine things are said with reference to the divine nature, and human things with reference to the human nature.[58] Now the specific reason why he here calls him the Son of God is that he set forth that gift as a sign of the divine love, through which the fruit of eternal life comes to us. And so, he should have been called by that name which indicates the power that produces eternal life; and this power is not in Christ as Son of Man but as Son of God: "This is the true God and eternal life," as we read in 1 John (5:20); "in him was life" (above 1:4).

480. Note also that he says, *should not perish*. Someone is said to be perishing when he is hindered from arriving at the end to which he is ordained. But the end to which man is ordained is eternal life, and as long as he sins, he turns himself from that end. And although while he is living he cannot entirely perish in the sense that he cannot be restored, yet when he dies in sin, then he entirely perishes: "The way of the wicked will perish" (Ps 1:6).

55. See *ST* I, q. 37, a. 2.
56. See *ST* III, q. 49, a. 3, especially ad 3.
57. See *ST* III, q. 47, a. 3.
58. See *ST* III, q. 16, a. 5.

He indicates the immensity of God's love in saying, *have eternal life*: for by giving eternal life, he gives himself. For eternal life is nothing else than enjoying God.[59] But to give oneself is a sign of great love: "But God, who is rich in mercy, has brought us to life in Christ" (Eph 2:5), i.e., he gave us eternal life.

481. Here the Lord excludes an objection that might be made. For in the Old Law it was promised that the Lord would come to judge: "The Lord will come to judge" (Is 3:14). So someone might say that the Son of God had not come to give eternal life but in order to judge the world. The Lord rejects this. First, he shows that he has not come to judge. Secondly, he proves it (v. 18).

482. So he says: The Son of God has not come to judge, because *God did not send his Son*, referring to his first coming, *into the world to judge the world, but that the world might be saved through him*. The same thing is found below (12:47): "I did not come to judge the world, but to save the world."

Now man's salvation is to attain to God: "My salvation is in God" (Ps 61:8). And to attain to God is to obtain eternal life; hence to be saved is the same as to have eternal life. However, because the Lord says, "I did not come to judge the world," men should not be lazy or abuse God's mercy, or give themselves over to sin: because although in his first coming he did not come to judge but to forgive, yet in his second coming, as Chrysostom[60] says, he will come to judge but not to forgive. "At the appointed time I will judge with rigor" (Ps 74:3).

483. However, this seems to conflict with what is said below (9:39): "I came into this world to judge." I answer that there are two kinds of judgment. One is the judgment of distinction, and the Son has come for this in his first coming; because with his coming men are distinguished, some by blindness and some by the light of grace. The other is the judgment of condemnation; and he did not come for this as such.

484. Now he proves what he had said, as though by a process of elimination, in the following way: Whoever will be judged will be either a believer or an unbeliever. But I have not come to judge unbelievers, because they are already judged. Therefore, from the outset, God did not send his Son to judge the world.[61] So first he shows that believers are not judged. Secondly, that unbelievers are not judged (v. 18).

485. He says therefore: I have not come to judge the world: because he did not come to judge believers, for *Whoever believes in him is not judged*, with the judgment of condemnation, with which no one who believes in him with faith informed by love is judged: "Whoever believes . . . will not encounter judgment, but will pass from death to

---

59. See *ST* I-II, q. 3, a. 8; I-II, q. 4, a. 1.
60. *Hom. in Io.* 28. 1; PG 59, col. 162; cf. *Catena aurea*, 3:16–18.
61. See *ST* III, q. 1, aa. 1–4.

life" (below 5:24). But he is judged with the judgment of reward and approval, of which the Apostle says: "It is the Lord who judges me" (1 Cor 4:4).

486. But will there be many believing sinners who will not be damned? I reply that some heretics [e.g., Origen] have said that no believer, however great a sinner he may be, will be damned, but he will be saved by reason of his foundation of salvation, namely, his faith, although he may suffer some [temporary] punishment. They take as the basis of their error the statement of the Apostle: "No one can lay a foundation other that the one that has been laid, that is, Jesus Christ" (1 Cor 3:11); and further on: "If a man's building burns . . . he himself will be saved as one fleeing through fire" (3:15).

But this view is clearly contrary to what the Apostle says in Galatians (5:1): "It is obvious what proceeds from the flesh: lewd conduct, impurity, licentiousness . . . Those who do such things will not inherit the kingdom of God." Therefore we must say that the foundation of salvation is not faith without charity (unformed faith), but faith informed by charity.[62] Significantly therefore the Lord did not say, "whoever believes him," but *whoever believes in him*, that is, whoever by believing tends toward him through love *is not judged*, because he does not sin mortally, thereby removing the foundation.[63]

Or one could say, following Chrysostom,[64] that everyone who acts sinfully is not a believer: "They profess to know God, but they deny him by their actions" (Ti 1:16); but only one who acts worthily: "Show me your faith by your works" (Jas 2:18). It is only such a one who is not judged and not condemned for unbelief.

487. Here [the Lord] shows that unbelievers are not judged. First he makes the statement; secondly, he explains it (v. 19).

488. Concerning the first we should note, according to Augustine, that Christ does not say, "whoever does not believe is judged," but rather *is not judged*. This can be explained in three ways. For, according to Augustine,[65] whoever does not believe is not judged, because he is already judged, not in fact, but in God's foreknowledge, that is, it is already known to God that he will be condemned: "The Lord knows who are his" (2 Tim 2:19). In another way: according to Chrysostom,[66] *whoever does not believe is already judged*, that is, the very fact that he does not believe is for him a condemnation: for not to believe is not to adhere to the light—which is to live in darkness, and this is a momentous condemnation: "All were bound with one chain of darkness"

62. See *ST* II-II, q. 4, a. 3.
63. See *ST* II-II, q. 2, a. 2.
64. *Hom. in Io.* 28. 1; PG 59, col. 163; cf. *Catena aurea*, 3:16–18.
65. *Tract. in Io.* 12. 12; PL 35, col. 1490; cf. *Catena aurea*, 3:16–18.
66. *Hom. in Io.* 28. 2; PG 59, col. 163; cf. *Catena aurea*, 3:16–18.

(Wis 17:17). "What kind of joy can I have; I who sit in darkness and do not see the light of heaven?" (Tb 5:12). In a third way: also according to Chrysostom,[67] *whoever does not believe is not judged*, that is, being already condemned, he displays the obvious reason for his condemnation. This is like saying that a person who is proven guilty of death is already dead, even before the sentence of death has been passed on him, because he is as good as dead.

Hence Gregory[68] says that in passing judgments there is a twofold order. Some will be sentenced by a trial; such are the ones who have something not deserving of condemnation, namely, the good of faith, that is, sinners who believe. But unbelievers, whose reason for condemnation is manifest, are sentenced without trial; and of these it is said, *whoever does not believe is already judged*. "In judgment the wicked will not stand" (Ps 1:5), that is, stand in trial.

489. It should be noted that to be judged is the same as to be condemned; and to be condemned is to be shut out from salvation, to which only one road leads, that is, the name of the Son of God: "There is no other name under heaven given to men, by which we are saved" (Acts 4:12); "O God, save me by your name" (Ps 53:3). Therefore, those who do not believe in the Son of God are cut off from salvation, and the cause of their damnation is evident.[69]

490. Here the Lord explains his statement that unbelievers have an evident cause for their condemnation. First, he sets forth the sign which shows this. Secondly, the fittingness of this sign (v. 20).

491. In the sign he sets forth he does three things. First, he mentions the gift of God. Secondly, the perversity of mind in unbelievers. Thirdly, the cause of this perversity.

So he says: It is abundantly clear that *whoever does not believe is already judged*, because *the light came into the world*. For men were in the darkness of ignorance, and God destroyed this darkness by sending a light into the world so that men might know the truth: "I am the light of the world. He who follows me does not walk in darkness, but will have the light of life" (below 8:12), "To enlighten those who sit in darkness and in the shadow of death" (Lk 1:78). Now the light came into the world because men could not come to it: for "He dwells in inaccessible light, whom no man has seen or is able to see" (1 Tim 6:16).

It is also clear from the perversity of mind in unbelievers who *loved darkness more then the light*, i.e., they preferred to remain in the darkness of ignorance rather than be instructed by Christ: "They have rebelled against the light" (Jb 24:13); "Woe to you who substitute darkness for light, and light for darkness" (Is 5:20).[70]

67. Ibid.; cf. *Catena aurea*, 3:16–18.
68. See *Mor.* 26. 27; PL 76, col. 379C; cf. *Catena aurea*, 3:16–18.
69. See *ST* II-II, q. 2, a. 7.
70. See *ST* II-II, q. 10, a. 1.

And the cause of this perversity is that *their deeds were evil*: and such deeds do not conform to the light but seek the darkness: "Let us cast off the works of darkness" (Rom 13:12), i.e., sins, which seek the darkness; "Those who sleep, sleep at night" (1 Thes 5:7); "The eye of the adulterer watches for the darkness," as we read in Job (24:15). Now it is by withdrawing from the light, which is unpleasant to him, that one does not believe the light.

492. But do all unbelievers produce evil works? It seems not: for many Gentiles have acted with virtue; for example, Cato, and many others. I answer, with Chrysostom,[71] that is it one thing to work by reason of virtue, and another by reason of a natural aptitude or disposition. For some act well because of their natural disposition, because their temperament is not inclined in a contrary way. And even unbelievers can act well in this way. For example, one may live chastely because he is not assailed by concupiscence; and the same for the other virtues. But those who act well by reason of virtue do not depart from virtue, in spite of inclinations to the contrary vice, because of the rightness of their reason and the goodness of their will; and this is proper to believers.[72]

Or, one might answer that although unbelievers may have done good things, they do not do them for love of virtue but out of vainglory. Further, they did not do all things well; for they failed to render to God the worship due him.

493. Then when he says, *Everyone who practices evil hates the light,* he shows the appropriateness of the sign he used. First, with respect to those who are evil. Secondly, with respect to the good.

494. So he says: The reason why they did not love the light is that their works were evil. And this is plain because *Everyone who practices evil hates the light.* He does not say, "practiced," but rather *practices*: because if someone has acted in an evil way, but has repented and is sorry, seeing that he has done wrong, such a person does not hate the light but comes to the light. But *Everyone who practices evil,* i.e., persists in evil, is not sorry, nor does he come to the light, but he hates it, not because it reveals truth, but because it reveals a person's sins. For an evil person still wants to know the light and the truth; but he hates to be unmasked by it. "If the dawn suddenly appears, they regard it as the shadow of death" (Jb 24:17). And so he *does not approach the light;* and this *for fear that his deeds might be exposed.* For no one who is unwilling to desert evil wants to be rebuked; this is fled from and hated. "They hate the one who rebukes at the city gate" (Am 5:10); "A corrupt man does not love the one who rebukes him" (Prv 15:12).

71. *Hom. in Io.* 28. 2; PG 59, col. 164; cf. *Catena aurea,* 3:19–21.
72. See *ST* I-II, q. 63, a. 2; I-II, q. 65, a. 2; I-II, q. 109, aa. 2 and 8; II-II, q. 4, a. 7; II-II, q. 10, a. 4.

495. Now he shows the same things with respect to the good, who practice the truth, i.e., perform good works. For truth is found not only in thought and words, but also in deeds. Every one of these *comes to the light.*

But did anyone practice the truth before Christ? It seems not, for to practice the truth is not to sin; and "before Christ all have sinned" (Rom 3:23). I answer, according to Augustine,[73] that he practices the truth in himself who is displeased at the evil he has done; and after leaving the darkness, keeps himself from sin, and repenting of the past, *comes to the light,* with the special intention of making his actions known.

496. But this conflicts with the teaching that no one should make public the good he has done; and this was a reason why the Lord rebuked the Pharisees. I answer that it is lawful to want one's works to be seen by God so that they may be approved: "It is not the one who commends himself who is approved, but the one whom God commends" (2 Cor 10:18); "My witness is in heaven," as is said in Job (16:20). It is also lawful to want them to be seen by one's own conscience, so that one may rejoice: "Our glory is this: the testimony of our conscience" (2 Cor 1:12). But it is reprehensible to want them to be seen by men in order to be praised or for one's own glory.[74] Yet, holy persons desire that their good works be known to men for the sake of God's glory and for the good of the faith: "Let your light so shine before men that they may see your good works, and glorify your Father in heaven" (Mt 5:16).[75] Such a person *comes to the light to make clear that his deeds are done in God,* that is, according to God's commandment or through the grace of God. For whatever good we do, whether it be avoiding sin, repenting of what has been done, or doing good works, it is all from God: "You have accomplished all our works" (Is 26:12).[76]

LECTURE 4

22 After this Jesus and his disciples came to Judean territory; he stayed there with his disciples and was baptizing. 23 But John also was baptizing at Aenon near Salim, where the water was plentiful, and people kept coming and were baptized. 24 John, of course, had not yet been thrown into prison. 25 A controversy arose between the disciples of John and the Jews concerning purification. 26 They went to

---

73. *Tract. in Io.* 12. 13; PL 35, col. 1491; cf. *Catena aurea,* 3:19–21.
74. See *ST* II-II, q. 132, a. 1.   75. See *ST* II-II, q. 129, a. 3.
76. See *ST* I, q. 105, a. 5.

John and said to him, "Rabbi, the man who was with you across the Jordan, the one of whom you have given testimony, he is here baptizing, and all the people are flocking to him."[77]

497. Above, the Lord gave us his teaching on spiritual regeneration in words; here he completes his teaching through action, by baptizing. First, two kinds of baptism are mentioned. Secondly, a question about their relationship is raised (v. 25). As to the first, two things are done. Mention is first made of the baptism of Christ. Secondly, of the baptism of John.

498. He says first, *After this*, i.e., the teaching on spiritual regeneration, *Jesus and his disciples came to Judean territory*. There is a question here about the literal meaning. For above, the Evangelist had said that the Lord had come from Galilee to Jerusalem, which is in Judean territory, where he taught Nicodemus. So how, after teaching Nicodemus, can he come into Judea, since he was already there?

Two answers are given to this. According to Bede,[78] after his discussion with Nicodemus, Christ went to Galilee, and after remaining there for a time, returned to Judea. And so *After this Jesus and his disciples came to Judean territory*, should not be understood to mean that he came into Judea immediately after his talk with Nicodemus. Another explanation, given by Chrysostom,[79] is that he did come into the territory of Judea immediately after this discussion: for Christ wanted to preach where the people gathered, so that many might be converted: "I have declared your justice in the great assembly" (Ps 39:10); "I have spoken openly to the world" (below 18:20).[80] Now there were two places in Judea where the Jewish people gathered: Jerusalem, where they went for their feasts, and the Jordan, where they gathered on account of John's preaching and his baptism. And so the Lord used to visit both places; and after the feast days were over in Jerusalem, which is in one part of Judea, he went to another part, to the Jordan, where John was baptizing.

499. As for the moral sense, Judea means "confession," to which Jesus came, for Christ visits those who confess their sins or speak in praise of God: "Judea became his sanctuary" (Ps 113:2). *He stayed there*, because he did not make a merely temporary visit: "We will come to him, and make our abode with him," as it says below (14:23). *And was baptizing*, i.e., cleansing from sin; because unless one confesses his sins he

77. St. Thomas refers to Jn 3:22 in *ST* III, q. 69, a. 7, obj. 2; III, q. 73, a. 5, ad 4; and Jn 3:22–23 in *ST* III, q. 38, a. 5, *sed contra*.
78. See *Glossa ordinaria, Evang. Ioannis*; PL 114, col. 368 D; cf. *Catena aurea*, 3:22–26.
79. *Hom. in Io.* 29. 1; PG 59, col. 166–167; cf. *Catena aurea*, 3:22–26.
80. See *ST* III, q. 42, a. 3.

does not obtain forgiveness: "He who hides his sins will not prosper" (Prv 28:13).[81]

500. Then when he says, **But John also was baptizing**, the Evangelist presents the baptism of John. And in regard to this he does four things. First, he presents the person who is baptizing. Secondly, the place of the baptism. Thirdly, its fruit. Fourthly, the time.

501. John is the person who is baptizing; so he says, John also was **baptizing**. There is a question about this: Since John's baptism was ordained to the baptism of Christ, it seems that John should have stopped baptizing when Christ started to baptize, just as the symbol does not continue when the truth comes. Three reasons are given for this.[82] The first is in relation to Christ, for John baptized in order that Christ might be baptized by him. But it was not fitting that John baptize just Christ; otherwise, on this point alone, it might seem that John's baptism was superior to Christ's. Accordingly, it was expedient that John baptize others before Christ, because before Christ's teaching was to be made public it was necessary that men be prepared for Christ by John's baptism. In this way, the baptism of John is related to the baptism of Christ as the catechesis or religious instruction given to prospects to teach and prepare them for baptism is related to the true baptism. It was likewise important that John baptize others after he had baptized Christ, so that John's baptism would not seem to be worthless. For the same reason, the practice of the ceremonies of the Old Law was not abolished as soon as the truth came, but as Augustine[83] says, the Jews could lawfully observe them for a time.

The second reason relates to John. For if John had stopped baptizing at once after Christ began baptizing, it might have been thought that he stopped out of envy or anger. And because, as the Apostle says, "We ought to look after what is good, not only before God, but also before all men" (Rom 12:17), this is the reason why John did not stop at once.

The third reason relates to John's disciples, who were already beginning to act like zealots toward Christ and his disciples, because they were baptizing. So if John had entirely stopped from baptizing, it would have provoked his disciples to an even greater zeal and opposition to Christ and his disciples. For even while John continued baptizing, they were hostile to Christ's baptism, as later events showed. And so John did not stop at once: "Take care that your freedom does not become a hindrance to those who are weak," as is said in 1 Corinthians (8:9).

502. The place of his baptism was **at Aenon near Salim, where the water was plentiful**. Another name for Salim is Salem, which is the vil-

81. See *ST* III, q. 90, a. 2.
82. See *ST* III, q. 38, a. 5.
83. See *Ep.* 82. 15–16; PL 33, col. 281–82.

lage from which the king Melchizedek came. It is called Salim here because among the Jews a reader may use any vowel he chooses in the
middle of his words; hence it made no difference to the Jews whether it was pronounced Salim or Salem. He added, *where the water was
plentiful*, to explain the name of this place, i.e., *Aenon*, which is the
same as "water."

503. The fruit of his baptism is the remission of sins; thus he says,
people kept coming and were baptized, i.e., cleansed: for as is stated in
Matthew (3:5) and in Luke (3:7), great crowds came to John.[84]

504. The time is indicated when he says, *John had not yet been
thrown into prison*. He says this so that we may know that he began
his narrative of Christ's life before the other Evangelists. For the others began their account only from the time of John's imprisonment. So
Matthew (4:12) says: "When Jesus heard that John had been arrested,
he withdrew into Galilee." And so, because they had passed over the
things that Christ did before John's imprisonment, John, who was the
last to write a Gospel, supplied these omissions. He suggests this when
he says: *John had not yet been thrown into prison*.

505. Note that by divine arrangement it came about that when
Christ began to baptize, John did not continue his own baptizing and
preaching for very long, in order not to create disunion among the people. But he was granted a little time so that it would not seem that he
deserved to be repudiated, as was mentioned before. Again, by God's
arrangement, it came about that after the faith had been preached and
the faithful converted, the temple was utterly destroyed, in order that
all the devotion and hope of the faithful could be directed to Christ.

506. Then when he says, *A controversy arose*, he brings in the issue of the two baptisms. First, the issue is mentioned. Secondly, it is
brought to John's attention (v. 26). Thirdly, the issue is resolved.

507. Because both John and Christ were baptizing, the disciples of
John, out of zeal for their teacher, started a controversy over this. And
this is what he says, *A controversy arose*, i.e., a dispute, *between the
disciples of John*, who were the first to raise the issue, *and the Jews*,
whom the disciples of John had rebuked for preferring Christ, because
of the miracles he did, to John, who did not do any miracles. The issue was concerning purification, i.e., baptizing. The cause of their envy
and the reason why they started the controversy was the fact that
John sent those he baptized to Christ, but Christ did not send those he
baptized to John. It seemed from this, and perhaps the Jews even said
so, that Christ was greater than John. Thus, the disciples of John, having not yet become spiritual, quarreled with the Jews over the baptisms. "While there is envy and fighting among you, are you not carnal?" (1 Cor 3:3).

84. See *ST* III, q. 38, a. 2.

508. They referred this issue to John; hence he says, *They went to John*. If we examine this closely, we see that they were trying to incite John against Christ. Indeed, they are like the gossip and the double-tongued: "Those who gossip and are double-tongued are accursed, for they disturb many who are at peace" (Sir 28:15).

So they bring up four things calculated to set John against Christ. First, they recall the previous unimportant status of Christ. Secondly, the good John did for him. Thirdly, the role which Christ took on. Fourthly, the loss to John because of Christ's new role.

509. They recall Christ's unimportance when they say, *the man who was with you*, as one of your disciples; and not the one you were with as your teacher. For there is no good reason for envy if honor is shown to one who is greater; rather, envy is aroused when honor is given to an inferior: "I have seen slaves on horses, and princes walking like slaves" (Ecc 10:7); "I called my servant, and he did not answer me" (Jb 19:16). For a master is more disturbed at the rebellion of a servant and a subject than of anyone else.

510. Secondly, they remind John of the good he did Christ. Thus they do not say, "the one whom you baptized," because they would then be admitting the greatness of Christ which was shown during his baptism when the Holy Spirit came upon him in the form of a dove and in the voice of the Father speaking to him. So they say, *the one of whom you have given testimony*, i.e., we are very angry that the one you made famous and admired dares to repay you in this way: "The one who ate my bread has lifted his heel against me" (Ps 40:10). They said this because those who seek their own glory and personal profit from their office become dejected if their office is taken over by someone else.

511. And so thirdly, they even add that Christ took over John's office for himself, when they say, *he is here baptizing*, i.e., he is exercising your office; and this also disturbed them very much. For we generally see that men of the same craft are envious and underhanded with respect to one another; a potter envies another potter, but does not envy a carpenter. So, even teachers, who are seeking their own honor, become sad if another teaches the truth. In opposition to them, Gregory[85] says: "The mind of a holy pastor wishes that others teach the truth which he cannot teach all by himself." So also Moses: "Would that all the people might prophesy," as we read in Numbers (11:29).

512. Yet they were not satisfied with merely disturbing John, rather they report something that should really excite him, that is, the loss that John seemed to be having because of the office Christ took over. They give this when they say: *and all the people are flocking to him*, i.e., the ones who used to come to you. In other words, they have re-

85. See *Mor.* 22. 23; PL 76, col. 247 C.

jected and disowned you, and now are all going to his baptism. It is clear from Matthew (11:7) that they used to go to John: "What did you go into the desert to see?" The same envy affected the Pharisees against Christ; so they said: "Look, the whole world has gone after him" (below 12:19). However, all this did not set John against Christ, for he was not a reed swaying in the wind; and this is clear from John's answer to their question.

LECTURE 5

27 John replied and, said: "No one can lay hold of anything unless it is given to him from heaven. 28 You yourselves are witnesses to the fact that I said: I am not the Christ, but the one sent before him. 29 It is the groom who has the bride. The groom's friend waits there and listens to him, rejoicing at hearing his voice. Therefore in this case my joy is complete. 30 He must increase, and I must decrease. 31 The One who came from above is above all things. He who is of earth is earthly, and speaks of earthly things. 32a The One who comes from heaven is above all things, and he testifies to what he sees, and to what he hears."[86]

513. Here we have John's answer to the question presented to him by his disciples. Their question contained two points: a complaint about the office Christ took on, and so they said, *he is here baptizing*; and about Christ's increasing fame and reputation among the people, and so they said, *all the people are flocking to him.* Accordingly, John directs his answer to these two complaints. First he answers the complaint about the office Christ took on. Secondly, the complaint about Christ's increasing reputation (v. 30). As to the first he does two things. First, he shows the source of Christ's office and of his own. Secondly, their difference (v. 28). Thirdly, how Christ and he are related to these offices.

514. As to the first, note that although John's disciples broach their question maliciously, and so deserve to be rebuked, John nevertheless does not sharply reprove them; and this because of their imperfection. For he feared that they might be provoked by a rebuke, leave him, and, joining forces with the Pharisees, publicly harass Christ. In acting this way he was putting into practice what is said of the Lord: "The bruised reed he will not break" (Is 42:3). Again, we should also note that he begins his answer not by telling them what is great and wonderful about Christ, but what is common and obvious; and he did this on account of their envy. For since the excellence of a person provokes others to envy, if John had stressed Christ's excellence at once, he would have fed the fire of their envy.

86. St. Thomas refers to Jn 3:31 in *ST* III, q. 14, a. 3.

515. Thus he states something unpretentious, and says, *No one can lay hold of anything unless it is given to him from heaven*; and he said this to them in order to inspire them with reverence. As if to say: If all men are going to him, it is God's doing, because *no one can lay hold of anything*, in the order of perfection and goodness, *unless it is given to him from heaven*. Therefore, if you oppose him, you oppose God. "If this plan or work is from men, it will fail," as is said in Acts (5:38). This is the way Chrysostom[87] explains it, applying these words to Christ.

Augustine,[88] on the other hand, does much better when he refers them to John. *No one can lay hold of anything unless it is given to him from heaven*: as if to say: You are zealous on my behalf and you want me to be greater than Christ; but that has not been given to me, and I do not wish to usurp it: "No one takes this honor on himself" (Heb 5:4). This is the origin of their offices.

516. Then follows the difference of their offices, when he says, *You yourselves are witnesses*. As if to say: From the testimony which I bore to him, you can know the office committed to me by Christ: for *You yourselves are witnesses*, i.e., you can testify, *to the fact that I said: I am not the Christ*—"He declared openly and did not deny" (above 1:20)—*but the one sent before him*, as a herald before a judge. And so from my own testimony you can know my office, which is to go before Christ and prepare the way for him: "There was a man sent by God, whose name was John" (above 1:6). But the office of Christ is to judge and to preside. If we look at this closely we can see that John, like a skillful disputant, answers them with their own arguments: "I judge you out of your own mouth," as said in Luke (19:12).

517. He shows how John is related to his own office when he says: *It is the groom who has the bride*. First, he gives a simile. Secondly, he applies it to his own situation. With respect to the first he does two things. First, he gives a simile which applies to Christ; and secondly, to himself.

518. As to the first, we should note that on the human level it is the groom who regulates, governs and has the bride. Hence he says, *It is the groom who has the bride*. Now the groom is Christ: "Like a bridegroom coming out of his bridal chamber" (Ps 18:6). His bride is the Church, which is joined to him by faith: "I will espouse you to myself in faith" (Hos 2:20). In keeping with this figure, Zipporah said to Moses: "You are a spouse of blood to me" (Ex 4:25). We read of the marriage: "The marriage of the Lamb has come" (Rv 19:7). So, because Christ is the groom, he has the bride, that is, the Church; but my part is only to rejoice in the fact that he has the bride.

519. Consequently he says, *The groom's friend waits there and listens to him, rejoicing at hearing his voice*. Although John had said ear-

87. *Hom. in Io.* 29. 2; PG 59, col. 168; cf. *Catena aurea*, 3:27–30.
88. *Tract. in Io.* 13. 9; PL 35, col. 1497; cf. *Catena aurea*, 3:27–30.

lier that he was not worthy to unfasten the strap of Jesus' sandal, he here calls himself the friend of Jesus in order to bring out the faithfulness of his love for Christ. For a servant does not act in the spirit of love in regard to the things that pertain to his master, but in a spirit of servitude; while a friend, on the other hand, seeks his friend's interests out of love and faithfulness. Hence a faithful servant is like a friend to his master: "If you have a faithful servant, treat him like yourself" (Sir 33:31). Indeed, it is proof of a servant's faithfulness when he rejoices in the prosperity of his master, and when he obtains various goods, not for himself, but for his master. And so because John did not keep the bride entrusted to his care for himself, but for the groom, we can see that he was a faithful servant and a friend of the groom. It is to suggest this that he calls himself *the groom's friend*.[89]

Those who are friends of the truth should act in the same way, not turning the bride entrusted to their care to their own advantage and glory, but treating her honorably for the honor and glory of the groom; otherwise they would not be friends of the groom but adulterers. This is why Gregory[90] says that a servant who is sent by the groom with gifts for the bride is guilty of adulterous thoughts if he himself desires to please the bride. This is not what the Apostle did: "I espoused you to one husband in order to present you to Christ as a chaste virgin" (2 Cor 11:2). And John did the same, because he did not keep the bride, i.e., the faithful, for himself, but brought them to the groom, that is, to Christ.

520. And so by saying, *the groom's friend*, he suggests the faithfulness of his love. Further, he suggests his constancy when he says, *waits*, firm in friendship and faithfulness, not extolling himself above what he really is: "I will stand my watch" (Hb 2:1); "Be steadfast and unchanging" (1 Cor 15:58); "A faithful friend, if he is constant, is like another self" (Sir 6:11).

He suggests his attention when he says, *and listens to him*, i.e., attentively considers the way in which the groom is united to the bride. For according to Chrysostom,[91] these words explain the manner of this marriage, for it is accomplished through faith, and "faith comes through hearing" (Rom 10:17). Or, he *listens to him*, i.e., reverently obeys him, by caring for the bride according to the commands of the groom: "I will listen to him as my master," as is said in Isaiah (50:4). This is in opposition to those evil prelates who do not follow Christ's command in governing the Church.[92]

Likewise, he hints at his spiritual joy when he says, *rejoicing at hearing his voice*, that is, when the groom talks to his bride. And he

89. See *ST* II-II, q. 23, a. 1.
90. *Reg. pastor. liber*, II. 8; PL 77, col. 42C.
91. *Hom. in Io.* 29. 3; PG 59, col. 170; cf. *Catena aurea*, 3:27–30.
92. See *ST* II-II, q. 105, a. 2.

says, rejoicing (literally, "rejoicing with joy"), to show the truth and perfection of his joy.[93] For one whose rejoicing is not over the good, does not rejoice with true joy. And so, if it made me sad that Christ, who is the true groom, preaches to the bride, i.e., the Church, I would not be a friend of the groom; but I am not sad.

521. *Therefore in this case my joy is complete*, namely, in seeing what I have so long desired, that is, the groom speaking to his bride. Or, my joy is complete, i.e., brought to its perfect and due measure, when the bride is united to the groom, because I now have my grace and I have completed my work: "I will rejoice in the Lord, and I will take joy in God, my Jesus" (Hb 3:18).

522. Then when he says, *He must increase, and I must decrease*, he answers their question as to their complaint about the increasing esteem given to Christ. First, he notes that such an increase is fitting. Secondly, he gives the reason for it (v. 31).

523. So he says: You say that all the people are flocking to him, i.e., to Christ, and therefore that he is growing in honor and esteem among the people. But I say that this is not unbecoming, because *He must increase*, not in himself, but in relation to others, in the sense that his power become more and more known. *And I must decrease*, in the reverence and esteem of the people: for esteem and reverence are not due to me as if I were a principal, but they are due to Christ. And therefore since he has come, the signs of honor are diminishing in my regard, but increasing in regard to Christ, just as with the coming of the prince, the office of the ambassador ceases: "When the perfect comes, what is imperfect will pass away" (1 Cor 13:10). And just as in the heavens the morning star appears and gives light before the sun, only to cease giving light when the sun appears, so John went before Christ and is compared to the morning star: "Can you bring out the morning star?" (Jb 38:32).

This is also signified in John's birth and in his death. In his birth, because John was born at a time when the days are getting shorter; Christ, however, was born when the days are growing longer, on the twenty-fifth of December. In his death, because John dies shortened by decapitation; but Christ died raised up by the lifting up of the cross.

524. In the moral sense, this should take place in each one of us. Christ *must increase* in you, i.e., you should grow in the knowledge and love of Christ, because the more you are able to grasp him by knowledge and love, the more Christ increases in you; just as the more one improves in seeing one and the same light, the more that light seems to increase. Consequently, as men advance in this way, their self-esteem decreases; because the more one knows of the divine greatness, the

---

93. See *ST* II-II, q. 28, a. 1.

less he thinks of his human smallness.[94] As we read in Proverbs (30:1): "The revelation spoken by the man close to God"; and then there follows: "I am the most foolish of men, and the wisdom of men is not in me." "I have heard you, but now I see you, and so I reprove myself, and do penance in dust and ashes," as we read in Job (42:5).

525. Then when he says, *The One who came from above is above all things*, he gives the reason for what he has just said. And he does this in two ways. First, on the basis of Christ's origin. And secondly, by considering Christ's teaching.

526. Regarding the first, we should note that in order for a thing to be perfect, it must reach the goal fixed for it by its origin; for example, if one is born from a king, he should continue to progress until he becomes a king. Now Christ has an origin that is most excellent and eternal; therefore he must increase by the manifestation of his power, in relation to others, until it is recognized that he is above all things. Thus he says, *The One who came from above*, that is, Christ, according to his divinity. "No one has gone up to heaven except the One who came down from heaven" (above 3:13); "You are from below, I am from above" (below 8:23).

527. Or, he *came from above*, as to his human nature, i.e., from the "highest" condition of human nature, by assuming it according to what was predominant in it in each of its states. For human nature is considered in three states. First, is the state of human nature before sin; and from this state he took his purity by assuming a flesh unmarked by the stain of original sin: "A lamb without blemish" (Ex 12:5). The second state is after sin; and from this he took his capability to suffer and die by assuming the likeness of sinful flesh as regards its punishment, but not in its guilt: "God sent his own Son in the likeness of sinful flesh" (Rom 8:3). The third state is that of resurrection and glory; and from this he took his impossibility of sinning and his joy of soul.[95]

528. Here we must be on guard against the error of those who say that there was left in Adam something materially unmarked by the original stain, and this was passed on to his descendants; for example, to the Blessed Virgin, and that Christ's body was formed from this. This is heretical, because whatever existed in Adam in a material way was marked by the stain of original sin. Further, the matter from which the body of Christ was formed was purified by the power of the Holy Spirit when he sanctified the Blessed Virgin.[96]

529. *The One who came from above*, according to his divinity as well as his human nature, *is above all things*, both by eminence of rank: "The Lord is high above all nations" (Ps 112:4), and by his authority

94. See *ST* II-II, q. 161, a. 6.
95. See *ST* III, q. 14, a. 1; III, q. 15, a. 1.
96. See *ST* III, q. 31, a. 1; III, q. 32, a. 4.

and power: "He has made him the head of the Church," as is said in Ephesians (1:22).

530. Now he gives the reason for what he had said above (v. 30), by considering the teaching of Christ. First, he describes the doctrine of Christ and its grandeur. Secondly, the difference in those who receive or reject this doctrine (v. 32b). He does two things with respect to the first. First, he describes John's doctrine. Secondly, he describes the doctrine of Christ (v. 32).

531. As to the first we should note that a man is known mainly by what he says: "Your accent gives you away" (Mt 26:73); "Out of the abundance of the heart the mouth speaks" (Mt 12:34). This is why the quality of a teaching or doctrine is considered according to the quality of its origin. Accordingly, in order to understand the quality of John's doctrine, we should first consider his origin. So he says, *He who is of earth*, that is John, not only as to the matter from which he was made, but also in his efficient cause: because the body of John was formed by a created power: "They dwell in houses of clay, and have a foundation of earth" (Jb 4:19). Secondly, we should consider the quality of John himself, which is earthly; and so he says, *is earthly*. Thirdly, the quality of his teaching is described: he *speaks of earthly things*. "You will speak of the earth" (Is 29:4).

532. But since John was full of the Holy Spirit while still in his mother's womb, how can he be said to speak of earthly things? I answer that, according to Chrysostom,[97] John says he speaks of earthly things by comparison with the teaching of Christ. As if to say: The things I speak of are slight and inferior as becomes one of an earthly nature, in comparison to him "in whom are hidden all the treasures of wisdom and knowledge" (Col 2:3); "As the heavens are high above the earth, so my ways are high above your ways" (Is 55:9).

Or we could say according to Augustine,[98] and this is a better explanation, that we can consider what any person has of himself and what he has received from another. Now John and every mere human of himself is of the earth. Therefore, from this standpoint, he has nothing to speak of except earthly things. And if he does speak of divine things, it is due to a divine enlightenment: "Your heart has visions, but unless they come from the Almighty, ignore them" (Sir 34:6). So the Apostle says, "It is not I, but the grace of God which is with me" (1 Cor 15:10); "For it is not you who speak, but the Holy Spirit who is speaking through you" (Mt 10:20). Accordingly, as regards John, he *is earthly and speaks of earthly things*. And if there was anything divine in him, it did not come from him, as he was the recipient, but from the one enlightening him.[99]

97. *Hom. in Io.* 30. 1; PG 59, col 171; cf. *Catena aurea*, 3:31–32.
98. *Tract. in Io.* 14. 6; PL 35, col. 1505; cf. *Catena aurea*, 3:31–32.
99. See *ST* I, q. 105, a. 3; II-II, q. 172, aa. 1–2.

533. Now he describes the doctrine of Christ. And he does three things. First, he shows its origin, which is heavenly; hence he says, *The One who comes from heaven is above all things*. For although the body of Christ was of the earth as regards the matter of which it was made, yet it came from heaven as to its efficient cause, inasmuch as his body was formed by divine power. It also came from heaven because the eternal and uncreated person of the Son came from heaven by assuming a body. "No one has gone up to heaven except the One who came down from heaven, the Son of Man, who lives in heaven" (above 3:13).[100]

Secondly, he shows the dignity of Christ, which is very great; so he says, *is above all things*. This was explained above.

Thirdly, he infers the dignity of Christ's doctrine, which is most certain, because *he testifies to what he sees and to what he hears*. For Christ, as God, is truth itself; but as man, he is its witness: "For this was I born, and for this I came into the world: to testify to the truth" (below 18:37). Therefore, he gives testimony to himself: "You testify to yourself" (below 8:13). And he testifies to what is certain, because his testimony is about what he has heard with the Father: "I speak to the world what I have heard from my Father" (below 8:26): "What we have seen and heard" (1 Jn 1:3).[101]

534. Note that knowledge of a thing is acquired in one way through sight and in another way through hearing. For by sight, a knowledge of a thing is acquired by means of the very thing seen; but by hearing, a thing is not made known by the very voice that is heard, but by means of the understanding of the one speaking. And so, because the Lord has knowledge which he has received from the Father, he says, *to what he sees*, insofar as he proceeds from the essence of the Father; *and to what he hears*, insofar as he proceeds as the Word of the Father's intellect. Now because among intellectual beings, their act of being is other than their act of understanding, their knowledge through sight is other than their knowledge through hearing. But in God the Father, the act of being (*esse*) and the act of understanding (*intelligere*) are the same.[102] Thus in the Son, to see and hear are the same thing. Moreover, since even in one who sees there is not the essence of the thing seen in itself but only its similitude, as also in the hearer there is not the actual thought of the speaker but only an indication of it, so the one who sees is not the essence of the thing in itself, nor is the listener the very thought expressed. In the Son, however, the very essence of the Father is received by generation, and he himself is the Word; and so in him to see and to hear are the same.[103]

And so John concludes that since the doctrine of Christ has more

100. See *ST* III, q. 2, a. 8.   101. See *ST* III, q. 7, a. 8.
102. See *ST* I, q. 3, a. 4; I, q. 14, a. 4.   103. See *ST* I, q. 34, a. 2.

grandeur and is more certain than his, one must listen to Christ rather than to him.

LECTURE 6

32b "And his testimony no one accepts. 33 But whoever accepts his testimony has given a sign [or certifies] that God is true. 34 For the One whom God sends speaks the words of God, for God does not bestow the Spirit in fractions. 35 The Father loves the Son, and has put everything into his hands. 36 Whoever believes in the Son has eternal life. But whoever is unbelieving in the Son will not see life; rather, the anger of God rests on him."[104]

535. Above, John the Baptist commended the teaching of Christ, here, however, he considers the difference in those who receive it. Thus, he treats of the faith that must be given to this teaching. And he does three things. First, he shows the scarcity of those who believe. Secondly, the obligation to believe (v. 33). Lastly, the reward for belief (v. 36).

536. He says therefore: I say that Christ has certain knowledge and that he speaks the truth. Yet although few accept his testimony, that is no reflection on his teaching, because it is not the fault of the teaching but of those who do not accept it: namely, the disciples of John, who did not yet believe, and the Pharisees, who slandered his teaching. Thus he says, *And his testimony no one accepts.*

537. *No one* can be explained in two ways. First, so that it implies a few; and so some did accept his testimony. He shows that some did accept it when he adds, "But whoever accepts his testimony." The Evangelist used this way of speaking before when he said: "He came unto his own, and his own did not receive him" (above 1:11): because a few did receive him.

In another way, to accept his testimony is understood as to believe in God. But no one can believe of himself, but only due to God: "You are saved by grace" (Eph 2:8). And so he says, *his testimony no one accepts,* i.e., of himself, but it is given to him by God.[105]

This can be explained in another way by realizing that Scripture refers to people in two ways. As long as we are in this world the wicked are mingled with the good; and so Scripture sometimes speaks of "the people," or "they," meaning those who are good; while at other times, the same words can refer to the wicked. We can see this in Jeremiah

---

104. St. Thomas refers to Jn 3:34 in *ST* III, q. 7, a. 11, obj. 1; and Jn 3:36 in *ST* I-II, q. 88, a. 4, obj. 1.

105. See *ST* I-II, q. 109, aa. 5–7; I-II, q. 112, a. 1; II-II, q. 6, a. 1.

(26): for first it says that all the people and the priests sought to kill Jeremiah, and this referred to those who were evil; then at once it says that all the people sought to free him, and this referred to those who were good. In the same way, John the Baptist says, looking to the left, i.e., toward those who are evil, *And his testimony no one accepts*; and later, referring to those on the right, i.e., to the good, he says, *But whoever accepts his testimony.*

538. *But whoever accepts his testimony.* Here he speaks of the obligation to believe, i.e., to submit oneself to divine truth.[106] As to this he does four things. First, he presents the divine truth. Secondly, he speaks of the proclamation of the divine truth (v. 34). Thirdly, of the ability to proclaim it (v. 34b). Fourthly, he gives the reason for this ability (v. 35).

539. Man's obligation to the faith is to submit himself to divine truth, and so he says that if few accept his testimony that means that some do. Hence he says, *whoever accepts his testimony*, i.e., whoever he may be, *has given a sign*, i.e., he ought to affix a certain sign or has in fact placed a seal in his own heart, that Christ is God. And he [Christ] *is true*, because he said that he is God. If he were not, he would not be true, but it is written: "God is true" (Rom 3:4). Concerning this seal it is said: "Set me as a seal on your heart" (Sg 8:6), and "The foundation of God stands firm, bearing a seal, etc.," as we read in 2 Timothy (2:19).

Or, following Chrysostom,[107] he *has given a sign*, i.e., he has shown *that God*, that is, the Father, is true, because he sent his Son whom he promised to send. The Evangelist says this to show that those who do not believe Christ deny the truthfulness of the Father.

540. Then, immediately he adds a commendation of divine truth, saying, *For the One whom God sends speaks the words of God.* As if to say: He has given this as a sign, namely, that Christ, whose testimony he accepts, *the One whom God sends speaks the words of God.* Consequently, one who believes Christ believes the Father: "I speak to the world what I have heard from the Father" (below 8:26). So he expressed verbally nothing but the Father and the words of the Father, because he has been sent by the Father, and because he is the Word of the Father. Hence, he says that he even bespeaks the Father.

Or, if the statement *God is true* refers to Christ, we understand the distinction of persons; for since the Father is true God, and Christ is true God, it follows that the true God sent the true God, who is distinct from him in person, but not in nature.[108]

541. The ability to proclaim divine truth is present in Christ in the highest degree, because he does not receive the Spirit in a partial way; and so he says, *for God does not bestow the Spirit in fractions.*

106. See *ST* II-II, q. 10, a. 1.
107. *Hom. in Io.* 30. 2; PG 59, col. 173; cf. *Catena aurea*, 3:32b–36.
108. See *ST* I, q. 39, a. 4.

You might say that although God sent Christ, yet not all that Christ says is from God, but only some of the things; for even the prophets spoke at times from their own spirit, and at other times from the Spirit of God. For example, we read that the prophet Nathan (2 Sm 7:3), speaking out of his own spirit, advised David to build a temple, but that later, under the influence of the Spirit of God, he retracted this. However, the Baptist shows that such is not the case with Christ. For the prophets receive the Spirit of God only fractionally, i.e., in reference to some things, but not as to all things. Consequently, not all they say are the words of God. But Christ, who received the Spirit fully and in regards to all things, speaks the words of God as to all things.[109]

542. But how can the Holy Spirit be given in fractions, since he is immense or infinite, according to the Creed of Athanasius:[110] "Immense is the Father, immense the Son, immense the Holy Spirit"? I answer that the Holy Spirit is given in fractions, not in respect to his essence or power, according to which he is infinite, but as to his gifts, which are given fractionally: "Grace has been given to each of us according to degree" (Eph 4:7).

543. We should note that we can understand in two ways what is said here, namely, that God the Father did not give the Spirit to Christ in a partial way. We can understand it as applying to Christ as God, and, in another way, as applying to Christ as man. Something is given to someone in order that he may have it: and it is appropriate to Christ to have the Spirit, both as God and as man. And so he has the Holy Spirit with respect to both. As man, Christ has the Holy Spirit as Sanctifier: "The Spirit of the Lord is upon me, because the Lord has anointed me" (Is 61:1), namely, as man. But as God, he has the Holy Spirit only as manifesting himself, inasmuch as the Spirit proceeds from him: "He will give glory to me," that is, make known, "because he will have received from me," as is said below (16:14).

Therefore, both as God and as man, Christ has the Holy Spirit beyond measure. For God the Father is said to give the Holy Spirit without out measure to Christ as God, because he gives to Christ the power and might to bring forth (*spirandi*) the Holy Spirit, who, since he is infinite, was infinitely given to him by the Father: for the Father gives it just as he himself has it, so that the Holy Spirit proceeds from him as much as from the Son. And he gave him this by an everlasting genera-

109. See *ST* III, q. 7, aa. 9–11.

110. Athanasian Creed (*Quicumque vult*); PG 28, col. 1581. The Athanasian Creed is a Western, Latin creed attributed to St. Athanasius but composed after his death, probably in southern Gaul or Spain in the late fifth or early sixth century. Its expansive treatment of the Trinity reflects Augustine's trinitarian teaching (including the Filioque), and its statement of the Incarnation follows the Christological affirmations of the Council of Chalcedon (451).

tion. Similarly, Christ as man has the Holy Spirit without measure, for the Holy Spirit is given to different men in differing degrees, because grace is given to each "by measure" [cf., e.g., Mk 4:24; Mt 7:2]. But Christ as man did not receive a certain amount of grace; and so he did not receive the Holy Spirit in any limited degree.[111]

544. It should be noted, however, that there are three kinds of grace in Christ: the grace of [the hypostatic] union, the grace of a singular person, which is habitual, and the grace of headship, which animates all the members. And Christ received each of these graces without measure.

The grace of union, which is not habitual grace, but a certain gratuitous gift, is given to Christ in order that in his human nature he be the true Son of God, not by participation, but by nature, insofar as the human nature of Christ is united to the Son of God in person. This union is called a grace because he had it without any preceding merits. Now the divine nature is infinite; hence from that union he received all infinite gift. Thus it was not by degree or measure that he received the Holy Spirit, i.e., the gift and grace of union which, as gratuitous, is attributed to the Holy Spirit.[112]

His grace is termed habitual insofar as the soul of Christ was full of grace and wisdom: "the Only Begotten of the Father, full of grace and truth" (above 1:14). We might wonder if Christ did receive this grace without measure. For since such grace is a created gift, we must admit that it has a finite essence. Therefore, as far as its essence is concerned, since it is something created, this habitual grace was finite. Yet Christ is not said to have received this in a limited degree for three reasons.[113]

First, because of the one who is receiving the grace. For it is plain that each thing's nature has a finite capacity, because even though one might receive an infinite good by knowing, loving and enjoying it, nevertheless one receives it by enjoying it in a finite way. Further, each creature has, according to its species and nature, a finite amount of capacity. But this does not make it impossible for the divine power to make another creature possessing a greater capacity; but then such a creature would not be of a nature which is specifically the same, just as when one is added to three, there is another species of number. Therefore, when some nature is not given as much of the divine goodness as its natural capacity is able to contain, then it is seen to be given to it by measure; but when its total natural capacity is filled, it is not given to it by measure, because even though there is a measure on the part of the one receiving, there is none on the part of the one giving, who is prepared to give all. Thus, if someone takes a pail to a river,

111. See *ST* III, q. 7, a. 11, especially ad 1.
112. See *ST* III, q. 2, aa. 10 and 12.
113. See *ST* III, q. 7, a. 11.

he sees water present without measure, although he takes the water by measure on account of the limited dimensions of the pail. Thus, the habitual grace of Christ is indeed finite according to its essence, but it is said to be given in an infinite way and not by measure or partially, because as much was given to him as created nature was able to hold.

Secondly, Christ did not receive habitual grace in a limited way by considering the gift which is received. For every form or act, considered in its very nature, is not finite in the way in which it is made finite by the subject in which it is received. Nevertheless, there is nothing to prevent it from being finite in its essence, insofar as its existence (*esse*) is received in some subject. For that is infinite according to its essence which has the entire fullness of being (*essendi*): and this is true of God alone, who is the Supreme *esse*. But if we consider some "spiritual" form as not existing in a subject, for example, whiteness or color, it would not be infinite in essence, because its essence would be confined to some genus or species—nevertheless it would still possess the entire fullness of that species. Thus, considering the nature of the species, it would be without limit or measure, since it would have everything that can pertain to that species. But if whiteness or color should be received into some subject, it does not always have everything that pertains necessarily and always to the nature of this form, but only when the subject has it as perfectly as it is capable of being possessed, i.e., when the way the subject possesses it is equivalent to the power of the thing possessed. Thus, Christ's habitual grace was finite according to its essence; yet it is said to have been in him without a limit or measure because he received everything that could pertain to the nature of grace. Others, however, do not receive all this; but one receives in one way, and another in another way: "There are different graces" (1 Cor 12:4).

The third reason for saying that the habitual grace of Christ was not received in a limited way is based on its cause. For an effect is in some way present in its cause. Therefore, if someone has an infinite power to produce something, he is said to have what can be produced without measure and, in a way, infinitely. For example, if someone has a fountain which could produce an infinite amount of water, he would be said to have water in an infinite way and without measure. Thus, the soul of Christ has infinite grace and grace without measure from the fact that he has united to himself the Word, which is the infinite and unfailing source of the entire emanation of all created things.

From what has been said, it is clear that the grace of Christ which is called capital grace, insofar as he is head of the Church, is infinite in its influence. For from the fact that he possessed that from which the gifts of the Spirit could flow out without measure, he received the power to pour them out without measure, so that the grace of Christ is sufficient not merely for the salvation of some men, but for all the people of the entire world: "He is the offering for our sins; and not for ours only, but also for those of the entire world" (1 Jn 2:2), and even for many worlds, if they existed.[114]

545. Christ also had the ability appropriate for declaring divine truth, because all things are in his power; hence he says, **The Father loves the Son, and has put everything into his hands**. This can refer to Christ both as man and as God, but in different ways. If it refers to Christ according to his divine nature, then **loves** does not indicate a principle but a sign: for we cannot say that the Father gives all things to the Son because he loves him. There are two reasons for this. First, because to love is an act of the will; but to give a nature to the Son is to generate him. Therefore, if the Father gave a nature to the Son by his will, the will of the Father would be the principle of the generation of the Son; and then it would follow that the Father generated the Son by will, and not by nature; and this is the Arian heresy.[115]

Secondly, because the love of the Father for the Son is the Holy Spirit.[116] So, if the love of the Father for the Son were the reason why the Father put everything into his hands, it would follow that the Holy Spirit would be the principle of the generation of the Son; and this is not acceptable. Therefore, we should say that **loves** implies only a sign. As if to say: The perfect love with which **the Father loves the Son**, is a sign that the Father **has put everything into his hands**, i.e., everything which the Father has: "All things have been given to me by my Father" (Mt 11:27); "Jesus, knowing that the Father had given all things into his hands" (below 13:3).

But if **loves** refers to Christ as man, then it implies the notion of a principle, so that the Father is said to have put everything into the hands of the Son, everything, that is, that is in heaven and on earth: "All authority has been given to me, in heaven and on earth," as he says in Matthew (28:18); "He has appointed him [the Son] the heir of all things" (Heb 1:2). And the reason why the Father gives to the Son is because he loves the Son; hence he says, **The Father loves the Son**, for the Father's love is the reason for creating each creature: "You love everything which exists, and hate nothing which you have made" (Wis 11:25).[117] Concerning his love for the Son we read in Matthew (3:17): "This is my beloved Son, in whom I am well pleased"; "He has brought us into the kingdom of the Son of his love," that is, i.e., of his beloved Son (Col 1:13).

546. Then when he says, **Whoever believes in the Son has eternal life**, he shows the fruit of faith. First, he sets forth the reward for faith. Secondly, the penalty for unbelief (v. 36b).

---

114. See *ST* III, q. 8, a. 3; III, q. 48, a. 1.
115. See *ST* I, q. 41, a. 2.
116. See *ST* I, q. 37, a. 2.
117. See *ST* I, q. 20, a. 2; I-II, q. 87, a. 3.

547. The reward for faith is beyond our comprehension, because it is eternal life. Hence he says, **Whoever believes in the Son has eternal life**. And this is shown from what has already been said. For if the Father has given everything he has to the Son, and the Father has eternal life, then he has given to the Son to be eternal life: "Just as the Father possesses life in himself, so he has given it to the Son to have life in himself" (below 5:26): and this belongs to Christ insofar as he is the true and natural Son of God. "That you may be in his true Son, Christ. This is the true God and eternal life" (1 Jn 5:20).[118] **Whoever believes in the Son** has that toward which he tends, that is, the Son, in whom he believes. But the Son is eternal life; therefore, whoever believes in him has eternal life. As it says below (10:27): "My sheep hear my voice . . . and I give them eternal life."

548. The penalty for unbelief is unendurable, both as to the punishment of loss and as to the punishment of sense.[119] As to the punishment of loss, because it deprives one of life; hence he says, **whoever is unbelieving in the Son will not see life**. He does not say, "will not have," but **will not see**, because eternal life consists in the vision of the true life: "This is eternal life: that they may know you, the only true God, and Jesus Christ, whom you have sent" (below 17:3): and unbelievers will not have this vision and this knowledge: "Let him not see the brooks of honey" (Jb 4:19), that is, the sweetness of eternal life. And he says, **will not see**, because to see life itself is the proper reward for faith united with love.

The punishment of sense is unendurable because one is severely punished; so he says: **the anger of God rests on him**. For in the Scriptures anger indicates the pain with which God punishes those who are evil. So when he says, **the anger of God**, the Father, **rests on him**, it is the same as saying: They will feel punishment from God the Father.[120]

Although the Father "has given all judgment to the Son," as we read below (5:22), the Baptist refers this to the Father in order to lead the Jews to believe in the Son. It is written about this judgment: "It is a terrible thing to fall into the hands of the living God" (Heb 10:31). He says, **rests on him**, because this punishment will never be absent from the unbelieving, and because all who are born into this mortal life are the objects of God's anger, which was first felt by Adam: "We were by nature," that is, through birth, "children of anger" (Eph 2:3).[121] And we are freed from this anger only by faith in Christ; and so the anger of God rests on those who do not believe in Christ, the Son of God.[122]

118. See *ST* III, q. 53, a. 4.
119. See *ST* II-II, q. 10, a. 3.
120. See *ST* I, q. 23, a. 3; I-II, q. 87, aa. 3–5.
121. See *ST* I-II, q. 81, aa. 1, 3.
122. See *ST* III, q. 49, aa. 3–4.

CHAPTER 4

LECTURE 1

1 When, therefore, Jesus learned that the Pharisees had heard that he was making more disciples and baptizing more than John 2 (although Jesus did not himself baptize, but his disciples did), 3 he left Judea, and went again to Galilee. 4 He had, however, to pass through Samaria. 5 He came therefore to a city of Samaria, called Sychar, near the plot of land which Jacob had given to his son Joseph. 6 This was the site of Jacob's well. Jesus, tired from his journey, rested there at the well. It was about the sixth hour. 7 When a Samaritan woman came to draw water, Jesus said to her, "Give me a drink." 8 (His disciples had gone to the town to buy some food.) 9 So the Samaritan woman said to him, "How is it that you, being a Jew, ask me, a woman of Samaria, for a drink?" (Recall that the Jews had nothing to do with the Samaritans.)[1]

549. Having set forth the teaching of Christ on spiritual regeneration, and that Christ had given this grace of spiritual regeneration to the Jews, he now shows how Christ gave this grace to the Gentiles. Now the salutary grace of Christ had been dispensed in two ways to the Gentiles: through teaching and through miracles. "Going forth, they preached everywhere": this is the teaching; "the Lord cooperated with them, and confirmed the word with signs": these are the miracles (Mk 16:20).

First, he shows the future conversion of the Gentiles through teaching. Secondly, their future conversion through miracles (v. 43). As to the first, he does two things. First, he sets down certain matters preliminary to the teaching. Secondly, he presents the teaching and its effect (v. 10). As to the first, he sets down three preliminary facts. First, what relates to the one teaching. Secondly, something about the matter taught. Thirdly, something about who received the instruction (v. 7). As to the person teaching, the preliminary remark is about his journey to the place where he taught. Here he does three things. First, he gives the place which he left, that is, from Judea. Secondly, the place where he was going, to Galilee. Thirdly, the place through which he passed,

---

1. St. Thomas quotes Jn 4:2 in *ST* III, q. 38, a. 6, obj. 2; III, q. 67, a. 2, ad 1; III, q. 72, a. 6, obj. 2; III, q. 84, a. 7, ad 4; Jn 4:7 in *ST* III, q. 42, a. 1, obj 3; and Jn 4:8 in *ST* II-II, q. 188, a. 7.

Samaria. As to the first, he does three things. First, he gives the reason for his leaving Judea. Secondly, he explains certain facts included in this reason. Thirdly, he describes Christ's departure from Judea (v. 3).

550. The Evangelist says, **When, therefore, Jesus learned that the Pharisees had heard**, because he wished to show that after the Baptist had calmed the envy of his disciples, Jesus avoided the ill will of the Pharisees.

551. Since we read: "All things were known to the Lord God before they were created" (Sir 23:29), and "All things are naked and open to his eyes" (Heb 4:13), it seems that we should ask why Jesus is said to acquire new knowledge. We must answer that Jesus, in virtue of his divinity, knew from eternity all things, past, present and to come, as the scriptural passages cited above indicate. Nevertheless, as man, he did begin to know certain things through experiential knowledge. And it is this experiential knowledge that is indicated when it says here, **When Jesus learned**, after the news was brought to him, **that the Pharisees had heard**. And Christ willed to acquire this knowledge anew as a concession, to show the reality of his human nature, just as he willed to do and endure many other things characteristic of human nature.[2]

552. Why does he say: **the Pharisees had heard that he was making more disciples and baptizing more than John**, when this would seem to be of no concern to them? For they persecuted John and did not believe in him: for as Matthew says (21:25), when the Lord questioned them about the source of John's baptism, they said: "If we say from heaven, he will say to us, 'Why then did you not believe him?'" Thus they did not believe in John.

There are two answers to this. One is that those disciples of John who had spoken against Christ were either Pharisees or allies of the Pharisees. For we see in Matthew (9:11, 14), that the Pharisees along with the disciples of John raised questions against the disciples of Christ. And so according to this explanation, then, the Evangelist says that **When, therefore, Jesus learned that the Pharisees had heard**, that is, after he learned that John's disciples, who were Pharisees or allied with the Pharisees, had raised questions and had been disturbed about his baptism and that of his disciples, **he left Judea**.

Or, we might say that the Pharisees were disturbed at John's preaching due to their envy, and for this reason they persuaded Herod to arrest him. This is plain from Matthew (17:12), where Christ, speaking of John, says, "Elijah has already come . . . and they did with him whatever they wanted," and then he adds, "so also will the Son of Man suffer from them." The Gloss[3] comments on this that it was the Pharisees who incited Herod to arrest John and put him to death. Thus

2. See *ST* III, q. 12, a. 2; III, q. 14, a. 1; III, q. 15, a. 4.
3. See Bede, *In S. Matthaei Evang. expos.* 3. 17; PL 92, col 82A.

it seems probable that they felt the same way toward Christ because of what he was preaching. And this is what it says, that is, the envious Pharisees and persecutors of Christ *had heard*, with the intention of persecuting him, *that he was making more disciples and baptizing more than John*.

553. This kind of hearing is described by Job (28:22): "Death and destruction have said: We have heard of his deeds." The good, on the other hand, hear in order to obey: "We have heard him in Ephrathah" (Ps 131:6), followed by, "We will adore at his footstool."

The Pharisees heard two things. First, that Christ made more disciples than John. This was right and reasonable, for as we read above (3:30), Christ must increase and John must decrease. The second thing was that Christ baptized; and rightly so, because he cleanses: "Wash me from my injustice" (Ps 50:4), and again in Psalm (7:7): "Rise up, O Lord," by baptizing, "in the command you have given," concerning baptism, "and a congregation of people," united through baptism, "will surround you."

554. Then when he says, *although Jesus did not himself baptize*, he explains what he has just said about Christ's baptizing. Augustine[4] says that there is an apparent inconsistency here: for he had stated that Jesus was baptizing, whereas now he says, as though correcting himself, *Jesus did not himself baptize*.

There are two ways to understand this. This first way is that of Chrysostom.[5] What the Evangelist now says is true, i.e., that Christ did not baptize. When he said above that Jesus was baptizing, this was the report received by the Pharisees. For certain people came to the Pharisees and said: You are envious of John because he has disciples and is baptizing. But Jesus is making more disciples than John and is also baptizing. Why do you put up with him? So the Evangelist is not himself saying that Jesus was baptizing, but only that the Pharisees heard that he was. It is with the intention of correcting this false rumor that the Evangelist says: It is true that the Pharisees heard that Christ was baptizing, but this is not true. So he adds: *although Jesus did not himself baptize, but his disciples did*. And so for Chrysostom,[6] Christ did not baptize, because the Holy Spirit was not given at any time before the passion of Christ in the baptism of John and his disciples. The purpose of John's baptism was to accustom men to the baptism of Christ and to gather people in order to instruct them, as he says.[7] Moreover, it would not have been fitting for Christ to baptize if the Holy Spirit were not given in his baptism; but the Spirit was not given until after

4. *Tract. in Io.* 15. 3; PL 35, col. 1511; cf. *Catena aurea*, 4:1–6.
5. *Hom. in Io.* 31. 1; PG 59, col. 176; cf. *Catena aurea*, 4:1–6.
6. Ibid., 29. 1, col. 167–168; cf. *Catena aurea*, 4:1–6.
7. See *ST* III, q. 38, a. 1.

the passion of Christ, as we read below (7:39): "The Spirit had not yet been given, because Jesus had not yet been glorified."

According to Augustine,[8] however, one should say, and this is the preferable way, that the disciples did baptize with the baptism of Christ, that is, in water and the Spirit, and the Spirit was given in this baptism, and also that Christ did and did not baptize. Christ did baptize because he performed the interior cleansing; but he did not baptize because he did not wash them externally with the water. It was the office of the disciples to wash the body, while Christ gave the Spirit which cleansed within. So in the proper sense Christ did baptize, according to: "The man on whom you see the Spirit come down and rest is the one who is to baptize with the Holy Spirit," as was said above (1:33).[9]

With respect to the opinion of Chrysostom that the Holy Spirit was not yet given and so on, we might say that the Spirit was not yet given in visible signs, as he was given to the disciples after the resurrection; nevertheless, the Spirit had been given and was being given to believers through an interior sanctification.[10]

The fact that Christ was not always baptizing gives an example to us that the major prelates of the churches should not occupy themselves with things that can be performed by others, but should allow them to be done by those of lesser rank: "Christ did not send me to baptize, but to preach the Gospel" (1 Cor 1:17).

555. If someone should ask whether Christ's disciples had been baptized, it could be said, as Augustine[11] answered Stelentius, that they had been baptized with the baptism of John, because some of Christ's disciples had been disciples of John. Or, which is more likely, they were baptized with the baptism of Christ, in order that Christ might have baptized servants through whom he would baptize others. This is the meaning of what is said below (13:10): "He who has bathed does not need to wash, except his feet," and then follows, "and you are clean, but not all."

556. He then mentions Christ's going away, **he left Judea**. He left for three reasons. First, to get away from the envy of the Pharisees, who were disturbed because of what they had heard about Christ, and were preparing to harass him. By this he gives us the example that we should, with gentleness, yield ground to evil for a time: "Do not pile wood on his fire" (Sir 8:4). Another reason was to show us that it is not sinful to flee from persecution: "If they persecute you in one town, flee to another" (Mt 10:23). The third reason was that the time of his passion had not yet come: "My time has not yet come" (above

---

8. *Tract. in Io.* 15. 3-4; PL 35, col. 1511; cf. *Catena aurea,* 4:1–6.

9. See *ST* III, q. 64, a. 3.

10. See *ST* III, q. 61, a. 3.

11. *Ep.* 265. 5; PL 33, col. 1087–88; see also *Ep.* 44. 10; PL 33, col. 178; cf. *Catena aurea,* 4:1–6.

2:4). And there is an additional reason, a mystical one: he indicated by his leaving that because of persecution the disciples were destined to abandon the Jews and go to the Gentiles.

557. Then when he says, *and went again to Galilee*, he shows where he was going. He says, *again*, because above (2:12) he had mentioned another time when Christ went to Galilee: when he went to Capernaum after the miracle at the wedding. Since the other three evangelists did not mention this first trip, the Evangelist says again to let us know that the other evangelists had mentioned none of the matters he mentions up to this point, and that he is now beginning to give his account contemporaneous with theirs. According to one interpretation, Galilee is understood to signify the Gentile world, to which Christ passed from the Jews; for Galilee means "passage." According to another interpretation,[12] Galilee signifies the glory of heaven, for Galilee also means "revelation."

558. Then he describes the intermediate place through which Christ passed; first in a general way, then specifically.

559. On his way to Galilee, Christ passes through Samaria; hence he says, *He had to pass through Samaria*. He says, *had to pass*, lest he seem to be acting contrary to his own teaching, for Christ says in Matthew (10:5): "Do not go on the roads of the Gentiles." Now since Samaria was Gentile territory, he shows that he went there of necessity and not by choice. Thus he says, *had to pass*, the reason being that Samaria was between Judea and Galilee.

It was Omri, the king of Israel, who bought the hill of Samaria from a certain Shemer (1 Kgs 16:24); and it was there he built the city which he called Samaria, after the name of the person from whom he bought the land. After that, the kings of Israel used it as their royal city, and the entire region surrounding this city was called Samaria. When we read here that Christ *had to pass through Samaria*, we should understand the region rather than the city.

560. Describing it in more detail, he adds, *He came therefore to a city of Samaria*, i.e., of the region of Samaria, *called Sychar*. This Sychar is the same as Shechem. Genesis (33:18) says that Jacob camped near here and that two of his sons, enraged at the rape of Dinah, Jacob's daughter, by the son of the king of Shechem, killed all the males in that city. And so Jacob took possession of the city, and he lived there and dug many wells. Later, as he lay dying, he gave the land to his son Joseph: "I am giving you a portion more than your brothers" (Gn 48:22). And this is what he says: *near the plot of land which Jacob had given to his son Joseph*.

The Evangelist is so careful to record all these matters in order to show us that all the things which happened to the patriarchs were

___

12. See Erigena, *Comm. in S. Evang. sec. Io.*, frag. 2; PL 122, col. 330D–331C.

leading up to Christ, and that they pointed to Christ, and that he descended from them according to the flesh.

561. Then when he says, **This was the site of Jacob's well**, the Evangelist gives the material setting for the spiritual doctrine about to be taught. And this was most fitting: for the doctrine about to be taught was about water and a spiritual font, and so he mentions the material well, thus giving rise to a discussion of the spiritual font, which is Christ: "For with you is the fountain of life" (Ps 35:10), namely, the Holy Spirit, who is the spirit of life. Likewise, the well symbolizes baptism: "On that day a fountain will be open to the house of David, to cleanse the sinner and the unclean" (Zec 13:1).

He does three things here. First, he describes the well. Secondly, Christ's rest at the well. Thirdly, the time.

562. He describes the water source saying, **the site of Jacob's well**. Here one might object that further on (v. 11) he says this source is deep; thus it did not gush water like a fountain. I answer, as does Augustine,[13] that it was both a well and gushed water like a fountain. For every well is a fountain, although the converse is not true. For when water gushes from the earth we have a fountain; and if this happens just on the surface, the source is only a fountain. But if the water gushes both on the surface and below, we have a well; although it is also still called a fountain. It is called Jacob's well because he had dug this well there due to a shortage of water, as we read in Genesis (chap. 34).

563. **Jesus, tired from his journey, rested there at the well**. Jesus reveals his weakness (even though his power was unlimited), not because of a lack of power, but to show us the reality of the [human] nature he assumed.[14] According to Augustine,[15] "Jesus is strong, for 'In the beginning was the Word' (above 1:1); but he is weak, for 'the Word was made flesh'" (above 1:14). And so Christ, wishing to show the truth of his human nature, allowed it to do and to endure things proper to men; and to show the truth of his divine nature, he worked and performed things proper to God. Hence when he checked the inflow of divine power to his body, he became hungry and tired; but when he let his divine power influence his body, he did not become hungry in spite of a lack of food, and he did not become tired in his labors. "He had fasted forty days and forty nights, and was hungry" (Mt 4:2).

564. Seeing Jesus becoming tired from his journey is an example to us not to shrink from our work for the salvation of others: "I am poor, and have labored since my youth" (Ps 87:16). We also have an example of poverty, as Jesus **rested there**, upon the bare earth.

In its mystical meaning, this resting [literally, a sitting] of Christ in-

---

13. See *Tract in Io.* 15. 5; PL 35, col. 1512; cf. *Catena aurea,* 4:1–6.
14. See *ST* III, q. 14, a. 2.
15. *Tract. in Io.* 15. 6; PL 35, col. 1512; cf. *Catena aurea,* 4:1–6.

dicates the abasement of his passion: "You know when I sit down (i.e., the passion), and when I rise" (Ps 138:2). Also, it indicates the authority of his teaching, for he speaks as one having power; thus we read in Matthew (5:1) that Christ, "sitting down, taught them."

565. He indicates the time, saying, **It was about the sixth hour.** There are both literal and mystical reasons for fixing the time. The literal reason was to show the cause of his tiredness: for men are more weary from work in the heat and at the sixth hour [at noon]. Again, it shows why Christ was resting: for men gladly rest near the water in the heat of the day.

There are three mystical reasons for mentioning the time. First, because Christ assumed flesh and came into the world in the sixth age of the world. Another is that man was made on the sixth day, and Christ was conceived in the sixth month. Third, at the sixth hour the sun is at its highest, and there is nothing left for it but to decline. In this context, the "sun" signifies temporal prosperity, as suggested by Job (31:26): "If I had looked at the sun when it shone, etc." Therefore Christ came when the prosperity of the world was at its highest, that is, it flourished through love in the hearts of men; but because of him natural love was bound to decline.

566. Next, we have a preliminary remark concerning the one who listens to Christ. First, we are introduced to the person who is taught. Secondly, we are given her preparation for his teaching.

567. The teaching is given to a Samaritan woman; so he says, **a Samaritan woman came to draw water.** This woman signifies the Church, not yet justified, of the Gentiles. It was then involved in idolatry, but was destined to be justified by Christ. She **came** from foreigners, i.e., from the Samaritans, who were foreigners, even though they lived in the neighboring territory: because the Church of the Gentiles, foreign to the Jewish race, would come to Christ: "Many will come from the East and the West, and will sit down with Abraham, and Isaac, and Jacob, in the kingdom of heaven," as we find in Matthew (8:11).

568. Christ prepares this woman for his teaching when he says, **Give me a drink.** First, we have the occasion for his asking her. Secondly, the Evangelist suggests why it was opportune to make this request (v. 8).

569. The occasion and the preparation of the woman was the request of Christ; thus he says, **Give me a drink.** He asks for a drink both because he was thirsty for water on account of the heat of the day, and because he thirsted for the salvation of man on account of his love. Accordingly, while hanging on the cross he cried out: "I thirst."

570. Christ had the opportunity to ask this of the woman because his disciples, whom he would have asked for the water, were not there; thus the Evangelist says, **His disciples had gone to the town.** Here we might notice three things about Christ. First, his humil-

ity, because he was left alone.[16] This is an example to his disciples that
they should suppress all pride. Someone might ask what need there
was to train the disciples in humility, seeing that they had been but
lowly fishermen and tentmakers. Those who say such things should
remember that these very fishermen were suddenly made more deserving of respect than any king, more eloquent than philosophers and
orators, and were the intimate companions of the Lord of creation.
Persons of this kind, when they are suddenly promoted, ordinarily become proud, not being accustomed to such great honor.[17]

Secondly, note Christ's temperance: for he was so little concerned
about food that he did not bring anything to eat.[18] Thirdly, note that
he was also left alone on the cross: "I have trodden the wine press
alone, and no one of the people was with me" (Is 63:3).

571. Our Lord prepared the woman to receive his spiritual teaching
by giving her an occasion to question him. First, her question is given.
Secondly, her reason for asking it (v. 9).

572. Here we should point out that our Lord, when asking the
woman for a drink, had in mind more a spiritual drink than a merely physical one. But the woman, not yet understanding about such a
spiritual drink, thought only of a physical drink. So she responds: *How
is it that you, being a Jew, ask me, a woman of Samaria, for a drink?*
For Christ was a Jew, because it was promised that he would be from
Judah: "The scepter will not be taken away from Judah . . . until he
who is to be sent comes" (Gn 49:10); and he was born from Judah:
"It is evident that our Lord came from Judah" (Heb 7:14). The woman knew that Christ was Jewish from the way he dressed: for as Numbers (15:37) says, the Lord commanded the Jews to wear tassels on the
corners of their garments, and put a violet cord on each tassel, so that
they could be distinguished from other people.

573. Then the reason for this question is given: either by the Evangelist, as the Gloss[19] says, or by the woman herself, as Chrysostom[20]
says; the reason being, *the Jews had nothing to do with Samaritans*.

Apropos of this, we should note that, as mentioned in 2 Kings, it
was on account of their sins that the people of Israel, i.e., of the ten
tribes, who were worshipping idols, were captured by the king of the
Assyrians, and led as captives into Babylonia. Then, so that Samaria
would not remain unpopulated, the king gathered people from various
nations and forced them to live there. While they were there, the Lord
sent lions and other wild beasts to trouble them; he did this to show
that he let the Jews be captured because of their sins, and not because

16. See also *ST* III, q. 46, a. 3.   17. See also *ST* II-II, q. 162, a. 4.
18. See also *ST* II-II, q. 147, a. 1.
19. See Bede, *In S. Ioannis Evang. expos.* 4; PL 92, col. 682A.
20. *Hom. in Io.* 31. 4; PG 59, col. 180.

of any lack in his own power. When news of their trouble reached the
Assyrian king and he was informed that this was happening because
these people were not observing the rites of the God of that territory,
he sent them a priest of the Jews who would teach them God's law as
found in the law of Moses. This is why, although these people were
not Jewish, they came to observe the Mosaic law. However, along with
their worship of the true God, they also worshipped idols, paid no attention to the prophets, and referred to themselves as Samaritans,
from the city of Samaria which was built on a hill called Shemer (1 Kgs
16:24). After the Jews returned to Jerusalem from their captivity, the
Samaritans were a constant source of trouble, and as we read in Ezra,
interfered with their building of the temple and the city. Although the
Jews did not mix with other people, they especially avoided these Samaritans and would have nothing to do with them. And this is what
we read: **Jews had nothing to do with the Samaritans.** He does not
say that the Samaritans do not associate with Jews, for they would
have gladly done so and have cooperated with them. But the Jews re-
buffed them in keeping with what is said in Deuteronomy (7:2): "Do
not make agreements with them."

574. If it was not lawful for the Jews to associate with Samaritans,
why did God ask a Samaritan woman for a drink? One might answer,
as Chrysostom[21] does, that the Lord asked her because he knew that
she would not give him the drink. But this is not an adequate answer,
because one who asks what is not lawful is not free from sin—not to
mention the scandal—even though what he asks for is not given to
him. So we should say, as we find in Matthew (12:8): "The Son of Man
is Lord even of the sabbath." Thus, as Lord of the law, he was able to
use or not use the law and its observances and legalities as it seemed
suitable to him.[22] And because the time was near when the nations
would be called to the faith, he associated with those nations.

LECTURE 2

*10 Jesus replied and said: "If you knew the gift of God, and real-
ized who it is who says to you, 'Give me a drink,' you perhaps would
have asked him that he give you living water." 11 The woman challenged him: "You, sir, have no bucket, and the well is deep. How then
could you have living water? 12 Are you greater than our father Jacob, who gave us this well and drank from it with his sons and his
flocks?" 13 Jesus replied and said: "Whoever drinks this water will be
thirsty again, but whoever drinks the water that I give, will never be*

21. Ibid.; cf. *Catena aurea*, 4:7–12.
22. See *ST* III, q. 40, a. 4.

thirsty again. 14 The water that I give will become a fountain within him, leaping up to provide eternal life." 15 "Lord," the woman said, "Give me this water so that I shall not grow thirsty and have to keep coming here to draw water." 16 Jesus said to her: "Go, call your husband, and then come back here." 17 "I have no husband," replied the woman. Jesus said, "You are right in saying you have no husband, 18 for you have had five, and the man you are living with now is not your husband. What you said is true." 19 "Sir," said the woman, "I see that you are a prophet. 20 Our ancestors worshiped on this mountain, but you people claim that Jerusalem is the place where men must worship God." 21 Jesus said to her: "Believe me, woman, the hour is coming when you will worship the Father neither on this mountain nor in Jerusalem. 22 You people worship what you do not understand, while we understand what we worship, since salvation is from the Jews. 23 But the hour is coming, and is now here, when true worshipers will worship the Father in spirit and in truth. Indeed, it is just such worshipers the Father seeks. 24 God is spirit, and those who worship him ought to worship in spirit and truth." 25 The woman said to him: "I know that the Messiah is coming, the one called Christ; when he comes he will tell us everything." 26 Jesus replied: "I who speak to you am he."[23]

575. Now (v. 10), the Evangelist gives us Christ's spiritual teaching. First, he gives the teaching itself. Secondly, the effect it had (v. 27). As to the first, he does two things. First, a summary of the entire instruction is given. Secondly, he unfolds it part by part (v. 11).

576. He said therefore: You are amazed that I, a Jew, should ask you, a Samaritan woman, for water; but you should not be amazed, because I have come to give drink, even to the Gentiles. Thus he says: **If you knew the gift of God, and realized who it is who says to you, Give me a drink, you perhaps would have asked him.**

577. We may begin with what is last, and we should know first what is to be understood by water. And we should say that water signifies the grace of the Holy Spirit. Sometimes this grace is called fire, and at other times water, to show that it is neither one of these in its nature, but like them in the way it acts.[24] It is called fire because it lifts up our hearts by its ardor and heat: "ardent in Spirit" (Rom 12:11), and because it burns up sins: "Its light is fire and flame" (Sg 8:6). Grace

23. St. Thomas quotes Jn 4:13 in *ST* I-II, q. 2, a. 1, ad 3; I-II, q. 30, a. 4; I-II, q. 33, a. 2, *sed contra*; Jn 4:14 in *ST* I-II, q. 114, a. 3; Jn 4:21 in *ST* I-II, q. 108, a. 3, ad 3; II-II, q. 84, a. 3, obj. 1; Jn 4:23 in *ST* I-II, q. 108, a. 3, ad 3; II-II, q. 83, a. 5, ad 1; II-II, q. 84, a. 2, obj. 1; II-II, q. 93, a. 1, ad 1; II-II, q. 94, a. 2, obj. 3; and Jn 4:24 in *ST* I, q. 3, a. 1 *sed contra*; I-II, q. 101, a. 2, obj. 4; I-II, q. 101, a. 3, obj. 3; II-II, q. 81, a. 7, obj. 1; II-II, q. 83, a. 13, obj. 1; III, q. 58, a. 1, obj. 1; III, q. 60, a. 4, obj. 2; III, q. 63, a. 4, ad 1. See also III, q. 42, a. 1, obj. 3.
24. See *ST* I, q. 1, a. 9; see also I, q. 36, a. 1.

is called water because it cleanses: "I will pour clean water upon you, and you will be cleansed from all your uncleanness" (Ez 36:25), and because it brings a refreshing relief from the heat of temptations: "Water quenches a flaming fire" (Sir 3:33), and also because it satisfies our desires, in contrast to our thirst for earthly things and all temporal things whatever: "Come to the waters, all you who thirst" (Is 55:1).[25]

Now water is of two kinds: living and non-living. Non-living water is water which is not connected or united with the source from which it springs, but is collected from the rain or in other ways into ponds and cisterns, and there it stands, separated from its source. But living water is connected with its source and flows from it. So according to this understanding, the grace of the Holy Spirit is correctly called living water, because the grace of the Holy Spirit is given to man in such a way that the source itself of the grace is also given, that is, the Holy Spirit. Indeed, grace is given by the Holy Spirit: "The love of God is poured out into our hearts by the Holy Spirit, who has been given to us" (Rom 5:5). For the Holy Spirit is the unfailing fountain from whom all gifts of grace flow: "One and the same Spirit does all these things" (1 Cor 12:11).[26] And so, if anyone has a gift of the Holy Spirit without having the Spirit, the water is not united with its source, and so is not living but dead: "Faith without works is dead" (Jas 2:20).

578. Then we are shown that in the case of adults, living water, i.e., grace, is obtained by desiring it, i.e., by asking. "The Lord has heard the desire of the poor" (Ps 10:17), for grace is not given to anyone without their asking and desiring it. Thus we say that in the justification of a sinner an act of free will is necessary to detest sin and to desire grace, according to Matthew (7:7): "Ask and you will receive." In fact, desire is so important that even the Son himself is told to ask: "Ask me, and I will give to you" (Ps 2:8). Therefore, no one who resists grace receives it, unless he first desires it; this is clear in the case of Paul who, before he received grace, desired it, saying: "Lord, what do you want me to do?" (Acts 9:6). Thus it is significant that he says, *you perhaps would have asked him*. He says *perhaps* on account of free will, with which a person sometimes desires and asks for grace, and sometimes does not.[27]

579. There are two things which lead a person to desire and ask for grace: a knowledge of the good to be desired and a knowledge of the giver. So, Christ offers these two to her. First of all, a knowledge of the gift itself; hence he says, *If you knew the gift of God*, which is every desirable good which comes from the Holy Spirit: "I know that I cannot control myself unless God grants it to me" (Wis 8:21). And this is a gift of God, and so forth. Secondly, he mentions the giver; and he says,

25. See *ST* III, q. 66, a. 3.   26. See *ST* I, q. 38, aa. 1–2.
27. See *ST* I-II, q. 112, a. 2.

and realized who it is who says to you, i.e., if you knew the one who can give it, namely, that it is I: "When the Paraclete comes, whom I will send you from the Father, the Spirit of truth . . . he will bear witness to me" (below 15:26); "You have given gifts to men" (Ps 67:19).[28]

Accordingly, this teaching concerns three things: the gift of living water, asking for this gift, and the giver himself.

580. When he says, *The woman challenged him*, he treats these three things explicitly. First, the gift; secondly, asking for the gift (v. 19); and thirdly, the giver (v. 25). He does two things about the first. First, he explains the gift by showing its power. Secondly, he considers the perfection of the gift (v. 15). About the first he does two things. First, he gives the woman's request. Secondly, Christ's answer (v. 13).

581. We should note, with respect to the first, that this Samaritan woman, because she was sensual, understood in a worldly sense what the Lord understood in a spiritual sense: "The sensual man does not perceive those things that pertain to the Spirit of God" (1 Cor 2:14). Consequently, she tried to reject what our Lord said as unreasonable and impossible with the following argument: You promise me living water; and it must come either from this well or from another one. But it cannot come from this well because *You, sir, have no bucket, and the well is deep*; and it does not seem probable that you can get it from some other well, because you are not *greater than our father Jacob, who gave us this well*.

582. Let us first examine what she says, *You, sir, have no bucket*, i.e., no pail to use to draw water from the well, *and the well is deep*, so you cannot reach the water by hand without a bucket.

The depth of the well signifies the depth of Sacred Scripture and of divine wisdom: "It has great depth. Who can find it out?" (Ecc 7:25).[29] The bucket with which the water of wisdom is drawn out is prayer: "If any of you lack wisdom, ask God" (Jas 1:5).[30]

583. The second point is given at, *Are you greater than our father Jacob, who gave us this well?* As if to say: Have you better water to give us than Jacob? She calls Jacob her father not because the Samaritans were descendants of the Jews, as is clear from what was said before, but because the Samaritans had the Mosaic law, and because they occupied the land promised to the descendants of Jacob.

The woman praised this well on three counts. First, on the authority of the one who gave it; so she says: *our father Jacob, who gave us this well*. Secondly, on account of the freshness of its water, saying: *Jacob drank from it with his sons*: for they would not drink it if it were not fresh, but only give it to their cattle. Thirdly, she praises its abun-

---

28. See *ST* I, q. 43, aa. 3, 6.   29. See *ST* I, q. 1, a. 10.
30. See *ST* II-II, q. 45, a. 1.

dance, saying, *and his flocks*: for since the water was fresh, they would not have given it to their flocks unless it were also abundant.

So, too, Sacred Scripture has great authority: for it was given by the Holy Spirit. It is delightfully fresh: "How sweet are your words to my palate" (Ps 118:103). Finally, it is exceedingly abundant, for it is given not only to the wise, but also to the unwise.[31]

584. Then when he says, *Jesus replied and said*, he sets down the Lord's response, in which he explains the power of his doctrine. First, with respect to the fact that he had called it water. Secondly, with respect to the fact that he called it living water (v. 14).

585. He shows that his doctrine is the best water because it has the effect of water, that is, it takes away thirst much more than does that natural water. He shows by this that he is greater than Jacob. So he says, *Jesus replied and said*, as if to say: You say that Jacob gave you a well; but I will give you better water, because *whoever drinks this water*, that is, natural water, or the water of sensual desire and concupiscence, although it may satisfy his appetite for a while, *will be thirsty again*, because the desire for pleasure is insatiable: "When will I wake up and find wine again?" (Prv 23:35). *But whoever drinks the water*, that is, spiritual water, *that I give, will never be thirsty again*. "My servants will drink, and you will be thirsty," as said in Isaiah (65:13).

586. Since we read in Sirach (24:29): "Those who drink me will still thirst," how is it possible that we will never be thirsty if we drink this water of divine wisdom, since this Wisdom itself says we will still thirst? I answer that both are true: because he who drinks the water that Christ gives still thirsts and does not thirst. But whoever drinks natural water will become thirsty again for two reasons. First, because material and natural water is not eternal, and it does not have an eternal cause, but an impermanent one; therefore its effects must also cease: "All these things have passed away like a shadow" (Wis 5:9). But spiritual water has an eternal cause, that is, the Holy Spirit, who is the unfailing fountain of life. Accordingly, he who drinks of this will never thirst; just as someone who had within himself a fountain of living water would never thirst.

The other reason is that there is a difference between a spiritual and a temporal thing. For although each produces a thirst, they do so in different ways. When a temporal thing is possessed it causes us to be thirsty, not for the thing itself, but for something else; while a spiritual thing when possessed takes away the thirst for other things, and causes us to thirst for it. The reason for this is that before temporal things are possessed, they are highly regarded and thought satisfying; but after they are possessed, they are found to be neither so great as

31. See *ST* I, q. 1, a. 8.

thought nor sufficient to satisfy our desires, and so our desires are not satisfied but move on to something else. On the other hand, a spiritual thing is not known unless it is possessed: "No one knows but he who receives it" (Rv 2:17). So, when it is not possessed, it does not produce a desire; but once it is possessed and known, then it brings pleasure and produces desire, but not to possess something else. Yet, because it is imperfectly known on account of the deficiency of the one receiving it, it produces a desire in us to possess it perfectly. We read of this thirst: "My soul thirsted for God, the living fountain" (Ps 41:2). This thirst is not completely taken away in this world because in this life we cannot understand spiritual things; consequently, one who drinks this water will still thirst for its completion. But he will not always be thirsty, as though the water will run out, for we read (Ps 35:9): "They will be intoxicated from the richness of your house." In the life of glory, where the blessed drink perfectly the water of divine grace, they will never be thirsty again: "Blessed are they who hunger and thirst for what is right," that is, in this world, "for they will be satisfied," in the life of glory" (Mt 5:6).[32]

587. Then when he says, *The water that I give will become a fountain within him, leaping up to provide eternal life*, he shows from the movement of the water that his doctrine is living water: thus he says that it is a leaping fountain: "The streams of the river bring joy to the city of God" (Ps 45:5).

The course of material water is downward, and this is different from the course of spiritual water, which is upward. Thus he says: I say that material water is such that it does not slake your thirst; but the water that I give not only quenches your thirst, but it is a living water because it is united with its source. Hence he says that this water *will become a fountain within* one: a fountain leading, through good works, to eternal life. So he says, leaping up, that is, making us leap up, *to eternal life*, where there is no thirst: "He who believes in me, out of his heart there will flow rivers" that is, of good desires, "of living water" (below 7:38); "With you is the fountain of life" (Ps 35:10).[33]

588. Then when he says, *The woman said*, he states her request for the gift. First, her understanding of the gift is noted. Secondly, the woman is found guilty (v. 17). As was said, the way to obtain this gift is by prayer and request. And so first, we have the woman's request. Secondly, Christ's answer (v. 16).

589. We should note with respect to the first that at the beginning of this conversation the woman did not refer to Christ as "Lord," but simply as a Jew, for she said: "How is it that you, being a Jew, ask me, a woman of Samaria, for a drink?" But now as soon as she hears that

---

32. See *ST* I, q. 26, a. 3; I-II, q. 2, a. 6; I-II, q. 2, a. 8; I-II, q. 3, a. 8.
33. See *ST* I-II, q. 4, a. 3.

he can be of use to her and give her water, she calls him "Lord": *Lord, give me this water.* For she was thinking of natural water, and was subject to the two natural necessities of thirst and labor, that is, of going to the well and of carrying the water. So she mentions these two things when asking for the water: saying in reference to the first, *so that I shall not grow thirsty*; and in reference to the second, *and have to keep coming here to draw water*, for man naturally shrinks from labor: "They do not labor as other men" (Ps 72:5).

590. Then (v. 16), the answer of Jesus is given. Here we should note that our Lord answered her in a spiritual way, but she understood in a sensual way. Accordingly, this can be explained in two ways. One way is that of Chrysostom,[34] who says that our Lord intended to give the water of spiritual instruction not only to her, but especially to her husband, for as is said, "Man is the head of woman" (1 Cor 11:3), so that Christ wanted God's precepts to reach women through men, and "If the wife wishes to learn anything, let her ask her husband at home" (1 Cor 14:35).[35] So he says, *Go, call your husband, and then come back here*; and then I will give it to you with him and through him.

Augustine[36] explains it another way, mystically. For as Christ spoke symbolically of water, he did the same of her husband. Her husband, according to Augustine, is the intellect: for the will brings forth and conceives because of the cognitive power that moves it; thus the will is like a woman, while the reason, which moves the will, is like her husband. Here the woman, i.e., the will, was ready to receive, but was not moved by the intellect and reason to a correct understanding, but was still detained on the level of sense. For this reason the Lord said to her, *Go*, you who are still sensual, *call your husband*, call in the reasoning intellect so you can understand in a spiritual and intellectual way what you now perceive in a sensual way; *and then come back here*, by understanding under the guidance of reason.

591. Here (v. 17), the woman is found guilty by Christ. First, her answer is set down. Secondly, the encounter in which she is found guilty by Christ.

592. As to the first, we should note that the woman, desiring to hide her wrongdoing, and regarding Christ as only a mere man, did answer Christ truthfully, although she keep silent about her sin, for as we read, "A fornicating woman will be walked on like dung in the road" (Sir 9:10). She said, *I have no husband.* This was true, for although she previously had a number of husbands, five of them, she did not now have a lawful husband, but was just living with a man; and it is for this that the Lord judges her.[37]

---

34. *Hom. in Io.* 32. 2; PG 59, col. 186; cf. *Catena aurea*, 4:13–18.
35. See *ST* III, q. 55, a. 1, ad 3.
36. *Tract. in Io.* 15. 18–19; PL 35, col. 1516–17; cf. *Catena aurea*, 4:13–18.
37. See *ST* II-II, q. 154, a. 8.

593. Then the Evangelist reports that Jesus said to her: *You are right in saying you have no husband*, a legitimate husband; *for you have had five*, before this one, *and the man you are living with now*, using as a husband, *is not your husband. What you said is true*, because you do not have a husband. The reason our Lord spoke to her about these things he had not learned from her and which were her secrets, was to bring her to a spiritual understanding so that she might believe there was something divine about Christ.

594. In the mystical sense, her five husbands are the five books of Moses: for, as was said, the Samaritans accepted these. And so Christ says, *you have had five*, and then follows *and he whom you now have*, i.e., he to whom you are now listening, i.e., Christ, *is not your husband*, because you do not believe.

This explanation, as Augustine[38] says, is not very good. For this woman came to her present "husband" after having left the other five, whereas those who come to Christ do not put aside the five books of Moses. We should rather say, *you have had five*, i.e., the five senses, which you have used up to this time; but *the man you are living with now*, i.e., an erring reason, with which you still understand spiritual things in a sensual way, is not your lawful husband, but an adulterer who is corrupting you. *Call your husband*, i.e., your intellect, so that you may really understand me.

595. Now the Evangelist treats of the request by which the gift is obtained, which is prayer. First there is the woman's inquiry about prayer. Secondly, Christ's answer (v. 21). Concerning the first the woman does two things. First, she admits that Christ is qualified to answer her question. Secondly, she asks the question (v. 20).

596. And so this woman, hearing what Christ had told her about things that were secret, admits that the one who up to now she believed was a mere man, is a prophet, and capable of settling her doubts. For it is characteristic of prophets to reveal what is not present, and hidden: "He who is now called a prophet was formerly called a seer" (1 Sm 9:9). And so she says, *Sir, I see that you are a prophet.* As if to say: You show that you are a prophet by revealing hidden things to me. It is clear from this, as Augustine[39] says, that her husband was beginning to return to her. But he did not return completely because she regarded Christ as a prophet: for although he was a prophet, "A prophet is not without honor except in his own country" (Mt 13:57), he was more than a prophet, because he produces prophets: "Wisdom produces friends of God and prophets" (Wis 7:27).[40]

597. Then she asks her question about prayer, saying: *Our ancestors worshiped on this mountain, but you people claim that Jerusa-*

38. *De div. quaest. 83*, q. 64. 6–7; PL 40, col. 57; cf. *Catena aurea*, 4:13–18.
39. *Tract. in Io.* 15. 23; PL 35, col. 1518; cf. *Catena aurea*, 4:19–24.
40. See *ST* I-II, q. 174, a. 1; III, q. 7, a. 8; III, q. 31, a. 2; III, q. 42, a. 1.

lem is the place where men must worship God. Here we should admire the woman's diligence and attention: for women are considered curious and unproductive, and not only unproductive, but also lovers of ease (1 Tim 5), whereas she did not ask Christ about worldly affairs, or about the future, but about the things of God, in keeping with the advice, "Seek first the kingdom of God" (Mt 6:33)

She first asks a question about a matter frequently discussed in her country, that is, about the place to pray; this was the subject of argument between Jews and Samaritans. She says, *Our ancestors worshiped on this mountain.* We should mention that the Samaritans, worshiping God according to the precepts of the law, built a temple in which to adore him; and they did not go to Jerusalem where the Jews interfered with them. They built their temple on Mount Gerizim, while the Jews built their temple on Mount Zion. The question they debated was which of these places was the more fitting place of prayer; and each presented reasons for its own side. The Samaritans said that Mount Gerizim was more fitting, because their ancestors worshiped the Lord there. So she says, *Our ancestors worshiped on this mountain.*

598. How can this woman say, *our ancestors,* since the Samaritans were not descended from Israel? The answer, according to Chrysostom,[41] is that some claim that Abraham offered his son on that mountain; but others claim that is was on Mount Zion. Or, we could say that *our ancestors* means Jacob and his sons, who as stated in Genesis (33) and as mentioned before, lived in Shechem, which is near Mount Gerizim, and who probably worshiped the Lord there on that mountain. Or it could be said that the children of Israel worshiped on this mountain when Moses ordered them to ascend Mount Gerizim that he might bless those who observed God's precepts, as recorded in Deuteronomy (6). And she calls them her ancestors either because the Samaritans observed the law given to the children of Israel, or because the Samaritans were now living in the land of Israel, as said before.

The Jews said that the place to worship was in Jerusalem, by command of the Lord, who had said: "Take care not to offer your holocausts in every place, but offer them in the place the Lord will choose" (Dt 12:13). At first, this place of prayer was in Shiloh, and then after, on the authority of Solomon and the prophet Nathan, the Ark was taken from Shiloh to Jerusalem, and it was there the temple was built: so we read: "He left the tabernacle in Shiloh," and a few verses later, "But he chose the tribe of Judah, Mount Zion, which he loved" (Ps 77:68). Thus the Samaritans appealed to the authority of the patriarchs, and the Jews appealed to the authority of the prophets, whom the Samaritans did not accept. This is the issue the woman raises. It is not surprising that she was taught about this, for it often happens in

41. *Hom. in Io.* 32. 2; PG 59, col. 186; cf. *Catena aurea,* 4:19–24.

places where there are differences in beliefs that even the simple people are instructed about them. Because the Samaritans were continually arguing with the Jews over this, it came to the knowledge of the
women and ordinary people.

599. Christ's answer is now set down (v. 21). First he distinguished
three types of prayer. Secondly, he compares them to each other (v. 22).

600. As to the first, he first of all gains the woman's attention, to indicate that he was about to say something important, saying, *Believe
me*, and have faith, for faith is always necessary: "To come to God, one
must believe" (Heb 11:6); "If you do not believe, you will not understand" (Is 7:9).[42]

Secondly, he mentions the three kinds of worship: two of these
were already being practiced, and the third was to come. Of the two
that were current, one was practiced by the Samaritans, who worshiped on Mount Gerizim; he refers to this when he says, *the hour is
coming when you will worship the Father neither on this mountain*, of
Gerizim. The other way was that of the Jews, who prayed on Mount
Zion; and he refers to this when he says, *nor in Jerusalem*.

The third type of worship was to come, and it was different from
the other two. Christ alludes to this by excluding the other two: for if
the hour is coming when they will no longer worship on Mount Gerizim or in Jerusalem, then clearly the third type to which Christ refers
will be a worship that does away with the other two.[43] For if someone
wishes to unite two people, it is necessary to eliminate that over which
they disagree, and give them something in common on which they
will agree. And so Christ, wishing to unite the Jews and Gentiles, eliminated the observances of the Jews and the idolatry of the Gentiles; for
these two were like a wall separating the peoples. And he made the
two people one: "He is our peace, he who has made the two of us one"
(Eph 2:14). Thus the ritual observances [of the Jews] and the idolatry of the Gentiles were abolished, and the true worship of God established by Christ.

601. As for the mystical sense, and according to Origen,[44] the three
types of worship are three kinds of participation in divine wisdom.
Some participate in it under a dark cloud of error, and these adore on
the mountain: for every error springs from pride: "I am against you,
destroying mountain" (Jer 51:25). Others participate in divine wisdom
without error, but in an imperfect way, because they see in a mirror
and in an obscure way; and these worship in Jerusalem, which signifies the present Church: "The Lord is building Jerusalem" (Ps 146:2).
But the blessed and the saints participate in divine wisdom without er-

42. See *ST* II-II, q. 2, a. 5.
43. See *ST* I-II, q. 103, a. 3; III, q. 62, a. 4.
44. *Comm. in Io.* XIII. 14, nos. 86–89; 15, no. 113; PG 14, col. 420B–C; 429C;
cf. *Catena aurea*, 4:19–24.

ror in a perfect way, for they see God as he is, as said in 1 John (3:2). And so Christ says, *the hour is coming,* i.e., is waited for, when you will participate in divine wisdom neither in error nor in a mirror in an obscure way, but as it is.[45]

602. Then (v. 22), he compares the different kinds of worship to each other. First, he compares the second to the first. Secondly, the third to the first and second (v. 23). As to the first he does three things. First, he shows the shortcomings of the first type of worship. Secondly, the truth of the second (v. 22b). Thirdly, the reason for each statement.

603. As to the first he says, *You people worship what you do not understand.*

Some might think that the Lord should have explained the truth of the matter and solved the woman's problem. But the Lord does not bother to do so because each of these kinds of worship was due to end.

As to his saying, *You people worship,* and so on, it should be pointed out that, as the Philosopher[46] says, knowledge of complex things is different than knowledge of simple things. For something can be known about complex things in such a way that something else about them remains unknown; thus there can be false knowledge about them. For example, if someone has true knowledge of an animal as to its substance, he might be in error touching the knowledge of one of its accidents, such as whether it is black or white; or of a difference, such as whether it has wings or is four-footed. But there cannot be false knowledge of simple things: because they are either perfectly known inasmuch as their quiddity is known; or they are not known at all, if one cannot attain to a knowledge of them. Therefore, since God is absolutely simple, there cannot be false knowledge of him in the sense that something might be known about him and something remain unknown, but only in the sense that knowledge of him is not attained. Accordingly, anyone who believes that God is something that he is not, for example, a body, or something like that, does not adore God but something else, because he does not know him, but something else.[47]

Now the Samaritans had a false idea of God in two ways. First of all, because they thought he was corporeal, so that they believed that he should be adored in only one definite corporeal place. Further, because they did not believe that he transcended all things, but was equal to certain creatures, they adored along with him certain idols, as if they were equal to him.[48] Consequently, they did not know him, because they did not attain to a true knowledge of him. So the Lord says, *You people worship what you do not understand,* i.e., You do not

45. See *ST* I, q. 26, a. 3; I-II, q. 3, a. 8.
46. See Aristotle, *Metaphysics,* θ 10, 1051 b 1–32.
47. See *ST* I, q. 3, a. 1; II-II, q. 2, a. 2, ad 3.
48. See *ST* I, q. 3, a. 5; II-II, q. 94, a. 3.

adore God because you do not know him, but only some imaginary being you think is God, "as the Gentiles do, with their foolish ideas" (Eph 4:17).

604. As to the second, i.e., the truth of the worship of the Jews, he says, *we understand what we worship*. He includes himself among the Jews, because he was a Jew by race, and because the woman thought he was a prophet and a Jew. *We understand what we worship*, because through the law and the prophets the Jews acquired a true knowledge or opinion of God, in that they did not believe that he was corporeal nor in one definite place, as though his greatness could be enclosed in a place: "If the heavens, and the heavens of the heavens cannot contain you, how much less this house that I have built" (1 Kgs 8:27). And neither did they worship idols: "God is known in Judah" (Ps 75:2).[49]

605. He gives the reason for this when he says, *since salvation is from the Jews*. As if to say: The true knowledge of God was possessed exclusively by the Jews, for it had been determined that salvation would come from them. And as the source of health should itself be healthy, so the source of salvation, which is acquired by the true knowledge and the true worship of God, should possess the true knowledge of God. Thus, since the source of salvation and its cause, i.e., Christ, was to come from them, according to the promise in Genesis (22:18): "All the nations will be blessed in your descendents," it was fitting that God be known in Judah.[50]

606. Salvation comes from the Jews in three ways. First in their teaching of the truth, for all other peoples were in error, while the Jews held fast to the truth, according to Romans (3:2): "What advantage do Jews have? First, they were entrusted with the words of God." Secondly, in their spiritual gifts: for prophecy and the other gifts of the Spirit were given to them first, and from them they reached others: "You," i.e., the Gentiles, "a wild olive branch, are ingrafted on them," i.e., on the Jews (Rom 11:17); "If the Gentiles have become sharers in their (i.e., the Jews') spiritual goods, they ought to help the Jews as to earthly goods" (Rom 15:27). Thirdly, since the very author of salvation is from the Jews, since "Christ came from them in the flesh" (Rom 9:5).[51]

607. Now (v. 23), he compares the third kind of worship to the first two. First, he mentions its superiority to the others. Secondly, how appropriate this kind of worship is (v. 23b).

608. As to the first point, we should note, as Origen[52] says, that when speaking above of the third kind of worship, the Lord said, *the hour is coming when you will worship the Father neither on this mountain nor in Jerusalem*; but he did not then add, *and is now here*.

49. See *ST* I-II, q. 98, a. 2.
50. See *ST* II-II, q. 16, aa. 1–2.
51. See *ST* I-II, q. 98, a. 4.
52. *Comm. in Io.* XIII. 14, no. 86; PG 14, col. 420B. cf. *Catena aurea*, 4:19–24.

But now, in speaking of it, he does say, *the hour is coming, and is now here*. The reason is because the first time he was speaking of the worship found in heaven, when we will participate in the perfect knowledge of God, which is not possessed by those still living in this mortal life. But now he is speaking of the worship of this life, and which has now come through Christ.

609. So he says, *But the hour is coming, and is now here, when true worshipers will worship the Father in spirit and in truth*.

We can understand this, as Chrysostom[53] does, as showing the superiority of this worship to that of the Jews. So that the sense is: Just as the worship of the Jews is superior to that of the Samaritans, so the worship of the Christians is superior to that of the Jews. It is superior in two respects. First, because the worship of the Jews is in bodily rites: "Rites for the body, imposed only until the time they are reformed" (Heb 9:10); while the worship of the Christians is in spirit. Secondly, because the worship of the Jews is in symbols: for the Lord was not pleased with their sacrificial victims insofar as they were things; so we read, "Shall I eat the flesh of bulls, or drink the blood of goats?" (Ps 49:13), and again, "You would not be pleased with a holocaust" (Ps 50:18), that is, as a particular thing; but such a sacrificial victim would be pleasing to the Lord as a symbol of the true victim and of the true sacrifice: "The law has only a shadow of the good things to come" (Heb 10:1). But the worship of the Christians is in truth, because it is pleasing to God in itself: "grace and truth have come through Jesus Christ," as we saw above (1:17). So he is saying here that *true worshipers will worship in spirit*, not in bodily rites, *and in truth*, not in symbols.[54]

610. This passage can in interpreted in a second way, by saying that when our Lord says, *in spirit and in truth*, he wants to show the difference between the third kind of worship and not just that of the Jews, but also that of the Samaritans. In this case, *in truth*, refers to the Jews: for the Samaritans, as was said, were in error, because they worshiped what they did not understand. But the Jews worshiped with a true knowledge of God.

611. *In spirit and in truth* can be understood in a third way, as indicating the characteristics of true worship. For two things are necessary for a true worship: one is that the worship be spiritual, so he says, *in spirit*, i.e., with fervor of spirit: "I will pray with spirit, and I will pray with my mind" (1 Cor 14:15); "Singing to the Lord in your hearts" (Eph 5:19). Secondly, the worship should be *in truth*. First, in the truth of faith, because no fervent spiritual desire is meritorious unless united to the truth of faith, "Ask with faith, without any doubt-

53. *Hom. in Io.* 33. 2; PG 59, col. 190; cf. *Catena aurea*, 4:19–24.
54. See *ST* I-II, q. 108, a. 1; III, q. 62, aa. 1 and 3.

ing" (Jas 1:6). Secondly, *in truth*, i.e., without pretense or hypocrisy; against such attitudes we read: "They like to pray at street corners, so people can see them" (Mt 6:5).[55]

This prayer, then, requires three things: first, the fervor of love: secondly, the truth of faith, and thirdly, a correct intention.

He says, the true worshipers will worship **the Father** in spirit and in truth, because under the law, worship was not given to the Father, but to the Lord. We worship in love, as sons; whereas they worshiped in fear, as slaves.[56]

612. He says *true* worshipers, in opposition to three things mentioned in the above interpretations. First, in opposition to the false worship of the Samaritans: "Put aside what is not true, and speak the truth" (Eph 4:25). Secondly, in opposition to the fruitless and transitory character of bodily rites: "Why do you love what is without profit, and seek after lies" (Ps 4:3). Thirdly, it is opposed to what is symbolic: "Grace and truth have come through Jesus Christ" (above 1:17).

613. Then when he says, **Indeed, it is just such worshipers the Father seeks**, he shows that this third kind of worship is appropriate for two reasons. First, because the One worshiped wills and accepts this worship. Secondly, because of the nature of the One worshiped (v. 24).

614. Concerning the first, we should note that for a man to merit receiving what he asks, he should ask for things which are not in opposition to the will of the giver, and also ask for them in a way which is acceptable to the giver. And so when we pray to God, we ought to be such as God seeks. But God seeks those who will worship him in spirit and in truth, in the fervor of love and in the truth of faith; "And now, Israel, what does the Lord your God want from you, but that you fear the Lord your God, and walk in his ways, and love him, and serve the Lord your God with all your heart" (Dt 10:12); and in Micah (6:8): "I will show you, man, what is good, and what the Lord requires of you: to do what is right, and to love mercy, and to walk attentively with your God."

615. Then he shows that the third type of worship is appropriate from the very nature of God, saying, **God is spirit**. As is said in Sirach (13:19), "Every animal loves its like"; and so God loves us insofar as we are like him. But we are not like him by our body, because he is incorporeal, but in what is spiritual in us, for **God is spirit**: "Be renewed in the spirit of your mind" (Eph 4:23).[57]

In saying, **God is spirit**, he means that God is incorporeal: "A spirit does not have flesh and bones" (Lk 24:39); and also that he is a life-giver, because our entire life is from God, as its creative source.

55. See ST II-II, q. 111, a. 3.
56. See *ST* I-II, q. 91, a. 5; I-II, q. 99, aa. 1 and 6.
57. See Thomas Aquinas, *Super Eph.*, chap. 4, lec. 7, no. 243; *ST* I, q. 3, a. 1; I, q. 93, a. 1, ad 1.

God is also truth: "I am the way, and the truth, and the life" (below 14:6). Therefore, we should worship him in spirit and in truth.

616. When he says, *The woman said to him,* he mentions the one who gives the gift, and this corresponds to what our Lord said before, *If you knew the gift of God, and realized who it is who says to you, Give me a drink, you perhaps would have asked him.* First, we have the woman's profession. Secondly, the teaching of Christ (v. 26). As to the first, he does two things. First, the woman professes her faith in the Christ to come. Secondly, in the fullness of his teaching, *he will tell us everything.*

617. The woman, wearied by the profound nature of what Christ was saying, was confused and unable to understand all this. She says: *I know that the Messiah is coming, the one called Christ.* As if to say: I do not understand what you are saying, but a time will come when the Messiah will arrive, and then we will understand all these things. For "Messiah" in Hebrew means the same as "Anointed One" in Latin, and "Christ" in Greek. She knew that the Messiah was coming because she had been taught by the books of Moses, which foretell the coming of Christ: "The scepter will not be taken away from Judah . . . until he who is to be sent comes" (Gn 49:10). As Augustine says,[58] this is the first time the woman mentions the name "Christ": and we see by this that she is now beginning to return to her lawful husband.

618. When this Messiah comes, he will give us a complete teaching. Hence she says, *when he comes he will tell us everything.* This was foretold by Moses: "I will raise up a prophet for them, from among their own brothers, like them; and I will put my words in his mouth, and he will tell them all I command him" (Dt 18:18). Because this woman had now called her husband, i.e., intellect and reason, the Lord now offers her the water of spiritual teaching by revealing himself to her in a most excellent way.

619. And so Jesus says: *I who speak to you am he,* i.e., I am the Christ: "Wisdom goes to meet those who desire her, so she may first reveal herself to them" (Wis 6:14), and below (14:21): "I will love him, and reveal myself to him."

Our Lord did not reveal himself to this woman at once because it might have seemed to her that he was speaking out of vainglory. But now, having brought her step by step to a knowledge of himself, Christ revealed himself at the appropriate time: "Words appropriately spoken are like apples of gold on beds of silver" (Prv 25:11). In contrast, when he was asked by the Pharisees whether he was the Christ, "If you are the Christ, tell us clearly" (below 10:24), he did not reveal himself to them clearly, because they did not ask to learn but to test him. But this woman is speaking in all simplicity.

58. *Tract. in Io.* 15. 21–23; PL 35, col. 1517–19; *De div. quaest. 83,* q. 64. 8; PL 40, col. 59.

LECTURE 3

27 His disciples, returning at this point, were amazed that Jesus was speaking with a woman. But no one said, "What do you want?" or "Why are you talking to her?" 28 The woman then left her water jar and went off to the town. And she said to the people: 29 "Come, and see the man who told me everything that I have done. Could he not be the Christ?" 30 At that they set out from the town to meet him. 31 Meanwhile, his disciples asked him saying, "Rabbi, eat something." 32 But he said to them, "I have food to eat of which you do not know." 33 At this the disciples said to one another, "Do you suppose that someone has brought him something to eat?"

620. After presenting the teaching on spiritual water, the Evangelist now deals with the effect of this teaching. First, he sets down the effect itself. Secondly, he elaborates on it (v. 31). The effect of this teaching is its fruit for those who believe. And first we have its fruit which relates to the disciples, who were surprised at Christ's conduct. Secondly, its fruit in relation to the woman, who proclaimed Christ's power (v. 28).

621. We are told three things about the disciples. First, their return to Christ: he says, **His disciples, returning at this point.** As Chrysostom[59] reminds us, it was very convenient that the disciples returned after Christ had revealed himself to the woman, since this shows us that all events are regulated by divine providence: "He made the small and the great, and takes care for all alike" (Wis 6:8); "There is a time and fitness for everything" (Ecc 8:6).

622. Secondly, we see their surprise at what Christ was doing; he says, they **were amazed that Jesus was speaking with a woman.** They were amazed at what was good; and as Augustine[60] says, they did not suspect any evil. They were amazed at two things. First, at the extraordinary gentleness and humility of Christ: for the Lord of the world stooped to speak with a poor woman, and for a long time, giving us an example of humility: "Be friendly to the poor" (Sir 4:7). Secondly, they were amazed that he was speaking with a Samaritan and a foreigner, for they did not know the mystery by which this woman was a symbol of the Church of the Gentiles; and Christ sought the Gentiles, for he came "to seek and to save what was lost" (Lk 19:10)

623. Thirdly, we see the disciples' reverence for Christ, shown by their silence. For we show our reverence for God when we do not presume to discuss his affairs: "It is to the glory of God to conceal things;

and to the glory of kings to search things out" (Prv 25:2). So the Evangelist says that although his disciples were surprised, none of them said, *What do you want?* or asked him, *Why are you talking to her?* "Listen in silence" (Sir 32:9). Yet the disciples had been so trained to observe order, because of their reverence and filial fear toward Christ, that now and then they would question him about matters that concerned themselves, i.e., when Christ said things relating to them, but which were beyond their understanding: "Young men, speak if you have to" (Sir 32:10). At other times they did not question him; in those matters that were not their business, as here.

624. Then (v. 28), we have the fruit which relates to the woman; by what she said to her people, she was taking on the role of an apostle. From what she says and does, we can learn three things. First, her affective devotion; secondly, her way of preaching; thirdly, the effect her preaching had (v. 30).

625. Her affection is revealed in two ways. First, because her devotion was so great that she forgot why she had come to the well, and left without the water and her water jar. So he says, *the woman then left her water jar and went off to the town*, to tell of the wonderful things Christ had done; and she was not now concerned for her own bodily comfort but for the welfare of others. In this respect she was like the apostles, who "leaving their nets, followed the Lord" (Mt 4:20). The water jar is a symbol of worldly desires, by which men draw out pleasures from the depths of darkness—symbolized by the well—i.e., from a worldly manner of life. Accordingly, those who abandon worldly desires for the sake of God leave their water jars: "No soldier of God becomes entangled in the business of this world" (2 Tim 2:4). Secondly, we see her affection from the great number of those to whom she brings the news: not to just one or two, but to the entire town; we read that she *went off to the town*. This signifies the duty Christ gave to the apostles: "Go, teach all nations" (Mt 28:19); and "I have chosen you to go and bring forth fruit" (below 15:16).

626. Next we see her manner of preaching (v. 29). She first invites them to see Christ, saying, *Come and see the man*. Although she had heard Christ say that he was the Christ, she did not at once tell the people that they should come to the Christ, or believe, so as not to give them a reason for scoffing. So at first she mentions things that were believable and evident about Christ, as that he was a man: "made in the likeness of men" (Phil 2:7). Neither did she say, "believe," but *Come, and see*; for she was convinced that if they were to taste from that well by seeing him, they would be affected in the same way she was: "Come, and I will tell you the great things he has done for me" (Ps 65:16). In this she is imitating the example of a true preacher, not calling men to himself, but to Christ: "What we preach is not ourselves, but Jesus Christ" (2 Cor 4:5).

627. Secondly, she mentions a clue to Christ's divinity, saying, *who told me everything that I have done*, that is, how many husbands she had had. For it is the function and sign of the divinity to disclose hidden things and the secrets of hearts. Although the things she had done would cause her shame, she is still not ashamed to mention them; for as Chrysostom[61] says: "When the soul is on fire with the divine fire, it no longer pays attention to earthly things, neither to glory nor to shame, but only to that flame that holds it fast."

628. Thirdly, she infers the greatness of Christ, saying, *Could he not be the Christ?* She did not dare to say that he was the Christ, lest she seem to be trying to teach them; they could have become angry at this and refuse to go with her. Yet she was not entirely silent on this point, but submitting it to their judgment, set it forth in the form of a question, saying, *Could he not be the Christ?* For this is an easier way to persuade someone.

629. This insignificant woman signifies the condition of the apostles, who were sent out to preach: "Not many of you are learned in the worldly sense, not many powerful ... But God chose the simple ones of the world to embarrass the wise" (1 Cor 1:26). Thus in Proverbs (9:3) the apostles are called handmaids: "She," divine wisdom, i.e., the Son of God, "sent out her handmaids," the apostles, "to summon to the tower."

630. The fruit of her preaching is given when he says, *At that they set out from the town*, to where she had returned, to meet him, Christ. We see by this that if we desire to come to Christ, we must set out from the town, i.e., leave behind our carnal desires: "Let us go out to him outside the camp, bearing the abuse he took," as we read in Hebrews (13:13).

631. Now the effect of this spiritual teaching is elaborated. First, by what Christ said to his disciples; secondly, by the effect of all this on the Samaritans (v. 39). Concerning the first he does two things. First, we have the situation in which Christ speaks to his disciples; secondly, what he said (v. 32).

632. The situation is the insistence of the apostles that Christ eat. He says, *Meanwhile*, i.e., between the time that Christ and the woman spoke and the Samaritans came, *his disciples asked him*, that is, Christ, *Rabbi, eat something*: for they thought that then was a good time to eat, before the crowds came from the town. For the disciples did not usually offer Christ food in the presence of strangers: so we read in Mark (6:31), that so many people came to him that he did not even have time to eat.

633. After presenting the situation, he gives its fruit. First, it is given in figurative language. Secondly, we see the disciples are slow in

61. *Hom. in Io.* 34. 1; PG 59, col. 193; cf. *Catena aurea*, 4:27–30.

understanding this. Thirdly, the Lord explains what he meant (v. 34).

634. The fruit of his spiritual teaching is proposed under the symbols of food and nourishment; so the Lord says, *I have food to eat*. We should note that just as bodily nourishment is incomplete unless there is both food and drink, so also both should be found in spiritual nourishment: "The Lord fed him with the bread of life and understanding," this is the food, "and gave him a drink of the water of saving wisdom," and this is the drink (Sir 15:3). So it was appropriate for Christ to speak of food after having given drink to the Samaritan woman. And just as water is a symbol for saving wisdom, so food is a symbol of good works.

The food that Christ had to eat is the salvation of men; this was what he desired. When he says that he has food to eat, he shows how great a desire he has for our salvation. For just as we desire to eat when we are hungry, so he desires to save us: "My delight is to be with the children of men" (Prv 8:31). So he says, *I have food to eat*, i.e., the conversion of the nations, *of which you do not know*; for they had no way of knowing beforehand about this conversion of the nations.

635. Origen[62] explains this in a different way, as follows. Spiritual food is like bodily food. The same amount of bodily food is not enough for everyone; some need more, others less. Again, what is good for one is harmful to another. The same thing happens in spiritual nourishment: for the same kind and amount should not be given to everyone, but adjusted to what is appropriate to the disposition and capacity of each. "Like newborn babes, desire spiritual milk" (1 Pt 2:2). Solid food is for the perfect; thus Origen says that the man who understands the loftier doctrine, and who has charge of others in spiritual matters, can teach this doctrine to those who are weaker and have less understanding. Accordingly, the Apostle says in 1 Corinthians (3:2): "Being little ones in Christ, I gave you milk, not solid food." And Jesus could say this with much more truth: *I have food to eat*; and "I have many things to tell you, but you cannot bear them now" (below 16:12).[63]

636. The slowness of the disciples to understand these matters is implied by the fact that what our Lord said about spiritual food, they understood as referring to bodily food. For even they were still without understanding, as we see from Matthew (15:16). It is not surprising that this Samaritan woman did not understand about spiritual water, for even the Jewish disciples did not understand about spiritual food.

In their saying to each other, *Do you suppose that someone has brought him something to eat?* we should note that it was customary

---

62. *Comm. in Io.* XIII. 33, nos. 205–13; PG 14, col. 456C–457B; cf. *Catena aurea*, 4:31–34.

63. See *ST* III, q. 42, a. 4.

for Christ to accept food from others; but not because he needs our goods: "He does not need our goods" (Ps 15:2), nor our food, because it is he who gives food to every living thing.

637. Then why did he desire and accept goods from others? For two reasons. First, so that those who give him these things might acquire merit. Secondly, in order to give us an example that those engrossed in spiritual matters should not be ashamed of their poverty, nor regard it burdensome to be supported by others.[64] For it is fitting that teachers have others provide their food so that, being free from such concerns, they may carefully pay attention to the ministry of the word, as Chrysostom[65] says, and as we find in the Gloss.[66] "Let the elders who rule well be regarded as worthy of a double compensation; especially those concerned with preaching and teaching" (1 Tim 5:17).

LECTURE 4

34 Jesus explained to them, "My food is to do the will of him who sent me, to accomplish his work. 35 Do you not have a saying: 'There are still four months, and it will be harvest time'? So I say to you: Lift up your eyes, look at the fields, because they are already white for the harvest! 36 He who reaps receives his wages and gathers fruit for eternal life, so that the sower can rejoice at the same time as the reaper. 37 For here the saying is verified: 'One man sows, another reaps.' 38 I have sent you to reap what you have not worked for. Others have done the work, and you have entered into their labors."[67]

638. Since the disciples were slow to understand the Lord's figure of speech, the Lord now explains it. First, we have its explanation, secondly, its application (v. 35).

639. As to the first, we should note that just as Christ explained to the Samaritan woman what he had told her in figurative language about water, so he explains to his apostles what he told them in figurative language about food. But he does not do so in the same way in both cases. Since the apostles were able to understand these matters more easily, he explains to them at once and in few words; but to the Samaritan woman, since she could not understand as well, our Lord leads her to the truth with a longer explanation.

640. It is perfectly reasonable for Christ to say, *My food is to do the will of him who sent me, to accomplish his work.* For as bodily food

64. See *ST* III, q. 40, a. 3.
65. *Comm. ad Gal.* 6. 2; PG 61, col. 676.
66. See Peter Lombard, *In Ep. I ad Tim.*, ch. 5; PL 192, col. 354 C–D.
67. St. Thomas quotes Jn 4:36 in *ST* I-II, q. 70, a. 1, obj. 1.

sustains a man and brings him to perfection, the spiritual food of the
soul and of the rational creature is that by which he is sustained and
perfected; and this consists in being joined to his end and following a
higher rule. David, understanding this, said: "For me, to adhere to God
is good" (Ps 72:28). Accordingly, Christ, as man, fittingly says that his
food is to do the will of God, to accomplish his work.[68]

641. These two expressions can be understood as meaning the same
thing, in the sense that the second is explaining the first. Or, they can
be understood in different ways.

If we understand them as meaning the same, the sense is this: *My
food is*, i.e., in this is my strength and nourishment, *to do the will of
him who sent me*; according to, "My God, I desired to do your will,
and your law is in my heart" (Ps 39:9), and, "I came down from heaven
not to do my own will, but the will of him who sent me" (below
6:38). But because "to do the will" (*facere voluntatem*) of another can be
understood in two ways—one, by making him will it, and second, by
fulfilling what I know he wills—therefore, explaining what it means
to do the will of him who sent him, the Lord says, to *accomplish his
work*, that is, that I might complete the work I know he wants: "I must
do the works of him who sent me while it is day" (below 9:4).

If these two expressions are understood as different, then we should
point out that Christ did two things in this world. First, he taught the
truth, in inviting and calling us to the faith; and by this he fulfilled the
will of the Father: "This is the will of my Father, who sent me: that everyone who sees the Son and believes in him should have eternal life"
(below 6:40). Secondly, he accomplished the truth by opening in us,
by his passion, the gate of life, and by giving us the power to arrive at
complete truth: "I have accomplished the work which you gave me to
do" (below 17:4). Thus he is saying: *My food is to do the will of him
who sent me*, by calling men to the faith, *to accomplish his work*, by
leading them to what is perfect.[69]

642. Another interpretation, given by Origen,[70] is that every man
who does good works should direct his intention to two things: the
honor of God and the good of his neighbor: for as it is said: "The end
of the commandment is love" (1 Tim 1:5), and this love embraces both
God and our neighbor. And so, when we do something for God's sake,
the end of the commandment is God; but when it is for our neighbor's good, the end of the commandment is our neighbor. With this
in mind, Christ is saying, *My food is to do the will of him who sent me*,

68. See *ST* III, q. 18, aa. 5–6.
69. See *ST* III, q. 49, a. 5.
70. This interpretation, ascribed to Origen by Thomas, is found neither in the
Catena aurea for Jn 4:34, nor in Origen's own comments on this text in his *Commentary on John*: XIII. 37, nos. 236–46; PG 14, col. 461D–465A.

God, i.e., to direct and regulate my intention to those matters that concern the honor of God, *to accomplish his work*, i.e., to do things for the benefit and perfection of man.

643. On the other hand, since the works of God are perfect, it does not seem proper to speak of accomplishing or completing them. I answer that among lower creatures, man is the special work of God, who made him to his own image and likeness (Gn 1:26). And in the beginning God made this a perfect work, because as we read in Ecclesiastes (7:30): "God made man upright." But later, man lost this perfection by sin, and abandoned what was right. And so, this work of the Lord needed to be repaired in order to become right again; and this was accomplished by Christ, for "Just as by the disobedience of one man, many were made sinners, so by the obedience of one man, many will be made just" (Rom 5:19). Thus Christ says, *to accomplish his work*, i.e., to bring man back to what is perfect.[71]

644. Then when he says, *Do you not have a saying: There are still four months, and it will be harvest time?* he makes use of a simile. Note that when Christ asked the Samaritan woman for a drink, "Give me a drink," he made use of a simile concerning water. But here, the disciples are urging the Lord to eat, and now he makes use of a simile concerning spiritual food.

There are some persons whom God asks for a drink, as this Samaritan woman; and there are some who offer a drink to God. But no one offers food to God unless God first asks him for it: for we offer spiritual food to God when we ask him for our salvation, that is, when we ask, "Your will be done on earth as it is in heaven" (Mt 6:10). We cannot obtain salvation of ourselves, unless we are pre-moved by "prevenient grace," according to the statement in Lamentations (5:21): "Make us come back to you, O Lord, and we will come back" (Lam 5:21). The Lord himself, therefore, first asks for that which makes us ask through "prevenient grace."[72]

In this simile, we have first, the harvest. Secondly, those who reap the harvest (v. 36). He does two things concerning the first. First, he states the simile concerning the natural harvest; secondly, concerning the spiritual harvest (v. 35b).

645. *Do you not have a saying: There are still four months, and it will be harvest time?* We can see from this that, as stated in Matthew (4:12), Christ left Judea and traveled through Samaria right after John was arrested, and that all this happened during the winter. So, because the harvests ripen there more according to the season, there were four months from that time till the harvest. Thus he says, *Do you not have a saying*, about the natural harvest, *There are still four months* that

71. See *ST* I-II, q. 106, a. 3.
72. See *ST* I-II, q. 111, a. 3.

must pass, *and it will be harvest time?* i.e., the time for gathering up
the harvest. *So I say to you,* speaking of the spiritual harvest, *Lift up
your eyes, look at the fields, because they are already white for the harvest.*

646. Here we should point out that harvest time is the time when
the fruit is gathered; and so whenever fruit is gathered can be regarded
as a harvest time. Now fruit is gathered at two times: for both in temporal and in spiritual matters there is nothing to prevent what is fruit
in relation to an earlier state from being seed in relation to something
later. For example, good works are the fruit of spiritual instruction, as
is faith and other such things; but these in turn are seeds of eternal life,
because eternal life is acquired through them.[73] So Sirach (24:23) says:
"My blossoms," in relation to the fruit to follow, "bear the fruit of hon-
or and riches," in relation to what preceded.

With this in mind, there is a certain gathering of a spiritual harvest;
and this concerns an eternal fruit, i.e., the gathering of the faithful into
eternal life, of which we read: "The harvest is the end of the world"
(Mt 13:39). We are not here concerned with this harvest. Another
spiritual harvest is gathered in the present; and this is understood in
two ways. In the first, the gathering of the fruit is the converting of the
faithful to be assembled in the Church; in the second, the gathering is
the very knowing of the truth, by which a person gathers the fruit of
truth into his soul. And we are concerned with these two gatherings of
the harvest, depending on the different expositions.

647. Augustine[74] and Chrysostom[75] understand the gathering of
the harvest in the first way, as follows. You say that it is not yet the
time for the natural harvest; but this is not true of the spiritual harvest. Indeed, *I say to you: Lift up your eyes,* i.e., the eyes of your mind,
by thinking, or even your physical eyes, *look at the fields, because they
are already white for the harvest*: because the entire countryside was
full of Samaritans coming to Christ.

The statement that the fields *are already white* is metaphorical: for
when sown fields are white, it is a sign that they are ready for harvest.
And so he only means to say by this that the people were ready for salvation and to hear the word. He says, *look at the fields,* because not only
the Jews, but the Gentiles as well, were ready for the faith: "The harvest
is great, but the workers are few" (Mt 9:37). And just as harvests are
made white by the presence of the burning heat of the summer sun, so
by the coming of the Sun of justice, i.e., Christ, and his preaching and
power, men are made ready for salvation. Malachi (4:2) says: "The sun
of justice will rise on you who fear my name." Thus it is that the time

73. See *ST* I-II, q. 5, a. 7.
74. *Tract. in Io.* 15. 32; PL 35, col. 1521–22.
75. *Hom. in Io.* 34. 2; PG 59, col. 194; cf. *Catena aurea,* 4:35–38.

of Christ's coming is called the time of plenitude or fullness: "When the
fullness of time had come, God sent his Son" (Gal 4:4).[76]

648. Origen[77] deals with the second gathering of the harvest, i.e.,
the gathering of truth in the soul. He says that one gathers as much of
the fruit of truth in the harvest as the truths he knows. And he says
that everything said here (v. 35) was presented as a parable. In this interpretation, the Lord does two things. First, he mentions a false doctrine held by some. Secondly, he rejects it, *I say to you.*

Some thought that man could not acquire any truth about anything. This opinion gave rise to the heresy of the Academicians, who
maintained that nothing can be known as certain in this life;[78] about
which we read: "I tested all things by wisdom. I said: 'I will acquire
wisdom,' and it became further from me" (Ecc 7:24). Our Lord mentions this opinion when he says, *Do you not have a saying: There are
still four months and it will be harvest time?* i.e., this whole present
life, in which man serves under the four elements, must end, so that
after it truth may be gathered in another life.

Our Lord rejects this opinion when he says: This is not true, *I say
to you: Lift up your eyes.* Sacred Scripture usually uses this expression
when something subtle and profound is being presented; as, "Lift up
your eyes on high, and see who has created these things" (Is 40:26).
For when our eyes are not lifted away from earthly things or from
the desires of the flesh, they are not fit to know spiritual fruit. For
sometimes they are prevented from considering divine things because
they have stooped to earthly things: "They have fixed their eyes on the
earth" (Ps 16:11); sometimes they are blinded by concupiscence: "They
have averted their eyes so as not to look at heaven or remember the
judgments of God" (Dn 13:9).[79]

649. So he says, *Lift up your eyes, look at the fields, because they
are already white for the harvest,* i.e., they are such that the truth
can be learned from them: for by the "fields" we specifically understand all those things from which truth can be acquired, especially the
Scriptures: "Search the Scriptures . . . they bear witness to me" (below
5:39). Indeed, these fields existed in the Old Testament, but they were
not white for the harvest because men were not able to pick spiritual fruit from them until Christ came, who made them white by open-

76. See *ST* III, q. 1, aa. 5–6.

77. *Comm. in Io.* XIII. 40, nos. 262–63; PG 14, col. 469B; cf. *Catena aurea,* 4:35–
38.

78. The Academicians that Aquinas refers to here are those that Augustine
writes against in his early work, *Against the Academicians* (written in 386). The
Academicians were part of the New Academy that looked to Cicero as its patron.
They adopted a skeptical philosophy, denying that we could have true knowledge of things.

79. See *ST* II-II, q. 15, a. 1.

ing their understanding: "He opened their minds so they could under-stand the Scriptures" (Lk 24.45).[80] Again, creatures are harvests from which the fruit of truth is gathered: "The invisible things of God are clearly known by the things that have been made" (Rom 1:20). None the less, the Gentiles who pursued a knowledge of these things gath-ered the fruits of error rather than of truth from them; because as we read, "they served the creature rather than the Creator" (Rom 1:25).[81] So the harvests were not yet white; but they were made white for the harvest when Christ came.

650. Next (v. 36), he deals with the reapers. First, he gives their re-ward. Secondly, he mentions a proverb. And thirdly, he explains it, i.e., applies it (v. 38).

651. Concerning the first, we should note that when the Lord was explaining earlier about spiritual water, he mentioned the way in which spiritual water differs from natural water: a person who drinks natural water will become thirsty again, but one who drinks spiritual water will never be thirsty again. Here, too, in explaining about the harvest, he points out the difference between a natural and a spiritual harvest. Three things are mentioned.

First, the way in which the two harvests are similar: namely, in that the person who reaps either harvest receives a wage. But the one who reaps spiritually is the one who gathers the faithful into the Church, or who gathers the fruit of truth into his soul. Each of these will receive a wage, according to: "Each one will receive his own wage according to his work" (1 Cor 3:8).

The two other points he mentions concern the ways the two har-vests are unlike each other. First, the fruit gathered from a natural harvest concerns the life of the body; but the fruit gathered by one who reaps a spiritual harvest concerns eternal life. So he says, he who reaps, i.e., he who reaps spiritually, *gathers fruit for eternal life*, that is, the faithful, who will obtain eternal life: "Your fruit is sanctification, your end is eternal life" (Rom 6:22). Or, this fruit is the very knowing and explaining of the truth by which man acquires eternal life: "Those who explain me will have eternal life," as we read in Sirach (24:31).[82] Secondly, the two harvests are unlike because in a natural harvest it is considered a misfortune that one should sow and another reap; hence he who sows is saddened when another reaps. But it is not this way when the seed is spiritual, for the sower can rejoice at the same time as the reaper.

According to Chrysostom[83] and Augustine,[84] the ones who sow

80. See *ST* I, q. 1, a. 10; I-II, q. 107, a. 3.
81. See *ST* I, q. 2, aa. 2–3; II-II, q. 1, a. 8, ad 1.
82. See *ST* II-II, q. 180, a. 5; II-II, q. 181, a. 3.
83. *Hom. in Io*. 34. 2; PG 59, col. 195–96; cf. *Catena aurea*, 4:35–38.
84. *Tract. in Io*. 15. 32; PL 35, col. 1521–22; cf. *Catena aurea*, 4:35–38.

spiritual seed are the fathers and prophets of the Old Testament, for "The seed is the word of God" (Lk 8:11), which Moses and the prophets sowed in the land of Judah. But the apostles were the reapers, because the former were not able to accomplish what they wanted to do, i.e., to bring men to Christ; this was done by the apostles. And so both the apostles and the prophets rejoice together, in one mansion of glory, over the conversion of the faithful: "Joy and gladness will be found there, thanksgiving and the voice of praise" (Is 51:3). This refutes the heresy of the Manicheans who condemn the fathers of the Old Testament; for as the Lord says here, they will rejoice with the apostles.[85]

According to Origen,[86] however, the "sowers" in any faculty [of the soul] are those who confer the very first principles of that faculty; but the reapers are those who proceed from these principles to further truths. And this is all the more true of the science of all the sciences. The prophets are sowers, because they handed down many things concerning divine matters; but the apostles are the reapers, because in preaching and teaching they revealed many things which the prophets did not make known: "which was not made known to the sons of men in other generations as it has now been revealed to his holy apostles" (Eph 3:5).[87]

652. Then when he says, *For here the saying is verified*, we are given a proverb. As if to say: *For here*, i.e., in this fact, *the saying is verified*, i.e., the proverb in current use among the Jews is fulfilled: *One man sows, another reaps*. This proverb seems to have grown out of a statement in Leviticus (26:16): "You will sow your seed in vain for it will be devoured by your enemies." As a result, the Jews used this proverb when one person labored on something, but another received the pleasure from it. This then is what our Lord says: The proverb is verified here because it was the prophets who sowed and labored, while you are the ones to reap and rejoice.

Another interpretation would be this. *For here the saying is verified*, i.e. what I am saying to you, *One man sows, another reaps*, because you will reap the fruits of the labor of the prophets. Now the prophets and the apostles are different, but not in faith, for they both had faith: "But now the justice of God has been manifested outside the law; the law and the prophets bore witness to it" (Rom 3:21).[88] They are different in their manner of life, for the prophets lived under the ceremonies of the law, from which the apostles and Christians have been freed: "When we were children, we were slaves un-

85. See *ST* III, q. 49, a. 5.
86. *Comm. in Io.* XIII. 46, nos. 302–5; PG 14, col. 480D–481B; cf. *Catena aurea*, 4:35–38.
87. See *ST* II-II, q. 174, a. 6.
88. See *ST* I-II, q. 107, aa. 2–3; II-II, q. 1, a. 7.

der the elements of this world. But when the fullness of time came, God sent his Son, made of a woman, made under the law, to redeem those who were under the law, so that we could receive adoption as sons" (Gal 4:3). And although the apostles and prophets labor at different times, nevertheless they will rejoice equally and receive wages *for eternal life, so that the sower can rejoice at the same time as the reaper.* This was prefigured in the transfiguration of Christ, where all had their own glory, both the fathers of the Old Testament, that is, Moses and Elijah, and the fathers of the New Testament, that is, Peter, John and James. We see from this that the just of the New and of the Old Testaments will rejoice together in the glory to come.[89]

653. Then (v. 38), he applies the proverb. First, he calls the apostles reapers. Secondly, he says they are laborers (v. 38b).

654. He says concerning the first: I say that it is one who reaps, because you are reapers, and another who sows, for *I have sent you to reap what you have not worked for.* He does not say, "I will send you," but *I have sent you.* He says this because he sent them twice. One time was before his passion, when he sent them to the Jews, saying: "Do not go on the roads of the Gentiles . . . but go rather to the lost sheep of the house of Israel" (Mt 10:5). In this case, they were sent to reap that on which they did not work, that is, to convert the Jews, among whom the prophets worked. After the resurrection, Christ sent them to the Gentiles, saying: "Go to the whole world, and preach the good news to every creature," as we find in Mark (16:15). This time they were sent to sow for the first time; for as the Apostle says: "I have preached the good news, but not where Christ was already known, so as not to build on another's foundation. But as it is written: 'They to whom he was not proclaimed will see, and they who have not heard will understand'" (Rom 15:20). And so Christ says, *I have sent you,* referring to the first time they were sent. This is the way, then, the apostles are reapers, and others, the prophets, are the sowers.

655. Accordingly, he says, *Others have done the work,* by sowing the beginnings of the doctrine of Christ, *and you have entered into their labors,* to collect the fruit: "The fruit of good labors is glorious" (Wis 3:15). The prophets labored, I say, to bring men to Christ: "If you believed Moses, you would perhaps believe me, for he wrote of me" (below 5:46). If you do not believe his written words, how will you believe my spoken words? But the prophets did not reap the fruit; so Isaiah said with this in mind: "I have labored for nothing and without reason: in vain I have exhausted my strength" (Is 49:4).

89. See *ST* III, q. 45, a. 3.

LECTURE 5

39 Many Samaritans of that town believed in him on the testimo-
ny of the woman who said, "He told me everything I ever did." 40 So
when the Samaritans came to him, they begged him to stay with them
awhile. So he stayed there two days. 41 And many more believed in him
because of his own words. 42 And they said to the woman, "Now we be-
lieve not just because of your story, but because we have heard him our-
selves, and we know that here is truly the Savior of the world."[90]

656. Above, the Lord foretold to the apostles the fruit to be produced among the Samaritans by the woman's witness. Now the Evangelist deals with this fruit. First, the fruit of the woman's witness is giv-
en. Secondly, the growth of this fruit produced by Christ (v. 41). The
fruit of the woman's witness is shown in three ways.

657. First, by the faith of the Samaritans, for they believed in Christ.
Thus he says, **Many Samaritans of that town**, to which the woman
had returned, **believed in him**, and this, **on the testimony of the wom-**
an, from whom Christ asked for a drink of water, who said, **He told me**
everything I ever did: for this testimony was sufficient inducement to
believe Christ. For since Christ had disclosed her failures, she would
not have mentioned them if she had not been brought to believe. And
so the Samaritans believed as soon as they heard her. This indicates
that faith comes by hearing.[91]

658. Secondly, the fruit of her witness is shown in their coming to
Christ: for faith gives rise to a desire for the thing believed.[92] Accordingly, after they believed, they came to Christ, to be perfected by him.
So he says, **So when the Samaritans came to him.** "Come to him, and
be enlightened" (Ps 33:6); "Come to me, all you who labor and are
burdened, and I will refresh you" (Mt 11:28).

659. Thirdly, the fruit of her witness is shown in their desire: for a
believer must not only come to Christ, but desire that Christ remain
with him. So he says, **they begged him to stay with them awhile. So he**
stayed there two days.

The Lord remains with us through charity: "If anyone loves me, he
will keep my word" (below 14:23), and further on he adds, "and we
will make our abode with him." The Lord remains for two days because
there are two precepts of charity: the love of God and the love of our
neighbor, "On these two commandments all the law and the prophets
depend" (Mt 22:40). But the third day is the day of glory: "He will re-

90. St. Thomas quotes Jn 4:42 in *ST* II-II, q. 2, a. 10; II-II, q. 27, a. 3, ad 2.
91. See *ST* II-II, q. 6, a. 1.
92. See *ST* III, q. 45, a. 3.

vive us after two days; on the third day he will raise us up" (Hos 6:3). Christ did not remain there for that day because the Samaritans were not yet capable of glory.

660. Then (v. 41), the Evangelist says that the fruit resulting from the witness of the woman was increased by the presence of Christ; and this in three ways. First, in the number of those who believed. Secondly, in their reason for believing. Thirdly, in the truth they believed.

661. The fruit was increased as to the number of those who believed because while many believed in Christ on account of the woman, *many more believed in him because of his own words*, i.e., Christ's own words. This signifies that although many believed because of the prophets, many more were converted to the faith after Christ came, according to the Psalm (7:7): "Rise up, O Lord, in the command you have given, and a congregation of people will surround you."

662. Secondly, this fruit was increased because of the way in which they believed: for they say to the woman: *Now we believe not just because of your story*.

Here we should note that three things are necessary for the perfection of faith; and they are given here in order. First, faith should be right; secondly, it should be prompt; and thirdly, it should be certain.

Now faith is right when it obeys the truth not for some alien reason, but for the truth itself; and as to this he says that they said to the woman, *Now we believe*, the truth, *not just because of your story*, but because of the truth itself. Three things lead us to believe in Christ. First of all, natural reason: "Since the creation of the world the invisible things of God are clearly known by the things that have been made" (Rom 1:20). Secondly, the testimony of the law and the prophets: "But now justification from God has been manifested outside the law; the law and the prophets bore witness to it" (Rom 3:21). Thirdly, the preaching of the apostles and others: "How will they believe without someone to preach to them?" as Romans (10:14) says. Yet when a person, having been thus instructed, believes, he can then say that it is not for any of these reasons that he believes: i.e., neither on account of natural reason, nor the testimony of the law, nor the preaching of others, but solely on account of the truth itself: "Abram believed God, who regarded this as his justification" (Gn 15:6).[93]

Faith is prompt if it believes quickly; and this was verified in these Samaritans because they were converted to God by merely hearing him; so they say: we have heard him ourselves, and believe in him, and we know that here is truly the Savior of the world, without seeing miracles, as the Jews saw. And although to believe men quickly is an indication of thoughtlessness, according to Sirach (19:4): "He who be-

93. See *ST* II-II, q. 1, a. 1; II-II, q. 2, aa. 2, 4, 10.

lieves easily is frivolous," yet to believe God quickly is more praisewor-
thy: "When they heard me, they obeyed me" (Ps 17:45).

Faith should be certain, because one who doubts in the faith is an
unbeliever: "Ask with faith, without any doubting" (Jas 1:6). And so
their faith was certain; thus they say, *and we know*. Sometimes, one
who believes is said to know (*scire*), as here, because *scientia* [science,
knowledge in a more perfect state] and faith agree in that both are certain. For just as *scientia* is certain, so is faith; indeed, the latter is much
more so, because the certainty of *scientia* rests on human reason, which
can be deceived, while the certainty of faith rests on divine reason,
which cannot be contradicted. However they differ in mode: because
faith possesses its certainty due to a divinely infused light, while *scientia* possesses its certainty due to a natural light. For as the certitude of
scientia rests on first principles naturally known, so the principles of
faith are known from a light divinely infused: "You are saved by grace,
through faith; and this is not due to yourselves, for it is the gift of God"
(Eph 2:8).[94]

663. Thirdly, the fruit was increased in the truth believed; so they
say, *here is truly the Savior of the world*. Here they are affirming that
Christ is the unique, true and universal Savior.

He is the unique Savior for they assert that he is different from others when they say, *here is*, i.e., here he alone is who has come to save:
"Truly, you are a hidden God, the God of Israel, the Savior" (Is 45:15);
"There is no other name under heaven given to men, by which we are
saved" (Acts 4:12).[95]

They affirm that Christ is the true Savior when they say, *truly*. For
since salvation, as Dionysius[96] says, is deliverance from evil and pres-
ervation in good, there are two kinds of salvation: one is true, and the
other is not true. Salvation is true when we are freed from true evils
and preserved in true goods. In the Old Testament, however, although
certain saviors had been sent, they did not truly bring salvation, for
they set men free from temporal evils, which are not truly evils, nor
true goods, because they do not last. But Christ is truly the Savior, because he frees men from true evils, that is, sins: "He will save his people from their sins" (Mt 1:21), and he preserves them in true goods,
that is, spiritual goods.[97]

They affirm that he is the universal Savior because he is not just for
some, i.e., for the Jews alone, but is the Savior of the world. "God did
not send his Son into the world to judge the world, but that the world
might be saved through him" (above 3:17).[98]

94. See *ST* II-II, q. 4, a. 8; II-II, q. 6, a. 1.
95. See *ST* III, q. 26, a. 1; III, q. 48, a. 5.
96. *De div. nom.* 8. 9; PG 3, col. 896D–897B.
97. See *ST* III, q. 1, a. 2.
98. See *ST* III, q. 47, a. 4, ad 1; III, q. 49, a. 1.

LECTURE 6

43 After two days he left that place and went to Galilee. 44 Jesus himself had testified that a prophet has no honor in his own country. 45 When however he arrived in Galilee, the Galileans welcomed him, because they had seen all the things he had done in Jerusalem on the festive day, where they too had gone. 46a He therefore went to Cana in Galilee once more, where he had made the water wine.[99]

664. Having described the conversion of the Gentiles due to teaching, their conversion due to miracles is now given. The Evangelist mentions a miracle performed by Christ: first, giving the place: secondly, describing the miracle; and thirdly, its effect (v. 53). He does two things about the first. First, he gives the general location of the miracle, that is, Christ's own homeland. Secondly, the specific place (v. 46). With respect to the first he does two things. First, he mentions the general place. Secondly, he tells how Christ was received there (v. 45). Concerning the first he does two things. First, he indicates the general place. Secondly, he gives a certain reason, at (v. 44).

665. He says first of all: I say that Jesus remained with these Samaritans for two days, and *after two days he left that place*, i.e., Samaria, *and went to Galilee*, where he had been raised. This signifies that at the end of the world, when the Gentiles have been confirmed in the faith and in the truth, a return will be made to convert the Jews, according to: "until the full number of the Gentiles enters, and so all Israel will be saved" (Rom 11:25).

666. Then he gives a certain reason, saying: *Jesus himself had testified that a prophet has no honor in his own country.* There are two questions here: one is about the literal meaning; and the other about the continuity of this passage with the first.

The problem about the literal meaning is that it does not seem to be true, as stated here, that a prophet has no honor in his own country: for we read that other prophets were honored in their own land. Chrysostom[100] answers this by saying that the Lord is speaking here about the majority of cases. So, although there might be an exception in some individual cases, what is said here should not be considered false: for in matters concerning nature and morals, that rule is true which is verified in most cases: and if a few cases are otherwise, the rule is not considered to be false.

Now what the Lord says was true with respect to most of the prophets, because in the Old Testament it is hard to find any prophet

99. St. Thomas refers to Jn 4:44 in *ST* III, q. 7, a. 8, *sed contra*.
100. *Hom. in Io.* 35. 2; PG 59, col. 200.

who did not suffer persecution, as stated in Acts (7:52): "Which of the
prophets did your fathers not persecute?"; and in Matthew (23:37):
"Jerusalem, Jerusalem, you kill the prophets and stone those who are
sent to you." Further, this statement of our Lord holds true not only in
the case of the prophets among the Jews, but also, as Origen[101] says,
with many among the Gentiles, because they were held in contempt
by their fellow citizens and put to death: for living with men in the
usual way, and too much familiarity, lessen respect and breed contempt. So it is that those with whom we are more familiar we come to
reverence less, and those with whom we cannot become acquainted
we regard more highly.

However, the opposite happens with God: for the more intimate we
become with God through love and contemplation, realizing how superior he is, the more we respect him and the less do we esteem ourselves. "I have heard you, but now I see you, and so I reprove myself,
and do penance in dust and ashes" (Jb 42:5). The reason for this is that
man's nature is weak and fragile; and when one lives with another for
a long time, he notices certain weaknesses in him, and this results in
a loss of respect for him. But since God is infinitely perfect, the more a
person knows him the more he admires his superior perfection, and as
a result the more he respects him.[102]

667. But was Christ a prophet? At first glance it seems not, because
prophecy involves an obscure knowledge: "If there is a prophet of the
Lord among you, I will appear to him in a vision" (Nm 12:6). Christ's
knowledge, however, was not obscure. Yet he was a prophet, as is clear
from, "The Lord your God will raise up a prophet for you, from your
nation and your brothers; he will be like me. You will listen to him"
(Dt 18:15). This text is referred to Christ.

I answer that a prophet has a twofold function. First, that of seeing: "He who is now called a prophet was formerly called a seer" (1
Sm 9:9). Secondly, he makes known, announces; Christ was a prophet
in this sense for he made known the truth about God: "For this was I
born, and for this I came into the world: to testify to the truth" (below
18:37). As for the seeing function of a prophet, we should note that
Christ was at once both a "wayfarer" and a "comprehensor," or blessed.
He was a wayfarer in the sufferings of his human nature and in all the
things that relate to this. He was a blessed in his union with the divinity, by which he enjoyed God in the most perfect way.[103] There are two
things in the vision or seeing of a prophet. First, the intellectual light
of his mind; and as regards this Christ was not a prophet because his
light was not at all deficient, his light was that of the blessed. Secondly,

101. *Comm. in Io.* XIII. 54, nos. 376–77; PG 14, 504A; cf. *Catena aurea*, 4:43–45.
102. See *ST* II-II, q. 161, a. 3.
103. See *ST* III, q. 9, a. 2.

all imaginary vision is also involved; and with respect to this Christ did have a likeness to the prophets insofar as he was a wayfarer and was able to form various images with his imagination.[104]

668. Secondly, there is the problem about continuity. For the Evangelist does not seem to be right in connecting the fact that *After two days he left that place and went to Galilee*, with the statement of Jesus that a *prophet has no honor in his own country*. It would seem that the Evangelist should have said that Christ did not go into Galilee, for if he was not honored there, that would be a reason for not going there.

Augustine[105] answers this by suggesting that the Evangelist said this to answer a question that could have been raised, namely: Why did Christ return to Galilee since he had lived there for a long time, and the Galileans were still not converted to him; while the Samaritans were converted in two days? It is the same as saying: Even though the Galileans had not been converted, still Jesus went there, for *Jesus himself had testified that a prophet has no honor in his own country.*

Chrysostom[106] explains this in a different way: *After two days he left*, not for Capernaum, which was his homeland because of his continuous residence there, nor for Bethlehem, where he was born, nor for Nazareth, where he was educated. Thus he did not go to Capernaum; hence in Matthew (11:23) he upbraids them, saying: "And you, Capernaum, will you be exalted to heaven? You will descend even to hell." He went rather to Cana in Galilee. And he gives the reason here [for not going to Capernaum]: because they were ill-disposed toward him. This is what he says: *Jesus himself had testified that a prophet has no honor in his own country.*

669. Was Christ seeking glory from men? It seems not, for he says: "I do not seek my own glory" (below 8:50). I answer that it is only God who seeks his own glory without sin. A man should not seek his own glory from men, but rather the glory of God.[107] Christ, however, as God, fittingly sought his own glory, and as man, he sought the glory of God in himself.

670. Then he shows that Christ was received by the Galileans more respectfully than before, saying, *When however he arrived in Galilee, the Galileans welcomed him*, respectfully. The reason behind this was because they had seen all the things he had done in Jerusalem on the festive day, where they too had gone, as the law commanded.

This seems to conflict with the fact that we did not read above of any miracles being performed by Christ at Jerusalem. I answer, with

104. See *ST* II-II, q. 173, aa. 2–3.
105. *Tract. in Io.* 16. 3–7; PL 35, col. 1523–27; cf. *Catena aurea,* 4:43–45.
106. *Hom. in Io.* 35. 1–2; PG 59, col. 200; cf. *Catena aurea,* 4:43–45.
107. See *ST* II-II, q. 132.

the opinion of Origen,[108] that the Jews thought it a great miracle that Christ drove the traders from the temple with such authority (above 2:14). Or, we could say that Christ performed many miracles which were not written down, according to, "Jesus did many other signs . . . which are not written down in this book" (below 20:30).

671. In its mystical sense, this gives us an example that if we wish to receive Jesus Christ within ourselves, we should go up to Jerusalem on a festive day, that is, we should seek tranquility of mind, and examine everything which Jesus does there: "Look upon Zion, the city of our festive days" (Is 33:20); "I have meditated on all your works" (Ps 142:5).

672. Note that as men were lesser in dignity, they were better with respect to God. The Judeans were superior in dignity to the Galileans: "Look at the Scriptures and see that the Prophet will not come from Galilee" (below 7:52); and the Galileans were superior in dignity to the Samaritans: "The Jews had nothing to do with the Samaritans" (above 4:9). On the other hand, the Samaritans were better than the Galileans because more of them believed in Christ in two days without any miracles than the Galileans did in a long period of time and even with the miracle of the wine: for none of them believed in him except his disciples. Finally, the Judeans were worse than the Galileans, because none of them believed in Jesus, except perhaps Nicodemus.

673. Then he says, *He therefore went to Cana in Galilee.* According to Chrysostom,[109] this is given as a conclusion from what went before; it is as though he were saying: Christ did not go to Capernaum because he was not held in honor there. But he was under an obligation to go to Cana in Galilee: for on the first occasion he had been invited to the wedding, and now he goes again without being invited. The two trips to Cana are mentioned by the Evangelist to show their hardness of heart: for at the first miracle of the wine, only his disciples believed in Christ; and at the second miracle, only the official and his household believed. On the other hand, the Samaritans believed on Christ's words alone.

674. In the mystical sense, the two visits to Cana signify the effect of God's words on our minds. First of all they cause delight, because they who hear the word "receive the word with joy" (Mt 13:20). This is signified in the miracle of the wine, which as the Psalm (103:15) says, "gladdens the heart of man." Secondly, the word of God heals: "It was neither a herb nor a poultice that healed them, but your word, O Lord, which heals all things" (Wis 16:12). And this is signified by the curing of the sick son.

---

108. *Comm. in Io.* XIII. 56, nos. 381–88; PG 14, col. 504C–505C cf. *Catena aurea,* 4:43–45.

109. *Hom. in Io.* 35. 2; PG 59, col. 200; cf. *Catena aurea,* 4:43–45.

Further, these two visits to Cana indicate the two comings of the
Son of God. The first coming was in all gentleness to bring joy: "Rejoice and give praise, people of Zion, for he is great who is in your
midst, the Holy One of Israel" (Is 12:6). So the angel said to the shepherds: "I bring you good news of great joy . . . this day a Savior has
been born to you" (Lk 2:10). This is signified by the wine. His second
coming into the world will be in majesty, when he will come to take
away our weaknesses and our punishments, and to make us like his
radiant body. And this is signified in the cure of the sick son.

LECTURE 7

*46b There happened to be a certain official, whose son lay sick at
Capernaum. 47 When he heard that Jesus had come to Galilee from
Judea, he went to him, and begged him to come down and heal his son,
who was at the point of death. 48 But Jesus said to him, "Unless you
see signs and wonders, you do not believe." 49 The official said to him,
"Lord, come down before my child dies." 50 Jesus told him, "Go, your
son lives." The man took Jesus at his word, and started for home. 51
While he was on his way down, his servants ran up to meet him with
word that his son was going to live. 52 He asked them at what time his
boy got better. And they told him that yesterday at the seventh hour the
fever left him. 53 The father then realized that it was at that very hour
when Jesus told him, "Your son lives." He and his whole household became believers. 54 This was the second sign Jesus had performed on returning from Judea to Galilee.*[110]

675. Having told us the place of this miracle, the Evangelist now describes the miracle itself: telling us of the person who was ill; the one
who interceded for him; and the one who healed him. The one who
was ill was the son of the official; his father interceded for him; and it
was Christ who was to heal him.

676. About the person who was ill, he first tells us of his status, a
son of an official; secondly, where he was, *at Capernaum*; thirdly, his
illness, a *fever*.

He says about the first, *There happened to be a certain official,
whose son lay sick.* Now one can be called an official for a variety of
reasons. For example, if one is in charge of a small territory. This is not
its meaning here for at this time there was no king in Judea: "We have
no king but Caesar" (below 19:15). One is also called an official, as

---

110. St. Thomas quotes Jn 4:48 in *ST* III, q. 43, a. 1, obj. 3; III, q. 55, a. 5, ad 3;
and Jn 4:53 in *ST* II-II, q. 6, a. 1, obj. 2.

Chrysostom[111] says, because he is from a royal family; and this is also not its meaning here. In a third way, an official is some officer of a king or ruler; and this is its meaning here.

Some think, as Chrysostom[112] reports, that this official is the same as the centurion mentioned by Matthew (8:5). This is not so, for they differ in four ways. First, because the illness was not the same in each. The centurion was concerned with a paralytic, "My servant is lying paralyzed at home" (Mt 8:6); while this official's son is suffering from a fever, *yesterday at the seventh hour the fever left him*. Secondly, those who are sick are not the same. In the first case, it was a servant, "my servant"; but now we have a son, as it says, *whose son*. Thirdly, what is requested is different. For when Christ wanted to go to the home of the centurion, the centurion discouraged him, and said: "Lord, I am not worthy to have you come under my roof; but only say the word and my servant will be healed" (Mt 8:8). But this official asked Christ to come to his house, *Lord, come down before my child dies*. Fourthly, the places are different. For the first healing took place at Capernaum, while this one is at Cana in Galilee. So this official is not the same as the centurion, but was from the household of Herod the Tetrarch, or some kind of a herald, or an official of the Emperor.

677. In its allegorical sense, this official is Abraham or one of the fathers of the Old Testament, in so far as he adheres by faith to the king, that is, to Christ, about which we read, "I was made king by him over Zion" (Ps 2:6). Abraham adhered to him, for as is said below (8:56): "Abraham, your father, rejoiced that he might see my day." The son of this official is the Jewish people: "We are the descendants of Abraham, and we have never been slaves to any one" (below 8:33). But they are sick from evil pleasures and incorrect doctrines. They are sick at Capernaum, i.e., in the abundance of goods which caused them to leave their God, according to, "The beloved grew fat and rebellious . . . he deserted the God who made him, and left God his Savior" (Dt 32:15).

678. In the moral sense, in the kingdom of the soul, the king is reason itself: "The king, who sits on his throne of judgment" (Prv 20:8). But why is reason called the king? Because man's entire body is ruled by it: his affections are directed and informed by it, and the other powers of the soul follow it. But sometimes it is called an official [not the king], that is, when its knowledge is obscured, with the result that it follows inordinate passions and does not resist them; "They live with their foolish ideas, their understanding obscured by darkness" (Eph 4:17).[113] Consequently, the son of this official, i.e., the affections, are sick, that is, they deviate from good and decline to what is evil. If reason were the king, that is, strong, its son would not be sick; but being only an of-

111. *Hom. in Io.* 35. 2; PG 59, col. 201.
112. Ibid.; cf. *Catena aurea*, 4:46–54.
113. See *ST* I-II, q. 85, a. 3.

ficial, its son is sick. This happens at Capernaum because a great many temporal goods are the cause of spiritual sickness: "This was the crime of your sister Sodom: richness, satiety in food, and idleness" (Ez 16:49).

679. Now we see the person making his request (v. 47). First, we have the incentive for making his request. Secondly, the request itself. Thirdly, the need for the request.

680. The incentive for making the request was the arrival of Christ. So he says, *When he,* the official, *heard that Jesus had come to Galilee from Judea, he went to him.* For as long as the coming of Christ was delayed, men's hope of being healed from their sins was that much fainter; but when it is reported that his coming is near, our hope of being healed rises, and then we go to him. For he came into this world to save sinners: "The Son of Man came to seek and to save what was lost" (Lk 19:22).[114] Further, as Sirach says (18:23), we should prepare our soul by prayer, and we do this by going to God through our desires. And this is what the official did, as we read, *he went to him.* Amos (4:12) says, "Be prepared to meet your God, O Israel."

681. The request of the official was that Christ heal his son. So the Evangelist says that he *begged him to come down,* out of compassion: "O that you would rend the heavens, and come down" (Is 64:1), *and heal his son.* We, too, ought to ask to be healed from our sins: "Heal my soul, for I have sinned against you" (Ps 40:5). For no one of himself can return to the state of justice; rather, he has to be healed by God: "I cannot help myself" (Jb 6:13).[115] The fathers of the Old Testament interceded for the people of Israel in the same way; for as we read of one: "He loves his brothers, because he prays much for the holy city and for the people of Israel, Jeremiah, the prophet of God" (2 Mc 15:14).

682. The need for this request was urgent, for the son *was at the point of death.* When a person is tempted, he is beginning to become sick; and as the temptation grows stronger and takes the upper hand, inclining him to consent, he is near death. But when he has consented, he is at the point of death and beginning to die.[116] Finally, when he completes his sin, he dies; for as we read: "Sin, when it is completed, brings forth death" (Jas 1:15). The Psalm (33:22) says about this: "The death of sinners is the worst," because it begins here and continues into the future without end.

683. Now he deals with the request for Christ to heal the son of the official. First, our Lord's criticism is given. Secondly, the official's request. Thirdly, the granting of the request.

684. Our Lord criticizes him for his lack of faith, saying, *Unless you see signs and wonders, you do not believe.* This raises a question, for

114. See *ST* II-II, q. 17, a. 7.   115. See *ST* I-II, q. 113, a. 2.
116. See *ST* I-II, q. 74, a. 7.

it does not seem right to say this to this official, for unless he had believed that Christ was the Savior, he would not have asked him to heal his son.

The answer to this is that this official did not yet believe perfectly; indeed, there were two defects in his faith. The first was that although he believed that Christ was a true man, he did not believe that he had divine power; otherwise he would have believed that Christ could heal one even while absent, since God is everywhere, as Jeremiah (23:24) says: "I fill heaven and earth." And so he would not have asked Christ to come down to his house, but simply give his command. The second defect in his faith, according to Chrysostom,[117] was that he was not sure that Christ could heal his son: for had he been sure, he would not have waited for Christ to return to his homeland, but would have gone to Judea himself. But now, despairing of his son's health, and not wishing to overlook any possibility, he went to Christ like those parents who in their despair for the health of their children consult even unskilled doctors.

685. In the second place, it does not seem that he should have been criticized for looking for signs, for faith is proved by signs. The answer to this is that unbelievers are drawn to Christ in one way, and believers in another way. For unbelievers cannot be drawn to Christ or convinced by the authority of Sacred Scripture, because they do not believe it; neither can they be drawn by natural reason, because faith is above reason. Consequently, they must be led by miracles: "Signs are given to unbelievers, not to believers" (1 Cor 14:22). Believers, on the other hand, should be led and directed to faith by the authority of Scripture, to which they are bound to assent. This is why the official is criticized: although he had been brought up among the Jews and instructed in the law, he wanted to believe through signs, and not by the authority of the Scripture. So the Lord reproaches him, saying, **Unless you see signs and wonders,** i.e., miracles, which sometimes are signs insofar as they bear witness to divine truth. Or **wonders** (*prodigia*), either because they indicate with utmost certitude, so that a prodigy is taken to be a "portent" or some "sure indication"; or because they portend something in the future, as if something were called a wonder as if showing at a great distance some future effect.

686. Now we see the official's persistence, for he does not give up after the Lord's criticism, but insists, saying. **Lord, come down before my child dies:** "We should pray always, and not lose heart" (Lk 18:1). This shows an improvement in his faith in one respect, that is, in that he calls him "Lord." But there is not a total improvement, for he still thought that Christ had to be physically present to heal his son; so he asked Christ to come.

117. *Hom. in Io.* 35. 2; PG 59, col. 201; cf. *Catena aurea,* 4:46–54.

687. His request is granted by the Lord, for persevering prayer is answered.[118] Jesus said to him: *Go, your son lives.* Here we have first, the statement by Christ, who cured the boy, that the boy was cured. Secondly, we are told of the persons who witnessed the cure (v. 51). Two things are mentioned concerning the first: the command of the Lord and the obedience of the official (v. 50b).

688. As to the first, the Lord does two things. First, he orders; secondly, he affirms. He orders the official to go: hence he says, *Go,* i.e., prepare to receive grace by a movement of your free will toward God: "Turn to me, and you will be saved" (Is 45:22); and by a movement of your free will against sin. For four things are required for the justification of an adult sinner: the infusion of grace, the remission of guilt, a movement of the free will toward God, which is faith, and a movement of the free will against sin, which is contrition.[119]

Then the Lord says that his son is healed, which was the request of the official: *Your son lives.*

689. One may ask why Christ refused to go down to the home of this official as asked, while he promised to go see the servant of the centurion. There are two reasons for this. One, according to Gregory,[120] is to blunt our pride; the pride of us who offer our services to great men, but refuse to help the insignificant: since the Lord of all offered to go to the servant of the centurion, but refused to go to the son of an official: "Be well-disposed to the poor" (Sir 4:7). The other reason, as Chrysostom[121] says, was that the centurion was already confirmed in the faith of Christ, and believed that he could heal even while not present; and so our Lord promised to go to show approval of his faith and devotion. But this official was still imperfect, and did not yet clearly know that Christ could heal even while absent. And so our Lord does not go, in order that he may realize his imperfection.

690. The obedience of this official is pointed out in two ways. First, because he believed what Christ said; so he says. **The man took Jesus at his word**, that is, *Your son lives.* Secondly, because he did obey the order of Christ; so he says, **he started for home**, progressing in faith, although not yet fully or soundly, as Origen[122] says. This signifies that we must be justified by faith: "Justified by faith, let us have peace with God, through our Lord Jesus Christ" (Rom 5:1).[123] We also must go and start out by making progress: because he who stands still runs the risk of being unable to preserve the life of grace. For, along the road to God, if we do not go forward we fall back.

118. See *ST* II-II, q. 83, a. 14.
119. See *ST* I-II, q. 113, aa. 3–5.
120. *XL hom. in Evang.* II, *Hom.* 28. 2; PL 76, col. 1212; cf. *Catena aurea*, 4:46–54.
121. *Hom. in Io.* 35. 3; PG 59, col. 202; cf. *Catena aurea*, 4:46–54.
122. See *Comm. in Io.* XIII. 59, no. 409; PG 14, col. 512A.
123. See *ST* I-II, q. 113, a. 4; II-II, q. 7, a. 2.

691. Next we see the servants bringing news of the healing. First, the news of the healing is given. Secondly, there is an inquiry about the time of the healing (v. 52).

692. He says, *While he was on his way down*, from Cana of Galilee to his own home, *his servants ran up to meet him*—which shows that this official was wealthy and had many servants—*with word that his son was going to live*: and they did this because they thought that Christ was coming, and his presence was no longer necessary as the boy was already cured.

693. In the mystical sense, the servants of the official, i.e., of reason, are a man's works, because man is master of his own acts and of the affections of his sense powers, for they obey the command and direction of reason. Now these servants announce that the son of the official, that is, of reason, lives, when a man's good works shine out, and his lower powers obey reason, according to: "A man's dress, and laughter, and his walk, show what he is" (Sir 19:27).

694. Because this official did not yet believe either fully or soundly, he still wanted to know whether his son had been cured by chance or by the command of Christ. Accordingly, he asks about the time of the cure. *He asked them*, the servants, *at what time his boy got better*. And he found that his son was cured at exactly the same hour that our Lord said, *Go, your son lives*. And no wonder, because Christ is the Word, through whom heaven and earth were made: "He spoke and they were made; he commanded and they were created" (Ps 148:5).

695. *And they*, his servants, *told him that yesterday at the seventh hour the fever left him*. In the mystical sense, the seventh hour, when the boy is cured of his fever, signifies the seven gifts of the Holy Spirit, through whom sins are forgiven, according to: "Receive the Holy Spirit; whose sins you forgive, are forgiven" (below 20:22), and through whom spiritual life is produced in the soul: "It is the Spirit that gives life" (below 6:64).[124] Again, the seventh hour signifies the appropriate time for rest, for the Lord rested from all his work on the seventh day.[125] This indicates that the spiritual life of man consists in spiritual rest or quiet, according to: "If you remain at rest, you will be saved" (Is 30:15). But of the evil we read: "The heart of the wicked is like the raging sea, which cannot rest" (Is 57:20).

696. Next, we are given the effect of this miracle (v. 53). First, its fruit is mentioned. Secondly, this miracle is linked with another one (v. 54).

697. He says, *The father then realized*, by comparing the hour mentioned by the servants with the hour of Christ's affirmation, *that it was at that very hour when Jesus told him, Your son lives*. Because of this

---

124. See *ST* I-II, q. 68, aa. 1–2, 5.
125. See *ST* I, q. 73, a. 3.

he was converted to Christ, realizing that it was by his power that the miracle was accomplished. *He and his whole household became believers*, that is, his servants and his aides, because the attitude of servants depends on the condition, whether good or wicked, of their masters: "As the judge of the people is himself, so also are his ministers" (Sir 10:2); and in Genesis (18:19) we read: "I know that he will direct his sons."

This also shows that the faith of the official was constantly growing: for at the beginning, when he pleaded for his sick son, it was weak; then it began to grow more firm, when he called Jesus "Lord," then when he believed what the Lord said and started for home, it was more perfect, but not completely so, because he still doubted. But here, clearly realizing God's power in Christ, his faith is made perfect, for as Proverbs (4:18) says: "The way of the just goes forward like a shining light, increasing to the full light of day."[126]

698. Finally, this miracle is linked with the previous one, *This was the second sign Jesus had performed on returning from Judea to Galilee.* We can understand this in two ways. In one way, that our Lord performed two miracles during this one trip from Judea to Galilee; but the first of these was not recorded, only the second. In the other way, we could say that Jesus worked two signs in Galilee at different times: the one of the wine, and this second one about the son of this official after he returned again to Galilee from Judea.

We also see from this that the Galileans were worse than the Samaritans. For the Samaritans expected no sign from the Lord, and many believed in his word alone; but as a result of this miracle, only this official and his whole household believed: for the Jews were converted to the faith little by little on account of their hardness, according to: "I have become as one who harvests in the summer time, like a gleaner at the vintage: not one cluster to eat, not one of the early figs I desire" (Mi 7:1).

---

126. See *ST* II-II, q. 4, a. 5; II-II, q. 5, a. 4.

CHAPTER 5

LECTURE 1

1 After this there was a Jewish festival, and Jesus went up to Jerusalem. 2 Now at Jerusalem there is a Sheep Pool, called in Hebrew Bethsaida, having five porticoes. 3 In these porticoes lay a great number of people: feeble, blind, lame and withered, waiting for the movement of the water. 4 From time to time an angel of the Lord used to come down into the pool and the water was stirred up, and the first one into the pool after it was stirred was healed of whatever ailment he had. 5 There was one man lying there who had been sick for thirty-eight years with his infirmity. 6 Jesus, seeing him lying there and knowing that he had been sick a long time, said to him, "Do you wish to be healed?" 7 The sick man said, "Sir, I have no one to plunge me into the pool once the water is stirred up. By the time I get there, someone else has gone in before me." 8 Jesus said to him, "Stand up, pick up your mat and walk!" 9a The man was immediately cured; he picked up his mat, and walked.[1]

699. Above, our Lord dealt with spiritual rebirth; here he deals with the benefits God gives to those who are spiritually reborn. Now we see that parents give three things to those who are physically born from them: life, nourishment, and instruction or discipline. And those who are spiritually reborn receive these three from Christ: spiritual life, spiritual nourishment, and spiritual teaching. And so these three things are considered here: first, the giving of spiritual life; secondly, the giving of spiritual food (chap. 6); and thirdly, spiritual teaching (chap. 7).

About the first he does three things. First, he sets forth a visible sign in which he shows Christ's power to produce and to restore life. This is the usual practice in this Gospel: to always join to the teaching of Christ some appropriate visible action, so that what is invisible can be made known through the visible. Secondly, the occasion for this teaching is given (v. 9b). Thirdly, the teaching itself is given (v. 19). As to the first he does three things. First, the place of the miracle is given. Secondly, the illness involved. Thirdly, the restoration of the sick person to health (v. 8).

700. The place of this miracle is described in two ways: in general and in particular. The general place is Jerusalem; so he says, *After*

---

1. St. Thomas quotes Jn 5:4 in *ST* III, q. 73, a. 1, ad 2.

this, i.e., after the miracle performed in Galilee, *there was a Jewish festival*, that is Pentecost, according to Chrysostom.[2] For above, when Christ went to Jerusalem, it was the Passover that was mentioned; and now, on the following festival of Pentecost, *Jesus went up to Jerusalem* again. For as we read in Exodus (23:17), the Lord commanded that all Jewish males be presented in the temple three times a year: on the festival days of the Passover, Pentecost, and Tabernacles.

There were two reasons why our Lord went up to Jerusalem for these festivals. First, so that he would not seem to oppose the law, for he said himself: "I have not come to destroy the law, but to complete it" (Mt 5:17);[3] and in order to draw the many people gathered there on the feast days to God by his signs and teaching: "I will praise him in the midst of the people" (Ps 108:30); and again, "I have declared your justice in the great assembly" (Ps 39:10). So Christ himself says, as we read below (18:20): "I have spoken openly to the world."[4]

701. The specific place of the miracle was the pool called the Sheep Pool; so he says, *Now at Jerusalem there is a Sheep Pool.* This is described here in four ways: by its name, its structure, from its occupants, and from its power.

702. First, it is described from its name when he says, *there is a Sheep Pool* (*probatica piscina*), for *probaton* is Greek for "sheep." It was called the Sheep Pool for it was there that the priests washed the sacrificial animals; especially the sheep, who were used more than the other animals. And so in Hebrew it was called *Bethsaida*, that is, the "house of sheep." This pool was located near the temple, and formed from collected rainwater.

703. In its mystical sense, this pool, according to Chrysostom,[5] has prefigured baptism. For the Lord, wishing to prefigure the grace of baptism in different ways, first of all chose water: for this washes the body from the uncleanness which came from contact with what was legally unclean (Nm 19). Secondly, he gave this pool a power that expresses even more vividly than water the power of baptism: for it not only cleansed the body from its uncleanness, but also healed it from its illness, for symbols are more expressive, the closer they approach the reality. Thus it signified the power of baptism: for as this water when applied to the body had the power (not by its own nature, but from an angel) to heal its illness, so the water of baptism has the power to heal and cleanse the soul from sins: "He loved us, and washed us from our sins" (Rev 1:5). This is the reason why the passion of Christ, prefigured by the sacrifices of the Old Law, is represented in baptism: "All of us

2. *Hom. in Io.* 36. 1; PG 59, col. 203; cf. *Catena aurea*, 5:1–13.
3. See *ST* III, q. 40, a. 4; III, q. 47, a. 2.
4. See *ST* III, q. 42, a. 3.
5. *Hom. in Io.* 36. 1; PG 59, col. 203–4; cf. *Catena aurea*, 5:1–13.

who have been baptized into Christ Jesus, have been baptized into his death" (Rom 6:3).[6]

According to Augustine,[7] the water in this pool signified the condition of the Jewish people, according to: "The waters are the peoples" (Rev 17:15). The Gentiles were not confined within the limits of the divine law, but each of them lived according to the vanity of his heart (Eph 4:17). But the Jews were confined under the worship of the one God: "We were kept under the law, confined, until the faith was revealed" (Gal 3:23). So this water, confined to the pool, signified the Jewish people. And it was called the Sheep Pool, for the Jews were the special sheep of God: "We are his people, his sheep" (Ps 94:7).[8]

704. The pool is described in its structure as *having five porticoes*, i.e., round about, so that a number of the priests could stand and wash the animals without inconvenience. In the mystical sense these five porticoes, according to Chrysostom, signify the five wounds in the body of Christ; about which we read: "Put your hand into my side, and do not be unbelieving, but believe" (below 20:27). But according to Augustine,[9] these five porticoes signify the five books of Moses.

705. The pool is also described from its occupants, for *in these porticoes lay a great number of people: feeble, blind, lame and withered*. The literal explanation of this is that since all the afflicted persons gathered because of the curative power of the water, which did not always cure nor cure many at the same time, it was inevitable that there be many hanging around waiting to be cured. The mystical meaning of this, for Augustine,[10] was that the law was incapable of healing sins: "It is impossible that sins be taken away by the blood of bulls and goats" (Heb 10:4). The law merely shed light on them, for "The knowledge of sin comes from the law" (Rom 3:20).[11]

706. And so, subject to various illnesses, these people lay there, unable to be cured. They are described in four ways. First, by their posture: for there they *lay*, i.e., clinging to earthly things by their sins; for one who is lying down is in direct contact with the earth: "He had compassion on them, for they were suffering, and lying like sheep without a shepherd" (Mt 9:36). But the just do not lie down, but stand upright, toward the things of heaven: "They," i.e., sinners, "are bound, and have fallen down; but we," the just, "have stood and are erect" (Ps 19:9).

Secondly, they are described as to their number, for there was *a great number* of them: "The evil are hard to correct, and the number

6. See *ST* III, q. 62, a. 5; III, q. 66, aa. 2–3.
7. *Tract. in Io.* 17. 2; PL 35, col. 1528; cf. *Catena aurea*, 5:1–13.
8. See *ST* I-II, q. 98, a. 4.
9. *Tract. in Io.* 17. 2; PL 35, col. 1528; cf. *Catena aurea*, 5:1–13.
10. Ibid.
11. See *ST* I-II, q. 103, a. 2.

of fools is infinite" (Ecc 1:15); and in Matthew (7:13): "The road that leads to destruction is wide, and many go this way."

Thirdly, these sick people are described as to their condition. And he mentions four things which a person brings on himself through sin. First, a person who is ruled by sinful passions is made listless or feeble; and so he says, *feeble*. So it is that Cicero[12] calls certain passions of the soul, such as anger and concupiscence and the like, illnesses of the soul. And the Psalm says: "Have mercy on me, O Lord, for I am weak" (Ps 6:3).

Secondly, due to the rule and victory of a man's passions, his reason is blinded by consent; and he says as to this, *blind*, that is, through sins. According to Wisdom (2:21): "Their own evil blinded them"; and in the Psalm (57:9): "Fire," that is the fire of anger and concupiscence, "fell on them, and they did not see the sun."[13]

Thirdly, a person who is feeble and blind is inconstant in his works and is, in a way, lame. So we read in Proverbs (11:18): "The work of the wicked is unsteady." With respect to this the Evangelist says, *lame*. "How long will you be lame?" (1 Kgs 18:21).

Fourthly, a man who is thus feeble, blind in understanding, and lame in his exterior actions, becomes dry in his affections, in the sense that all the fatness of devotion withers within him. This devotion is sought in the Psalm (62:6): "May my soul be filled with fat and marrow." With respect to this the Evangelist says, *withered*. "My strength is dried up like baked clay" (Ps 21:16).

But there are some so afflicted by the lassitude of sin, who do not wait for the motion of the water, wallowing in their sins, according to Wisdom (14:22): "They live in a great strife of ignorance, and they call so many and great evils peace." We read of such people: "They are glad when they do evil, and rejoice in the worst of things" (Prv 2:14). The reason for this is that they do not hate their sins: they do not sin from ignorance or weakness, but from malice.[14] But others, who do not sin from malice, do not wallow in their sins, but wait by desire for the motion of the water. So he says, *waiting*. "Every day of my service I wait for my relief to come" (Jb 14:14). This is the way those in the Old Testament waited for Christ: "I will wait for your salvation, O Lord" (Gn 49:18).

707. Finally, the power of the pool is described, for it healed all physical illnesses in virtue of an angel who came to it; so he says. *From time to time an angel of the Lord used to come down into the pool.* In certain ways, the power of this pool is like that of baptism. It is like it, first, in the fact that its power was unperceived: for the power of

12. *Tusculan Disputations* III. 5. 10–11.
13. See *ST* II-II, q. 153, a. 1; II-II, q. 158, a. 2.
14. See *ST* I-II, q. 78, a. 2.

the water in this pool did not come from its very nature, otherwise it
would have healed at all times; its power was unseen, being from an
angel. So he says, *From time to time an angel of the Lord used to come
down into the pool.* The water of baptism is like this in that precisely
as water it does not have the power to cleanse souls, but this comes
from the unseen power of the Holy Spirit, according to: "Unless one is
born again of water and the Holy Spirit, he cannot enter the kingdom
of God" (above 3:5). It is like it, in a second way, in its effect: for as the
water of baptism heals, so also the water of that pool healed.[15] So he
says, *the first one into the pool was healed.* Further, God gave to that
water the power to heal so that men by washing might learn through
their bodily health to seek their spiritual health.

Yet the water of this pool differs from the water of baptism in three
ways. First, in the source of its power: for the water in the pool produced health because of an angel, but the water of baptism produces
its effect by the uncreated power not only of the Holy Spirit, but of
the entire Trinity. Thus the entire Trinity was present at the baptism of
Christ: the Father in the voice, the Son in person, and the Holy Spirit
in the form of a dove.[16] This is why we invoke the Trinity in our baptism.

Secondly, this water differs in its power: for the water in the pool
did not have a continuous power to cure, but only *from time to time*;
while the water of baptism has a permanent power to cleanse, according to: "On that day a fountain will be open to the house of David, and
to the inhabitants of Jerusalem, to cleanse the sinner and the unclean"
(Zec 13:1).

Thirdly, this water differs as regards the number of people healed:
for only one person was cured when the water of this pool was moved;
but all are healed when the water of baptism is moved. And no wonder: for the power of the water in the pool, since it is created, is finite
and has a finite effect; but in the water of baptism there is an infinite
power capable of cleansing an infinite number of souls, if there were
such: "I will pour clean water upon you, and you will be cleansed from
all your uncleanness" (Ez 36:25).

708. According to Augustine,[17] however, the angel signifies Christ,
according to this reading of Isaiah (9:6): "He will be called the angel of
the great counsel." Just as the angel descended at certain times into the
pool, so Christ descended into the world at a time fixed by the Father:
"The time is near" (Is 14:1); "When the fullness of time had come God
sent his Son, made from a woman, made under the law" (Gal 4:4).[18]
Again, just as the angel was not seen except by the motion of the wa-

15. See *ST* III, q. 69, aa. 2–3.
16. See *ST* III, q. 39, aa. 6, 8.
17. *Tract. in Io.* 17. 3; PL 35, col. 1528; cf. *Catena aurea*, 5:1–13.
18. See *ST* III, q. 1, aa. 5–6.

ter, so Christ was not known as to his divinity, for "If they had known, they would never have crucified the Lord of glory" (1 Cor 2:8). For as Isaiah (45:15) says: "Truly, you are a hidden God." And so the motion of the water was seen, but not the one who set it in motion, because, seeing the weakness of Christ, the people did not know of his divinity. And just as the one who went into the pool was healed, so a person who humbly believes in God is healed by his passion: "Justified by faith, through the redemption which is in Christ, whom God put forward as an expiation" (Rom 3:24).[19] Only one was healed, because no one can be healed except in the oneness or unity of the Church: "One Lord, one faith, one baptism" (Eph 4:5). Therefore, woe to those who hate unity, and divide men into sects.

709. Then (v. 5), the Evangelist mentions the disability of a man who lay by the pool. First, we are told how long he was disabled; and secondly, why it was so long (v. 7).

710. He was disabled for a long time, for *There was one man lying there who had been sick for thirty-eight years with his infirmity.* This episode is very aptly mentioned: the man who could not be cured by the pool was to be cured by Christ, because those whom the law could not heal, Christ heals perfectly, according to: "God did what the law, weakened by the flesh, could not do: by sending his own Son in the likeness of sinful flesh, and as a sin-offering, he condemned sin in his flesh" (Rom 8:3); and in Sirach (36:6): "Perform new signs and wonders."[20]

711. The number thirty-eight is well-suited to his infirmity, for we see it associated with sickness rather than with health. For, as Augustine[21] says, the number forty signifies the perfection of justice, which consists in observing the law. But the law was given in ten precepts, and was to be preached to the four corners of the world, or be completed by the four Gospels, according to: "The end of the law is Christ" (Rom 10:4). So since ten times four is forty, this appropriately signifies perfect justice. Now if two is subtracted from forty, we get thirty-eight. This two is the two precepts of charity, which effects perfect justice. And so this man was sick because he had forty minus two, that is, his justice was imperfect, for "On these two commandments all the law and the prophets depend" (Mt 22:40).

712. Now the reason for the length of the man's illness is considered. First, we have the Lord's query; secondly, the sick man's answer (v. 7).

713. John says, *Jesus, seeing him,* the man, *lying there.* Jesus saw him not only with his physical eyes, but also with the eyes of his mercy; this is the way David begged to be seen, saying: "Look at me, O

19. See *ST* III, q. 49, a. 1.
20. See *ST* III, q. 44, a. 3.
21. *Tract. in Io.* 17. 4, 6; PL 35, col. 1529, 1530; cf. *Catena aurea,* 5:1–13.

Lord, and have mercy on me" (Ps 85:16). And Jesus *knowing that he had been sick a long time*—which was repugnant to the heart of Christ as well as to the sick man himself: "A long illness is a burden to the physician" (Sir 10:11)—said to him, *Do you wish to be healed?* He did not say this because he did not know the answer, for it was quite evident that the man wanted to be healed; he said it to arouse the sick man's desire, and to show his patience in waiting so many years to be cured of his sickness, and in not giving up. We see from this that he was all the worthier to be cured: "Act bravely, and let your heart be strengthened, all you who hope in the Lord" (Ps 30:25). Jesus incites the man's desires because we keep more securely what we perceive with desire and more easily acquire. "Knock," by your desire, "and it will be opened to you," as we read in Matthew (7:7).[22]

Note that in other situations the Lord requires faith: "Do you believe that I can do this for you" (Mt 9:28); but here he does not make any such demand. The reason is that the others had heard of the miracles of Jesus, of which this man knew nothing. And so Jesus does not ask faith from him until after the miracle has been performed.[23]

714. Then (v. 7), the answer of the sick man is given. Two reasons are given for the length of his illness: his poverty and his weakness. As he was poor, he could not afford a man to plunge him into the pool; so he says, *Sir, I have no one to plunge me into the pool.* Perhaps he thought, as Chrysostom[24] says, that Christ might even help to put him into the water. Someone else always reached the pool before him because he was weak and not able to move fast; so he says, *By the time I get there, someone else has gone in before me.* He could say with Job: "I cannot help myself" (Jb 6:13). This signifies that no mere man could save the human race, for all had sinned and needed the grace of God. Mankind had to wait for the coming of Christ, God and man, by whom it would be healed.[25]

715. Now we see the man restored to health, i.e., the working of the miracle. First, the Lord's command is given; secondly, the man's obedience (v. 9).

716. The Lord commanded both the nature of the man and his will, for both are under the Lord's power. He commanded his nature when he said, *Stand up.* This command was not directed to the man's will, for this was not within the power of his will. But it was within the power of his nature, to which the Lord gave the power to stand by his command. He gave two commands to the man's will: *pick up your mat and walk!* The literal meaning for this is that these two things were

22. See *ST* I-II, q. 112, a. 2.
23. See *ST* III, q. 43, aa. 1, 4.
24. *Hom. in Io.* 37. 1; PG 59, col. 207; cf. *Catena aurea,* 5:1–13.
25. See *ST* III, q. 1, a. 2.

commanded in order to show that the man had been restored to perfect health. For in all his miracles the Lord produced a perfect work,
according to what was best in the nature of each case: "The works of
God are perfect" (Dt 32:4). Now this man was lacking two things: first,
his own energy, since he could not stand up by himself, thus our Lord
found him lying by the pool. Secondly, he lacked the help of others; so
he said, *I have no one*. So our Lord, in order that this man might recognize his perfect health, ordered him who could not help himself to
pick up his mat, and him who could not walk to walk.

717. These are the three things which the Lord commands in the
justification of a sinner. First, he should *stand up*, by leaving his sinful
ways: "Rise up, you who sleep, and arise from the dead" (Eph 5:14).
Secondly, he is commanded to *pick up your mat*, by making satisfac-
tion for the sins he has committed. For the mat on which a man rests
signifies his sins. And so a man takes up his mat when he begins to do
the penance given to him for his sins.[26] "I will bear the anger of God,
because I have sinned against him" (Mic 7:9). Thirdly, he is commanded to *walk*, by advancing in what is good, according to: "They will go
from strength to strength" (Ps 83:8).

718. According to Augustine,[27] this sick man was lacking two
things: the two precepts of charity. And so our Lord gives two commands to his will, which is perfected by charity: to take up his mat,
and to walk. The first concerns the love of neighbor, which is first in
the order of doing; the second concerns the love of God, which is first
in the order of precept.[28] Christ says, with respect to the first, *pick up
your mat*. As if to say: When you are weak, your neighbor bears with
you and, like a mat, patiently supports you: "We who are stronger
ought to bear with the infirmities of the weak, and not seek to please
ourselves" (Rom 15:1). Thus, after you have been cured, *pick up your
mat*, i.e., bear and support your neighbor, who carried you when you
were weak: "Carry each other's burdens" (Gal 6:2). About the second
he says, *walk*, by drawing near God; so we read: "They will go from
strength to strength" (Ps 83:8); "Walk while you have the light" (below 12:35).

719. Next we see the man's obedience. First, the obedience of his
nature, because, *The man was immediately cured*. And no wonder, because Christ is the Word through whom heaven and earth were made:
"He commanded and they were created" (Ps 148:5): "By the Word of
the Lord the heavens were made" (Is 32:6).[29] Secondly, we see the obedience of the man's will: first, because *he picked up his mat*, and sec-

26. See *ST* III, q. 85, a. 3; III, q. 86, a. 1.
27. *Tract. in Io.* 17. 8–9; PL 35, col. 1531–32; cf. *Catena aurea,* 5:1–13.
28. See *ST* II-II, q. 25, a. 1.
29. See *ST* I, q. 45, a. 6.

ondly, because he *walked.* "We will do everything that the Lord commands, and obey him" (Ex 24:7).[30]

LECTURE 2

9b That day, however, was a Sabbath. 10 Therefore the Jews told the man who had been cured, "It is the Sabbath; it is not permitted for you to carry your mat." 11 He replied to them, "He who cured me said to me: 'Pick up your mat and walk.'" 12 They then asked him, "Who is this man who told you to pick up your mat and walk?" 13 But he who was cured had no idea who it was, for Jesus had slipped away from the crowd that had gathered in that place. 14 Later, Jesus found the man in the temple and said to him, "Remember, you have been made well; now do not sin again lest something worse happen to you." 15 The man went off and related to the Jews that it was Jesus who had cured him. 16 For reasons like this the Jews began to persecute Jesus, because he performed such works on the Sabbath. 17 But Jesus had a reply for them: "My Father works even until now, and so do I." 18 Consequently, the Jews tried all the harder to kill him, because he not only broke the Sabbath rest, but even called God his own Father, making himself equal to God.[31]

720. Having seen a visible miracle which shows the power of Christ to restore spiritual life, we now see an opportunity given to him to teach. This opportunity was the persecution launched against him by the Jews. These Jews, who were envious of Christ, persecuted him for two reasons: first, the above act of his mercy; secondly, his teaching of the truth (v. 17). As to the first, the Evangelist does three things. First, he gives the occasion for their persecution. Secondly, the false accusation against the man who was just cured (v. 10). And thirdly, their attempt to belittle Christ (v. 12).

721. Their opportunity to persecute Christ was the fact that he cured the man on the Sabbath; accordingly, the Evangelist says, *That day, however, was a Sabbath*, when Christ performed the miracle of commanding the man to pick up his mat.

Three reasons are given why our Lord began to work on the Sabbath. The first is given by Ambrose, in his commentary, *On Luke.*[32] He says that Christ came to renovate the work of creation, that is, man, who had become deformed. And so he should have begun where the Creator had left off the work of creation, that is, on a Sabbath, as men-

30. See *ST* II-II, q. 104, a. 4.
31. St. Thomas quotes Jn 5:14 in *ST* III, q. 44, a. 3, ad 3; Jn 5:17: I, q. 73, a. 2, obj. 1; q. 118, a. 3, obj. 1; III, q. 40, a. 4, ad 1; Jn 5:18: III, q. 47, a. 4, obj. 3.
32. *Expos. Evang. sec. Luc.* IV. 58; PL 15, col. 1629–30.

tioned in Genesis (chap. 1). Thus Christ began to work on the Sabbath to show that he was the renovator of the whole creature.

Another reason was that the Sabbath day was celebrated by the Jews in memory of the first creation. But Christ came to make, in a way, a new creation, according to Galatians (6:15): "In Christ Jesus, neither circumcision nor the lack of circumcision is a benefit; what counts is a new creation," i.e., through grace, which comes through the Holy Spirit: "You will send forth your Spirit, and they will be created; and you will renew the face of the earth" (Ps 103:30). And so Christ worked on the Sabbath to show that a new creation, a recreation, was taking place through him: "that we might be the first-fruits of his creatures" (Jas 1:18).[33]

The third reason was to show that he was about to do what the law could not do: "God did what the law, weakened by the flesh, could not do: by sending his own Son in the likeness of sinful flesh, he condemned sin in his flesh, in order that the requirements of the law might be accomplished in us" (Rom 8:3).[34]

The Jews, however, did not do any work on the Sabbath, as a symbol that there were certain things pertaining to the Sabbath which were to be accomplished, but which the law could not do. This is clear in the four things which God ordained for the Sabbath: for he sanctified the Sabbath day, blessed it, completed his work on it, and then rested. These things the law was not able to do. It could not sanctify; so we read: "Save me, O Lord, for there are no holy people left" (Ps 11:1). Nor could it bless; rather, "Those who rely on the works of the law are under a curse" (Gal 3:10). Neither could it complete and perfect, because "the law brought nothing to perfection" (Heb 7:19). Nor could it bring perfect rest: "If Joshua had given them rest, God would not be speaking after of another day" (Heb 4:8).

These things, which the law could not do, Christ did.[35] For he sanctified the people by his passion: "Jesus, in order to sanctify the people with his own blood, suffered outside the gate" (Heb 13:12).[36] He blessed them by an inpouring of grace: "Blessed be God, the Father of our Lord Jesus Christ, who has blessed us with every spiritual blessing of heaven, in Christ" (Eph 1:3).[37] He brought the people to perfection by instructing them in the ways of perfect justice: "Be perfect, as your heavenly Father is perfect" (Mt 5:48). He also led them to true rest: "We who have believed will find rest," as is said in Hebrews (4:3).[38] Therefore, it is proper for him to work on the Sabbath, who is able to make perfect those things that pertain to the Sabbath, from which an impotent law rested.[39]

33. See *ST* I-II, q. 100, a. 5, ad 2.
34. See *ST* III, q. 47, a. 2, ad 2.
35. See *ST* I-II, q. 107, a. 2.
36. See *ST* III, q. 49, a. 1.
37. See *ST* III, q. 48, a. 1.
38. See *ST* III, q. 46, a. 3.
39. See *ST* III, q. 40, a. 4, ad 1.

722. Then (v. 10), the Evangelist gives the accusation brought against the man who was healed. First, we have the accusation; and secondly, the explanation given by the man who was healed (v. 11).

723. The man was accused for carrying his mat on the Sabbath, and not for being healed; so they say: *It is the Sabbath; it is not permitted for you to carry your mat.* There are several reasons for this. One is that the Jews, although frequently charging Christ with healing on the Sabbath, had been embarrassed by him on the ground that they themselves used to pull their cattle from ditches on the Sabbath in order to save them. For this reason the Jews did not mention his healing, as it was useful and necessary; but they charge him with carrying his mat, which did not seem to be necessary. As if to say: Although your cure need not have been postponed, there was no need for you to carry your mat, or for the order to carry it. Another reason was that the Lord had shown, contrary to their opinion, that it was lawful to do good on the Sabbath. And so, because being healed is not the same as doing good, but being done a good, they attack the one healed rather than the one healing. The third reason was that the Jews thought that they were forbidden by the law to do any work on the Sabbath; and it was the carrying of burdens that was especially forbidden on the Sabbath: "Do not carry a burden on the Sabbath" (Jer 17:21). Accordingly, they made a special point of being against the carrying of anything on the Sabbath, as being opposed to the teaching of the prophet. But this command of the prophet was mystical: for when he forbade them to carry burdens, he wanted to encourage them to rest from the burdens of their sins on the Sabbath. Of these sins it is said: "My iniquities are a heavy burden and have weighed me down" (Ps 37:5). Therefore, since the time had come to explain the meaning of obscure symbols, Christ commanded him to take up his mat, i.e., to help his neighbors in their weaknesses: "Bear one another's burdens, and so you will fullfil the law of Christ" (Gal 6:2).[40]

724. Then (v. 11), we see the man who was healed defending himself. His defense is wisely taken: for a doctrine is never so well proved to be divinely inspired as by miracles which can be accomplished only by divine power: "Going out, they preached everywhere, and the Lord worked with them and confirmed the word by the signs that followed" (Mk 16:20).[41] Thus he argued with those who were defaming the one who healed him, saying: *He who cured me said to me.* As if to say: You say that I am forbidden to carry a burden on the Sabbath, and this on divine authority; but I was commanded by the same authority to pick up my mat. For, he who cured me, and by restoring my health showed that he had divine power, said to me, *Pick up your mat*

40. See *ST* I-II, q. 100, a. 8, ad 4.
41. See *ST* III, q. 43, a. 1.

and walk. Therefore, I was duty bound to obey the commands of one who has such power and who had done me such a favor. "I will never forget your precepts because you have brought me to life by them" (Ps 118:93).

725. Then, since they could not very well charge the man who was cured, they try to belittle Christ's cure, for this man defended himself through Christ. But since he did not indicate precisely who he was, they maliciously ask him who it was. With respect to this, first, the search for Christ is set down. Secondly, his discovery. And thirdly, his persecution (v. 16).

726. Three things are mentioned about the first: the Jews' interrogation; the ignorance of the man who was cured; and the cause of that ignorance.

As to the first, we read: ***They then asked him,*** not with the good intention of making progress, but for the evil purpose of persecuting and destroying Christ: "You will seek me, and you will die in your sin" (below 8:21). Their very words show their malice: for while our Lord had commanded the man who was sick to become healed and to pick up his mat, they ignored the first, which is an undeniable sign of divine power, and harped on the second, which seemed to be against the law, saying, ***Who is this man who told you to pick up you mat and walk?*** "He lies in wait, and turns good into evil, and he will put blame," i.e., attempt to put blame, "on the elect" (Sir 11:33).

727. As to the second, the Evangelist says, ***But he who was cured had no idea who it was.*** This cured man signifies those who believe and have been healed by the grace of Christ: "You are saved by grace" (Eph 2:8). Indeed, they do not know who Christ is, but they know only his effects: "While we are in the body, we are absent from the Lord: for we walk by faith, and not by sight" (2 Cor 5:6). We will know who Christ is when "we shall see him as he is," as said in 1 John (3:2).

728. Next, the Evangelist gives the reason for the man's ignorance, saying, ***for Jesus had slipped away from the crowd that had gathered in that place.*** There are both literal and mystical reasons why Christ left. Of the two literal reasons, the first is to give us the example of concealing our good deeds and of not using them to seek the applause of men: "Take care not to perform your good actions in the sight of men, in order to be seen by them" (Mt 6:1). The second literal reason is to show us that, in all our actions, we should leave and avoid those who are envious, so as not to feed and increase their envy: "Do not be provoked by one who speaks evil of you, so he will not trap you by your own words" (Sir 8:14).

There are also two mystical reasons why Christ slipped away. First, it teaches us that Christ is not easy to find in the midst of men, or in the whirlwind of temporal cares; rather, he is found in spiritual seclusion: "I will lead her into the wilderness, and there I will speak to her heart" (Hos 2:14); and in Ecclesiastes (9.17): "The words of the wise are heard in silence."[42] Secondly, this suggests to us that Christ was to leave the Jews for the Gentiles: "He hid his face for a while from the house of Jacob" (Is 8:17), i.e., he withdrew the knowledge of his truth from the Jewish people.

729. Then (v. 14), the Evangelist tells us how Jesus was found. First, he says that he was found. Secondly, that after having been found, he taught. Thirdly, that after having taught, his identity was reported to the Jews.

730. The Evangelist tells us both where and the way in which Christ was found. The way in which he was found was remarkable, for Christ is not found unless he first finds; hence he says, *Later*, after the above events, *Jesus found the man*. For we cannot find Jesus by our own power unless Christ first presents himself to us; so we read: "Seek your servant" (Ps 118:176); and, "She [wisdom] goes to meet those who desire her" (Wis 6:14).

The place Christ was found was holy, *in the temple*, according to: "The Lord is in his holy temple" (Ps 10:5).[43] For his mother had also found him in the temple (Lk 2:46); and he was there for he had to be concerned with his Father's affairs. We see from this that this man was not cured in vain, but having been converted to a religious way of life, he visited the temple and found Christ: because if we desire to come to a knowledge of the Creator, we must run from the tumult of sinful affections, leave the company of evil men, and flee to the temple of our heart, where God condescends to visit and live.

731. After Christ was found, he began to teach (v. 14). First, Christ reminded the man of the gift he was given. Secondly, he offered him sound advice. And thirdly, he pointed out an imminent danger.

732. The gift was remarkable, for it was a sudden restoration to health; so he says, *Remember, you have been made well*. Therefore, you should always keep this in mind, according to: "I will remember the tender mercies of the Lord" (Is 63:7).

733. His advice, too, was useful, that is, *do not sin again*. "My son, you have sinned. Do not sin again" (Sir 21:1).

Why did our Lord mention sin to this paralytic and to certain others that he cured, and not to the rest? He did this to show that illness comes to certain people as a result of their previous sins, according to: "For this reason many of you are weak and sick, and many have died" (1 Cor 11:30). In this way he even showed himself to be God, pointing out sins and the hidden secrets of the heart: "Hell and destruction are open to the Lord; how much more the hearts of the children of men" (Prv 15:11). And so Christ mentioned sin only to some he cured

---

42. See *ST* II-II, q. 83, a. 2; II-II, q. 182, a. 3.
43. See *ST* I-II, q. 102, a. 4, ad 1.

and not to all, for not all infirmities are due to previous sins: some
come from one's natural disposition, and some are permitted as a trial,
as with Job.[44] Or, Christ might have brought up sin to some because
they were better prepared for his correction: "Do not rebuke one who
mocks, lest he hate you; rebuke a wise man, and he will love you"
(Prv 9:8). Or, we could say, in telling some not to sin, he intended his
words for all the others.

734. The imminent danger was great; so he says, *lest something
worse happen to you*. This can be understood in two ways, according
to the two events that preceded. For this man was first punished with
a troublesome infirmity, and then received a marvelous favor. Accordingly, Christ's statement can refer to each. To the first, for when anyone is punished for his sin, and the punishment does not check him
from sinning, it is just for him to be punished more severely. So Christ
says, *do not sin again*, because if you do sin, something worse will
happen to you: "I have struck your children in vain" (Jer 2:30). It can
refer to the second, for one who falls into sin after receiving favors
deserves a more severe punishment because of his ingratitude, as we
see in 2 Peter (2:20): "It would be better for them not to know the
way of truth, than to turn back after knowing it."[45] Also, because after a man has once returned to sin, he sins more easily, according to
Matthew (12:45): "The last state of that man becomes worse than the
first"; and in Jeremiah (2:20): "You broke your yoke a long time ago,
and snapped off your chains, and said: 'I will not serve.'"

735. Then when he says, *The man went off and related to the Jews*,
we see Jesus identified. Some think, as Chrysostom[46] reports, that this
man identified Jesus out of malice. But this does not seem probable:
that he would be so ungrateful after receiving such a favor. He *related
to the Jews that it was Jesus who had cured him*, in order to make it
clear that Christ had the power to heal: "Come . . . and I will tell you
what great things the Lord has done for me," as we read in the Psalm
(65:16). This is obvious, for they had asked him who commanded him
to pick up his mat, but he told them that *it was Jesus who had cured
him*.

736. Next (v. 16), we have the persecution of Christ, begun because
he performed a work of mercy on the Sabbath. Thus the Evangelist
says, *For reasons like this the Jews began to persecute Jesus, because
he performed such works on the Sabbath*. "Princes have persecuted me
without cause" (Ps 118:161).

737. Then (v. 17), the second reason for his persecution is given:
what he taught. First, we are given the truth he taught; and secondly,
the perversity of his persecutors (v. 18).

44. See *ST* I-II, q. 85, a. 6; III, q. 44, a. 3, ad 3.
45. See *ST* II-II, q. 12, a. 1.
46. *Hom. in Io.* 38. 2; PG 59, col. 213–14; cf. *Catena aurea*, 5:14–18.

738. Our Lord taught the truth, while justifying his breaking of the Sabbath. Here we should note that our Lord justified both himself and his disciples from breaking the Sabbath. He justified his disciples, since they were men, by comparing them to other men: as the priests who, although they worked in the temple on the Sabbath, did not break the Sabbath; and to David, who, while Ahimelech was priest, took the consecrated bread from the temple on the Sabbath when he was running from Saul (1 Sm 21:1).

Our Lord, who was both God and man, sometimes justified himself in breaking the Sabbath by comparing himself to men, as in Luke (14:5): "Which of you; if his donkey or ox falls into a pit, will not take him out on the Sabbath?" And sometimes he justified himself by comparing himself to God: particularly on this occasion, when he said: *My Father works even until now, and so do I.* As if to say: Do not think that my Father rested on the Sabbath in such a way that from that time he does not work; rather, just as he is working even now without laboring, so I also am working.

By saying this, Christ eliminated the misunderstanding of the Jews: for in their desire to imitate God, they did not do any work on the Sabbath, as if God entirely ceased from work on that day. In fact, although God rested on the Sabbath from producing new creatures, he is working always and continuously even till now, conserving creatures in existence. Hence it is significant that Moses used the word "rest," after recounting the works of God from which he rested: for this signifies, in its hidden meaning, the spiritual rest which God, by the example of his own rest, promised to the faithful, after they have done their own good works. So we may say that this command was a foreshadowing of something that lay in the future.[47]

739. He expressly says, *works even until now*, and not "has worked," to indicate that God's work is continuous. For they might have thought that God is the cause of the world as a craftsman is the cause of a house, i.e., the craftsman is responsible only for the making or coming into existence of the house: in other words, just as the house continues in existence even when the craftsman has ceased working, so the world would exist if God's influence ceased. But according to Augustine,[48] God is the cause of all creatures in such a way as to be the cause of their existing: for if his power were to cease even for a moment, all things in nature would at once cease to be, just as we may say that the air is illuminated only as long as the light of the sun remains in it. The reason for this is that things which depend on a cause only for their coming into existence, are able to exist when that cause ceases; but things that depend on a cause not only for their coming into existence but also to

47. See *ST* I, q. 73, aa. 2–3; I-II, q. 100, a. 5, ad 2; III, q. 40, a. 4.
48. *De Gen. ad litt.* IV. 12. 22; PL 34, col. 304; cf. *Catena aurea,* 5:14–18.

exist, need that cause for their continuous conservation in existence.[49]

740. Further, in saying that *My Father works even until now,* he rejects the opinion of those who say that God creates through the instrumentality of secondary causes.[50] This opinion conflicts with Isaiah (26:12): "O Lord, you have accomplished all our works for us." Therefore, just as *my Father,* who in the beginning created nature, *works even until now,* by preserving and conserving his creation by the same activity, so do I work, because I am the Word of the Father, through whom he accomplishes all things: "God said: 'Let there be light'" (Gn 1:3). Thus, just as he accomplished the first production of things through the Word, so also their conservation. Consequently, if he works even until now, so do I, because I am the Word of the Father, through whom all things are made and conserved.[51]

741. Then (v. 18), the Evangelist mentions the persecution of Christ, which resulted from his teaching: for it was because of his teaching that *the Jews tried all the harder,* i.e., with greater eagerness and a higher pitch of zeal, *to kill him.* For in the law two crimes were punished by death: the crime of breaking the Sabbath—thus anyone who gathered wood on the Sabbath was stoned, as we see from Numbers (15:32); and the crime of blasphemy—so we read: "Bring the blasphemer outside the camp . . . and let all the children of Israel stone him" (Lv 24:14). Now they thought it was blasphemy for a man to claim that he was God: "We are not stoning you for any good work, but for blasphemy: because although you are a man, you make yourself God" (below 10:33). It was these two crimes they imputed to Christ: the first because he broke the Sabbath; the second because he said he was equal to God. So the Evangelist says that *the Jews tried all the harder to kill him, because he not only broke the Sabbath rest, but even called God his own Father.*[52]

Because other just men had also called God their Father, as in "You will call me 'Father'" (Jer 3:19), they do not just say that he called God his own Father, but added what made it blasphemy, making himself equal to God, which they understood from his statement: *My Father works even until now, and so do I.* He said that God was his Father so that we might understand that God is his Father by nature, and the Father of others by adoption.[53] He referred to both of these when he said: "I am going to my Father," by nature, "and to Your Father," by grace (below 20:17). Again, he said that as the Father works, so he works. This answers the accusation of the Jews about his breaking the Sabbath: for this would not be a valid excuse unless he had equal au-

49. See *ST* I, q. 8, a. 1.
50. See *ST* I, q. 44, aa. 1–2; I, q. 45, a. 5.
51. See *ST* I, q. 34, a. 4.
52. See *ST* II-II, q. 13, a. 3; III, q. 47, a. 5.
53. See *ST* III, q. 23, a. 4, ad 2.

thority with God in working. It was for this reason they said he made himself equal to God.

742. How great then is the blindness of the Arians when they say that Christ is less than God the Father: for they cannot understand in our Lord's words what the Jews were able to understand. For the Arians say that Christ did not make himself equal to God, while the Jews saw this. There is another way to settle this, from the very things mentioned in the text. For the Evangelist says that the Jews persecuted Christ because he broke the Sabbath, because he said God is his Father, and because he made himself equal to God. But Christ is either a liar or equal to God. But if he is equal to God, Christ is God by nature.

743. Finally, the Evangelist says, *making himself equal to God*, not as though he was making himself become equal to God, because he was equal to God through an eternal generation. Rather, the Evangelist is speaking according to the understanding of the Jews who, not believing that Christ was the Son of God by nature, understood him to say that he was the Son of God in the sense of wishing to make himself equal to God; but they could not believe he was such: "because although you are a man, you make yourself God" (below 10:33), i.e., you say that you are God, understanding this as you wish to make yourself God.

LECTURE 3

19 Jesus therefore replied and said to them: "Amen, amen, I say to you, the Son cannot do anything of himself, but only what he sees the Father doing. For whatever the Father does, the Son does likewise. 20a For the Father loves the Son, and shows him everything that he does."[54]

744. Here we have Christ's teaching on his life-giving power. First, his teaching is presented. Secondly, it is confirmed (v. 31). Two things are done with the first. First, Christ's teaching on his life-giving power in general is given. Secondly, it is presented in particular (v. 20b). As to the first, three things are done. First, the origin of this power is mentioned. Secondly, the greatness of this power, at (v. 19b). Thirdly, the reason for each is given (v. 20).

745. We should point out, with respect to the first, that the Arians use what Christ said here, *the Son cannot do anything of himself*, to support their error that the Son is less than the Father. As the Evangelist said, the Jews persecuted Christ for making himself equal to God. But the Arians say that when our Lord saw that this disturbed

54. St. Thomas quotes Jn 5:19 in *ST* I, q. 27, a. 1; I, q. 46, a. 6, obj. 1 and *sed contra*; III, q. 23, a. 2; III, q. 43, a. 4; Jn 5:20 in I, q. 42, a. 6, obj. 2.

the Jews, he tried to correct this by stating that he was not equal to the Father, saying, *Amen, amen, I say to you, the Son cannot do anything of himself, but only what he sees the Father doing.* As if to say: Do not interpret what I said, "My Father works even until now, and so do I," as meaning that I work as though I am equal to the Father, for I cannot do anything of myself. Therefore, they say, because the Son can do *only what he sees the Father doing*, he is less than the Father. But this interpretation is false and erroneous. For if the Son were not equal to the Father, then the Son would not be the same as the Father; and this is contrary to: "I and the Father are one" (below 10:30). For equality is considered with respect to greatness, which in divine realities is the essence itself. Hence, if the Son were not equal to the Father, he would be different from him in essence.[55]

746. To get the true meaning of Christ's statement, we should know that in those matters which seem to imply inferiority in the Son, it could be said, as some do, that they apply to Christ according to the nature he assumed; as when he said: "The Father is greater than I" (below 14:28). According to this, they would say that our Lord's statement, *the Son cannot do anything of himself*, should be understood of the Son in his assumed nature. However, this does not stand up, because then one would be forced to say that whatever the Son of God did in his assumed nature, the Father had done before him. For example, that the Father had walked upon the water as Christ did: otherwise, he would not have said, *but only what he sees the Father doing.*

And if we say that whatever Christ did in his flesh, God the Father also did in so far as the Father works in him, as said below (14:10): "The Father, who lives in me, he accomplishes the works," then Christ would be saying that *the Son cannot do anything of himself*, but only what he sees the Father doing in him, i.e., in the Son. But this cannot stand either, because Christ's next statement, *For whatever the Father does, the Son does likewise*, could not, in this interpretation, be applied to him, i.e., to Christ. For the Son, in his assumed nature, never created the world, as the Father did. Consequently, what we read here must not be understood as pertaining to Christ's assumed nature.

747. According to Augustine,[56] however, there is another way of understanding statements which seem to, but do not, imply inferiority in the Son: namely, by referring them to the origin of the Son coming or begotten from the Father. For although the Son is equal to the Father in all things, he receives all these things from the Father in an eternal begetting. But the Father gets these from no one, for he is unbegotten.[57] According to this explanation, the continuity of thought is

55. See *ST* I, q. 42, aa. 1–2.
56. *Tract. in Io.* 19. 13; PL 35, col. 1550, and 20. 4; col. 1558; cf. *Catena aurea*, 5:19–20. See *ST* I, q. 33, a. 4; I, q. 42, a. 4.
57. See *ST* I, q. 33, a. 4.

the following: Why are you offended because I said that God is my Father, and because I made myself equal to the Father? *Amen, amen, I say to you, the Son can do nothing of himself.* As if to say: I am equal to the Father, but in such a way as to be from him, and not he from me; and whatever I may do, is in me from the Father.

748. According to this interpretation, mention is made of the power of the Son when he says, *can,* and of his activity when he says, *do.* Both can be understood here, so that, first of all, the derivation of the Son's power from the Father is shown, and secondly, the conformity of the Son's activity to that of the Father.

749. As to the first, Hilary[58] explains it this way: Shortly above our Lord said that he is equal to the Father. Some heretics, basing themselves on certain scriptural texts which assert the unity and equality of the Son to the Father, claim that the Son is unbegotten. For example, the Sabellians, who say that the Son is identical in person with the Father. Therefore, so you do not understand this teaching in this way, he says, *the Son cannot do anything of himself,* for the Son's power is identical with his nature. Therefore the Son has his power from the same source as he has his being (*esse*); but he has his being (*esse*) from the Father: "I came forth from the Father, and I have come into the world" (Jn 16:28). He also has his nature from the Father, because he is God from God; therefore, it is from him that the Son has his power (*posse*).

So his statement, *the Son cannot do anything of himself, but only what he sees the Father doing,* is the same as saying: The Son, just as he does not have his being (*esse*) except from the Father, so he cannot do anything except from the Father. For in natural things, a thing receives its power to act from the very thing from which it receives its being: for example, fire receives its power to ascend from the very thing from which it receives its form and being. Further, in saying, *the Son cannot do anything of himself,* no inequality is implied, because this refers to a relation; while equality and inequality refer to quantity.[59]

750. Someone might misunderstand his saying, *but only what he sees the Father doing,* and take it to mean that the Son works or acts in the way he sees the Father acting, i.e., that the Father acts first, and when the Son sees this, then the Son begins to act. It would be like two carpenters, a master and his apprentice, with the apprentice making a cabinet in the way he saw the master do. But this is not true for the Word, for it was said above (1:3): "All things were made through him." Therefore, the Father did not make something in such a way that the Son saw him doing it and so learned from it.

58. *De Trin.* 7. 17–18, 21; PL 10, col. 212D–214A, 216A–217A; cf. *Catena aurea,* 5:19–20.
59. See *ST* I, q. 42, a. 1.

But this is said so that the communication of paternity to the Son might be designated in terms of begetting or generation, which is fittingly described by the verb *sees*, because knowledge is conveyed to us by another through seeing and hearing. For we receive our knowledge from things through seeing, and we receive knowledge from words through hearing. Now the Son is not other than Wisdom, as we read: "I came forth out of the mouth of the Most High, the first-born before all creatures" (Sir 24:5). Accordingly, the derivation of the Son from the Father is nothing other than the derivation of divine Wisdom. And so, because the act of seeing indicates the derivation of knowledge and wisdom from another, it is proper for the generation of the Son from the Father to be indicated by an act of seeing; so that for the Son to see the Father doing something is nothing other than to proceed by an intellectual procession from the acting Father.[60]

Another possible explanation of this is given by Hilary.[61] For him, the word *sees* eliminates all imperfection from the generation of the Son or Word. For in physical generation, what is generated changes little by little in the course of time from what is imperfect to what is perfect, for such a thing is not perfect when it is first generated. But this is not so in eternal generation, since this is the generation of what is perfect from what is perfect. And so he says, *but only what he sees the Father doing.* For since the act of seeing is the act of a perfect thing, it is plain that the Son was begotten as perfect at once, as seeing at once, and not as coming to perfection over a course of time.

751. Apropos of the second point, Chrysostom[62] explains it as showing the conformity of the Father to the Son in operation. So that the sense is: I say that it is lawful for me to work on the Sabbath, because my Father, too, continues to work, and I cannot do anything opposed to him: and this is because *the Son cannot do anything of himself.* For one does something of himself when he does not conform himself to another in his actions. But whoever is from another sins, if he is opposed to him: "Whoever speaks on his own, seeks his own glory" (below 7:18). Therefore, whoever exists from another, but acts of himself, sins. Now the Son is from the Father; thus, if he acts of himself, he sins; and this is impossible. So by saying, *the Son cannot do anything of himself,* he means nothing more than that the Son cannot sin. As if to say: You are persecuting me unjustly for breaking the Sabbath, because I cannot sin, since I do not act in a way opposed to my Father.[63]

Augustine[64] makes use of both of these explanations, that of Hilary and the one given by Chrysostom, but in different places.

60. See *ST* I, q. 27, a. 2.
61. *De Trin.* 7. 17; PL 10, col. 213; cf. *Catena aurea,* 5:19–20.
62. *Hom. in Io.* 38. 4; PG 59, col. 216–18; cf. *Catena aurea,* 5:19–20.
63. See *ST* III, q. 15, a. 1; III, q. 18, a. 5.
64. *De Trin.* 2. 1, no. 3; PL 42, col. 847.

752. Then when he says, *For whatever the Father does, the Son does likewise*, he affirms the greatness of Christ's power. He excludes three things in the power of Christ: limitation, difference, and imperfection.

First, limitation is excluded. Since there are diverse agents in the world, and the first universal agent has power over all other agents, but the other agents, which are from him, have a limited power in proportion to their rank in the order of causality, some might think that since the Son is not of himself, that he must have a power limited to certain existents rather than a universal power over all, as the Father has. And so to exclude this he says, *whatever the Father does*, i.e., to all the things to which the Father's power extends, the Son's power also extends: "All things were made through him" (above 1:3).

Secondly, difference is excluded. For sometimes a thing that exists from another is able to do whatever that from which it exists does. And yet the things the former does are not the same as those done by that from which it is. For example, if one fire which exists from another can do whatever that other does, i.e., cause combustion, the act of causing combustion would be specifically the same in each, even though one fire ignites certain things and the other fire ignites different things. And so that you do not think that the Son's activity is different from the activity of the Father in this way, he says, *whatever* the Father does, the Son does, i.e., not different things, but the very same.

Thirdly, imperfection is excluded. Sometimes one and the same thing comes from two agents: from one as the principal and perfect agent, and from the other as an instrumental and imperfect agent. But it does not come in the same way, because the principal agent acts in a different way from the instrumental agent: for the instrumental agent acts imperfectly, and in virtue of the other. And so that no one thinks that this is the way the Son does whatever the Father does, he says that whatever the Father does, the Son does likewise, i.e., with the same power by which the Father acts, the Son also acts; because the same power and the same perfection are in the Father and the Son: "I was with him, forming all things" (Prv 8:30).[65]

753. Then when he says, *For the Father loves the Son*, he gives the reason for each, i.e., for the origin of the Son's power and for its greatness. This reason is the love of the Father, who loves the Son. Thus he says, *For the Father loves the Son*.

In order to understand how the Father's love for the Son is the reason for the origin or communication of the Son's power, we should point out that a thing is loved in two ways. For since the good alone is loveable, a good can be related to love in two ways: as the cause of love, or as caused by love. Now in us, the good causes love: for the cause of our loving something is its goodness, the goodness in it.

65. See *ST* I, q. 25, a. 2; I, q. 42, a. 6.

Therefore, it is not good because we love it, but rather we love it because it is good. Accordingly, in us, love is caused by what is good. But it is different with God, because God's love itself is the cause of the goodness in the things that are loved. For it is because God loves us that we are good, since to love is nothing else than to will a good to someone.[66] Thus, since God's will is the cause of things, for "whatever he willed he made" (Ps 113:11), it is clear that God's love is the cause of the goodness in things. Hence Dionysius[67] says that the divine love did not allow itself to be without issue.[68] So, if we wish to consider the origin of the Son, let us see whether the love with which the Father loves the Son, is the principle of his origin, so that he proceeds from it.

In divine realities, love is taken in two ways: essentially, so far as the Father and the Son and the Holy Spirit love; and notionally or personally, so far as the Holy Spirit proceeds as Love. But in neither of these ways of taking love can it be the principle of origin of the Son. For if it is taken essentially, it implies an act of the will; and if that were the sense in which it is the principle of origin of the Son, it would follow that the Father generated the Son, not by nature, but by will—and this is false.[69] Again, love is not understood notionally, as pertaining to the Holy Spirit. For it would then follow that the Holy Spirit would be the principle of the Son—which is also false. Indeed, no heretic ever went so far as to say this. For although love, notionally taken, is the principle of all the gifts given to us by God, it is nevertheless not the principle of the Son; rather it proceeds from the Father and the Son.[70]

Consequently, we must say that this explanation is not taken from love as from a principle (ex principio), but as from a sign (ex signo). For since likeness is a cause of love (for every animal loves its like), wherever a perfect likeness of God is found, there also is found a perfect love of God. But the perfect likeness of the Father is in the Son, as is said: "he is the image of the invisible God" (Col 1:15): and "he is the brightness of the Father's glory, and the image of his substance" (Heb 1:3). Therefore, the Son is loved perfectly by the Father, and because the Father perfectly loves the Son, this is a sign that the Father has shown him everything and has communicated to him his very own [the Father's] power and nature.[71] And it is of this love that we read above (3:5): "The Father loves the Son, and has put everything into his hands"; and, "This is my beloved Son" (Mt 3:17).

754. With respect to what follows, **and shows him everything that he does**, we should point out that someone can show another his

66. See *ST* I, q. 20, a. 2.
67. *De div. nom.* 6. 2–3; PG 3, col. 856C–857B.
68. See *ST* III, q. 1, a. 1.
69. See *ST* I, q. 41, a. 2.
70. See *ST* I, q. 27, a. 4; I, q. 36, aa. 2–3; I, q. 37, a. 1.
71. See *ST* I, q. 42.

works in two ways: either by sight, as an artisan shows his apprentice the things he has made; or by hearing, as when he verbally instructs him. In whatever of these ways *shows* is understood, there can follow something which is not appropriate, that is, something that is not present when the Father shows things to the Son. For if we say the Father shows things to the Son by sight, then it follows, as with humans, that the Father first does something which he then shows to the Son; and that he does this by himself, without the Son. But the Father does not show the Son things which he did before, for the Son himself says: "The Lord possessed me at the beginning of his ways, before he made anything" (Prv 8:22). Nor does the Father show the Son things he has done without the Son, for the Father does all things through the Son: "All things were made through him" (above 1:3). If *shows* is understood as a kind of hearing, two things seem to follow. For the one who teaches by word first points out something to the one who is ignorant; again, the word is something intermediate between the one showing and the one being shown. But it is in neither of these ways that the Father shows things to the Son: for he does not do so to one who is ignorant, since the Son is the Wisdom of the Father: "Christ is the power of God, and the wisdom of God" (1 Cor 1:24); nor does the Father use some intermediate word, because the Son himself is the Word of the Father: "The Word was with God" (above 1:1).

Therefore, it is said that the Father shows all that he does to the Son, inasmuch as he gives the Son a knowledge of all of his works. For it is in this way that a master is said to show something to his disciple, inasmuch as he gives him a knowledge of the things he makes. Hence, according to Augustine,[72] for the Father to show anything to the Son is nothing more than for the Father to beget or generate the Son. And for the Son to see what the Father does is nothing more than for the Son to receive his being (*esse*) and nature from the Father.

Nevertheless, this showing can be considered similar to seeing insofar as the Son is the brightness of the paternal vision, as we read in Hebrews (1:3): for the Father, seeing and understanding himself, conceives the Son, who is the concept of this vision. Again, it can be considered similar to hearing insofar as the Son proceeds from the Father as the Word. As if to say: *The Father shows him everything*, insofar as he generates him as the brightness and concept of his own wisdom, and as the Word. Thus the words, *The Father shows*, refer to what was said before: *the Son cannot do anything of himself, but only what he sees the Father doing*. And the word, *everything*, refers to, *For whatever the Father does, the Son does likewise*. [73]

---

72. *Tract. in Io.* 21. 4; PL 35, col. 1566; cf. *Catena aurea*, 5:19–20.
73. See *ST* I, q. 34, aa. 1 and 2.

LECTURE 4

20b "Indeed, he will show him even greater works than these, such that you will be amazed. 21 For just as the Father raises the dead and grants life, so the Son grants life to those to whom he wishes. 22 The Father himself judges no one, but he has given all judgment to the Son, 23 so that all men may honor the Son as they honor the Father. Whoever does not honor the Son does not honor the Father who sent him. 24 Amen, amen, I say to you, that whoever hears my voice and believes in him who sent me, possesses eternal life; and he will not encounter judgment, but has passed from death to life. 25 Amen, amen, I say to you, the hour is coming, and is now here, when the dead shall hear the voice of the Son of God; and those who hear it will live."[74]

755. Having pointed out the power of the Son in general, he now shows it in more detail. First, the Lord discloses his life-giving power. Secondly, he clarifies what seemed obscure in what was said before (v. 26). As to the first he does two things. First, he shows that the Son has life-giving power. Secondly, he teaches how life is received from the Son (v. 24). Concerning the first he does three things. First, he presents the life-giving power of the Son. Secondly, he gives a reason for what he says (v. 22). Thirdly, he shows the effect of this (v. 23). With respect to the first he does two things. First, he sets forth this life-giving power in general. Secondly, he expands on it (v. 21).

756. He says, to the first, **Indeed, he will show even greater works than these**. As if to say: You are astonished and affected by the power of the Son in his healing of the sick man, but the Father will show **even greater works than these**, as in raising the dead, **such that you will be amazed**.

757. This passage gives rise to two difficulties. First, about his saying, **he will show**. For the earlier statement that the Father shows everything to the Son (5:20) refers to his eternal generation. How, then, can he say here, **he will show**, if the Son is coeternal with him and eternity does not allow of a future?[75] The second difficulty is over, **such that you will be amazed**. For if he intends to show something to amaze the Jews, then he will be showing it to the Son at the same time as to them; for they could not be amazed unless they saw it. And yet the Son saw all things from eternity with the Father.

758. We must say that this is explained in three ways. The first way is given by Augustine,[76] and in it this future showing is referred to the

74. St. Thomas quotes Jn 5:21 in *ST* III, q. 56, a. 1, obj. 3; III, q. 56, a. 1; Jn 5:22: III, q. 59, a. 4 *sed contra*; Jn 5: 23: III, q. 25, a. 1, obj. 1.
75. See *ST* I, q. 10, aa. 1–3; I, q. 42, a. 2.
76. *Tract. in Io.* 21. 7, 9; PL 35, col. 1568, 1569; cf. *Catena aurea*, 5:19–20.

disciples. For it is Christ's custom that now and then he says that what happens to his members happens to himself, as in Matthew (25:40): "As long as you did it to one of the least of my brethren, you did it to me." And then the meaning is this: You saw the Son do something great in healing the sick man, and you were amazed; but the Father *will show him even greater works than these*, in his members, that is, the disciples: "He will do greater things than these," as we read below (14:12). He then says, *such that you will be amazed*, for the miracles of the disciples so amazed the Jews that a great many of them were converted to the faith, as we see in the Acts.

759. The second explanation, also by Augustine,[77] refers this showing to Christ according to his assumed nature. For in Christ there is both a divine nature and a human nature, and in each he has life-giving power from the Father, although not in the same way. According to his divinity he has the power to give life to souls; but according to his assumed nature, he gives life to bodies. Hence Augustine[78] says: "The Word gives life to souls; but the Word made flesh gives life to bodies." For the resurrection of Christ and the mysteries which Christ fulfilled in his flesh are the cause of the future resurrection of bodies: "God, who is rich in mercy, has brought us to life in Christ" (Eph 2:5); "If it is preached that Christ rose from the dead, how can some of you say that there is no resurrection of the dead" (1 Cor 15:12).[79] The first life-giving power he has from eternity; and he indicated this when he said: "The Father shows him everything that he does" (above 4:20), all of which he shows to his flesh.

The other life-giving power he has in time, and concerning this he says: *he will show him even greater works than these*, i.e., his power will be shown by the fact that he will do greater works, by raising the dead. He will raise some of the dead here: as Lazarus, the young girl, and the mother's only son; and finally he will raise all on the day of judgment.

760. A third explanation refers this showing to Christ in his divine nature, according to the custom of Scripture in saying that a thing is beginning to take place when it is beginning to be known. For example: "All power has been given to me, in heaven and on earth" (Mt 28:18); for although Christ had the complete fullness of power from eternity (because "whatever the Father does, the Son does likewise"), he still speaks of this power as being given to him after the resurrection, not because he was then receiving it for the first time, but because it was through the glory of the resurrection that it became most known.[80] In this interpretation, then, he says that power is given to him insofar as

77. Ibid., 19. 5; col. 1545; 23. 12; col. 1590–91; cf. *Catena aurea*, 5:19–20.
78. Ibid., 19. 16; col. 1553.   79. See *ST* III, q. 56, a. 1.
80. See *ST* III, q. 59, a. 3.

he exercises it in some work. As if to say: *he will show him even greater works than these*, i.e., he will show by his works what has been given to him. And this will come about when you are amazed, i.e., when the one who seems to you to be a mere man is revealed to be a person of divine power and as God.

We could also take the word *show* as referring to an act of seeing, as was explained above [750].

761. Now he explains in more detail the life-giving power of the Son by indicating those greater works which the Father will show the Son (v. 21). Here we should point out that in the Old Testament the divine power is particularly emphasized by the fact that God is the author of life: "The Lord kills, and brings to life" (1 Sm 2:6); "I will kill, and bring to life again" (Dt 32:39). Now just as the Father has this power, so also does the Son; hence he says, *For just as the Father raises the dead and grants life, so the Son grants life to those to whom he wishes*. As if to say: These are those greater works that the Father will show the Son, that is, he will give life to the dead. Such works are obviously greater, for it is greater to raise the dead than for a sick man to become well. Thus *the Son grants life to those to whom he wishes*, i.e., by giving initial life to the living, and by raising the dead.

We should not think that some are raised up by the Father and others by the Son. Rather, the same ones who are raised and vivified by the Father, are raised and vivified by the Son also: because just as the Father does all things through the Son, who is his power, so he also gives life to all through the Son, who is life, as he says below: "I am the way, and the truth, and the life" (14:6).[81]

The Father does not raise up and give life through the Son as through an instrument, because then the Son would not have freedom of power. And so to exclude this he says, *the Son grants life to those to whom he wishes*, i.e., it lies in the freedom of his power to grant life to whom he wills. For the Son does not will anything different than the Father wills: for just as they are one substance, so they have one will; hence Matthew (20:15) says: "Is it not lawful for me to do as I will?"

762. Then when he says, *The Father himself judges no one*, he gives the reason for what was said above, and indicates his own power. It should be remarked that there are two expositions for the present passages: one is given by Augustine, and the other by Hilary and Chrysostom.

Augustine's[82] explanation is this. The Lord had said that just as the Father raises the dead, so also does the Son. But so that we do not think that this refers only to those miracles the Son performs in raising the dead to this life, and not to the Son's raising to eternal life, he leads

---

81. See *ST* III, q. 56, a. 1.
82. *Tract. in Io.* 21. 11; PL 35, col. 1570; cf. *Catena aurea*, 5:21–23.

them to the deeper consideration of the resurrection to occur at the future judgment. Thus he refers explicitly to the judgment, saying, *The Father himself judges no one.*

Another explanation by Augustine,[83] in which the same meaning is maintained, is that the earlier statement, *just as the Father raises the dead and grants life, so the Son,* should be referred to the resurrection of souls, which the Son causes inasmuch as he is the Word; but the text, *The Father himself judges no one,* should be referred to the resurrection of bodies, which the Son causes inasmuch as he is the Word made flesh. For the resurrection of souls is accomplished through the person of the Father and of the Son; and for this reason he mentions the Father and Son together, saying, *just as the Father raises the dead . . . so the Son.*[84] But the resurrection of bodies is accomplished through the humanity of the Son, according to which he is not coeternal with the Father. Consequently, he attributes judgment solely to the Son.

763. Note the wonderful variety of expressions. The Father is first presented as acting and the Son as resting, when it says: "the Son cannot do anything of himself, but only what he sees the Father doing" (5:19); but here, on the contrary, the Son is presented as acting and the Father as resting: The Father *himself judges no one, but he has given all judgment to the Son.* We can see from this that he is speaking from different points of view at different times. At first, he was speaking of an action which belongs to the Father and the Son; thus he says that "the Son cannot do anything of himself, but only what he sees the Father doing"; but here he is speaking of an action by which the Son, as man, judges, and the Father does not: thus he says that the Father *has given all judgment to the Son.* For the Father will not appear at the judgment because, in accord with what is just, God cannot appear in his divine nature before all who are to be judged: for since our happiness consists in the vision of God, if the wicked were to see God in his own nature, they would be enjoying happiness. Therefore, only the Son will appear, who alone has an assumed nature. Therefore, he alone will judge who alone will appear to all. Yet he will judge with the authority of the Father: "He is the one appointed by God to be the judge of the living and of the dead" (Acts 10:42); and in the Psalm (71:2) we read: "O Lord, give your judgment to the king."[85]

764. Then when he says, *so that all men may honor the Son,* he gives the effect which results from the power of the Son. First, he gives the effect. Secondly, he excludes an objection (v. 23b).

765. He says that the Father has given all judgment to the Son, according to his human nature, because in the Incarnation the Son emp-

83. Ibid., 23. 12–13; col. 1590–91; cf. *Catena aurea,* 5:21–23.
84. See *ST* III, q. 56, a. 2.
85. See *ST* III, q. 59, a. 2.

tied himself, taking the form of a servant, under which form he was dishonored by men, as is said below (8:49): "I honor my Father, and you have dishonored me." Therefore, judgment was given to the Son in his assumed nature in order *that all men may honor the Son as they honor the Father.* For on that day "they will see the Son of Man coming with great power and glory" (Lk 21:27); "They fell on their faces and worshipped, saying: 'Blessing and glory, and wisdom and thanks, and honor, power and strength, to our God' (Rev 7:11).

766. Someone might say: I am willing to honor the Father, but do not care about the Son. This cannot be, because whoever does not honor the Son does not honor the Father who sent him. For it is one thing to honor God precisely as God, and another to honor the Father. For someone may well honor God as the omnipotent and immutable Creator without honoring the Son. But no one can honor God as Father without honoring the Son, for he cannot be called Father if he does not have a Son. But if you dishonor the Son by diminishing his power, this also dishonors the Father: because where you give less to the Son, you are taking away from the power of the Father.

767. Another explanation, given by Augustine,[86] is this. A twofold honor is due to Christ. One, according to his divinity, in regard to which he is owed an honor equal to that given the Father; and with respect to this he says, *that all men may honor the Son as they honor the Father.* Another honor is due the Son according to his humanity, but not one equal to that given the Father; and with respect to this he says, *Whoever does not honor the Son does not honor the Father who sent him.* Thus in the first case he significantly used "as"; but now, the second time, he does not say "as," but states absolutely that the Son should be honored: "He who rejects you rejects me; and he who rejects me, rejects him who sent me," as we read in Luke (10:16).

768. Hilary[87] and Chrysostom[88] give a more literal explanation, but it is only slightly different. They explain it this way. Our Lord said above, *the Son grants life to those to whom he wishes.* Now whoever does anything according to the free decision of his will acts because of his own judgment. But it was stated above that "whatever the Father does, the Son does likewise" (5:19). Therefore, the Son enjoys a free decision of his own will in all things, since he acts because of his own judgment. Thus he immediately mentions judgment, saying that *the Father himself judges no one,* i.e., without or apart from the Son. Our Lord used this way of speaking below (12:47): "I do not judge him," i.e., I alone, "but the word that I have spoken will judge him on the

86. *Tract. in Io.* 23. 13; PL 35, col. 1591; cf. *Catena aurea,* 5:21–23.
87. *De Trin.* 7. 20; PL 10, col. 215; 8. 43; col. 268–69; 9. 50; col. 320–21; cf. *Catena aurea,* 5:19–20.
88. *Hom. in Io.* 38. 4; 39. 1; PG 59, col. 218, 220.

last day." *But he has given all judgment to the Son*, as he has given all things to him. For as he has given him life and begotten him as living, so he has given him all judgment, i.e., begotten him as judge: "I judge only as I hear it" (below 5:30), i.e., just as I have being (*esse*) from the Father, so also judgment. The reason for this is that the Son is nothing other than the conception of the paternal wisdom, as was said.[89] But each one judges by the concept of his wisdom. Hence, just as the Father does all things through the Son, so he judges all things through him. And the fruit of this is *that all men may honor the Son as they honor the Father*, i.e., that they may render to him the cult of "latria" as they do the Father.[90] The rest does not change.

769. Hilary[91] calls our attention to the remarkable relationship of the passages so that the errors concerning eternal generation can be refuted. Two heresies have arisen concerning this eternal generation. One was that of Arius, who said that the Son is less than the Father; and this is contrary to their equality and unity. The other was that of Sabellius, who said that that there is no distinction of persons in the divinity; and this is contrary to their origin.

So, whenever he mentions the unity and equality [of the Father and Son], he immediately also adds their distinction as persons according to origin, and conversely.[92] Thus, because he mentions the origin of the persons when he says, "the Son cannot do anything of himself, but only what he sees the Father doing" (5:19), then, so we do not think this involves inequality, he at once adds: "for whatever the Father does, the Son does likewise." Conversely, when he states their equality by saying: *For just as the Father raises the dead and grants life, so the Son grants life to those to whom he wishes*, then, so that we do not deny that the Son has an origin and is begotten, he adds, the Father *himself judges no one, but he has given all judgment to the Son*. Similarly, when he mentions the equality of the persons by saying, so *that all men may honor the Son as they honor the Father*, he immediately adds something about a "mission," which indicates an origin, saying: *Whoever does not honor the Son does not honor the Father who sent him*, but not in such a way that involves a separation.[93] Christ mentions such a mission below (8:29) in saying: "He who sent me is with me, and he has not left me alone."

89. See *ST* I, q. 27, aa. 1–2.
90. See *ST* III, q. 25, a. 1. "Latria" is the term used to denote the worship that is given to God alone and not to any creature, however exalted. In the eighth century John of Damascus used the distinction between *latreia* (worship given to God alone) and *proskynesis* (reverence that may be given to created beings and holy things) to defend the reverence that the Church gives to the holy icons, and to distinguish this from the worship that is rendered to God alone.
91. *De Trin.* 7. 17–18, 20; PL 10, col. 212–13, 215.
92. See *ST* I, q. 42, aa. 1, 3.
93. See *ST* I, q. 42, a. 5.

770. Above, our Lord showed that he had life-giving power; here he shows how someone can share in this life coming from him. First, he tells how one can share in this life through him. Secondly, he predicts its fulfillment (v. 25).

771. With respect to the first, we should point out that there are four grades of life.[94] One is found in plants, which take nourishment, grow, reproduce, and are reproduced. Another is in animals which only sense. Another in living things that move, that is, the perfect animals. Finally, there is another form of life which is present in those who understand. Now among those grades of life that exist, it is impossible that the foremost life be that found in plants, or in those with sensation, or even in those with motion. For the first and foremost life must be that which is *per se*, not that which is participated. This can be none other than intellectual life, for the other three forms are common to a corporal and spiritual creature [as man]. Indeed, a body that lives is not life itself, but one participating in life. Hence intellectual life is the first and foremost life, which is the spiritual life, that is immediately received from the first principle of life, whence it is called the life of wisdom. For this reason in the Scriptures life is attributed to wisdom: "He who finds me finds life, and has salvation from the Lord" (Prv 8:35). Therefore we share life from Christ, who is the Wisdom of God, insofar as our soul receives wisdom from him.[95]

Now this intellectual life is made perfect by the true knowledge of divine Wisdom, which is eternal life: "This is eternal life: that they may know you, the only true God, and Jesus Christ, whom you have sent" (below 17:3). But no one can arrive at any wisdom except by faith. Hence it is that in the sciences, no one acquires wisdom unless he first believes what is said by his teacher. Therefore, if we wish to acquire this life of wisdom, we must believe through faith the things that are proposed to us by it.[96] "He who comes to God must believe that he is and rewards those who seek him" (Heb 11:6); "If you do not believe, you will not understand," as we read in another version of Isaiah (28:16).

772. Thus, our Lord fittingly shows that the way of obtaining life is through faith, saying, **whoever hears my voice and believes in him who sent me, possesses eternal life.** First, he mentions the merit of faith. Secondly, the reward of faith, **eternal life.**

773. Concerning the merit of faith, he first indicates how faith is brought to us; and secondly, the foundation of faith, that on which it rests.

Faith comes to us through the words of men: "Faith comes through hearing, and hearing through the word of Christ" (Rom 10:17). But

---

94. See *ST* I, q. 18, a. 3.   95. See *ST* III, q. 3, a. 8.
96. See *ST* I, q. 1, a. 1; II-II, q. 2, a. 3.

faith does not rest on man's word, but on God himself: "Abram believed God, who counted this as his justification" (Gn 15:6); "You who fear the Lord, believe in him" (Sir 2:8). Thus we are led to believe through the words of men, not in the man himself who speaks, but in God, whose words he speaks: "When you heard the word we brought you as God's word, you did not receive it as the word of men, but, as what it really is, the word of God" (1 Thes 2:13).[97] Our Lord mentions these two things. First, how faith is brought to us, when he says, *whoever hears my voice* [literally, *word*], which leads to faith. Secondly, he mentions that on which faith rests, saying, *and believes in him who sent me*, i.e., not in me, but in him in virtue of whom I speak.

This text can apply to Christ, as man, insofar as it is through Christ's human words that men were converted to the faith. And it can apply to Christ, as God, insofar as Christ is the Word of God. For since Christ is the Word of God, it is clear that those who heard Christ were hearing the Word of God, and as a consequence, were believing in God. And this is what he says: *whoever hears my word*, i.e., me, the Word of God, *and believes in him*, i.e., the Father, whose Word I am.

774. Then when he says, *possesses eternal life*, he mentions the reward of faith, and states three things we will possess in the state of glory; but they are mentioned in reverse order. First, there will be the resurrection from the dead. Secondly, we will have freedom from the future judgment. Thirdly, we will enjoy everlasting life, for as we read in Matthew (chap. 25), the just will enter into everlasting life. He mentions these three as belonging to the reward of faith; and the third was mentioned first since it is desired more than the others.[98]

775. So he says, whoever believes, i.e., through faith, *possesses eternal life*, which consists in the full vision of God. And it is fitting that one who believes on account of God certain things that he does not see, should be brought to the full vision of these things: "These things are written that you may believe . . . and that believing you may have life in his name" (below 20:31).

776. He mentions the second when he says, *and he will not encounter judgment*. But the Apostle says something which contradicts this: "We must all appear before the judgment seat of Christ" (2 Cor 5:10), even the apostles. Therefore, even one who does believe will encounter judgment. I answer that there are two kinds of judgment. One is a judgment of condemnation, and no one encounters that judgment if he believes in God with a faith that is united with love [a "formed faith"]. We read about this judgment: "Do not enter into judgment with your servant, for no living man is just in your sight"; and it was said above (3:18): "Whoever believes is not judged." There is also

97. See *ST* II-II, q. 1, aa. 1–2.
98. See *ST* II-II, q. 4, a. 1.

a judgment of separation and examination; and, as the Apostle says, all must present themselves before the tribunal of Christ for this judgment. Of this judgment we read: "Judge me, O God, and distinguish my cause from those people who are not holy" (Ps 42:1).[99]

777. Thirdly, he mentions a reward when he says, **but has passed from death to life**, or "will pass," as another version says. This statement can be explained in two ways. First, it can refer to the resurrection of the soul. In this case the obvious meaning is that he is saying: Through faith we attain not only to eternal life and freedom from judgment, but also to the forgiveness of our sins as well. Hence he says, **but has passed**, from unbelief to belief, from injustice to justice: "We know that we have passed from death to life" (1 Jn 3:14).

Secondly, this statement can be explained as referring to the resurrection of the body. Then it is an elaboration of the phrase, **possesses eternal life**. For some might think from what was said, that whoever believes in God will never die, but live forever. But this is impossible, because all men must pay the debt incurred by the first sin, according to: "Where is the man who lives, and will not see death?" (Ps 88:49). Consequently, we should not think that one who believes has eternal life in such a way as never to die; rather, he will pass from this life, through death, to life, i.e., through the death of the body he will be revived to eternal life.

Or, "will pass," might refer to the cause [of one's resurrection]: for when a person believes, he already has the merit for a glorious resurrection: "Your dead will live, your slain will rise" (Is 26:19).[100] And then, once released from the death of the old man, we will receive the life of the new man, that is, Christ.

778. **Amen, amen, I say to you.** ... Since some might doubt if any would pass from death to life, our Lord predicts that this will happen, saying: I say that he [who believes] "will pass from death to life"; and I say it before it actually occurs. And this is what he states, saying: **Amen, amen, I say to you, the hour is coming**, not determined by a necessity of fate, but by God's decree: "It is the last hour" (1 Jn 2:18).[101] And so that we do not think that it is far off, he adds, **and is now here**—"It is now the time for us to rise from sleep" (Rom 13:11)—i.e., the hour is now here **when the dead shall hear the voice of the Son of God; and those who hear it will live.**

779. This can be explained in two ways. In one way as referring to the resurrection of the body, and so it is said that **the hour is coming, and is now here**, as if he had said: It is true that eventually all will rise, but even now is the hour when some, whom the Lord was about to

99. See *ST* III, q. 59, a. 5.
100. See *ST* I-II, q. 114, a. 3; II-II, q. 7, a. 2; III, q. 56, a. 1.
101. See *ST* I, q. 116, a. 1.

resuscitate, *shall hear the voice of the Son of God*. This is the way Lazarus heard it when it was said to him, "Come forth," as we read below (11:43); and in this way the daughter of the leader of the synagogue heard it (Mt 9:18); and the widow's son (Lk 7:12). Therefore, he says significantly, *and is now here*, because through me the dead already are beginning to be raised.

Another explanation is given by Augustine,[102] according to which *and is now here* refers to the resurrection of the soul. For as was said above, resurrection is of two kinds: the resurrection of bodies, which will happen in the future; this does not take place now, but will occur at the future judgment. The other is the resurrection of souls from the death of unbelief to the life of faith, and from the life of injustice to that of justice; and this *is now here*.[103] Hence he says, *the hour is coming, and is now here, when the dead*, i.e., unbelievers and sinners, *shall hear the voice of the Son of God; and those who hear it will live*, according to the true faith.

780. This passage seems to imply two strange occurrences. One, when he says that the dead will hear. The other, when he adds that it is through hearing that they will come to life again, as though hearing comes before life, whereas hearing is a certain function of life. However, if we refer this to the resurrection, it is true that the dead will hear, i.e., obey the voice of the Son of God. For the voice expresses the interior concept. Now all nature obeys the slightest command of the divine will: "He calls into existence what does not exist" (Rom 4:17). According to this, then, wood, stones, all things, not just the dry bones but also the dust of dead bodies, *shall hear the voice of the Son of God* so far as they obey his slightest will. And this belongs to Christ, not insofar as he is the Son of Man, but insofar as he is the Son of God, because all things obey the Word of God. And so he significantly says, *of the Son of God*; "What kind of man is this, for the sea and winds obey him?" (Mt 8:27).

If this statement (25b) is understood as referring to the resurrection of souls, then the reason for it is this: the voice of the Son of God has a life-giving power, that voice by which he moves the hearts of the faithful interiorly by inspiration, or exteriorly by his preaching and that of others: "The words that I have spoken to you are spirit and life" (below 6:64). And so he gives life to the dead when he justifies the wicked.[104] And since hearing is the way to life, either of nature through obedience, namely, by repairing nature, or the hearing of faith by repairing life and justice, he therefore says, *and those who hear it*, by obedience as to the resurrection of the body, or by faith as to the resurrection of

102. *Tract. in Io.* 19. 8–9, 22; PL 35, col. 1547; 22. 12, col. 1581; cf. *Catena aurea*, 5:25–26.
103. See *ST* I-II, q. 113, a. 1; III, q. 56, a. 2.
104. See *ST* I-II, q. 113, a. 9.

souls, *will live*, in the body in eternal life, and in justice in the life of grace.

LECTURE 5

26 *"Indeed, just as the Father possesses life in himself, so he has given it to the Son to have life in himself. 27 And he [the Father] gave him the power to pass judgment, because he is the Son of Man. 28 Do not be surprised at this, since the hour is coming when all those buried in tombs will hear the voice of the Son of God. 29 And those who have done well will come forth to a resurrection of life; those who have done evil will come forth to a resurrection of judgment [i.e., condemnation]. 30 I cannot do anything of myself, but I judge only as I hear it and my judgment is just, because I am not seeking my own will, but the will of him who sent me."*[105]

781. Above, our Lord showed that he had the power to give life and to judge; and he explained each by its effect. Here he shows how each of these powers belongs to him. First, he shows this with respect to his life-giving power. Secondly, with respect to his power to judge (v. 27).

782. So he says, first: I say that as the Father raises the dead, so I do also; and anyone who hears my word has eternal life. And I possess this because, *just as the Father possesses life in himself, so he has given it to the Son to have life in himself.*

Apropos of this, we should note that some who live do not have life in themselves: as Paul, "I am living by faith in the Son of God" (Gal 2:20); and again in the same place: "it is not I who now live, but Christ lives in me." Thus he lived, yet not in himself, but in another through whom he lived: as a body lives, although it does not have life in itself, but in a soul through which it lives. So that has life in itself which has an essential, non-participated life, i.e., that which is itself life. Now in every genus of things, that which is something through its essence is the cause of those things that are it by participation, as fire is the cause of all things afire. And so, that which is life through its essence, is the cause and principle of all life in living things. Accordingly, if something is to be a principle of life, it must be life through its essence. And so our Lord fittingly shows that he is the principle of all life by saying that he has life in himself, i.e., through his essence, when he says: *just as the Father possesses life in himself,* i.e., as he is living through his essence, so does the Son. Therefore, as the Father is the cause of life, so also is his Son.[106]

105. St. Thomas quotes Jn 5:27 in *ST* III, q. 59, a. 2 *sed contra*; 5:28: III, q. 51, a. 1; 5: 30: I, q. 42, a. 6, obj. 2.
106. See *ST* I, q. 18, aa. 3–4.

Further, he shows the equality of the Son to the Father when he says, *as the Father possesses life in himself*; and he shows their distinction when he says, *he has given it to the Son*.[107] For the Father and the Son are equal in life; but they are distinct, because the Father gives, and the Son receives. However, we should not understand this to mean that the Son receives life from the Father as if the Son first existed without having life, as in lower things a first matter, already existing, receives a form, and as a subject receives accidents: because in the Son there is nothing that exists prior to the reception of life. For as Hilary[108] says: "the Son has nothing unless it is begotten," i.e., nothing but what he receives through his birth. And since the Father is life itself, the meaning of, *he has given it to the Son to have life in himself*, is that the Father produced the Son as living. As if one were to say: the mind gives life to the word, not as though the word existed and then receives life, but because the mind produces the word in the same life by which it lives.

783. According to Hilary,[109] this passage destroys three heresies. First, that of the Arians, who said that the Son is inferior to the Father. They were forced by what was stated earlier, that is, "For whatever the Father does, the Son does likewise" (5:19), to say that, the Son is equal to the Father in power; but they still denied that the Son is equal to the Father in nature. But now, this too is refuted by this statement, namely, *just as the Father possesses life in himself, so he has given it to the Son to have life in himself*. For since life pertains to the nature, if the Son has life in himself as does the Father, it is clear that he has in himself, by his very origin, a nature indivisible from and equal to that of the Father.

The second error is also Arian: their denial that the Son is coeternal with the Father, when they say that the Son began to exist in time. This is destroyed when he says, *the Son has life in himself*. For in all living things whose generation occurs in time, it is always possible to find something that at some time or other was not living. But in the Son, whatever is, is life itself. Consequently, he so received life itself that he has life in himself, so as always to have been living.[110]

Thirdly, by saying, *he has given*, he destroys the error of Sabellius, who denied the distinction of persons. For if the Father gave life to the Son, it is obvious that the Father, who gave it, is other than the Son, who received it.[111]

---

107. See *ST* I, q. 42, aa. 1, 3–4.
108. *De Trin.* 4. 10; PL 10, col. 103; cf. *Catena aurea*, 5:25–26.
109. See *Liber de Syn.*, definit. II, IV, VI; PL 10, col. 491–95; *De Trin.* 2. 11; PL 10, col. 59; 5. 37, col. 154–55; 6. 35, col. 185; 9. 37, 53, 69; col. 308–9, 323–24.
110. See *ST* I, q. 42, a. 2.
111. See *ST* I, q. 27, a. 2; I, q. 31, a. 2; I, q. 33, a. 4.

784. Then (v. 27), he makes it clear that he has the power to judge. First, he reveals his judiciary power. Secondly, he gives a reason for what he has said (v. 30). As to the first he does two things. First, he indicates the origin of his judiciary power. Secondly, he shows that his judgment is just (v. 29).

785. With regard to the first, we should note that his statement, *he [the Father] gave him the power*, can be understood in two ways. One way is that of Augustine; the other is that of Chrysostom.

786. If we understand it as Chrysostom[112] does, then this section is divided into two parts. First, he reveals the origin of his judiciary power. Secondly, he settles a difficulty (v. 27b).

Chrysostom punctuates this section in the following way. *He gave him the power to pass judgment.* And then a new sentence begins: *Because he is the Son of Man, do not be surprised at this.* The reason for this punctuation is that Paul of Samosata, an early heretic, who like Photius said that Christ was only a man and took his origin from the Virgin, punctuated it as: *He gave him the power to pass judgment because he is the Son of Man.* And then he began a new sentence: *Do not be surprised at this, since the hour is coming.* It was as if he thought that it was necessary for judiciary power to be given to Christ because he is the Son of Man, that is, a mere man, who, of himself, cannot judge men. And so, if Christ is to judge others, he must be given the power to judge.

But this, according to Chrysostom, cannot stand, because it is not at all in agreement with what is stated. For if it is because he is a man that he receives judiciary power, then for the same reason, since it would belong to every man to have judiciary power in virtue of his human nature, it would not belong to Christ any more than to other men. So we should not understand it this way. Rather, we should say that because Christ is the ineffable Son of God, he is on that account also judge. And this is what he says: The Father not only gave him the power to give life, but also *he gave him the power*, through eternal generation, *to pass judgment*, just as he gave him, through eternal generation, to have life in himself: "He is the one appointed by God to be the judge of the living and of the dead," as we read in Acts (10:42).[113]

He settles a difficulty when he says, *Do not be surprised at this.* First, he mentions the difficulty. Secondly, he clears it up.

787. The difficulty arose in the minds of the Jews and they were surprised because while they thought that Christ was no more than a man, he was saying things about himself that surpassed man and even the angels. So he says, *Do not be surprised at this*, that is, that I have

112. *Hom. in Io.* 39. 3; PG 59, col. 223–24; cf. *Catena aurea*, 5:27–29.
113. See *ST* I, q. 59, a. 1.

said that the Son gives life to the dead and has the power to judge precisely *because he is the Son of Man*. They were surprised because, although they thought he was only a man, they saw that he accomplished divine effects: "What kind of man is this, for the sea and winds obey him?" (Mt 8:27).[114] And he gives a reason why they should not be surprised, which is, because he who is the Son of Man is the Son of God. Although, as Chrysostom[115] says, is it not said explicitly that the Son of Man is the Son of God, our Lord lays down the premises from which this statement necessarily follows: just as we notice that those who use syllogisms in their teaching do not express their main conclusion, but only that from which it follows with necessity. So our Lord does not say that he is the Son of God, but that the Son of Man is such that at his voice all the dead will rise. From this it necessarily follows that he is the Son of God: for it is a proper effect of God to raise the dead.[116] Thus he says, *Do not be surprised at this, since the hour is coming when all those buried in tombs will hear the voice of the Son of God*. But he does not say of this hour, as he said above, "and is now here" (5:25). Again, here he says, *all*, which he did not say above: because at the first resurrection he raised only some, as Lazarus, the widow's son and the young girl; but at the future resurrection, at the time of judgment, *all will hear the voice of the Son of God*, and will rise. "I will open your graves, and lead you out of your tombs" (Ez 37:12).

788. Augustine[117] punctuates this passage in the following way. *And he gave him the power to pass judgment because he is the Son of Man*. And then a new sentence follows: *Do not be surprised at this*. In this interpretation there are two parts. The first concerns the power to judge granted to the Son of Man. In the second, the granting of an even greater power is made clear, at *Do not be surprised at this*.

789. As to the first we should note that, according to the mind of Augustine,[118] he spoke above of the resurrection of souls, which is accomplished through the Son of God; but here he is speaking of the resurrection of bodies, which is accomplished through the Son of Man.[119] And because the general resurrection of bodies will take place at the time of judgment, he mentions the judgment first, in saying, *And he [the Father] gave him*, i.e., Christ, *the power to pass judgment*, and this, *because he is the Son of Man*, i.e., according to his human nature. Thus it is also after the resurrection that he says in Matthew (28:18): "All power has been given to me, in heaven and on earth."

There are three reasons why judiciary power has been given to

114. See *ST* III, q. 44, a. 4, especially ad 3.
115. *Hom. in Io.* 39. 3; PG 59, col. 223–24; cf. *Catena aurea*, 5:27–29.
116. See *ST* III, q. 56, a. 1.
117. *Tract. in Io.* 19. 16; PL 35, col. 1553; 22. 12, col. 1580.
118. Ibid., 23. 15; col. 1592. See also *ST* III, q. 59.
119. See *ST* III, q. 56, aa. 1–2.

Christ as man. First, in order that he might be seen by all: for it is necessary that a judge be seen by all who are to be judged. Now both the good and the wicked will be judged. And the good will see Christ in his divinity and in his humanity; while the wicked will not be able to see him in his divinity, because this vision is the happiness of the saints and is seen only by the pure in heart: "Happy are the pure in heart, for they will see God" (Mt 5:8). And so, in order that Christ can be seen at the judgment not only by the good, but also by the wicked, he will judge in human form: "Every eye will see him, and all who pierced him" (Rev 1:7).

Secondly, the power to judge was given to Christ as man because by the self-abasement of his passion he merited the glory of an exaltation. Thus, just as he who died arose, so that [human] form which was judged, will judge, and he who stood before a human judge will preside at the judgment of men. He who was falsely found guilty will condemn the truly guilty, as Augustine[120] remarks in his work, *The Sayings of the Lord*: "Your cause has been judged as that of the wicked; but cause and judgment you will recover" (Jb 36:17).

Thirdly, Christ as man was given judiciary power to suggest the compassion of the judge. For it is very terrifying for a man to be judged by God: "It is a terrible thing to fall into the hands of the living God" (Heb 10:31); but it produces confidence for a man to have another man as his judge. Accordingly, so you can experience the compassion of your judge, you will have a man as judge: "We do not have a high priest who cannot have compassion on our weakness" (Heb 4:15).[121]

Thus, *he gave him*, Christ, *the power to pass judgment because he is the Son of Man*.

790. *Do not be surprised at this*, for he has given him a greater power, that is, the power to raise the dead. Thus he says, *since the hour is coming*, that is, the last hour at the end of the world: "The time has come, the day of slaughter is near" (Ez 7:7), *when all those buried in tombs will hear the voice of the Son of God*. Above he did not say "all," because there he was speaking of the spiritual resurrection, in which all did not rise at his first coming, for we read: "All do not have faith" (2 Thes 3:2). But here he is speaking of the resurrection of the body, and all will rise in this way, as we read in 1 Corinthians (15:20). He adds, *those buried in tombs*, which he had not mentioned above, because only bodies, not souls, are in tombs, and it is the resurrection of bodies that will then take place.

All those buried in tombs will hear the voice of the Son of God. This voice will be a sense perceptible sign of the Son of God, at whose sound all will be raised: "The Lord will come with the cry of the arch-

120. *Serm. de Scrip.* 127. 7. 10; PL 38, col. 711; cf. *Catena aurea*, 5:27–29.
121. See *ST* III, q. 59, a. 2.

angel and with the trumpet of God" (1 Thes 4:15); we find the same in
1 Corinthians (15:52) and in Matthew (25:6): "There was a cry at mid-
night." This voice will derive its power from the divinity of Christ: "He
will make his voice a powerful voice," as the Psalm (67:34) says.

791. As we saw, Augustine says that the resurrection of the body
will be accomplished through the Word made flesh, but the resurrection of the soul is accomplished through the Word. One may wonder
how to understand this: whether we are talking about a first cause or
a meritorious cause. If we are referring to a first cause, then it is clear
that the divinity of Christ is the cause of the corporal and spiritual resurrection, i.e., of the resurrection of bodies and of souls, according to:
"I will kill, and I will bring to life again" (Dt 32:39). But if we are referring to a meritorious cause, then it is the humanity of Christ which
is the cause of both resurrections: because through the mysteries accomplished in the flesh of Christ we are restored not only to an incorruptible life in our bodies, but also to a spiritual life in our souls: "He
was put to death on account of our sins, and he rose for our justification" (Rom 4:25). Accordingly, what Augustine says does not seem to
be true.

I answer that Augustine is speaking of the exemplary cause and of
that cause by which that which is brought to life is made conformable
to that which brings it to life: for everything that lives through another is conformed to that through which it lives. Now the resurrection
of souls does not consist in souls being conformed to the humanity
of Christ, but to the Word, because the life of the soul is through the
Word alone; and so he says that the resurrection of souls takes place
through the Word. But the resurrection of the body will consist in our
bodies being conformed to the body of Christ through the life of glory,
that is, through the glory of our bodies, according to: "He will change
our lowly body so it is like his glorious body" (Phil 3:21). And it is from
this point of view that he says that the resurrection of the body will
take place through the Word made flesh.[122]

792. Then (v. 29), he shows the justness of his judgment: because
the good will be rewarded, and so he says, **And those who have done
well will come forth to a resurrection of life**, i.e., to living in eternal
glory; but the wicked will be damned, and so he says, **those who have
done evil will come forth to a resurrection of judgment**, i.e., they will
rise for condemnation: "These," the wicked, "will go into everlasting
punishment; but the just will go to eternal life" (Mt 25:46); "Many of
those who sleep in the dust of the earth will awake: some to an everlasting life, and others to everlasting shame" (Dn 12:2).[123]

---

122. See *ST* III, q. 56, aa. 1–2.
123. See *ST* III, q. 59, a. 5, especially ad 1.

793. Note than when he was speaking above of the resurrection of souls, he said, "those who hear it," the voice of the Son of God, "will live" (5:25); but here he says, *will come forth*. He says this because of the wicked, who will be condemned: for their life should not be called a life, but rather an eternal death. Again, above he mentioned only faith, saying, "Whoever hears my voice and believes in him who sent me, possesses eternal life; and he will not encounter judgment" (5:24). But here he mentions works, so that we do not think that faith alone, without works, is sufficient for salvation, saying: *And those who have done well will come forth to a resurrection of life*. As if to say: *Those will come forth to a resurrection of life* who do not just believe, but who have accomplished good works along with their faith: "Faith without works is dead," as we see from James (2:26).[124]

794. Then when he says, *I cannot do anything of myself*, he gives the reason for what he has just said. Now he had spoken of two things: the origin of his power, and the justness of his judgment. Consequently, he mentions the reason for each.

795. The first point, when he says, *I cannot do anything of myself*, can be understood in two ways, even according to Augustine.[125] First, as referring to the Son of Man in this manner: You say that you have the power to raise the dead because you are the Son of Man. But do you have this power precisely because you are the Son of Man? No, because *I cannot do anything of myself, but I judge only as I hear it*. He does not say, "as I see," as he said above: "The Son cannot do anything of himself, but only what he sees the Father doing" (5:19). But he does say, *as I hear it*: for in this context "to hear" is the same as "to obey." Now to obey belongs to one who receives a command, while to command pertains to one who is superior. Accordingly, because Christ, as man, is inferior to the Father, he says, *as I hear it*, i.e., as infused into my soul by God.[126] We read of this kind of hearing in Psalm 84 (v. 9): "I will hear what the Lord God says in me." But above he said "sees," because he was then speaking of himself as the Word of God.

796. Then when he says, *and my judgment is just*, he shows the justness of his judgment. For he had said: "Those who have done well will come forth to a resurrection of life." But some might say: Will he be partial and uneven when he punishes and rewards? So he answers: No, saying: *my judgment is just*; and the reason is *because I am not seeking my own will, but the will of him who sent me*. For there are two wills in our Lord Jesus Christ: one is a divine will, which is the same as the will of the Father; the other is a human will, which is proper to himself,

124. See *ST* II-II, q. 4, aa. 3–5.
125. *Tract. in Io.* 19. 19; PL 35, col. 1555; 22. 14–15, col. 1581–82; 23. 15, col. 1592; cf. *Catena aurea*, 5:30.
126. See *ST* III, q. 9, a. 3; III, q. 10, a. 2.

just as it is proper to him to be a man. A human will is borne to its own good; but in Christ it was ruled and regulated by right reason, so that it would always be conformed in all things to the divine will.[127] Accordingly he says: *I am not seeking my own will*, which as such is inclined to its own good, *but the will of him who sent me*, that is, the Father: "I have desired to do your will, my God" (Ps 39:9); "Not as I will, but as you will" (Mt 26:39).

If this is carefully considered, the Lord is assigning the true nature of a just judgment, saying: *because I am not seeking my own will*. For one's judgment is just when it is passed according to the norm of law. But the divine will is the norm and the law of the created will. And so, the created will, and the reason, which is regulated according to the norm of the divine will, is just, and its judgment is just.[128]

797. Secondly, it is explained as referring to the Son of God; and then the aforesaid division still remains the same. Thus Christ, as the Divine Word showing the origin of his power, says: *I cannot do anything of myself*, in the way he said above, "the Son cannot do anything of himself" (5:19). For his very doing and his power are his being (*esse*); but being (*esse*) in him is from another, that is, from his Father.[129] And so, just as he is not of himself (*a se*), so of himself he cannot do anything: "I do nothing of myself" (below 8:28).

His statement, *I judge only as I hear it*, is explained as his previous statement, "only what he sees the Father doing" (above 5:19). For we acquire science or any knowledge through sight and hearing (for these two senses are those most used in learning).[130] But because sight and hearing are different in us, we acquire knowledge in one way through sight, that is, by discovering things, and in a different way through hearing, that is, by being taught. But in the Son of God, sight and hearing are the same; thus, when he says either "sees" or "hears," the meaning is the same so far as the acquisition of knowledge is concerned. And because judgment in any intellectual nature comes from knowledge, he says significantly, *I judge only as I hear it*, i.e., as I have acquired knowledge together with being from the Father, so I judge: "Everything I have heard from my Father I have made known to you" (below 15:15).

798. Showing the justness of his judgment he says: *and my judgment is just*: the reason being, *because I am not seeking my own will*. But do not the Father and the Son have the same will? I answer that the Father and the Son do have the same will, but the Father does not have his will from another, whereas the Son does have his will from another, i.e., from the Father.[131] Thus the Son accomplishes his own

127. See *ST* III, q. 18, a. 5; III, q. 20, aa. 1–2.
128. See *ST* I-II, q. 19, aa. 4, 9–10; I-II, q. 91, a. 1; II-II, q. 60, a. 1.
129. See *ST* I, q. 27, a. 2.   130. See *ST* I, q. 84, a. 6.
131. See *ST* I, q. 42, aa. 2 and 4.

will as from another, i.e., as having it from another; but the Father accomplishes his will as his own, i.e., not having it from another. Thus he says: *I am not seeking my own will*, that is, such as would be mine if it originated from myself, but my will, as being from another, that is from the Father.

LECTURE 6

31 "If I were to bear witness to myself, my testimony would not be valid. 32 But there is someone else who testifies on my behalf, and I know that the witness he bears on my behalf is true. 33 You sent [messengers] to John; and he bore witness to the truth. 34 I myself do not need proof from men; but I say this in order that you may be saved. 35 He was a lamp, blazing and burning brightly. And for a time you yourselves exulted in his light. 36 But I have testimony that is greater than that of John. The very works which my Father has given me to perform—those works that I myself perform—they bear witness to me that the Father sent me. 37 Moreover, the Father who sent me has himself given testimony on my behalf, but you have neither heard his voice, nor seen his image; 38 and you do not have his word abiding in your hearts, for you do not believe in him whom he has sent. 39 Search the Scriptures, since you think you have eternal life in them; they too bear witness to me. 40 Yet you are unwilling to come to me in order to possess that life."[132]

799. Having given us the teaching on the life-giving power of the Son, he now confirms it. First, he confirms, with several testimonies, what he had said about the excellence of his power. In the second place, he reproves them because of their slowness to believe (v. 41). He does two things about the first. First, he states why there was a need to resort to such testimonies. Secondly, he invokes the testimonies (v. 32).

800. The need to appeal to testimony arose because the Jews did not believe in him; for this reason he says: *If I were to bear witness to myself, my testimony would not be valid* (*verum*, valid, true). Some may find this statement puzzling: for if our Lord says of himself, "I am the truth" (below 14:6), how can his testimony not be valid? If he is the truth, in whom shall one believe if the truth itself is not believed in? We may answer, according to Chrysostom,[133] that our Lord is speaking here of himself from the point of view of the opinion of

132. St. Thomas quotes Jn 5:36 in *ST* III, q. 43, a. 1; III, q. 43, a. 4 sed contra; Jn 5, 37: III, q. 39, a. 8 ad 2; Jn 5, 39: III, q. 39, a. 8, ad 3.
133. *Hom. in Io.* 40. 1; PG 59, col. 229; cf. *Catena aurea*, 5:31–40.

others, so that his meaning is: *If I were to bear witness to myself, my testimony would not be valid* so far as your outlook is concerned, because you do not accept what I say about myself unless it is confirmed by other testimony: "You are bearing witness to yourself; your testimony is not valid" (below 8:13).

801. Next, he presents these testimonies: first, a human testimony; secondly, a divine testimony. He does two things about the first. First, he mentions the testimony of John; secondly, he tells why this testimony was given (v. 34). With respect to the first he does two things. First, he brings in the testimony; secondly, he commends it (v. 32).

802. He brings on the witness when he says: *But there is someone else who testifies on my behalf.* This is, in the opinion of Chrysostom,[134] John the Baptist, of whom we read above: "There was a man sent by God, whose name was John. He came as a witness, that he might bear witness to the light" (1:6).

803. He commends John's testimony on two grounds: first, because of its truth; secondly, because of its authority, for the Jews had sought it (v. 33).

804. He commends his testimony because of its truth, saying: *And I know*, from certain experience, *that the witness he*, that is, John, *bears on my behalf is true.* His father, Zechariah, had prophesied this of him: "You will go before the face of the Lord to prepare his way, to give his people a knowledge of salvation" (Lk 1:76). Now it is obvious that false testimony is not a testimony that saves, because lying is a cause of death: "A lying mouth kills the soul" (Wis 1:11). Therefore, if John's testimony was for the purpose of giving knowledge of salvation to his people, his testimony is true.

805. The Gloss[135] has a different explanation of this: *If I were to bear witness to myself, my testimony would not be valid.* For above, Christ was referring to himself as God, but here he is referring to himself as a man. And the meaning is: *If I*, namely, a man, *were to bear witness to myself*, i.e., apart from God, that is, which God the Father does not certify, then it follows that *my testimony would not be valid*, for human speech has no truth unless it is supported by God, according to: "God is true, but every man is a liar" (Rom 3:4). Thus, if we take Christ as a man separated from the Deity and not in conformity with it, we find a lie both in his essence and in his words: "Although I bear witness to myself, my testimony is true" (below 8:14); "I am not alone, because the Father is with me" (below 16:32). And so, because he was not alone but with the Father, his testimony is true.

Accordingly, to show that his testimony is true, not in virtue of his

---

134. Ibid., col. 230; cf. *Catena aurea*, 5:31–40.
135. See Alcuin, *Comm. in S. Ioannis Evang.* 3. 10; PL 100, col. 815–16; cf. Bede, *In S. Ioannis Evang. expos.* 5; PL 92, col. 700D–701C.

humanity considered in itself, but in so far as it is united to his divinity and to the Word of God, he says, *But there is someone else who testifies on my behalf*: not John, but the Father, according to this explanation. Because if the testimony of Christ as man is not of itself true and productive, much less is the testimony of John. Therefore, the testimony of Christ is not verified by the testimony of John, but by the testimony of the Father. So this someone else who testifies is understood to be the Father. And I know that the witness he bears on my behalf is true, for he is truth: "God is light," i.e., truth, "and in him there is no darkness," i.e., lie (1 Jn 1:5).

The first explanation, which is that given by Chrysostom, is nearer to the letter of the text.

806. He also commends the testimony of John by reason of its authority, because it was sought after by the Jews, saying: *You sent [messengers] to John*. As if to say: I know that his testimony is true and you should not reject it, because the great authority John enjoyed among you led you to seek his testimony about me; and you would not have done this if you did not think that he was worthy of belief: "The Jews sent priests and Levites from Jerusalem to him" (above 1:19). And on this occasion, John *bore witness*, not to himself, but *to the truth*, i.e., to me. As a friend of the truth, he bore testimony to the truth, which is Christ: "He declared openly, and did not deny, and stated clearly, 'I am not the Messiah'" (above 1:20).

807. Then (v. 34), he gives the reason why an appeal was made to the testimony of John. First, he excludes a supposed reason. Next, he presents the true reason (v. 34b).

808. Someone might think that John's testimony was brought in to assure them about Christ, on the ground that Christ's own testimony was not sufficient. He excludes this reason when he says, *I myself do not need proof from men*. Here we should note that sometimes in the sciences a thing is proved by something else which is more evident to us, but which is less evident in itself; and at other times a thing is proved by something else which is more evident in itself and absolutely.[136] Now, in this case, the issue is to prove that Christ is God. And, although the truth of Christ is, in itself and absolutely, more evident, yet it is proved by the testimony of John, which was better known to the Jews. So Christ, of himself, did not have any need of John's testimony; and this is what he says: *I myself do not need proof from men*.

809. But this seems to conflict with: "You are my witnesses, said the Lord" (Is 40:10); and with "You will be my witnesses in Jerusalem and in all of Judea and Samaria, and to the remotest part of the world" (Acts 1:8). So how can he say: *I myself do not need proof from men*.

This can be understood in two ways. In the first way, the sense is: I

136. See *ST* I, q. 2, a. 1.

myself do not need proof from men, as relying on it alone; but I have stronger testimony, that is, divine testimony: "For me, it does not matter much if I am judged by you" (1 Cor 4:3); "You know that I have not desired the day of man," i.e., human glory (Jer 17:16).

Another interpretation is: I myself do not need proof from men, insofar as the one giving witness is a man, but insofar as he is enlightened by God in order to testify: "There was a man sent by God, whose name was John" (above 1:6); "We did not seek glory from men" (1 Thes 2:6); "I do not seek my own glory" (below 8:50). And so I receive the testimony of John not just as a man, but insofar as he was sent and enlightened by God in order to testify.

A third explanation, and a better one, is: I myself do not need proof from men, i.e., human testimony. As far as I am concerned, I receive my authority from no one but God, who proves that I am great.

810. Next (v. 34b), he gives the real reason for appealing to John's testimony. First, he states the reason. Secondly, he explains it. The reason for appealing to this testimony was so that the Jews might be saved by believing in Christ, and this because of John's testimony.[137] Thus he says: I do not need John's testimony for my sake, *but I say this in order that you may be saved*: "He desires the salvation of all men" (1 Tim 2:4); "Christ came into this world to save sinners" (1 Tim 1:15).

811. He explains his statement, *in order that you may be saved*: that is, because I am appealing to testimony you have accepted. And so he mentions that John was accepted by them: *He was a lamp, blazing and burning brightly*. First, he states that John was a witness accepted on his own merits. Secondly, he mentions to what degree he was accepted by them (v. 35b).

812. Three things perfected John and show that he was a witness accepted in his own right. The first concerns the condition of his nature, and he refers to this when he says, *He was a lamp*. The second concerns the perfection of his love, because he was a *blazing* lamp. The third is related to the perfection of his understanding, because he was a lamp that was *burning brightly*.

John was perfect in his nature because he was a *lamp*, i.e., enriched by grace and illumined by the light of the Word of God. Now a lamp differs from a light: for a light radiates light of itself, but a lamp does not give light of itself, but by participating in the light. Now the true light is Christ: "He was the true light, which enlightens every man coming into this world" (above 1:9). John, however, was not a light, as we read in the same place, but a lamp, because he was enlightened "in order to bear witness to the light" (above 1:8), by leading men to Christ. We read of this lamp: "I have prepared a lamp for my anointed" (Ps 131:17).

137. See *ST* III, q. 38, a. 2.

Further, he was blazing and impassioned in his affections, so he says, *blazing.* For some people are lamps only as to their office or rank, but they are snuffed out in their affections: for as a lamp cannot give light unless there is a fire blazing within it, so a spiritual lamp does not give any light unless it is first set ablaze and burns with the fire of love. Therefore, to be ablaze comes first, and the giving of light depends on it, because knowledge of the truth is given due to the blazing of love: "If any one loves me, he will keep my word, and my Father will love him, and we will come to him, and make our home with him" (below 14:23); and "I have called you friends, because everything I have heard from my Father I have made known to you" (below 15:15); "You who fear the Lord, love him, and your hearts will be enlightened" (Sir 2:20).[138]

The two characteristics of fire are that it both blazes and shines. Its blazing signifies love for three reasons. First, because fire is the most active of all bodies; so too is the warmth of love (charity), so much so that nothing can withstand its force: "The love of Christ spurs us on" (2 Cor 5:14). Secondly, because just as fire, because it is very volatile, causes great unrest, so also this love of charity makes a person restless until he achieves his objective: "Its light is fire and flame" (Sg 8:6). Thirdly, just as fire is inclined to move upward, so too is charity; so much so that it joins us to God: "He who abides in love abides in God, and God in him" (1 Jn 4:16).

Finally, John had an intellect that was *burning brightly.* First, it was bright within, because of his knowledge of the truth: "The Lord will fill your soul with brightness," i.e., he will make it shine (Is 58:11). Secondly, it was bright without, because of his preaching: "You will shine in the world among them like stars, containing the word of life" (Phil 2:15). Thirdly, it was bright because it manifested good works: "Let your light so shine before men that they may see your good works" (Mt 5:16).

813. And so, because John was of himself so acceptable—for he was a lamp, not smothered out but blazing, not dark but burning brightly—he deserved to be accepted by you, as indeed he was, because *for a time you yourselves exulted in his light.* He fittingly links their exulting or rejoicing with light; because a man rejoices most in that which most pleases him. And among physical things nothing is more pleasant than light, according to: "It is a delight for the eyes to see the sun" (Sir 11:7). He says, *you yourselves exulted in his light,* i.e., you rested in John and put your end in him, thinking that he was the Messiah. But you did this only *for a time,* because you wavered on this; for when you saw that John was leading men to another, and not to himself, you turned away from him. Thus we read in Matthew (21:32) that the Jews did

138. See *ST* II, q. 4, a. 4; II-II, q. 4, a. 7, especially ad 4, 5.

not believe in John. They belonged to that group referred to by Matthew (13:21) as believing "for a while."

814. Then (v. 36), he presents the divine testimony. First, he mentions its greatness; and then he continues on to describe it.

815. He says: I do not need proof from men for my sake, but for your sake, for **I have testimony that is greater than that of John**, that is, the testimony of God, which is greater than the testimony of John: "If we receive the testimony of men, the testimony of God is greater" (1 Jn 5:9). It is greater, I say, because of its greater authority, greater knowledge, and infallible truth, for God cannot deceive: "God is not like man, a liar" (Nm 23:19).[139]

816. God bore witness to Christ in three ways: by works, by himself, and by the Scriptures. First, he mentions his witness as given by the working of miracles; secondly, the way God gave witness by himself (v. 37); thirdly, the witness given through the Scriptures (v. 39).

817. He says first: **I have testimony that is greater than that of John**, that is, my works, i.e., the working of miracles, **the very works which my Father has given me to perform**. We should point out that it is natural for man to learn of the power and natures of things from their actions, and therefore our Lord fittingly says that the sort of person he is can be learned through the works he does. So, since he performed divine works by his own power, we should believe that he has divine power within him: "If I had not done among them the works which no one else did, they would not have sin," that is, the sin of unbelief (below 15:24). And so he leads them to a knowledge of himself by appealing to his works, saying, **the very works which my Father has given me** in the Word, through an eternal generation, by giving me a power equal to his own. Or we could say, **the very works which my Father has given me**, in my conception, by making me one person who is both God and man, **to perform**, i.e., to perform them by my own power. He says this to distinguish himself from those who do not perform miracles by their own power but have to obtain it as a favor from God; thus Peter says: "In the name of Jesus Christ of Nazareth: stand up" (Acts 3:6). Thus it was God, and not themselves, who accomplished these works; but Christ accomplished them by his own power: "Lazarus, come forth," as John reports below (11:43). Accordingly, **those works that I myself perform—they bear witness to me**; "If you do not believe me, at least believe my works" (below 10:38). We see from Mark (16:20) that God bears witness by the working of miracles: "The Lord worked with them and confirmed the word by the signs that followed."[140]

818. Then (v. 37), he presents the second way God bore witness to

139. See *ST* I, q. 16, a. 5.
140. See *ST* III, q. 43, a. 4.

Christ, namely, by himself. First, he mentions the way; secondly, he shows that they were not able to receive this testimony.

819. He says: It is not only the works which my Father has given me to perform that bear witness to me, *but the Father who sent me has himself given testimony on my behalf*: in the Jordan, when Christ was baptized (Mt 3:17): and on the mountain, when Christ was transfigured (Mt 17:5). For on both these occasions the voice of the Father was heard: "This is my beloved Son." And so they should believe in Christ, as the true and natural Son of God: "This is the testimony of God: he has borne witness to his Son" (1 Jn 5:9). Consequently, anyone who does not believe that he is the Son of God, does not believe in the testimony of God.[141]

820. Someone could say that God also gave testimony to others by himself: for example, to Moses, on the mountain, with whom God spoke while others were present. We, however, never heard his testimony, as the Lord says: *you have neither heard his voice*. On the other hand, we read in Deuteronomy (4:33): Did it ever happen before that the people heard the voice of God speaking from the midst of fire, as you heard, and have lived?" Then how can Christ say: *you have neither heard his voice*?

I reply, according to Chrysostom,[142] that the Lord wishes to show those established in a philosophical frame of mind that God gives testimony to someone in two ways, namely, sensibly and intelligibly. Sensibly, as by a sensible voice only; and in this way he gave witness to Moses on Mount Sinai: "You heard his voice, and saw no form at all" (Dt 4:12). Likewise, he gives testimony by a sensible form, as he appeared to Abraham (Gn 26), and to Isaiah: "I saw the Lord seated on a high and lofty throne" (Is 6:1). However, in these visions, neither the audible voice nor the visible figure were like anything in the animal kingdom, except efficiently, in the sense that these were formed by God. For since God is a spirit, he neither emits audible sounds nor can he be portrayed as a figure. But he does bear testimony in an intelligible manner by inspiring in the hearts of certain persons what they ought to believe and to hold: "I will hear what the Lord God will speak within me" (Ps 84:9); "I will lead her into the wilderness and there I will speak to her heart," as we read in Hosea (2:14).[143]

Now you were able to receive the testimony given in the first of these ways; and this is not surprising, because they were the words and image of God only efficiently, as was said. But they were not able to receive the testimony given in that intelligible voice; so he says: *you have neither heard his voice*, i.e., you were not among those who shared in

141. See *ST* III, q. 39, a. 8; III, q. 45, a. 4.
142. *Hom. in Io.* 40. 3; PG 59, col. 232–33; cf. *Catena aurea*, 5:31–40.
143. See *ST* II-II, q. 173, a. 2.

it. "Everyone who has heard the Father and has learned, comes to me" (below 6:45). But you do not come to me. Therefore, *you have neither heard his voice nor seen his image*, i.e., you do not have his intelligible testimony. Hence he adds: *and you do not have his word abiding in your hearts*, i.e., you do not have his word that is inwardly inspired. And the reason is, *for you do not believe in him whom he*, the Father, *has sent*. For the word of God leads to Christ, since Christ himself is the natural Word of God. But every word inspired by God is a certain participated likeness of that Word.[144] Therefore, since every participated likeness leads to its original, it is clear that every word inspired by God leads to Christ. And so, because you are not led to me, *you do not have his word*, i.e., the inspired word of God, *abiding in your hearts*. "He who does not believe in the Son of God does not have life abiding in him," as it says below (*sic*). He says *abiding*, because although there is no one who does not have some truth from God, they alone have the truth and the word abiding in them whose knowledge has progressed to the point where they have reached a knowledge of the true and natural Word.[145]

821. Or we could say that, *you have neither heard his voice*, can be taken as showing the three ways in which God reveals things. This is done either by a sensible voice, as he bore witness to Christ in the Jordan and on the mountain, as in 2 Peter (1:16): "We were eyewitnesses of his greatness. For he received honor and glory from God the Father, when a voice came from the heavens." And the Jews did not hear this. Or, God reveals things through a vision of his essence, which he reveals to the blessed. And they did not see this, because "while we are in the body, we are absent from the Lord" (2 Cor 5:6). Thirdly, it is accomplished by an interior word through an inspiration; and the Jews did not have this either.

822. Then when he says, *Search the Scriptures*, he gives the third way in which God bore witness to Christ, through the Scriptures. First, he mentions the testimony of the Scriptures. Secondly, he shows that they were not able to gather the fruit of this testimony (v. 40).

823. He says: *Search the Scriptures*. As if to say: You do not have the word of God in your hearts, but in the Scriptures; therefore, you must seek for it elsewhere than in your hearts. Hence, *Search the Scriptures*, that is, the Old Testament, for the faith of Christ was contained in the Old Testament, but not on the surface, for it lay hidden in its depths, under shadowy symbols: "Even to this day, when Moses is read, a veil is over their hearts" (2 Cor 3:15).[146] Thus he significantly says, *Search*, probe into the depths: "If you search for her [wisdom] like money, and

144. See *ST* I, q. 15, a. 2; I, q. 16, aa. 5–6; I, q. 34, a. 3.
145. See *ST* II-II, q. 10, a. 4, ad 3.
146. See *ST* I-II, q. 107, a. 3, especially ad 1.

dig for her like a treasure, you will understand the fear of the Lord and will find the knowledge of God" (Prv 2:4); "Give me understanding and I will search your commandments" (Ps 118:34).

The reason why you should search them I take from your own opinion, because *you think you have eternal life in them*, since we read in Ezekiel (8:19): "He who has kept my commands will live." But you are mistaken; because although the precepts of the Old Law are living, they do not contain life in themselves. They are said to be living only to the extent that they lead to me, the Christ.[147] Yet you use them as though they contained life in themselves, and in this you are mistaken, for *they bear witness to me*, i.e., they are living to the extent that they lead to a knowledge of me. And they lead to a knowledge of me either by plain prophecies, as in Isaiah (7:14): "A virgin will conceive" or in Deuteronomy (18:15): "The Lord your God will raise up a prophet for you"; and so Acts (10:43) says: "All the prophets bear witness to him." The Scriptures also lead to a knowledge of Christ through the symbolic actions of the prophets; thus we read: "I have used resemblances in the ministry of the prophets" (Hos 12:10). Knowledge of Christ is also given in their sacraments and figures, as in the immolation of the lamb, and other symbolic sacraments of the law: "The law has only a shadow of the good things to come" (Heb 10:1).[148] And so, because the Scriptures of the Old Testament gave much testimony about Christ, the Apostle says: "He promised the Good News before, through his prophets in the holy Scriptures; the Good News of his Son, a descendant of David in his human nature" (Rom 1:2).[149]

824. The fruit which you think you have in the Scriptures, that is, eternal life, you will not be able to obtain, because in not believing the testimonies of the Scriptures about me, *you are unwilling to come to me*, i.e., you do not wish to believe in me, in whom the fruit of these Scriptures exists, *in order to possess that life* in me, the life which I give to those who believe in me: "I give them eternal life" (below 10:28); "Wisdom infuses life into her children" (Sir 4:12); "He who finds me will find life, and will have salvation from the Lord" (Prv 8:35).

LECTURE 7

41 "Praise from men I do not need, 42 but I know you, and you do not have the love of God in your hearts. 43 I have come in my Father's name, and yet you do not accept me. If someone else came in his own name, you would be accepting him. 44 How can people like you believe,

147. See *ST* I-II, q. 107, a. 2.   148. See *ST* III, q. 73, a. 6.
149. See *ST* II-II, q. 174, a. 6.

when you crave praise from each other, and yet not even ask for that one praise which is from God alone? 45 Do not think that I will accuse you before my Father. The one who accuses you is Moses, in whom you place your trust. 46 If you believed Moses, you would perhaps believe me as well, for it was about me that he wrote. 47 But if you do not believe in his written statements, how will you believe in my spoken words?"[150]

825. After God confirmed the greatness of his power by the testimonies of men, of God, and of the Scriptures, he here rebukes the Jews for being slow to believe.[151] Now the Jews persecuted Christ on two grounds: for breaking the Sabbath, by which he seemed to go against the law, and for saying that he is the Son of God, by which he seemed to go against God. Thus they persecuted him on account of their reverence for God and their zeal for the law. And so our Lord wishes to show that their persecution of him was really inspired not by these motives, but by contrary reasons.

He first shows that the cause of their unbelief was their lack of reverence for God. Secondly, that another cause of their unbelief was their lack of reverence for Moses (v. 45). As to the first he does two things. First, he shows their irreverence for God. Secondly, he shows that this is the cause of their unbelief (v. 44). Concerning the first he does two things. First, he mentions their lack of reverence for God. Secondly, he makes this obvious by a sign (v. 43). With respect to the first he does two things. First, he rejects what they might have assumed to be his intention, from what he had said before. Secondly, he presents his real intention (v. 42).

826. The Jews might have assumed that Christ was seeking some kind of praise from men, since he had reminded them of so many witnesses to himself, as John, God, his own works, and the testimony of the Scriptures. Against this thought he says, **Praise from men I do not need**, i.e., I do not seek praise from men; for I have not come to be an example of one seeking human glory: "We did not seek glory from men" (1 Thes 2:6). Or, **Praise from men I do not need**, i.e., I do not need human praise, because from eternity I have glory with the Father: "Glorify me, Father, with the glory I had before the world was made" (below 17:5). For I have not come to be glorified by men, but rather to glorify them, since all glory proceeds from me (Wis 7:25) ["Wisdom is a pure emanation of the glory of the almighty God."] It is through this wisdom that I have glory. God is said to be praised and glorified by men—"Glorify the Lord as much as you are able; he will still surpass even that" (Sir 43:30)—not that he might become by

150. St. Thomas quotes Jn 5:46 in *ST* I-II, q. 98, a. 2; I-II, q. 106, a. 4, ad 3.
151. See *ST* II-II, q. 10, a. 6; III, q. 47, aa. 4–6.

this more glorious, but so that he might appear glorious among us.[152]

827. Thus Christ presented the various testimonies to himself not for the reason they thought, but for another one: because *I know you*, i.e., I have made known about you, that *you do not have the love of God in your hearts*, although you pretend to have it. And so you are not persecuting me because of your love for God. You would be persecuting me for the love of God if God and the Scriptures did not bear witness to me; but God himself bears witness to me by himself, his works and in the Scriptures, as has been said. Consequently, if you truly loved God, then so far from rejecting me, you would come to me. You, therefore, do not love God.

Another interpretation would be this. It is as though he were saying: I have not brought in these witnesses because I wanted your praise; but I know you do not love God and your waywardness makes me sad, and I want to lead you back to the way of truth: "Now they have seen and hated both me and my Father" (below 15:24); "The pride of those who hate you continuously rises," as the Psalm (73:23) says.

828. Here we should point out that God cannot be hated in himself by anyone, nor can he be hated with respect to all his effects, since every good in things comes from God, and it is impossible for anyone to hate all good, for he will at least love existence and life. But someone may hate some effect of God, insofar as this is opposed to what he desires: for example, he might hate punishment, and things of that sort. It is from this point of view that God is said to be hated.[153]

829. Then (v. 43), he gives a sign that they do not love God. First, a present sign; secondly, a future sign (v. 43b).

830. The present sign concerns his own coming; so he says, *I have come in my Father's name*. As if to say: What I say is obvious, for if one loves his Lord, it is clear that he will honor and receive one who comes from him, and seek to honor him. But *I have come in my Father's name*, and I make his name known to the world: "I have made your name known to those you have given me" (below 17:6), *and yet you do not accept me*. Therefore, you do not love him. The Son is said to make his Father known to men because, although the Father, as God, was known—"God is known in Judah" (Ps 75:1)—yet he was not known as the natural Father of the Son before Christ came. Thus Solomon asked: "What is his name? And what is the name of his son?" (Prv 30:4).

831. The future sign concerns the coming of the Antichrist.[154] For the Jews could say: Although you come in his name, we have not accepted you, because we will not accept anyone but God the Father. The Lord speaks against this, and says that it cannot be, because you will accept another, who will come, not in the Father's name, but in his own

152. See *ST* II-II, q. 91, aa. 1–2.   153. See *ST* II-II, q. 34, a. 1.
154. See *ST* III, q. 8, a. 8.

name; and what is more, he will come, not in the name of the Father, but *in his own name*, precisely because he will not seek the glory of the Father but his own. And whatever he does, he will attribute it, not to the Father, but to himself: "who opposes and is exalted above all that is called God, or is worshipped" (2 Thes 2:4). *You would be accepting him*; and so the Apostle continues in the same letter: "God will send them a misleading influence so that they might believe what is false" (2 Thes 2:11). And this, because they did not accept the true teaching, that they might be saved. So the Gloss says: "Because the Jews were unwilling to accept Christ, the penalty for this sin will be, fittingly enough, that they will receive the Antichrist; with the result that those who were unwilling to believe the truth, will believe a lie."

According to Augustine,[155] however, we can understand this text as applying to heretics and false teachers: who spread a teaching that comes from their own hearts and not from the mouth of God, and who praise themselves and despise the name of God.[156] Of such persons it is written: "You have heard that the Antichrist is coming; and now many antichrists have appeared" (1 Jn 2:18). So it is clear that your persecution of me does not spring from your love for God, but from your hatred and envy of him. And this was the reason why they did not believe.

832. He concludes: *How can people like you believe, when you crave praise from each other*, i.e., human praise, *and yet not even ask for that one praise which is from God alone?* which is true glory. The reason they could not believe in Christ was that, since their proud minds were craving their own glory and praise, they considered themselves superior to others in glory, and regarded it as a disgrace to believe in Christ, who seemed common and poor. And this was why they could not believe in him. The one who can believe in Christ is the person of humble heart, who seeks the glory of God alone, and who strives to please him. And so we read: "Many of the leaders believed in him; but they did not admit it because of the Pharisees, so that they would not be expelled from the synagogue" (below 12:42). We can see from this just how dangerous vainglory is.[157] For this reason Cicero[158] says: "Let a man beware of that glory that robs him of all freedom; that freedom for which a man of great spirit should risk everything." And the Gloss[159] says: "It is a great vice to boast and to strive for human praise: to desire that others think you have what you really do not have."

833. Then (v. 45), he shows that they do not have zeal for Moses.

155. *Serm. de Scrip.*, 129. 6. 7; PL 38, col. 723; cf. *Catena aurea*, 5:41–47.
156. See *ST* II-II, q. 11, aa. 1–2.
157. See *ST* II-II, q. 132, aa. 1, 3.
158. *De Officiis* 1. 20, sec. 68.
159. See Alcuin, *Comm. in S. Ioannis Evang.* 3. 11; PL 100, col. 818B; Bede, *In S. Ioannis Evang. expos.* 5; PL 92, col. 703C–D.

First, how Moses was against them. Secondly, he gives the reason for this opposition (v. 46). As to the first he does two things. First, he rejects their false zeal; secondly, he shows them true zeal, *The one who accuses you is Moses.*

834. As to the first he says: *Do not think that I will accuse you before my Father.* There are three reasons for his saying this. First, the Son of God did not come into the world to condemn the world, but to save it. So he says, *Do not think* that I have come to condemn; I have come to free: "God did not send his Son into the world to judge the world," that is, to condemn the world, "but that the world might be saved through him" (above 3:17). And so the blood of Christ cries out, not to accuse, but to forgive: "We have the blood of Christ, crying out better than that of Abel" (Heb 12:24), whose blood cried out to accuse; "Who will accuse God's elect? It is Christ who justifies. Who is it, then, who will condemn?" (Rom 8:33).[160] As to his second reason for saying this, he says: *Do not think that I will accuse you before my Father,* because I will not be the one to accuse you, but to judge you: "The Father has given all judgment to the Son" (above 5:22). The third reason is: *Do not think that I,* i.e., I alone, *will accuse you before my Father* for what you are doing to me; for even Moses will accuse you for not believing him in the things he said of me.

835. Consequently he adds: *The one who accuses you is Moses, in whom you place your trust,* because you believe you are saved through his precepts. Moses accuses them in two ways. Materially, because they deserved to be accused for transgressing his commands: "Those who have sinned under the law, will be judged by the law" (Rom 2:12). Again, Moses accuses them because he and the other saints will have authority in the judgment: "The two-edged swords will be in their hands" (Ps 149:6).

836. He presents the reason for this opposition when he says: If you believed Moses, you would perhaps believe me as well, as is clear from "The Lord your God will raise up a prophet for you, from your nation and your brothers; he will be like me: you will listen to him" (Dt 18:15), and from all the sacrifices, which were a symbol of Christ. He says, perhaps, to indicate that their will acts from a free judgment, and not to imply that there is any doubt on the part of God.

837. Then when he says, *But if you do not believe in his written statements, how will you believe in my spoken words?* he gives a sign of this opposition. He does this by comparing two things, and then denying of the lesser of them what is denied of the greater. First, there is a comparison between Moses and Christ: for although Christ, absolutely speaking, is greater than Moses, Moses was the greater in reputation among the Jews. Thus he says: If you do not believe Moses, you will

160. See *ST* III, q. 46, a. 5.

not believe me either. Secondly, he compares the way in which they presented their teaching: Moses gave his precepts in a written form; and so they can be studied for a long time, and are not easily forgotten. Hence they impose a stronger obligation to believe. But Christ presented his teachings in spoken words. Thus he says, *But if you do not believe in his written statements*, which you have preserved in your books, *how will you believe in my spoken words?*[161]

161. See *ST* III, q. 42, a. 4.

INDEX

This index covers the editors' introduction and the prologue and chapters 1–5 of Thomas Aquinas's commentary. References in roman numerals (in italics) denote pages in the introduction. Arabic numerals denote paragraphs of Aquinas's commentary.

active life, 1, 383
adoptionism, 64n66
Albert the Great, *xiii, xviii, xxvii*
Alcuin, 50, 51, 299, 392n54, 805n135, 832n159
Ambrose, *xixn28*, 96, 721
angels, 25, 57, 87, 98, 110–14, 125, 137, 167, 184, 186–89, 201, 210–14, 329–33, 368, 467, 703, 707–8, 787
Anselm of Canterbury, 26
Anslem of Laon, *xxixn38*, 40n41
Apollinarius, *xxvi*, 168, 413
apostles, 14, 123, 177, 179, 180, 183, 191, 200, 201, 272, 281–82, 306, 308, 330, 371, 383, 414, 625, 629, 639, 651–54, 776
Aristotle, *x, xxii, xxvii–xxix*, 25, 65, 160, 351, 603
Arius/Arians, *xx, xxvi*, 41, 61, 62, 64, 69, 126, 167, 168, 198, 262, 477, 545, 742, 745, 769, 783
Athanasian Creed, 542
Augustine, *xiv, xv, xixn28, xxi, xxii–xxiv, xxvi, xxvii, xxviii, xxix*, 1, 2, 6, 25, 26, 27, 32, 36, 37, 39, 55, 71, 72, 76, 77, 79, 87, 88, 91, 96, 102, 103, 130, 138, 160, 165, 174, 182, 189, 200, 206, 209, 241, 246, 271, 272, 275, 294, 297, 306, 307, 318, 323, 332, 333, 341, 349, 352, 357, 359, 371, 385, 392n54, 404, 409, 411, 420, 446, 451, 453, 464, 488, 495, 501, 515, 532, 542n110, 554, 555, 562, 563, 590, 594, 596, 617, 622, 647, 648n78, 651, 668, 703, 704, 705, 708, 711, 718, 739, 747, 751, 754, 758, 759, 762, 767, 779, 785, 788, 789, 791, 795, 831

baptism, 164, 243–44, 250, 252, 255, 266, 268–69, 272, 274–76, 433, 439–48, 456, 464, 472, 497–512, 553–55, 561, 703, 707–8

Basil of Caesarea, 37, 47, 51, 64n70
beatific vision, 101, 120, 211–14, 287, 379, 548, 763, 775, 789, 821
Bede, 50, 51, 341, 498, 552n3, 573n19, 805n135, 832n159
Bible. *See* Scripture
Blessed Virgin. *See* Mary
Body of Christ. *See* Church
Bonaventure, *xiii*

Catena aurea, *xiii, xviii–xix, xxiv, xxx*
causality: divine, 5, 73, 76, 87, 90, 133, 477, 739, 753, 782; efficient, 76, 133, 160, 161, 162, 448, 531, 533; eternal, 586; exemplary, 791; formal, 76; instrumental, 740, 752; intermediate, 119; material, 161, 162, 448; meritorious, 791
Cerinthus, 10, 64
charity/love, 159, 188–89, 201, 239, 272, 304, 347, 392, 485–86, 519, 524, 548, 577, 611, 614, 642, 659, 666, 711, 718, 753, 776, 812
chastity, 13
Christ: ascension, 330; baptism, 10n15, 253–79; 337, 376, 501; emotions of, 168; grace at work in, 8, 188–90, 201–2, 404, 544; human knowledge, 667; Lamb of God, 255–58, 283; merit of, 190, 276, 327, 544, 789; Messiah, 233, 246, 301, 617–18; passion and death, 190, 206, 352, 378, 402, 414, 474–75, 478, 554, 556, 703, 789; as priest, 789; as prophet, 233, 596, 618, 667–68, 823; redeemer, 92; resurrection, 397–98, 403–4, 414, 759–60; savior, 92, 139, 270, 275, 370, 662–63, 684; second coming, 232, 482, 665, 674; Son of God, 10, 66, 71, 77, 92, 93, 104, 106, 118, 123, 139, 144, 149, 162, 170, 174, 176, 196, 229, 270, 274–75, 278, 327–31, 375, 435, 468, 471, 477–79, 482, 489, 544, 547,

Commentary on the Gospel of John: Chapters 1–5 was designed and typeset in Meridien by Kachergis Book Design of Pittsboro, North Carolina. It was printed on 55-pound Natural and bound by Versa Press of East Peoria, Illinois.